THE SOUTHWESTERN JOURNALS
OF ADOLPH F. BANDELIER
1880–1882

ASSOCIATE PROFESSOR of anthropology at Southern Illinois University, Dr. Carroll L. Riley received his M.A. from the University of California at Los Angeles, and his B.A. and Ph.D. degrees from the University of New Mexico.

Dr. Riley's field researches have covered many parts of the world, including the Southwest, Mexico, Central America, and the Mediterranean. He has published some forty papers in several fields of anthropology, including linguistics and physical anthropology, archaeology and ethnohistory.

He has contributed important studies of the blowgun in the New World, anthropology and medicine, and the color-direction symbolism in the greater Southwest. Dr. Riley has three books and two monographs in preparation.

Adolph F. Bandelier as a young man

The Southwestern Journals

of Adolph F. Bandelier

1880-1882

EDITED AND ANNOTATED BY

CHARLES H. LANGE

AND

CARROLL L. RILEY

THE UNIVERSITY OF NEW MEXICO PRESS
ALBUQUERQUE

THE SCHOOL OF AMERICAN RESEARCH
MUSEUM OF NEW MEXICO PRESS
SANTA FE

ACKNOWLEDGMENT IS MADE TO

Edgar L. Hewett

Founding Director of the School of American Research
and the Museum of New Mexico
who encouraged publication of the Bandelier Journals
and

Wayne L. Mauzy

Formerly Acting Director of the School of American Research
and Director of the Museum of New Mexico
who initiated editorial and financial arrangements
which brought publication to fruition

Manufactured in the United States of America
by the University of New Mexico Printing Plant
Library of Congress Catalog Card No. 65-17862
First edition

CONTENTS

ILLUSTRATIONS

Frontispiece: Adolph Bandelier as a young man

Page xvii: Bandelier's journal entry for September 5, 1880

Facing page 1: Locale of Bandelier's research

Following page 62:

Bandelier, his wife Josephine, and his father

Bandelier, Josephine, her sister, and his father

Bandelier in mature years

Bandelier and his second wife, Fanny

Following page 254:

José Hilario Montoya of Cochiti Pueblo

Palace of the Governors

Fort Marcy

Pecos mission and monastery

Quarai mission and monastery

Ruins of Tyuonyi, Bandelier National Monument

Stone mountain lions of Cochiti

Painted Cave, Bandelier National Monument

Green Corn Dance at Santo Domingo Pueblo

Kiva at Santo Domingo Pueblo

Acoma Pueblo

Mission church at Acoma Pueblo

Ceremonial dance at Zuñi Pueblo

Gran Quivira mission ruins

Girls of Isleta Pueblo

All photographs are from the
archives of the Museum of New Mexico

DRAWINGS

From original sketches in Bandelier's journal

PREFACE

THE PRESENT VOLUME represents the fruition of plans, extending over two decades, to publish the daily journals of the famous scholar, Adolph F. Bandelier. These journals were begun in the year 1880 and were continued, more or less regularly; they documented the writer's adventures in the Southwest, in Mexico, and in South America for almost a quarter century. After Bandelier's death in 1914, the journals passed to his wife and fellow scholar, Fannie R. Bandelier, who in turn willed them to the Laboratory of Anthropology, Santa Fe, New Mexico. At present the original—mainly handwritten—manuscripts are kept in the Archives of the Governor's Palace, Museum of New Mexico.

A major difficulty in bringing these journals to the public in published form has been in the technical problems of editing. Suggestions for editing the journals have varied from plans to publish verbatim to suggestions that only certain data—ethnological, for example—be extracted and presented with extensive commentary. In editing the Southwestern portions of these journals (1880-1892), we have attempted to steer a middle course between the extremes of, on the one hand, presenting the journals as a mass of "raw" material and of, on the other hand, presenting only a portion of interest to specialists such as anthropologists or historians.

The journals contain day-by-day records of Bandelier's activities, serving as a combined field notebook and diary. Their range is amazing; Bandelier was interested in almost everything about him and a particular day's journal may contain information of interest to anthropologists, biographers, botanists, folklorists, geographers, geologists, historians, and zoologists. Some entries have considerable literary quality while others are written in a cursory manner in which phrases or even single words comprise the entire record on a given matter. Often, especially in the early years, Bandelier's Continental European background comes to light in the peculiar and frequently complicated structure of his sentences.

It is perfectly obvious that Bandelier never intended his journals for publication. Certain parts of them, much modified, later served as the basis for published material (cf. *Final Report, Islands of Lake Titicaca and Koati, Documentary History of Zuñi*, etc.). The most striking feature of the journals, however, is the candid, personal nature of many observations. Not only were field data given with on-the-spot comments, but Bandelier had much to say about the people around him, whether Indian informants, colleagues, friends, or relatives. We see, through Bandelier's eyes, the daily activities, virtues, and faults of a great many people—some historically famous, others known primarily from the journals themselves. The journals, thus, provide vignettes that are especially valuable to anyone interested in the Southwest. The often pungent opinions and criticisms of Bandelier must be taken for what they really are, one man's *private* comment on life about him.

In the edited journals, there is a considerable amount of annotation. This includes identification of historical figures and places, discussion of ethnographic data, etc. If no footnote is given for particular ethnographic information fully accepted by Bandelier, these data, in our opinion, are probably valid for Bandelier's time (in fact, many of the descriptions of everyday life, religious ceremonies, political structure, social relation-

ships, etc., apply equally today). On the other hand, Bandelier's interpretations of his data and reactions to his observations reveal the lack of sophistication in the social sciences
common to his day.

As a matter of editorial policy, the following modifications
in the original Bandelier journal entries have been made.

1. Certain types of entries, incidental information relating
to the weather, occasional descriptions of background scenery,
and unimportant calculations of elevations and distance, have
been deleted entirely with no indication of this given. Bandelier regularly started each day of his journal with weather data
and occasionally interspersed additional comments later in the
day. When these serve no practical value, they have been
dropped from the edited material. Where weather conditions
are pertinent to the activities of the day, the comments have
been retained. This policy applies to certain scenic descriptions
as well. For example, the skyline of the Sandia Mountains has
not changed in the past seventy years and incidental out-of-
context references to it do not add to the value of the journals.
The deletions are not indicated in the text, in part because such
indications reduce the readability of the journals. In addition,
the rather haphazard way in which weather comments are
introduced makes such deletion indicators as ellipses occasionally misleading. For example, we quote from the entry for
March 28, 1882: "Went to Governor Ritch at night. He was
exceedingly kind with me. Made some confidential communications." This was followed immediately by a comment on the
weather with no subsequent indication ever as to the nature
of the confidences. Ellipses at such a point would very likely
mislead the reader into thinking that the editors had withheld
secret or sensitive material. We would stress here that no such
censorship takes place at any point in the journals.

2. A number of sketches found in the original journals are
not included in the published version. These are drawings of
skylines, maps of ruins, ground plans of pueblos, or plots of

fields, some of which were later published in the *Final Report* or elsewhere. We recognize, however, that certain sketches might have particularistic value to specialists, and so we have indicated with an asterisk (*) each point at which a sketch deletion has been made. Such sketches, together with various measurements and azimuths, often give the illusion of considerable precision on Bandelier's part. In reality, these data were frequently so incomplete or without the necessary base points as to make them unusable. Similarly, notations of photographic plates have not been retained. Bandelier's collection of plates has never come to light, and retention here of his numbering system and notes seems pointless. Should this collection ever be found, the original journals could be consulted.

3. Certain types of entries have been deleted in entirety from the present volume of the journals. These include copies of archival documents and lists of Indian vocabularies. All such material is planned to be published as special appendices in the final volume of the journals. As this special material normally does not relate to the everyday entries in the journals, no note is made of its deletion. In the appendices in the last volume, however, the location of such materials in the original journals is expected to be noted.

4. A special problem exists in the spelling of certain Indian names. Many spellings used by Bandelier have since been changed—for example, Tewa for Tehua, Keres for Queres, Tiwa for Tihua, Zia for Cia. In these cases, we have shown the modern spelling at the first appearance of the term and from then on follow Bandelier's usage. In certain cases where Bandelier varied (Queres, QQueres, or Qqueres), we have retained only the most favored spelling and others are planned to appear as variants in the appendices of the final volume.

5. Foreign words and phrases are accompanied by translations in the text at their first appearance. In addition, a glossary of foreign terms will be appended to each volume for the convenience of the reader. Entries in a foreign language of two

lines or more are presented only in English, such translations being duly noted.

6. A few observations, recorded lineally by Bandelier, have been arranged in chart form for greater convenience.

7. The dating system used by Bandelier was somewhat variable. In editing the journals, such usages as "24 Oct. '80," and other forms have been standardized, e.g., "October 24."

8. The chaotic punctuation used by Bandelier has been somewhat modified to fit modern usage. Along these same lines, there have been occasional minor changes in sentence structure for the purposes of clarity. Paragraph breaks are primarily those of the present editors. The use of italics (for Spanish, German, and French phrases) is simply an editing policy. Bandelier, himself, was not consistent in handling these terms.

Finally, it should be stressed that it is the editors' aim to present each volume of the southwestern journals of Adolph F. Bandelier as a self-contained unit. Each volume is intended to stand alone and to be enjoyed without reference to earlier or later volumes of the set. The present volume contains an extended introductory sketch of Bandelier's life. The succeeding volumes will have shorter sketches which, in each case, provide context for the journal entries of that volume.

ACKNOWLEDGMENTS

THE EDITORS must first express their deep appreciation to officials of the Museum of New Mexico, the School of American Research, and the Laboratory of Anthropology, Santa Fe, especially to Mr. Bruce T. Ellis and Mr. Wayne L. Mauzy. Having entrusted to us the task of editing these journals, Mr. Ellis and Mr. Mauzy have cooperated in every way possible in seeing publication realized.

In our tedious search for identification of people and places mentioned by Bandelier, we have received considerable aid from notes compiled by Dr. A. J. O. Anderson, former member of the Museum of New Mexico staff. Dr. Bertha P. Dutton, Curator of Ethnology; Miss Gertrude Hill, Librarian; Dr. Myra Ellen Jenkins, Archivist; Miss Virginia Jennings, Editorial Assistant; Mrs. Marjorie Lambert, Curator of Archaeology; the late Stanley A. Stubbs of the Laboratory of Anthropology; and others of the Museum of New Mexico and Laboratory of Anthropology staffs have been most generous with their time and interest in our project.

Mrs. R. L. Ormsbee, the daughter of Mrs. Elizabeth Bandelier Kaune (the niece, "Lizzie," of Bandelier's journals), and her husband were most cordial during our weeks in Santa Fe in the summer of 1959. They showed us through their home (the former Bandelier residence) in the center of present-day Santa

Fe and brought out family photograph albums and other materials for us to examine. All of these contributed to our insight and knowledge concerning Adolph Bandelier.

The support from officials of Southern Illinois University—Dr. Walter W. Taylor, Chairman, Department of Anthropology; Dean T. W. Abbott, College of Liberal Arts and Sciences; Dr. J. Charles Kelley, Director, University Museum; Dean Willis G. Swartz, Graduate School; and Dr. John O. Anderson, Research Coordinator—has resulted both in released time from other university duties to hasten the completion of the editorial task and in other significant aid. A number of students at Southern Illinois University, Carolyn Kinsey, Barbara Miles, Mary Elizabeth Putt, Linda Souther, Ann Turner, Bonnie Gail Turner, Ruth Ann Wagner, H. Leslie Clendenen, Joseph J. Manak, and Philip Weigand have contributed to the completion of the manuscript.

Reverend Lowry J. Daly, S. J., and Mr. Charles J. Ermatinger of the Pius XII Vatican Microfilm Library, Saint Louis University, have been most cooperative in obtaining black-and-white and color slides of the Bandelier manuscript presented by Archbishop J. B. Salpointe of Santa Fe to the Vatican in honor of the Jubilee of Pope Leo XIII in 1888. They and their associates also undertook a vigorous search for the missing portion (1,200 pages of foolscap in French) of the manuscript as a part of their comprehensive search for important archival materials. Unfortunately, as was true in past searches (among which those of Professor Lansing B. Bloom were especially determined), their efforts have thus far failed to locate this manuscript. The effort is being continued as this was termed by Dr. Edgar L. Hewett as "probably the most important unpublished work left by Mr. Bandelier." (Letter to Mr. Postlethwaite, Colorado College, August 20, 1937.) The editors, though, of course, ignorant of the contents of this document, tend to challenge this evaluation in favor of the present journals.

Dr. W. W. Hill, Dr. France V. Scholes, and the late Dr. Leslie Spier, all of the University of New Mexico, have been of particular aid in the editing of the Bandelier journals, and their interest is greatly appreciated.

A special word of appreciation must be expressed for the invaluable aid provided by the typescripts of the original Bandelier journals which were prepared by Mrs. Hulda Hobbs Heidel during her service on the staff of the Museum of New Mexico. While all entries have again been checked against the original journals, these typescripts, meticulously done, have greatly facilitated our editorial task.

Finally, the editors wish to express their gratitude to the American Philosophical Society for a grant-in-aid from the Johnson Fund which made the preparation of this first volume possible.

June 1, 1962

1880.

5. Sept. Beautiful day. Walked over to Pecos. ab't 4 [nov 14]
mile, crossing high ridges with cedars & piñones. — Stopped
with E. K. Walters & talked with a number of mexicans. —
The owner of the "Rio Pecos" is the "Jicarito," ab't W.S. from
the ruins. — Dined with Juan Baca y Salazar & his
brother-in-law Ambrosio Pino. The latter lives at
Galisteo, where there are about 7. Tanos-Indians left.
They all say that when the bell was found on the mesa
of Pecos, were the winter = houses of the Pecos-Indians,
& that they carried the Bell along with them when they
destroyed the church in 1680. — Then called on Father
Léon Mailluchet / from French = Comté, & well known
ab't the Jura, near near Pontarlier.) He lives with
his brother & family, who are keeping house for him. No
church records back of 1862. — Has two paintings, one
on buffalo = hide representing N⁴ S⁴ de Guadalupe,
1. ft. long, & 1. ft. wide. the other of same size on cloth
representing N⁴ S⁴ de los Angeles. Sells them for $60. —
Both from old Pecos-church. The latter is remarkably
well done. — He says the grounds of the ruins of Pecos
were sold by the Indians to the Archbishop. —
Ret'd on foot, & met Thomas Munn. Interesting. —
He says that where the fragments of the Bell were found,
there is a circular basin (estufa.) and that a man
named Murphy noticed the ruins of what was like another
fortification, also an oblong chamber of cut stone, contigua
skeleton, looking to the East. Says also that the kirch is
cut in many places, like unto an opening — Train in time
at 5. P.M., but missed it. Compelled to stay. — In the P.M.
Shower East & N.E. across the mountains. — Made arrange-
= ments with Thos Munn to go to the mesa to-morrow.

Bandelier's journal entry for September 5, 1880

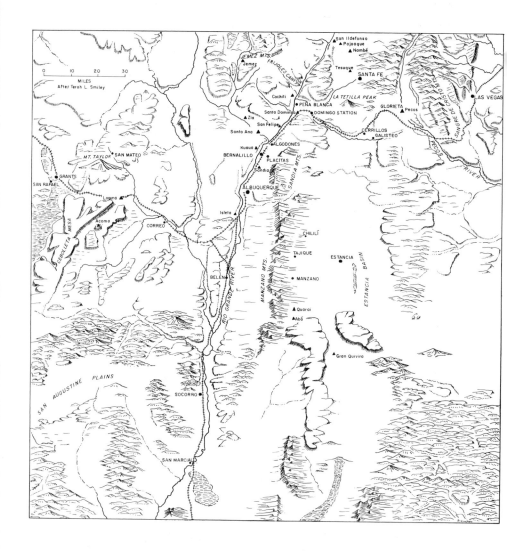

Locale of Bandelier's research during
the period covered by this volume

Courtesy of Geochronology Laboratories, The University of Arizona

INTRODUCTION

THE NAME OF Adolph Francis Alphonse Bandelier[1] has long been accorded prominence among the nineteenth-century scholars in anthropology, history, and related fields, especially those scholars interested in the American Indian. This prominence, it must be admitted, can be termed neither unanimous nor entirely enthusiastic. Bandelier's works, as is true of those produced by the pioneers in any discipline, have been subjected to periodic criticism by later scholars.

Such criticism—refutation and modification—has, in some instances, tended to categorically discredit Bandelier's researches and publications. This adverse evaluation may well have been initially reinforced by Bandelier's complex personality— aristocratic, confident, critical, impatient, inquisitive, keen, suspicious, and tense. He was anxious for friendships and respect, though a tendency to be sensitive rather than sensible produced variable moods which made it difficult to work with him. Fay-Cooper Cole (1952: 159), in a mid-twentieth-century reminiscence regarding early anthropologists, was moved to remark that Bandelier "was the one real Bohemian" among the early workers he had known in this field.

---

1. Bandelier was probably christened "Adolphe Francis Alphonse," according to Hobbs (1940: 122). Though using both "Adolphe" (French) and "Adolf" (German), as well as "A. F.," Bandelier, himself, seems to have preferred the abbreviated form, "Ad." In the literature, the German and English form, "Adolph," seemingly has become most common, and this form has been adopted here.

The journals of Adolph Bandelier, beginning in 1880 when Bandelier was forty years old, covered the latter half of his life excepting only the final years in New York and in Spain. The task of the editors has been to extract those entries from 1880 through 1892 which pertain to the Southwest, as this area is commonly envisioned in present-day anthropology. This region —New Mexico, Arizona, and the immediately adjacent portions of the United States and Mexico—was the locale of Bandelier's research for periods of varying lengths of time during these thirteen years.

In addition to the periods of research in the Southwest were sporadic trips made to the family home in Highland, Illinois, and also to Mexico and Europe. The present volume is concerned only with Bandelier's initial trip to the Southwest in the last quarter of 1880 and, after a year's absence (the year 1881 having been spent primarily in Mexico), with the first portion of his second visit that began in 1882. Three companion volumes are now projected; they will include Bandelier's seven subsequent trips which ranged from six weeks to a year and a half in duration. The present prospectus for these volumes is as follows: the second volume, 1883 and 1884; the third, 1885, 1886, 1887, 1888; and the fourth, 1889, 1890, 1891, 1892. Included in the fourth volume will be a compilation of vocabulary and other linguistic data, glossaries, and unpublished archival material extracted from the journals where they appear in haphazard fashion and merely disrupt the continuity of the entries.

Biographical sketches of some scope have been compiled by Brother Cassian Edmunds (1937) and Edgar F. Goad (1939). The first of these was limited to a consideration of the period from 1880 through 1892; the second treated Bandelier's entire life, extending from 1840 to 1914. Neither has been published. Among the published studies of Bandelier's life, mention should be made of those by George P. Hammond and Goad (1949), Hulda R. Hobbs (1940), and Frederick Webb Hodge (1932). Also of value are obituaries by Hiram Bingham (1914),

Frederick Webb Hodge (1914), Charles F. Lummis (1914), and Clark Wissler (1914). Other sketches may be found in *The Dictionary of American Biography* (Kidder 1928), in *Prominent Americans of Swiss Origin* (Bartholdi 1932), and in the Introduction (Lummis 1916) to the second edition of *The Delight Makers*. T. T. Waterman (1916-17) published an appraisal of Bandelier's use of sources in his earlier monographs, Leslie A. White (1940) edited the correspondence between Bandelier and Lewis Henry Morgan, and White and Ignacio Bernal (1960) edited another series of letters between Bandelier and Joaquín García Icazbalceta. The influence of Morgan upon the work of Bandelier becomes clearly evident from an examination of Bandelier's correspondence, publications, and journal entries.

Goad (p. 4) made the interesting observation that Bandelier "has been called an archaeologist by the historians, and a historian by the archaeologists." In a sense this may be true, but as Goad himself demonstrated, the comment has implications which seem unjustifiably harsh. In contrast is an appraisal credited to Alfred V. Kidder by Hodge (1940: 12) in a paper presented during a Memorial Conference, August 6-8, 1940, in Santa Fe, as a part of a centennial celebration of Bandelier's birth.

> No American archaeologist has depended as did Bandelier upon historical sources; and no American historian has checked his work so fully by a study of archaeological materials. He also realized the necessity of collecting from surviving aborigines all possible legendary data and of imbuing himself with a knowledge of their ways of life and habits of thought.

Today, several decades later and in the wake of extensive and intensive ethnohistorical and archaeological research prompted by the series of claims cases brought by many American Indian tribes before the Indian Claims Commission, the uniqueness of Bandelier's broad approach to cultural history no longer exists. No volume of research effort, however, can erase the pioneering efforts made by him along these specific lines.

Goad's brief summarization (pp. 5-6) of the situation as it was at the time Bandelier began his work merits repeating here.

> Until the latter decades of the nineteenth century, the pre-Columbian period of American history remained European in concept and, with few exceptions, romantic in treatment. The fiction of J. Fenimore Cooper and Captain Mayne Reid, no less than the serious histories of William Hickling Prescott and Francis Parkman, were accepted as final words on the condition of the American native races. In turn, even scholarly historical works were often based on uncritical acceptance of the journals of early explorers as to the social organization and methods of government of the American aborigines. This led to an exaggerated idea on the part of historians, at least, of both the heights of civilization reached by certain pre-Columbian Americans and an equal exaggeration of the depths of their degradation and savagery.
>
> In 1870, when Bandelier began his studies, there may be said to have been, with the possible exception of Lewis H. Morgan, no American ethnologists in the scientific sense. Such scientific approach to the history of the aborigines as existed was represented by the observations of such men as Charles Darwin, Alexander von Humboldt, and other traveling European scholars.

It is also worth noting at this point, in further providing context for the work of Bandelier, that although the Smithsonian Institution was established in Washington, D. C., in 1846, the Bureau of American Ethnology was not established until 1879, with Major J. W. Powell as its first Director. In a different vein, the American Anthropological Association began publication in 1888. The American Association for the Advancement of Science recognized anthropology by electing an anthropologist, Lewis Henry Morgan, President of the Association for 1879-80.

Paralleling his interest in utilizing a common archaeological-historical approach, Bandelier's awareness of the great value to be derived from an intimate knowledge of ethnological data in the interpretation of archaeological remains was again an essentionally "trail blazing" concept. At times clumsily and incompletely pursued, these insights were later discredited as "romanticism" (which Bandelier, himself, criticized) and, accordingly, shunned by subsequent generations of "scientifically" oriented scholars. Still later, there began a counter-movement (perhaps most fully expressed by Walter W. Taylor's *A Study of Archaeology* [1948]) which urged the interpretation of archaeological remains much more fully—beyond and above the mere time and space affiliations. This effort to make archaeologists more aware of total culture, "the anthropological viewpoint," by means of what Taylor termed "the conjunctive approach" (p. 7 *et seq.*), is currently widely endorsed.

Rudiments of this approach, however, may be clearly and repeatedly seen as the aspirations and goals overtly or covertly expressed in the entries of Bandelier's journals. It is quite evident, also, that the level of actual attainment was seldom high, but this, as noted previously, is the inevitable limitation of virtually all pioneers. There was, undeniably, a basic awareness of the advantages of such an approach.

Thus, returning to Goad's comment, it would appear to be of little real importance whether Bandelier's efforts should be properly classified as anthropology (archaeology), or history. Rather, the activities of Bandelier may be more sensibly viewed as early, and often fumbling, attempts to learn accurately and seriously everything possible about a particular segment of man and culture—the American Indians, and in the context of the present project, the Pueblo Indians of the American Southwest.

Bandelier, as the journals demonstrate, had an essentially untrained though insatiable and keen mind. He combined penetrating analysis and comprehensive perspective with a lack of sophistication and an unfortunate tendency to make premature correlations and conclusions.

In presenting this brief sketch of Bandelier's life, primarily to provide a suitable context for the journals, the editors regret that more of his rather voluminous correspondence was not available for reference. Aside from the already cited Bandelier-Morgan letters (White 1940) and Bandelier-García Icazbalceta correspondence (White and Bernal 1960) and a few travel accounts, or *Reisebriefe*, sent to various periodicals and intended for publication, Bandelier's personal correspondence for the earlier period of his life appears to have been largely destroyed or lost. For example, no letters to his first wife or to other family members have come to light. Such papers would unquestionably enhance one's insight, especially if used in conjunction with the journals themselves. It will become evident that considerable use has been made of Goad's study (1939). Goad examined newspaper files in the Highland area and in Santa Fe as well as certain correspondence in the files of the American Museum of Natural History, the Archaeological Institute of America, and Peabody Museum of Harvard University. More important perhaps, during the 1930's at the time of Goad's research, it was possible to interview or to correspond with a number of Bandelier's contemporaries who had known him rather well over a considerable period of time—an advantage no longer available to anyone.

The Early Years: 1840-1873

Adolphe Francis Alphonse Bandelier was born August 6, 1840, in Bern, the capital of Switzerland. His father, Adolphe Eugene, was of a distinguished family of that city as was Bandelier's mother, Marie Senn, who had married early and been widowed before her marriage to Bandelier's father.

Having been trained in law, Bandelier's father took some part in political affairs and was at least once elected to public office. Whether or not a turn in political fortunes directly prompted the move is not clear, but Bandelier's father left Switzerland with a friend to seek a new home in Brazil. Disappointed there, he went next to the Illinois prairies. Some forty miles east of St. Louis, he found the Swiss settlement of Highland to his liking. Originally called New Switzerland, the community had been plotted and renamed Highland in the 1830's. In 1850, the population was about 500, and in the next decade, it grew to 1,500 (Spencer 1937: 16-26).

Finding Highland to his satisfaction, Bandelier's father sent in 1848 for his wife, son, and the family maid, Annali, to join him. In time, a second son, Emil Frederick, was born to the family. Bandelier's mother apparently found it difficult to adjust to the unfamiliar life of a small community in a strange country and was homesick much of the time. She died in 1855. and Annali stayed on to help with the household.

Bandelier's father had erected a large, comfortable home on a forty-acre tract a mile northeast of Highland. This acreage, however, was primarily for fruit trees and vineyards. For the principal support of his family, Bandelier's father joined two partners, F. Ryhiner and Moritz Huegy, Sr., in the F. Ryhiner Bank of Highland, which became one of the largest banks in southern Illinois during the mid-nineteenth century. Bandelier's father's personal acquaintance with various moneyed interests in Switzerland was especially valuable as the bank participated in the development of this community. He also played a prominent role in diverse civic affairs, leading civil movements, serving as secretary of the school board, and helping with the organization of a French Evangelical Church. "Herr Professor," as he was known, was frequently called upon to speak at various civic occasions, such as the dedication of public buildings. He was, according to Goad (p. 16), "absolute master of his household," and further afield, "demanding and receiving the respect of all." Elsewhere (p. 14), Goad noted that Bandelier's father, "a pompous gentleman, stubborn and strong-willed, was the only man who dared to wear a silk hat on the muddy streets of the little southern Illinois town." It might be added that, under these circumstances, his desire to dress in this manner is equally revealing insofar as personality is concerned.

Within this family and community context, the earlier years of Adolph Bandelier's life assume added interest as the formulative base for his subsequent interests and activities. Quite effectively, it appears, Goad (p. 17) disputed the statements of Hodge (1914: 349-350; 1932: 353) and others (see Hobbs 1940: 123) to the effect that Bandelier was educated almost exclusively by family and private tutors. Goad claimed that Bandelier attended public school from the time of his arrival in Highland in 1848, though he also pointed out that Bandelier, as was the custom of the day, undoubtedly had private lessons in singing, art, elocution, and similar subjects. In addition, the family, according to Hobbs (p. 123),

> stimulated in him the spirit of scientific inquiry. They had a telescope, through which Adolph and his father used to study the heavenly bodies. They had a custom of reading aloud in the evenings. The remarkable breadth of Adolph's knowledge thus appears to have been built up from his early childhood. He and his father always spoke French together, unless others were present. They spoke perfect "Paris French"—not the Swiss patois. They were equally at home with German. Whether Adolph learned to speak Spanish in childhood is not known, but his first published works are based upon wide reading of Spanish documents.[2]

---

2. The flattering nature of Hobbs' appraisal of Bandelier's linguistic talents typifies the rather widespread deference paid him in this regard. More recently, however, Bernal has challenged these assumed talents (White and Bernal 1960: 99). Despite Bandelier's record of research, publishing, and/or corresponding in English, French, German, and Spanish, his mastery of these tongues was not complete. Because of his multilingual Swiss or European background, Bandelier apparently felt little hesitation in using these languages. To what extent his confidence deceived him is difficult to judge. Bernal cited situations in which contemporaries suggested to Bandelier that he use some idiom other than theirs. No vestige of an edited manuscript of Bandelier's numerous publications has come to light so there is no way of knowing to what extent these publications were reworked by editors.

Allowing for the customary laxities and deviations in a journal meant merely as a record of fieldwork and personal notation, Bandelier's journal entries contain many awkward and peculiar words and phrases. Some of these were, in fact, so awkward that (according to the policy set forth in the preface to this volume) it was necessary to rephrase them.

We now have data that Hobbs lacked regarding the circumstances of Bandelier's learning Spanish. In a letter dated November 9, 1875 (White and

In 1857, Bandelier's father sent him to Bern where he studied geology under Professor Studer (Hodge 1932: 353). How long he remained in Europe is not certain. On January 5, 1862, five years later, Bandelier was married to Josephine Huegy, several years his senior, who was the first Swiss child to be born in Highland and the daughter of one of his father's banking partners. In 1865, the couple visited Switzerland, and Adolph was in attendance at the University of Bern, in the School of Law, for the winter semester, 1865-66, the summer semester of 1866, and the winter semester of 1866-67 (Goad 1939: 18).

In 1867 Bandelier returned from Europe to Highland, and his life in the post-Civil War period followed much the same pattern as that already indicated for his father before him. He assisted at the bank though he apparently held no formal position in its organization. Like his father, he became active in

---

Bernal 1960: 112), Bandelier wrote of his desire to learn Nahuatl, expressing the suspicion that it would prove more difficult than Spanish. While ill and confined to bed in New Haven, Connecticut, he had begun by reading Acosta without the use of a dictionary. Two months later, he read Herrera and claimed to comprehend Italian and Portuguese at that time. Considering his prior familiarity with French, this is not too surprising. However, one can suspect that the finer points of grammar and semantics may have eluded Bandelier; this may well explain a basic distrust of Bandelier's archival work on the part of numerous scholars.

A case in point, minor perhaps though nonetheless suggestive, was Bandelier's mistranslation of a passage in the *Relacion del Suceso* (Bandelier, A. F., 1892: 48), as noted by Lange (1950: 204). In the original Spanish, the Puebloan use of turkeys was described as follows: "é algunas gallinas de las de México; y estos las tienen más para la pluma que para comer, porqué hacen della pellones, á causa que no tienen ningun algodón."

Bandelier's translation stated that turkeys were kept "for feathers rather than to eat" whereas the meaning is actually that turkeys were kept more for their feathers than for eating. Thus, a preference was transformed into a negation, misconstruing the sense of the original observation. Lange's comment is relevant in the present context: "While correct translations were made by Winship (1896: 573) and others, the reputation of Bandelier in Southwestern ethnology and history has resulted in perpetuating this error." It is precisely the cumulative recognition of such errors in Bandelier's work that has served to discredit it in the minds of some scholars. While one must unquestionably be cautious in using Bandelier's materials, there remains much that is of great value—and, again, it is the purpose of the present editors to present and evaluate such data so that they may be used without qualifications.

civic matters, speaking at numerous affairs, and serving as an official in various community organizations. Bandelier also was fond of discussing politics, books, and such matters with various colleagues, including Timothy Gruaz of the local newspaper, "professors" from the public school, and others, in the beer parlors of Highland. He and his father were both active in the local Schützenbund (Rifle Club) as well as in the national affairs of this group.

In 1868 and 1869, a series of meteorological articles by Bandelier appeared in the local newspapers.[3] These were accompanied by discussions of the local climate and its effect on life in central Illinois. According to Goad's account (pp. 20-21),

> During Christmas week, 1869, the newly erected *Turnhalle* was dedicated in Highland, with the senior Bandelier giving the principal address. A bust of Alexander von Humboldt smiled approvingly from the wall between portraits of William Tell and George Washington, according to the rather fullsome account in *Die Union*, of December 30, 1869. On January 14, 1870, "Herr Professor" Adolph F. Bandelier announced in *Die Union* a series of lectures in the *Turnhalle* on the subject, "Schilderungen aus der Anfangen," (Descriptions from Early Times), for which an admission charge of twenty-five cents was to be made, the receipts to be used to furnish the *Turnhalle*. John Springer, a public school teacher, alternated with Adolph F. in giving the lectures. "Professor" Springer spoke on the "Unprogressiveness of the Chinese Empire and its Causes."

3. Highland, in a pattern characteristic for this period, had a variety of local newspapers. Goad (p. 16) noted two German-language papers, *Der Highland Bote* and *Die Highland Union*. *Der Bote* appears to have antedated *Die Union* which Goad stated began in 1863 as an organ of the Republican Party. Files of these papers were in possession of the *Highland News-Leader* of which A. P. Spencer was the editor as of the time of Goad's research in the Highland area in the summers of 1937 and 1938. In addition (p. 108), the *Highland Telephone* was also listed as the first English-language paper in the community, having been started in 1884.

In the local newspapers of the 1870's, Bandelier's activities were reported in much the same vein. In 1871, "Herr" Adolph F. Bandelier gave a series of lectures to raise funds for Swiss relief; in 1872, Bandelier and his father both served on the national finance committee of the Schützenbund; also in 1872, Bandelier was listed as water carrier with the Volunteer Fire Company; in 1875, he was a member of the Turnverein's library committee; and in 1878, he served as vice president of a committee to arrange a German Protestant Church affair. (Goad 1939: 21). In November, 1877, Bandelier had become a naturalized citizen of the United States (White 1940: II, 81).

It is apparent that the Bandelier home was visited by many friends, both from the local community and from St. Louis and farther away. Undoubtedly the most significant of these visitors, in terms of Bandelier's future scholarly interests, was Lewis Henry Morgan, named by some authorities as the "Father of American Ethnology," and by others as the "Father of American Anthropology."

THE BEGINNINGS OF A CAREER: 1870-1880

To pinpoint the precise moment or event which is the starting point of a career is a difficult task whether one is involved with an autobiography or with a biography. The problem is a fascinating one, nonetheless, and one gains an impression that such interests are generally attributable to one or more personalities whose influence may or may not have been consciously exerted or received. From the limited details of the background sketch of Bandelier's formative years already presented here, it is clear that scholarly interests, in a wide sense, were cultivated by the family itself and also through the social relationships fostered by the family.

For Bandelier, one may well hypothesize significant early influence from the activities and publications of Baron Alexander von Humboldt, of whom it is known Bandelier became a great admirer. This influence appears to have been reinforced

in the course of his visits and studies in Bern in the decade between 1857 and 1867, during which period, in 1859, von Humboldt died. Whether there was personal contact between the
two or whether Bandelier was merely influenced through the
literature and by the renown of von Humboldt is uncertain.
Von Humboldt's interests in various aspects of natural history
and science as well as his explorations and studies in Latin
America, particularly those in Mexico, could easily have intensi-
fied Bandelier's curiosity and interest regarding this area and its
cultural history. Writing, of course many years after the event,
Bandelier's second wife stated that Adolph Bandelier had met
and corresponded with Alexander von Humboldt but in a fit of
despondence had destroyed that and other correspondence.
"Humboldt seems to have written him like a father would
write to his son concerning his prospects in the scientific field."
(Bandelier, Fanny R., n.d.) It is, indeed, unfortunate that this
correspondence did not survive in order that it might become
available to posterity as in the cases of the Bandelier-Morgan
letters (White 1940) and the Bandelier-García Icazbalceta
letters (White and Bernal 1960).

Goad (p. 23) raised the question as to why Bandelier should
have bypassed the great Cahokia mounds, "almost in his back-
yard," in favor of Mexico and the Southwest. Goad continued,

> The record is silent. Dr. Hodge suggests he may have
> been interested by Morgan's paper on "The Seven Cities
> of Cibola," published in 1869. Also, in 1865, *Der Bote* pub-
> lished, as a serial, Captain Mayne Reid's *The Scalp Hunt-
> ers*, a thrilling tale of the Southwestern Indians, which was
> very popular at the time and which Bandelier undoubtedly
> read. This may have aroused his interest in the Southwest.
> . . . Of all the ancient remains . . . undoubtedly those
> of Mexico, Peru, and New Mexico were in 1880 most invit-
> ing to one just entering the field of American historical
> research. Add to this the fact that Bandelier read Spanish,
> and was already familiar with the literature of the Con-

quest when he met Morgan; that distant pastures all look greener; that he was bored with business and Highland, and it is not hard to see why he turned toward the Southwest just then being widely advertised by the railroads.

On a more tangible basis than the influence of von Humboldt was that of Lewis Henry Morgan; here the details have been elucidated through the correspondence edited by White (1940). The circumstances prompting a meeting between Bandelier and Morgan remain obscure though it has been established that they were introduced in Rochester, New York, by the Reverend Dr. W. B. Anderson, President of the University of Rochester in 1873.[4] In any event, the men visited one another afterward in their respective homes, and a considerable correspondence developed. Morgan was the object of great esteem from the younger man, but it is equally apparent that the relationship was by no means a one-sided one. Goad (p. 25) observed that,

> Between December 20, 1873, when Bandelier wrote his first letter, and June 27, 1881, when the last letter was written from Mitla, his correspondence with Morgan fills 693 typewritten pages, transcribed. In all his writings, Bandelier never missed an opportunity to make obeisance to Morgan for his influence and encouragement. (After Morgan's death, December 17, 1881, Bandelier continued to correspond with Mrs. Morgan, the last letter in the Morgan file being dated July 18, 1883.)

As Goad (p. 22) noted, the correspondence between Bandelier and Morgan shows that Bandelier had already achieved a considerable measure of familiarity with the literature of the Spanish Conquest before his meeting with Morgan. In part, this was the result of visits to the universities and libraries of

---

4. The University of Rochester was founded in 1850. One of its early and important benefactors was Morgan who left the better part of his fortune to the institution to be used in the education of women. (Goad 1939: 27).

the east, and, in part, it was the result of personal purchases, often at what now appear to be amazingly low prices.[5]

As late as 1878, Bandelier appears to have remained content with his library research, or at least reconciled to it, as he compared his position to that of Johann Paul Richter's "Quintus Fixlein, who, whenever he heard of a book whose contents he would have liked to know, wrote it himself for himself. I am in about a similar position: writing about countries and peoples which I shall never be able to see." (White 1940: II, 113)

Despite the fact that Morgan, at the time he first met Bandelier in 1873, was already an acknowledged leader in the scientific comparative study of human societies,[6] Bandelier was in position to be of real assistance to him. Goad (pp. 39-40) summarized the situation as follows:

> Morgan had set out to interpret Mexican social organization in what he considered a universal pattern of Indian society. In reconstructing Aztec society, he proposed to use those portions of the early Spanish chronicles "which harmonize with what is known of actual Indian society" as it

---

5. Goad apparently did not realize that Bandelier only began reading Spanish the year he met Morgan and, at the time of the meeting, probably had no great command of that language. (See footnote 1a.)

6. White (1957:259) provided the following brief sketch of Morgan: "Lewis Morgan was born near Aurora, New York, in 1818. He was graduated from Union College in 1840. He went to Rochester, New York, in 1844 where he engaged in the practice of law. Profitable investments enabled him eventually to give up his law practice and to devote himself to ethnology. All his scientific work was done as a private citizen; he never held a position with an institution of higher learning, a museum, or other scientific organization. The two highest honors that American science can bestow were conferred on Morgan: election to the National Academy of Sciences, and the presidency of the American Association for the Advancement of Science. He died at his home in Rochester on December 17, 1881." Elsewhere (p. 257) in this paper, White stated that "In 1871, the Smithsonian Institution published one of the most significant anthropological treatises ever written: "Systems of Consanguinity and Affinity of the Human Family," by Lewis Henry Morgan. It has been called "monumental" by A. C. Haddon and A. R. Radcliffe-Brown, a "towering monument" by Robert H. Lowie. George P. Murdock has termed it "perhaps the most original and brilliant single achievement in the history of anthropology."

existed when he had studied it. Now, there came to him a man who had that thorough knowledge of the early chronicles of which Morgan doubtless felt a lack. Bandelier was a necessary complement to Morgan as Morgan was essential to the scholarly ambitions of the young corn-belt student.

It remained only for Bandelier to be converted to Morgan's views. This was not too difficult, but, like all genuine conversions, it did not come about without some soul-searching on the part of the convert and after several years of struggle. Bandelier admired Morgan from the first, but he was not ready to give up his beloved chroniclers and subscribe to the doctrine of Morgan that Indian institutions on the Iroquoian pattern were "substantially universal in the Indian family, and therefore existed, presumptively, among the Aztecs."

In the first Bandelier letter to Morgan (White 1940: I, 109 et seq.), Bandelier revealed an independence of thought, though apologizing for his reluctance to accept Morgan's views wholeheartedly—"Please, therefore, to accept this as an apology for many *apparent* tendencies toward objectionalism & contradiction and also excuse the inklings, not of *school*-philosophy, but of school-*boy's* philosophy." He continued,

> You have warned me seriously against placing too much reliance on the statements of the older authors. I heed this warning at every step, but, still, how can we judge of the unadulterated condition of the American aboriginees except by *their* statements. . . . What can the present study of such a race give us, which should be of more *critical* value than are the statements of cultivated minds which observed the same race at the time of its purity & comparative strength? Are not both branches: the ethnological (the present) & the historical (the past) to go rather parallel?

Having thus stated his variance with the master's views, Bandelier ended his first letter with a request to be corrected if Morgan was so inclined. He complained of his isolation, "Here

& at St. Louis I have no serious assistance to look to," an attitude often repeated in his correspondence with Morgan. Goad believed that from the beginning of Bandelier's contact with Morgan, there was a gradual withdrawal from the Highland friends and associates, and that (pp. 37-38) from this time on, Bandelier had "only two ambitions, one of which he thought necessary in order to realize the other. He wanted to get rich so that he might, like his new-made acquaintance, devote his time and attention solely to his beloved studies."

Hodge (1932: 353) stated that Bandelier in 1877 widened his knowledge by extensive travel in Mexico and Central America and that between 1877 and 1879 a number of papers were published which dealt with the ethnology of the ancient Mexicans.[7] Goad (p. 22) flatly rejected this statement, however, claiming that these monographs regarding the Mexican area were strictly the products of library research. All evidence and lines of reason support Goad on this point. (See, for example, White and Bernal 1960.)

Nevertheless, these publications impressed the Executive Committee of the newly organized Archaeological Institute of America (or at least they impressed Morgan who, in turn, influenced the committee). Goad (p. 28) cited a letter, dated April 10, 1939, which Hodge wrote to him, stating that Morgan, Frederick W. Putnam, and Francis Parkman supported the sending of Bandelier to the Southwest, against the opposition of the President, Charles Eliot Norton, who had little respect for American archaeology.[8] The committee (Hodge

---

7. These papers were:
"On the Art of War and the Mode of Warfare of the Ancient Mexicans," *Tenth Annual Report, Peabody Museum,* Cambridge, 1877, pp. 95-161.

"On the Distribution and Tenure of Lands, and the Customs with Respect to Inheritance, among the Ancient Mexicans," *Eleventh Annual Report, Peabody Museum,* Cambridge, 1878, pp. 385-448.

"On the Sources for Aboriginal History of Spanish America," *Proceedings, American Association for the Advancement of Science,* St. Louis Meeting, 1878, Salem, Massachusetts, 1879, pp. 315-337.

8. Charles Eliot Norton (1827-1908) was the founder and first president of the Archaeological Institute of America. He was at that time Professor of

1932: 354) considered Bandelier "marked by sound judgement and correct methods of historical interpretation," and also noted that he had "shown a minute and familiar acquaintance with the existing sources of information concerning the conditions of the native races at the time of the Spanish Conquest." Further, the committee stated that

> Thoroughly equipped in this respect and possessing a knowledge of several European languages, and a fondness for linguistic studies which qualified him for the steady acquisition of native dialects, he has also the advantage of an enthusiastic devotion to his favorite studies, a readiness to endure any hardship in their pursuit, and a capacity for adapting himself to any necessity.

This glowing appraisal may well have been the newly constituted committee's concern for justifying their appointment, especially in view of the divided sentiment reported by Hodge. It was apparent that Bandelier had never actually conducted field investigations of any kind. His travels up to that time had been mainly in the relatively secure and comfortable circumstances existing in the eastern United States and Europe as of that date. Perhaps we should simply consider Morgan and the others to have been swift and keen judges of character since, as the journal entries repeatedly reveal, their mention of "enthusiastic devotion" to his studies and "a readiness to endure any hardship in their pursuit" undeniably proved to be accurate predictions.

On the other hand, the journals reveal somewhat less of "a capacity for adapting himself to any necessity," though this probably was not a lack of this ability but rather a complete candidness on the part of Bandelier in reporting his thoughts, reactions, and emotions. Virtually without exception, Bandelier appears to have recorded his innermost feelings in regard to his

---

History and Art at Harvard University. Norton favored classical archaeology, the basis for his lack of enthusiasm about the American studies proposed by Morgan, Parkman, and Putnam.

surroundings—weather, accommodations, food, and fellow man. The status of his health, as well as that of his family, the degree of cooperation from informants, guides, comrades, and correspondents, his estimate of progress made, and similar factors are all recorded. It should certainly be pointed out, in all fairness, that Bandelier, despite his frequent complaints and expressions of dissatisfaction, never recorded a longing or a threat to abandon his field investigations in favor of a library, classroom, lecture platform, or any other means of livelihood. As Goad (pp. 56-67) noted, one of Bandelier's greatest weaknesses was his frequently expressed self-pity, "so much so that he often accuses people, usually innocent of any but the kindliest feelings toward him, with being his enemies." Typically, Bandelier generally forgot these rages soon after uttering them and returned to a friendly attitude. ·

In the years after meeting Morgan, Bandelier's discontent with conditions in Highland seems to have mounted steadily. During this period, Bandelier had become involved in business interests, together with C. H. Sebyt, in the Confidence Coal Mining Company ("That infernal hole," as he referred to it in a letter of April 26, 1878, to Morgan [White 1940: II, 97]) and the Highland Mechanical Works. He divided his time between the offices of these two enterprises and, in addition, carried on his research and writing in the evenings and other spare moments. His letters to Morgan revealed great unhappiness with these business ventures.

His exhausting self-imposed schedule resulted in a gradual withdrawal from the customary activities of a civic nature. Nevertheless, the strain and discontent weighed heavily upon him, and Elise,[9] Bandelier's niece, wrote Morgan on January 28, 1880,

---

9. Bandelier's brother, Emil, had moved to Breece, Illinois, with his family. Emil died a few months prior to the time Bandelier first met Morgan, and Emil's daughters, Elise (Lizzie) and Emma, returned to Highland to live with their Uncle Adolph and his wife.

> Uncle is sick, the physicians say it is nervous prostration
> and have expressly forbidden all literary work whatsoever
> for the space of one year at least. (White 1940: II, 158)

A few days later, Bandelier, himself, against the order of his
physician, wrote Morgan (White 1940: II, 158-159) that he
had to leave Highland for a year or two. He begged Morgan to
help him find a situation, "if possible as assistant librarian or
something similar to it." His condition, he added, was "very urgent, it is one of life & death, for if I cannot find a place then
I cannot leave here, & by staying here I have the perspective
of becoming a helpless idiot very soon. My strength is over for
me."

Goad (p. 58) evaluated this plea as an obvious exaggeration
since the Bandelier family, as of that time, could well take care
of itself. Nevertheless, Morgan appreciated the necessity of
finding a position which would at least divert Bandelier's mind
from his troubles, both real and fancied. Morgan apparently
acted swiftly as Bandelier's niece wrote again on February 3,
saying that Bandelier gratefully accepted his offer. This was
seemingly a proposal that Bandelier accompany Morgan on a
field trip to New Mexico. On February 5, Bandelier wrote confirmation of his acceptance, stating that he had abandoned his
business ventures and that he was eager to go, for as much as
two years of field work. He suggested (White 1940: II, 159-
160) that the proposed survey be extended

> so as to follow the supposed tracks of the Mexican tribe to
> the "Casas Grandes"[10] [in northern Chihuahua] . . . and
> finally to Michhuacan.

In conclusion, Bandelier proposed that he go on to Mexico

---

10. It is interesting to note both Bandelier's mention of this great complex
of ruins prior to his actual visitation and the fact that, despite the long-
recognized importance of Casas Grandes, serious excavation at Casas Grandes
did not begin until 1957-58 when Dr. Charles C. Di Peso of the Amerind
Foundation began extensive work at this site.

City where he would request that a dozen active young Americans join him in exploring Mitla, Palenque, Copan, and other sites.

To this letter of February 5, Bandelier added a postscript, in which he asked Morgan, "What kind of fire-arms shall I buy? What sort of clothing?" Goad (p. 59) aptly noted, "he was full of plans for the expedition, as excited as a boy on his first real hunting trip, and almost as naive." His health and spirit improved in the next few weeks although his recovery was hardly complete. He began writing again, despite a series of sleepless nights and similar difficulties. His impatience is revealed in a letter to Morgan, dated February 29, in which he said he had sent a review of C. C. Rau's "Palenque Tablet," to The Nation but had received no reply. He believed his review to have been "too long, and, besides, too bitter."[11]

Bandelier continued with a lengthy defense of Morgan and himself, and he concluded the letter, saying, "The key to aboriginal history of Mexico and Central America lies between the city of Mexico and the southern part of Colorado."[12]

---

11. This paper appeared in the series, Contributions to Knowledge (331: XXII), Smithsonian Institution, Washington, 1879. Rau, of the United States National Museum, had criticized the Morgan adherents for erring on the side of a too simple type of Mexican society in an effort to controvert the errors on the opposite side. Bandelier, in turn, severely criticized his ignorance of the Spanish-American literature. In his letter of February 29, 1880, to Morgan (White 1940:II, 163), Bandelier called Rau an "ignoramus." Bandelier's fears proved groundless as his review of the "Palenque Tablet" appeared in the June 3, 1880, number of The Nation.

12. This prediction, on the basis of library research alone, is interesting to contemplate in view of various research developments and findings of the last decade. Goad (p. 61) stated that Bandelier and Morgan "believed the Aztecs were merely Pueblo people who were related to, or migrated from, the Pueblo region of Northern New Mexico and Southern Colorado . . ."

There is, in addition, especially evident in the earlier years of Bandelier's southwestern investigations, a strong tendency to derive Puebloan culture from aboriginal Mexico. While some of his attempts were obviously naive and unwarranted by the data, it may well be that Bandelier's efforts will find increasing support and confirmation. A case in point, demonstrating this increasing willingness to consider Southwestern-Mexican connections, is the description, analysis, and discussion of the Kuaua kiva murals by Bertha P. Dutton in a forthcoming

(White 1940: II, 166) As the spring developed, Morgan found that he would not be able to go to the Southwest, but Bandelier continued with his preparations and plans. In March, he wrote that both his father and he had recognized his unsuitability for the business world and that arrangements had been completed whereby he could "cut loose altogether from business" and await the "call from science." (White 1940: II, 166; also see White and Bernal 1960:287.)

Bandelier's letters to Morgan during the spring of 1880 contained further plans and additional details. He proposed a thorough search of the church records, for which he needed a letter of introduction to the Bishop of Santa Fe in order to obtain, in turn, letters to the local priests to assist him in his searches. He hoped to "collect as many relations, reports of Missions, etc., as possible and besides ransack the baptismal and matrimonial registers for traces of the 'gens.'"

Bandelier fretted as the directors of the Archaeological Institute of America seemed unable to reach final decisions regarding the expedition. Learning of a French expedition being prepared for work in Mexico, Bandelier (White 1940: II, 169) wrote Morgan, urging haste—"Let Americans hurry up, else there will be another installment of ruined cities, palaces, &c., poured out over the world." In a following letter, he predicted that members of the Lorillard Expedition[13] will (among other things)

> take hold of these . . . "oldest records" of America and will prove that there are indications tending to show that at some very remote period there was a Scandinavian immigration which introduced the art of writing among savage hordes in this continent. (White 1940: II, 172)

---

publication. The extensive archaeological work in northern Mexico by J. Charles Kelley will, when published, fill many of the present "contact" gaps.

13. This expedition was financed by Pierre Lorillard, the American tobacco millionaire and by the French government. Later, in 1881, Bandelier was sent to Mexico to join this expedition which proved to have been a failure. (Goad 1939: 63)

He also again expressed unhappiness to Morgan (White 1940: II, 177) that the Peabody Museum had not printed his monograph, "On the Social Organization and Mode of Government of the Ancient Mexicans."[14]

In April (White 1940: II, 184), Bandelier wrote Morgan that he had turned down a possibility of joining the Lorillard Expedition, adding that he would prefer a position as assistant-librarian somewhere in the East in case the Institute's plans should not materialize. In the same letter, Bandelier expressed an interest in an alternative to Mexico, namely, that of going to Santa Fe and spending the winter in the archives and library there. He included a list of pueblos, churches, and missions which he had compiled from the literature and proceeded to explain to Morgan in some detail the method with which he would use the church records in studying the ethnology of the various pueblos. In a preceding letter (White 1940: II, 184), he had said:

> Lastly, it becomes clearer & clearer to me that if the history of aborigines in Spanish America rests on a frail and unsatisfactory basis, this is not at all due to any lack of material honestly collected . . . but much rather to the careless and superficial study of these Spanish sources by modern compilators or so-called historians.

In a letter of May 11 (White 1940: II, 187-188), Bandelier informed Morgan that he had written directly to Norton, mentioning the possibility of his New Mexico research. From this letter, it seems that Major J. W. Powell, Director of the Bureau of American Ethnology, was being considered as leader of the expedition, and Bandelier made known his pleasure at the prospect of working under him. He also mentioned a fourth monograph he was contemplating for the Mexican area, "On the Method of dividing and counting time used by the ancient

14. This paper finally appeared in the *Twelfth Annual Report, Peabody Museum*, Cambridge, 1879, pp. 557-699. White (1940: I, 77) stated that the reason for the delay was, in part, the length of the manuscript and, in part, typographical difficulties with the manuscript.

Mexicans, and their method of fixing dates graphically and in chronological order—or something like that. . . ."[15]

Further delays continued to frustrate Bandelier. He turned to Quito and Peru in his research, but hastened to make it clear that he had not abandoned Mexico. "I shall remain in the field of Mexican antiquities until every feature of them is thoroughly 'monographized.' " (White 1940: II, 194) His South American research at this time consisted of copying "two very scarce books on Peru and Quito which I shall never be able to purchase."[16] In these, he reported that he had found "additional evidence in regard to the 'gens.' "

Other letters of this period reveal more of Bandelier's viewpoint. The work in New Mexico and Mexico was of interest to him, not in the way of personal prestige but rather as an opportunity to learn basic data. "The main thing is to have an expedition sent out. . . ." (White 1940: II, 196-197) He expressed willingness to go or not to go, to lead the expedition or to be merely a member of the party. He hoped it would be possible for him to spend a week at Taos, one at Acoma, and then make a trip through the San Juan valley and the Rio Chaco area.[17] These experiences would provide:

> such practical knowledge of the ruins and of their builders as to enable me to undertake that far more important journey southward through the great "terra incognita," where

---

15. This paper was never published, and no manuscript has been found.
16. These two publications were:
Miguel Cavello Balboa, *Miscelanea Anartica y Origen de los Incas del Peru,* in the Ternaux-Compans collection. *Circa* 1570.
Juan de Valasco, *Historia del Reyno de Quito. Circa* 1800.
Goad (p. 67fn38) stated that it was unknown what edition of these works Bandelier used and also how he obtained them.
17. Here, Bandelier was quite obviously guilty of oversimplification, and at the same time, he was overly optimistic. His selection of these two pueblos and his designation of the particular concentrations of archaeological remains are interesting in terms of present-day perspectives. He simultaneously revealed an impressive familiarity with the area, based upon the available sources rather than personal first-hand acquaintance, and a somewhat surprising naiveté, or blindness, in respect to the limitations of the available early sources.

the Mexicans, the Maya, the Quiché went through the gradual transformation . . . which changed them from the northern "pueblo Indians" to southern "pueblo Indians."

The proposed journey south to Mexico City, which Bandelier never was able to make, was not a grandiose venture. If it proved to be a matter of finances, Bandelier was ready to make the trip alone. He believed that great value lay in studying the development and transition of architecture as a clue in tracing ethnic relationships. "As long as we cannot establish one connected string of evidence from Colorado to Guatemala, and then from Bogota to Bolivia, we have not gained our cause fully." Goad (p. 68) commented that to Bandelier, "our cause" meant "the establishment of the essential unity of the whole American Indian Pueblo culture." This statement might be clarified, insofar as modern context is concerned, by substituting some such phrase as "Nuclear America," or "High Civilization," for Goad's "Pueblo culture."

Goad (pp. 68-69) continued, somewhat over-pessimistically, perhaps:

It was in pursuit of this proof that Bandelier was to spend the rest of his life. The tragedy was, of course, that he was pursuing a will-o-the-wisp. Racial unity in general is admitted by anthropologists now, though it existed amid the greatest cultural heterogeneity in America.

In late June, plans came to a head. Bandelier was called to Washington to talk with Major Powell. He spent two weeks there with Powell and Rau, receiving instructions and historical material for his archaeological work in New Mexico. He also visited the Smithsonian Library as well as the Library of Congress. Later, he spent a week with Professor Norton in Cambridge, and then collected photographic supplies in New York.

In July, he wrote Morgan (White 1940: II, 203) that he

was to be allowed $1,200 per year by the Archaeological Institute of America for his expenses. "This is certainly not extravagant," he wrote, "since it includes *all purchases* & the expenses of nearly 40 days of *eastern* travel," as well as travel and other expenses in New Mexico. "I believe that this is the poorest outfit ever extended, but . . . the most valuable explorations have cost the *least money*." This sentiment has unquestionably been echoed by innumerable research scholars in virtually all fields in the years since Bandelier consoled himself with it.

In the travels through the East, Bandelier added to his documentary collection regarding the Spanish conquest and colonization of the Southwest.[18] His reactions to the people whom he met after earlier correspondence or other impersonal contact through publication have been summarized by Goad (pp. 71-72).

> Rau, with whom Bandelier had apparently made his peace, seemed to him "free and easy," despite the "Palenque Tablet" affair. Putnam, of Peabody Museum, and Rau explained to the novitiate archaeologist their systems of classifying museum material. He liked Norton, in fact all of them much better than he had expected. This is another characteristic of Bandelier. However much he might recite the faults of brother scholars in his letters, Bandelier usually liked people when he met them face to face. He thought both Powell and Putnam were in danger of being buried under details.

Bandelier wrote Morgan, "The same trouble is apparent in Europe. Lines of thought are superior, in the end, to lines of facts, because fact is dead without the constant action of thought upon it." (White 1940: II, 207)

---

18. According to Goad (pp. 70-71), Bandelier took a number of bibliographic items westward with him to New Mexico. The citations were not listed in detail, but included narratives of Jaramillo and Castañeda, the reports of Guzmán, Espejo, Herrera, Kino, Escalante, and numerous others.

Bandelier remained in Highland through the first half of August, working at his "Historical Introduction."[19] He concluded that Cibola was Zuñi, and he busied himself with the diary of Gaspar Castaño de Sosa and the documents pertaining to the Oñate colonization. Finally, in mid-August, he was prepared to depart for New Mexico—his principal regret being that he would be unable to attend the meeting of the American Association for the Advancement of Science, at which Morgan, as President, was to preside. (White 1940: II, 208)

On August 20, Bandelier left St. Louis for New Mexico by rail.

THE YEARS OF FIELD WORK: 1880-1903

Bandelier arrived in Santa Fe on the evening of August 23, 1880, and took a room at the Grand Central Hotel where, revealing something of his "adaptability," he slept "until 9 A.M. with bedbugs." The next several days were spent in trying to meet various individuals in the city and in gaining access to archival and documentary materials.[20] In at least some of these efforts he was successful, and seemingly, as an outcome of his conversations with priests whom he met at the Archbishop's, he decided to go to Pecos. Between this decision and his actual departure, three days rather than one passed as it took time to make the necessary arrangements for the buggy and horses.

Meanwhile, he made further contacts, collected informa-

---

19. This paper, "Historical Introduction to Studies among the Sedentary Indians of New Mexico," was written in Santa Fe, in September, 1880, according to Goad (p. 191). It was published along with "A Visit to the Aboriginal Ruins in the Valley of the Rio Pecos" in the *Papers of the Archaeological Institute of America*, Vol. 1, nos. 1 and 2, Boston, 1881.

20. The first portion of this section of the Introduction pertains to the same period of time, 1880-1892, as that covered by the journals being edited for this and the three projected companion volumes. An effort has been made to avoid needless duplication though a certain amount of material from the journals has been utilized in order to provide adequate context and continuity for data derived from the Morgan letters, local newspaper items, and other sources not covered in the journal entries.

tion, and widened his acquaintance with his new surroundings, not all of which met with his approval.

Bandelier spent a little more than a week at Pecos, talking with residents of the vicinity, examining the ruins there as well as others nearby, photographing, measuring, collecting specimens, and making notations—all in a pattern which Goad (p. 74) described as typifying the first trip westward.

> Delighted as a child, he rushed here and there, exploring, collecting pottery fragments, flint and obsidian flakes, arrowheads, and even samples of the adobe mud from between the stones of New Mexico's ruins. These he shipped to Putnam at Harvard with little rhyme or reason.[21]

This cursory survey served as a basis for a surprisingly lengthy report on these extensive remains. This "History of Pecos" was finished September 17, and his "Historical Introduction" was completed two days later. Accepted and retitled by the Institute's officers, this rather superficial study of Pecos, together with the "Historical Introduction," comprised the first of the Papers of the Institute (Bandelier, A. F., 1881: a and b). Perhaps the greatest value of the Pecos study was the attention it called to archaeological possibilities in the Southwest.

The report is also of interest in revealing Bandelier's attempt to further the cause advocated by Morgan and himself. In concluding his measurements and tally of rooms at Pecos, he commented,

> The entire structure therefore presents the appearance of a honeycomb, or rather of a beehive, and perfectly illustrates among the lower degrees of culture of mankind, the

---

21. Goad's appraisal was unfortunately all too accurate as of the time at which Bandelier was doing this initial field work. However, it is worth noting that techniques of analysis developed in recent decades and applied even more recently could utilize materials such as Bandelier collected, assuming that adequate notations on source, etc. were made. There would be real satisfaction in reporting such activities as evidence of Bandelier's unusual pioneering perception of significant evidence, but, unfortunately, it seems that Goad's appraisal was quite justified.

prevailing principle of communism in living, which finds
its parallel in the lower classes of animals. Tradition, historical relation, and analogy, tell us that this house was
used as a dwelling, and that consequently it was to all intents and purposes, a communal house. (Bandelier, A. F.,
1881b: 54)

Using various Spanish sources to reinforce his position here,
Bandelier went on elsewhere to quote Ruiz, who lived near the
Pecos ruins at the time of Bandelier's visit.

> Not only did the Pecos Indians live together, build their
> houses together, but they raised their crops in one com-
> mon field (though divided into individual or rather family
> plots, according to Ruiz), irrigated from one common
> water source which gathered its contents of moisture from
> the inhabited surface of the pueblo ground . . . It forcibly
> recalls the system of "distribution and tenure of lands"
> among the ancient Mexicans. (p. 90)

While overstating the communal aspects of puebloan life,
these reconstructions of Bandelier were essentially accurate.
However, he, himself, realized the superficiality and potential
error of his researches as he expressed an intention of returning
to Pecos at a later date for further investigations.

> Should, in the meantime, some archaeologist explore
> the same locality, correct my errors, and unravel the mys-
> teries hovering about the place, I heartily wish him as
> much pleasure and quiet enjoyment as I have had during
> my ten days' work, in which the dream of a life has at last
> begun to be a realization. (p. 103)[22]

This same enthusiastic pleasure was reported, more infor-

---

22. Bandelier, interestingly enough, never returned to Pecos to continue
his investigations there. Actually serious work at Pecos did not begin until
A. V. Kidder did his extensive and intensive excavations there in the 1920's
and 1930's. For major publications resulting from the work of this expedition,
see the following sources: Kidder 1924; 1931-36; 1932; and 1958; also, Hooton
1930 and Parsons 1925.

mally, in a letter which Bandelier wrote to Morgan (White 1940: II, 213) from Baughl's on September 5 (a letter which, interestingly, Bandelier failed to mention in his journal. It would seem that he recorded his correspondence quite meticulously, perhaps especially that with Morgan, but this, at least, was one exception.) To Morgan, he wrote, "I am dirty, ragged & sunburnt, but of best cheer. My life's work has at last begun." Having written in this spirit on the 5th, he opened his entry of the 6th with "Rather unwell' but then continued, "Started for the mesa with Thomas Munn at 8 A.M."

Before leaving for the Southwest, Bandelier had expressed his specific interest in Acoma and Taos. Upon arrival, he was urged to go to still other villages (Isleta, Tesuque, Laguna, etc.) by the Vicar-General, Padre Eguillon, and by Dr. Thomas. But on August 27, before leaving for Pecos, Bandelier recorded that he "saw and conversed with Padre Rómulo Ribera of Peña Blanca." From this meeting, presumably their first, came an invitation from Padre Ribera to visit and stay with him. Apparently this additional measure of cooperation or hospitality tipped the scales in favor of this venture, to be started as soon as Bandelier had completed his Pecos trip and consequent writing.

This seemingly insignificant shift actually introduced Bandelier to his ethnographic studies under exceedingly difficult circumstances. Arriving at Peña Blanca on September 23, Bandelier was taken the next day to Santo Domingo Pueblo by Padre Ribera. There he was left in the priest's quarters, alone among a people who even today have maintained a reputation of coolness to outsiders which turns to outright hostility when one would investigate their customs and beliefs.

Bandelier must have created quite a stir in the pueblo with his insatiable curiosity. Partly from lack of experience and background and partly from linguistic handicaps, Bandelier gathered obviously contradictory data on such points as the location, above or below, of the summer and winter houses, respectively. He inquired, in random fashion, into clan presence and structure, government, economics, food, and other topics. Initially, he seems to have been reasonably well accepted as he helped record some tribal affairs in writing. Some reservation was noted by Bandelier, however, insofar as the governor was concerned. Nevertheless, he pursued his inquiries, beginning on the 27th to measure and map the houses and the kivas. A dance took place, but Bandelier did not see it although he did record the alternate periods of drumming and silence. On a trip to Peña Blanca, together with a Spaniard and a Santo Domingo man, Bandelier foolishly attempted to question the Indian in regard to the existence and nature of the cacique.

On September 30, Bandelier clearly noted that relations between the Pueblo and himself had deteriorated although G. C. Bennett of Santa Fe arrived to do some photographic work, and Bandelier seemingly pursued his inquires disregarding this change in attitude. By October 2, a man confided that Bandelier was wrong in staying on in the pueblo. The photography and constant stream of questions on a wide range of topics were having their impact, especially on the older people (in whose hands lay the governing of the tribe). Directed to stay in his room during a funeral, Bandelier instead went elsewhere in the church where he could watch without being seen himself. Later, while showing Dr. Thomas the church, the sacristan objected strenuously. Finally, Bandelier went to Peña Blanca for consultation with Padre Ribera, relations with the Santo Domingans, in general, having worsened. While waiting for the return of the Padre, Bandelier explored the vicinity of Peña Blanca, measuring, collecting, and taking notes. On the 5th, he met his first Cochiti Indian who was noticeably more cordial and open than had been most of the people of Santo Domingo.

With the return of Padre Ribera, Bandelier's experiences were discussed, and a decision was reached to transfer his efforts to Cochiti. On the 6th of October, Bandelier visited Cochiti. Greatly pleased with the far more hospitable reception accorded him there, Bandelier moved to that pueblo on the 7th, making his home in that village until December. During this stay, which proved highly satisfactory, Bandelier made his first visit to the Rito de los Frijoles (October 23),[23] and he enthusiastically searched for antiquities in the area and studied the life around him at Cochiti.

From Cochiti, Bandelier wrote Morgan (White 1940: II, 214) that,

> At Sto. Domingo I could not stay any longer, I quarreled with the council of the tribe, after they had lied to me 3 times, & finally kicked the governor out of my room. This manner of protesting [?] was not to his taste, & the next morning came a declaration of war in the shape of a refusal to give me anything more to eat. To this I replied by simply *staying*, & supporting myself on watermelons, until at last the things grew obsolete and, unable to achieve anything more there, I moved to this pueblo of Cochití, also of Queres stock, where I have been rec'd with open arms and have been, for 2 weeks, staying with one of the "principales" of the tribe, & shall stay here until next spring.

Bandelier returned to Santa Fe, however, on December 15, made a number of visits there, and then left for Highland and his family on the 18th, arriving home on the 21st—in time for Christmas. From the journal, it seems that this was a surprise visit, and there was rejoicing all around with Bandelier's return. For the rest of the year, the journal entries are

---

23. Bandelier visited the Frijoles area again in 1880, on a three-day trip in December. Later, in August, 1885, he returned to the area briefly, and in 1890, he was there from October 12 to 16 and, perhaps, had one other short visit. All of these trips were exploratory in nature—observing, measuring, note-taking, and collecting. In a manner consistent with his Southwestern investigations generally, Bandelier did no excavating in the Frijoles region. Later, Bandelier made Frijoles Canyon the principal locale of his novel, *The Delight Makers*. The Frijoles area, with the country south to the Cañada de Cochiti Grant, was proclaimed a National Monument, named in honor of Bandelier, by President Woodrow Wilson on February 11, 1916.

minimal as Bandelier caught up loose ends from his previous months' work and joined in the season's activities. In his entry of December 31, Bandelier summarized his feelings in respect to his initial field work as follows:

> Thus the most important year of my entire life draws to a close. . . So far, so good, and there is hope for better. . . Have no reflections to record. Future action is all that occupies my thought.

On the 6th of January, 1881, Bandelier, rather than returning to the Southwest, went East. There, his plans changed completely; he was to go to Mexico as a member of the Lorillard-de Charney Expedition. Seemingly his eagerness to go to this new area outweighed his feelings of contempt expressed earlier. In a letter to Morgan, dated January 15 in Boston, Bandelier indicated that there was dissatisfaction with de Charney's leadership, and Professor Norton had been approached to suggest someone capable of taking charge, "in a quiet & unobtrusive manner." (White 1940: II, 223)

On January 20, he wrote Morgan (White 1940: II, 224), outlining his plans. The approach would be historical, following the trail of the early Spaniards: ground plans of pueblos inhabited in 1518 would be obtained; and he would study the living Maya. Sailing from New Orleans on February 20, he reached Mexico City on March 2 only to find that de Charney was returning to Europe, his expedition having been riddled with fever in Chiapas. The exploration of Yucatan was abandoned. Bandelier took the view, in which he was supported by de Charney (whom he liked upon meeting, despite earlier criticisms), that the Lorillard people would have to live up to the agreement and continue to support the Bandelier work.

Having corresponded earlier, Bandelier met his "dear friend," Joaquín García Icazbalceta,[24] the great bibliographer.

_____

24. Don Joaquín García Icazbalceta (1825-1894), a 19th-century Mexican scholar who spent much of his life collecting and publishing rare historical documents and writing on the colonial history of Mexico.

In a letter of March 3 (White 1940: II, 228), he informed Morgan that he had arranged to have a copy of "Social Organization" go to García Icazbalceta and that he would "watch the effects." In the same letter, he announced that he had found the transition from the New Mexican pueblo beehive to the isolated structure of Yucatan at Tula. He confided that de Charney "does not know it himself yet, but I saw it at a glance."

With the unexpected freedom of the altered plan, Bandelier visited the pyramids of Teotihuacan and other sites in the vicinity of Mexico City, and then he visited García Icazbalceta in La Puebla. In one of a series of *Reisebriefe* in the *Highland Union*, appearing between March 25 and August 19, he wrote from La Puebla on March 7, "I am consequently in a highly placed neighborhood and I myself live and move in high circles."

From March 8th until early June, Bandelier visited the Cholula area, studying the ruins and observing the country. The Indians of the region were despicable. His trip to Oaxaca was hot and uncomfortable, but Bandelier managed to retain some perspective, or humor, as evidenced in his account of the guide and horses for his trip from Tehuacan,

> On which ever side I would place my foot in the stirrup, the weight of my body threatened to demolish the horse. To leap into the saddle from behind would have resulted in breaking its spinal column, for the individual vertebrae seemed to hang loosely from the backbone like the beads of a rosary. Finally, I leaned the animal against the wall and so succeeded in the course of time and with great care to climb into the saddle. (*Die Highland Union*, June 10, 1881)

Bandelier's report (1884: 262-326) on the ruins of Mitla provided dimensions and methods of construction, with little or no speculation. He appeared, however, to have been more impressed with these remains than he had been with any in

New Mexico. These intimate reactions were expressed overtly in a *Reisebrief* (*Die Highland Union*, September 2, 1881).

> A stillness as of the grave rules in the well cleaned courtyard, . . . Not a bird sings, no cricket chirps in the "Ruins of Mitla." Lizards rustle over the stones, while the carrion vulture sits on the walls and watches the body of the intruder with a cold, inquiring look.
> . . . in the narrow passages, footsteps resound like a dull roar from the depths. But wherever the eye may turn, it is met not by ugly faces nor horridly twisted snake-like bodies, but by simple, geometric figures which, to be sure, reveal the stiffness of death, but, too, a striving for symmetric harmony. This was all so completely different than what I had thought; not larger or more imposing, but purer, more noble than I had imagined.
> Here lay questions, which could not be answered either by unthinking groping among the errors of the past three centuries or by a fantastic interpretation influenced by oriental dreams, even less by an exclusive holding to the conditions of the natives toward the north. Only exact study of details with continuous reference to the geographical relationships, could lead to the goal.

It is interesting, in view of this statement and others in a letter to Morgan (White 1940: II, 242), that in 1882 Bandelier could speak of ruins in the Acoma area as superior to those of Mitla.

In July, Bandelier returned to Cholula and planned to depart for home without delay. A yellow fever epidemic in Vera Cruz and his own illness, however, prevented the departure until September 18. On July 31, while in Cholula, he had officially become a member of the Catholic Church with a baptismal name of Agustín Vicente Adolfo Francisco Bandelier "de Berna, Suiza," García Icazbalceta acting as his sponsor (White and Bernal 1960: 248 et seq.) Arriving in the United States on October 1, he visited in Cambridge and with Morgan after which time, he returned to Highland on October 13.

Apparently Bandelier returned with the idea that the archaeological remains of Mexico were essentially the work of a primitive people, that they were of a higher order than those found in New Mexico and the United States generally, but that they were still Indian.

Two letters from Mitla, one dated April 14, the other June 27, provided Morgan with some of Bandelier's overall impressions (White 1940: II, 234-244). The combination of slabs and rocks in adobe which he had found in the walls of Mitla reminded him of pueblo ruins in New Mexico, though the walls of Mitla were better made and were of great beauty. The so-called "pyramids" (Bandelier felt that the word pyramid should not be used) were fortifications [sic] with a temple on top. It was his belief that the Nahuatl speakers of Mexico were not an originally sedentary people and, further, that aside from their belonging to the same race, "*they have nothing in common with the pueblos of New Mexico.*" Communal tenure of lands had disappeared except for a few traces. He expressed his faith in the early authors, with exception of their terminology. He placed Nahuatl, coming from the north, in the Athapascan linguistic stock. (Linguistic research of long standing has demonstrated that this last point is completely erroneous. Nahuatl belongs to the Uto-Aztecan stock, which is entirely distinct from the Athapascan stock.)

No further correspondence from Bandelier to Morgan has been preserved, but there were a number of letters written by Bandelier to Mrs. Morgan after her husband's death. From these letters to the Morgans and, to a lesser extent, from the journal entries, Bandelier's theories may be discerned. Goad (pp. 97-98) summarized this phase of Bandelier's career as follows.

> He was careful in his public utterances, for he knew he was on the defensive. Hence his endless footnotes and careful elision of everything but the observed facts in his archaeological reports. Only as opportunity offered did he slip into his scholarly writing pegs on which to hang

his and Morgan's theories of social evolution.

The trip to Mexico was a fine thing for Bandelier at this time. It helped to give him a broader viewpoint and it seems to have jarred his rather dogmatic views as to the relationship between New Mexican and Mexican culture. He returned to New Mexico, in 1882, a wiser man and a riper anthropologist.

Seemingly overlooked by Goad in his analysis of relationships between Bandelier and Morgan was the fact that Bandelier, in his *Reisebrief* of September 2, 1881, expressed a significant reliance on geographical relationships. Here, inferentially, he seems to have had in mind distributions and, probably, also environmental factors. In other words, Bandelier, as of that time, retained an appreciable measure of influence from von Humboldt and others which had been exerted prior to his relationships with Morgan. If this may be assumed, it follows that Bandelier, in the winter of 1881-82, experienced something of a reassessment of his beliefs.

Morgan's death forever closed the possibility of recurrent stimulation or of further conditioning from that source. Simutaneously, there can be little doubt that Bandelier felt less of a release from unwanted pressure than a dedication to the further strengthening of the thesis advanced by Morgan and himself, a strengthening that now rested largely on his own efforts. However, these emotions were inevitably confronted by the undeniable significance of yet other factors, such as those of geographical considerations, and also by the data gathered in the field, first in New Mexico and then in Mexico, through his own efforts. Thus, having spent the winter of 1881-82 in writing up his work on Mexico,[25] there is little doubt that Bandelier did, as Goad noted, return to New Mexico in the spring of 1882, "a wiser man." Multiple perspectives derived from diverse experiences and various sources have long

25. This research was presented in Bandelier's publication: "Report of an Archaeological Tour into Mexico in the Year 1881," which appeared in 1884 as one of the *Papers of the Archaeological Institute of America*.

been recognized as fundamental to the maturation of any scholar.

On March 17, 1882, Bandelier returned to Santa Fe, this time in the company of his wife, Josephine, or, as she is normally referred to in the journals, Joe. He renewed his acquaintances with friends in town and met Indians from various pueblos, including Cochiti, who brought him up to date on local events. In late April, after spending most of his time at Cochiti (while Joe went to Albuquerque), Bandelier rejoined his wife in Albuquerque briefly and then embarked upon an extended trip in the Laguna-Acoma-Grants area. After a number of shorter trips from a base at Albuquerque, the Bandeliers returned to Santa Fe at the end of June. Joe's health had steadily declined during the recent weeks, and after a series of visits in Santa Fe and a brief trip to Peña Blanca and Cochiti for farewells and for the celebration of the Cochiti major Feast Day, July 14, the Bandeliers left Santa Fe on July 15. They reached home, in Highland, July 22.

A quiet summer ensued. Friends were visited, and there was some writing. For a month, Bandelier offered to keep books. He lectured in St. Louis and traveled to Rochester for two weeks in October. By early November, however, the cumulative effect of his father's ill-temper and domination and the desire to go back to the field resulted in Bandelier's taking leave of Joe, "poor, dear, little wife," and returning to the Southwest.

Reaching Las Vegas on the 5th, Bandelier spent several days visiting people and sites in the region. He was attempting to locate the eastern periphery of the Puebloan area, a project that he had not had time enough to complete on his journey eastward the previous summer. By the 15th, he had arrived in Santa Fe and had started final preparations for the long trip which he had described to Mrs. Morgan prior to his departure from Highland (White 1940: II, 244-245) and one in which Morgan himself had expressed great interest and to which he had attached great value. The purpose was to attempt to trace a supposed migration from the Pueblo area to the Valley of Mexico. The Institute had provided photographic apparatus; otherwise, he was "foot-loose" and "absolutely independent from outside help—a guide excepted." He added, hopefully, "If nothing untoward happens, it ought to become a journey memorable for archaeological science."

Until the 18th of December, Bandelier was busy with a shipment of specimens (some eighteen cigar boxes of pottery, etc.) from Santa Fe, "cleaning up" affairs, buying a horse (for fifty dollars), and employing a guide, José Olivas. Among these preparations, Bandelier found time for a short trip to Peña Blanca, Zile, and Cochiti, in the course of which he witnessed several ceremonies. Traveling down the corridor east of the Sandia Mountains, Bandelier visited numerous ruins, some of which were inhabited within the historic period, and talked with residents of the region whose families, in a number of instances, had been in that area for several generations. Wind, snow, and cold hindered but did not halt their efforts to photograph, measure, and collect specimens from the numerous sites along their way. On the final day of the year, Bandelier recorded in his journal that the cold was "almost insupportable."

While filled with his usual enthusiasm and determination, the final paragraph of his last journal entry in 1882 reveals a loneliness for family, or homesickness, that Bandelier rarely expressed. As such, its tone is in rather sharp contrast to the feeling of complete satisfaction with the present and great optimism for the future expressed in the final entry of 1880.

The month of January, 1883, was also spent in the corridor east of the Sandia-Manzano mountain chain. From Albuquerque on February 1, Bandelier headed westward via Isleta and Belen to Laguna, Acoma, and ultimately, to Zuñi, on the 21st of February. Later (March 18), in a letter to Mrs. Morgan (White 1940: II, 249), he described this trip as follows.

I left Belen on the 11 of February on horseback and

traveled 50 miles to Laguna, a very pleasant journey, done leisurely in 2 days, measuring two interesting ruins on the road. At Laguna I was hospitably received and had the advantage of witnessing one of their chief dances. A young American, Mr. Bigler[26] from Santa Fe, had joined me there, & so I rode over to Acoma with him in a furious blizzard of snow, & then left for Zuñi by rail. I did this in order to gain time, leaving my horse at Laguna. At Bennett's Station no horse could be obtained, so I walked over to Zuñi (30 miles), where Mr. Cushing[27] & his people received me with open arms. I spent 15 days in the most pleasant and most profitable manner imaginable. . . My opinion of him [Cushing] is that he is the direct successor to Mr. Morgan in the study of Indian life. . . His discoveries are marvelous and, what is stranger still, they are perfectly within the scope of our views.

From Zuñi, Bandelier swung back to the Fort Wingate, Laguna, and Grants area, not returning until the end of March. In early April, he was again on the move, this time striking southwestward to Hawikuh, and thence to San Juan (St. Johns), Showlow, Fort Apache, San Carlos, Fort Thomas, Globe, and the Rio Salado area, reaching Fort Reno at the end of the month. In June, he visited Fort McDowell, Phoenix, Tempe, Sweetwater, the Pima Agency, Casa Grande, and Tucson. Leaving his horse at Fort Lowell, near Tucson, he returned by train to Santa Fe, and, after a few days of visiting and conducting some business matters, Bandelier returned to Illinois, leaving Santa Fe on July 12 and arriving in Highland on the 13th.

26. This was Frank Bigler, a friend of Cushing.

27. Frank H. Cushing (1857-1900). Cushing went with Major Powell's expedition to New Mexico in 1879, and he lived at Zuñi Pueblo until the spring of 1884. He wrote a number of major publications regarding various aspects of Zuñi culture. Bandelier was not always as complimentary in his views on Cushing, however, as he was here. In 1889, when the Hemenway Expedition was in financial difficulties (and Bandelier's own future was in jeopardy), Bandelier wrote, "Cushing, it seems, is in disgrace. Well—while I am very sorry for it, still it is his own fault. I worked and saved, what he did I do not know."

Remaining in the east, primarily in Highland, until October 22, Bandelier returned to Santa Fe on the 25th of October. Until early December (with the exception of a two-week trip in November to the El Paso area), Bandelier confined his activities to visiting ruins and pueblos in the region around Santa Fe and examining the archives there. In mid-December, Bandelier began to work his way down the Rio Grande valley, then westward until he reached Tucson in late January, 1884. At Fort Lowell, he reclaimed his horse, which had been cared for by the troops, and then traveled to the border, via Benson, Fort Huachuca, and Tombstone. Despite the advice of the garrison at Fort Huachuca to forego explorations in that area because of Geronimo and his renegade Apaches, Bandelier, with an Indian guide, crossed the border at Naco on February 21.

Traveling by way of Cananea, Arispe, and Bavícora, he penetrated a hundred miles or more south of the border before turning eastward into the mountains. At Oposura on the upper Rio Yaqui drainage, he left his horse, and, with two young guides as companions, reached the village of Nacori. From this village, he entered the western slopes of the Que-hua-ue-ri-chi range and then returned to Granados on the western fork of the upper Rio Yaqui. He joined a convoy to cross the Apache-infested mountains, spent a few days with the "remnants of church archives" at Haassavas and examining the traces of "ancient garden beds and dwellings." From Huachinera, he moved to Bacerac and Bavispe, searching out the remains as he went. Crossing into Chihuahua, he proceeded to Janos on the Upper Rio Casas Grandes. Turning south, he followed the valley to the ruins at Casas Grandes, measuring them and exploring the eastern slopes of the sierra as far as the Arroyo del Nombre de Dios where he visited the cave-dwellings. From May 8 until mid-June, he pursued his examination of the Casas Grandes valley. On June 14, 1884, he returned to the American side of the border, stopping at Deming.

With his return at this time, the long-planned and hopefully regarded tracing of an assumed Pueblo migration from
New Mexico to the Central Valley of Mexico came to a halt.
There is no substantial evidence explaining why he did not
follow through with the original plan to go all the way to
Mexico City. By the time he had reached Bavícora, he had
penetrated through the area of serious Apache trouble and
was more than halfway to Hermosillo. There were people in
Mexico City who could be depended upon for whatever assistance was necessary. However, from Deming, he swung westward to Tucson and from there returned to Santa Fe, which
he reached on July 2. With the usual visits and business affairs
tended to, he departed for the east, arriving in Highland on
July 20.

At this stage, Bandelier's examination of Mexican prehistoric remains in situ and his investigation of the Mexican
tribes in the field were concluded. His deepest penetration
of northern Mexico was about 150 miles below the border;
though he later worked in the archives of Mexico on several
occasions, this was the last of his field investigations in that
country. The rather extensive data on climate, biota, and
ethnology of northwestern Mexico were, as indicated in the
footnotes of such publications as his Final Report (Bandelier
A. F., 1890: 3-187), derived from archival and library sources.

Goad (pp. 107-108) summarized this aspect of Bandelier's
work in the following words.

> He, perhaps better than anyone in his time, knew the
> literature. He asked everyone he met for information, and
> he used that information when it suited his purpose. So
> Bandelier appears here, as always, the historian, the ar-
> chivist, not a field archaeologist or ethnologist. He says,
> speaking of the Indians of Chihuahua, "To search among
> these for remains of their ancient culture and traditions is
> the task of the practical ethnologist . . ."
> He missed no opportunity to delve into the Church
> archives, even in the little mountain villages of northeast-

ern Sonora. He was not fond of Indians, nor of roughing it. In spite of the heroic picture that Charles F. Lummis draws of Bandelier, he did not relish hardship. This is evident through all his journals, and in the life he lived when relieved of the necessity of working in the field. He liked to go to the "brewery" each afternoon while he lived in Santa Fe from 1885-1892; he loved to go calling, and to have friends drop in. He enjoyed conviviality and conversation and good food and drink. Bandelier liked to travel, but not where there were few of his kind who could talk with him. This may account for his abandonment of the trip through Mexico. Perhaps he simply became homesick.

The Highland newspaper of the summer and autumn of 1884 had several items regarding Bandelier. On July 9, *The Weekly Telephone*, the newly founded English-language paper, announced,

> Adolph Bandelier is expected home this week. His many friends will be glad to see him again after an absence of nearly ten months.

Arriving a bit later than expected, Bandelier remained in Highland until early September when he went East to consult with Putnam and Norton in regard to future research and publication. He did not return to Highland until early November, as noted in the *Telephone* of November 5, and in the next issue of November 12, another departure was noted.

> After a short stay of only about a week Prof. Bandelier has again left us. He had been absent about two months in the East, attending to the publication of his new book on Mexico, and lecturing at Boston, New York, and other Eastern cities. Since the illustrations for his grand work cannot be furnished as desired in this country, he now leaves for Europe to make arrangements there with the most prominent artists, the text of his books, however, will be printed in America. He will be absent about seven or

eight weeks, and after his return here will resume writing
his books, which will require several years.

This trip to Europe was not only for the purposes of consulting about illustrations and publications but also to discuss affairs with the Swiss creditors of the F. Ryhiner Bank which was
in difficulties (cf. White and Bernal 1960: 278, et seq.). Goad
(p. 110) was of the definite opinion that Bandelier visited the
representatives of these Swiss creditors, the Gruner-Haller and
Company of Bern.

While Bandelier was in Europe, a paper of his, "The Romantic School in American Archaeology," was read on February 3 before a meeting of the New York Historical Society.[28] It
is of significance here as it expressed views on the reconstruction
of prehistoric cultures more clearly and succinctly than any
other of Bandelier's writing. He considered the works of Clavi-
gero and Robertson as the beginning of a new era in the history of the Americas; the explorations of von Humboldt
amounted to a "rediscovery of tropical América."

Under such influences he believed that the popular interest
in America, both in Europe and at home, had become more
serious. People had not been previously interested in the au-
thentic history of aboriginal America because historians had not
given them the proper information. He envisioned the needs
of culture history, north of Mexico, as resting upon a study of
"What the Indian is, and how shall we treat him?" and also
"Has the Indian left any monuments from which useful lessons for our present and future benefit may be derived?"

Bandelier felt that south of the United States, studies of Indian culture were far more complex. Such questions as "What
did nature afford the inhabitant for his sustenance and progress?", "What use did the inhabitant make of such natural re-
sources?", and "What has been the effect of contact with

---

28. This appeared in the *Papers of the New York Historical Society*, February
5, 1885. The fourteen-page article was reprinted in New York by Trow's Printing
and Bookbinding Company, also in 1885.

European civilization with the aborigines up to the present time?" were of practical importance.[29]

After these questions, Bandelier added the following observations:

> The majority of writers of this day represent the Indian as a human being on the lowest scale of culture as to the arts of life, but endowed with the aspirations and moral principles sometimes in advance of those of actual society. Consequently we should be entitled to treat this Indian according to the moral and mental principles pervading civilized communities of today. We are thus led to ask him to become as we are now, while he is left to live as our ancestors may have lived untold centuries ago.

Because of such views, Bandelier noted,

> Our Indian policy has been kept vacillating between two extremes: the one treating the Indian as a mere savage and as an obstacle to civilization, only fit to be removed . . ., the other fondling him like a child endowed with the highest qualifications for rapid progress.

Urging historians to do more than merely copy the early authors, he continued,

> However carefully and honestly we copy their statements, as long as we do not dissect and compare, we remain but the faithful scribe only, and give the public a reflected picture not of things as they were, but as they were looked at and appreciated three centuries ago.

Closing with praise of Morgan, Bandelier stated that he had made ethnology and archaeology valuable sources for historical

---

29. From these questions it would seem that Bandelier revealed interests in problems of acculturation and applied anthropology which did not receive any appreciable degree of professional concern among anthropologists for at least another half century.

research in America. In addition, Bandelier credited Morgan with giving "historical study its most valuable ally, geography in its widest acceptance." In conclusion, he predicted, a bit over-enthusiastically, it would seem,

> The days of historical fiction are past, the progress of science in auxiliary branches [of history] is alone great enough to carry the history of America upward to those heights when it shall become a critical, and therefore a practically useful, branch of human knowledge.

Returning from Europe, Bandelier arrived in Highland in early April, 1885, to find the F. Ryhiner Bank's position had deteriorated even more. It had joined with others in the region in promoting the boom days of the post-Civil War period. However, a progressive slackening of trade in 1884 had resulted in a steadily declining business trend. The Ryhiner Bank had long depended on capital from Europe, utilizing bonds secured by mortgages on Illinois land. Fixed rates of interest could not be paid as farmers found themselves unable to sell their crops at a high enough price. The situation had worsened to the point that an agent was sent by the Gruner-Haller and Company of Bern to protect the interests of the European investors. An awareness of this development precipitated a run on the F. Ryhiner Bank which closed its doors. A statement on the first page of the *Highland Weekly Telephone* of May 6, 1885, indicated that the liabilities of the bank exceeded the assets by $290,767.22. Other information in this issue of the paper, under the heading of "Terrible Crash," indicated that Adolph F. Bandelier was in Highland, while Adolph E., "Father" Bandelier had departed two days earlier with the announced intention of visiting the New Orleans Exposition and, quite possibly, Cuba. Goad (p. 116) was convinced that the elder Bandelier knew the crash was imminent. Whether he passed this information along to his son is unknown. F. C. Ryhiner, Jr., a member of the firm, was then in Iowa, but another partner, Maurice

Huegy, was in Highland where he had other business interests. The public demanded some action from the authorities, and a warrant was issued for the arrest of F. C. Ryhiner, Ad. E. Bandelier, Maurice Huegy, and A. F. Bandelier on the 20th of May, 1885, though it seems clear from all available accounts that Adolph F. was not a partner in the bank. In the heat of the moment, especially with the senior Bandelier absent, this detail became irrelevant.

Maurice Huegy and Adolph F. Bandelier were immediately arrested and charged, before the Justice of the Peace, with receiving money on deposit knowing the bank was insolvent. Bond of $1,000 was established for each man, with an appearance arranged for May 28. F. C. Ryhiner, Jr., hearing of the charge, wrote from Dubuque, Iowa, offering to appear voluntarily. On the other hand, nothing was heard from Bandelier's father, though Goad (p. 116) stated that relatives were reported to have received a letter in which the senior Bandelier bade them good-bye, adding that he was stranded in New Orleans with only $30.00 but that he would make out somehow. Search for him would be fruitless, and he bade his relatives "farewell for life." (In reality, it seems that he went to Venezuela where he remained until joining his son in Santa Fe in 1888.)

On the morning of May 28, the day of the preliminary hearing, Maurice Huegy committed suicide. Despite this sensational development, Bandelier was arraigned, though the proceedings were delayed from 10:00 A.M. until 1:00 P.M. because of the death of his friend and brother-in-law. Goad (pp. 117-118), from information given by Carl Huegy, the son of Maurice, described the scene in the following words.

> It is not difficult to imagine the feelings of the anthropologist when he appeared before the desk of the township Justice of the Peace to hear the charge of ruining so many of his neighbors and friends. There was a large crowd at

the hearing. Bandelier probably knew as little of the affairs of the bank as any person in the room. He had just lost a boyhood and life-time friend, a man with whom his relationship had been closer even than with his blood brother. As boys Maurice Huegy and Adolph Bandelier had been taught natural history and geology by the elder Bandelier. They had gone into business together, and finally Adolph had married Huegy's sister. Now he was absolutely alone, accused of being responsible for the loss of the lifetime savings of his townsmen.

Black powder bombs had been exploded on Maurice Huegy's lawn. The town was in an ugly mood.

Bandelier was bound over to the grand jury, but bond, as before, was offered. He either could not or would not make the bond, and accordingly was placed in custody of the local officers to be delivered to the sheriff in Edwardsville, the county seat. According to the *Weekly Telephone* of June 2, 1885,

The prisoner was taken to the depot at 3:00 o'clock to be brought by train to Edwardsville, where he was to be placed in jail; but as the train was delayed several hours by washouts, a carriage was procured, in which the prisoner, constable Todd and W. P. Bradshaw drove off. The crowd which had gathered at Riniker's [the Justice's] office and at the depot, was of course more of less excited, but the threats of "hang him," etc., were not made in earnest, but intended only to scare. The man displaying the rope said he expected a bull calf to arrive with the train, and the fact is that he did receive the animal the next day. Bandelier was lodged in jail that night [Goad was told by Mr. Charles Boeschenstein, President of the Edwardsville National Bank, that Bandelier actually stayed in the sheriff's house as a guest.] but the following morning Athanas Hoffman, D. W. Mudge, and Chas. Boeschenstein signed his bond, whereupon he was released to appear again when his trial comes up. He is now at Santa Fe,

New Mexico where he has taken up his archaeological
researches.[30]

Bandelier's case never came to trial. Henceforth, his life was
devoted to scholarly pursuits though the bitter experiences of
the business world lingered on. Technically, he was not a partner in the bank, but as the article in the *Weekly Telephone*,
June 14, 1885, pointed out, he appeared to have enjoyed the
privileges of this status for many years. As evidence of such
status, the paper cited his trips to Switzerland to confer with

---

30. Goad (p. 119) reported that he found the name of Bandelier to have
been an "anathema" in Highland. "Even today [1937-38] he is remembered,
if at all, with bitterness, however proud the townspeople may have been of his
achievements as a scholar." An excellent example can be found in the *Highland
News-Leader*, as of 1927: "42 years ago, Ryhiner & Co. bank at Highland failed
for a large sum of money. Adolph F. Bandelier was cashier. At that date, the
people here wanted to hang him. The President of the United States later
named a large park in the West in his honor—'Bandelier Park.' Yes, times
changed!" (clipping in Archives, Museum of New Mexico) As indicated elsewhere in this brief sketch, the quoted item contained several misstatements: (1)
Bandelier was not cashier; (2) The *Telephone* account of events of the time
(June 2, 1885) maintained the threat to hang Bandelier was not in earnest
(rationalization in retrospect, perhaps?); and (3) President Wilson set aside
a national monument and not a park in Bandelier's honor.

The seriousness of such misrepresentations may be seen in a news item in
the *Highland News-Leader*, July 7, 1937. Announcing Goad's presence in the
community as a representative of the Museum of New Mexico in search of
Bandelier data, the announcement continued: "None but our older people
have any personal recollection of Mr. Bandelier, and theirs is not a very pleasant
one. Prior and up to 1885 he was active in the management of the F. Ryhiner &
Co. bank and after the failure of that institution he was held to the Madison
County grand jury on the charge of having solicited deposits for the bank
after he knew it was insolvent. No one in Highland would go his bail, and he
spent one night in jail at Edwardsville [Goad maintained this was as a guest
of the Sheriff]. The next day some Edwardsville people went his bail, and he
left for New Mexico. He was indicted by grand jury but never appeared for
trial. Whether or not his bondsmen paid, we do not know. Probably not. At
any rate he was never in Highland but once after that. About two years later he
came here one evening, but left before daylight and only a few of his most
intimate friends knew of his presence here. [Goad denied the accuracy of this
episode.] Time has lessened the bitterness that existed then, and Highland
people will likely give Mr. Goad every assistance in his investigations." (This
clipping, with marginal notations, is included among the files relating to Goad's
research in the archives of the Museum of New Mexico.)

the bank's creditors. Further, according to the *Telephone*, the Bandeliers, father and son, did not keep separate accounts. In the period between August, 1878, and December, 1880, the paper claimed the account had been overdrawn in the amount of $23,807.89. Much was made of this despite the fact that the Bandeliers owed but $2,569.99 at the time the bank closed. This sum was far less than the recognized value of the Bandelier farm and town residence of Adolph F. and Josephine Bandelier.

Returning to Santa Fe on June 2 (having left Edwardsville on May 30), Bandelier resumed his research under the auspices of the Archaeological Institute of America. His position, however, was precarious. Aside from the Illinois fiasco, the financial arrangement with the Institute was a source of continual worry. Since its founding, the Institute's major effort had been in the classical civilizations of the Eastern Mediterranean.[31] With the flight of his father, Bandelier had full responsibility for his orphaned nieces, Lizzie and Emma. In addition to his immediate household, there were other relatives and various friends who accepted the hospitality of the patriarchal Bandelier home. His $1,200 a year, never more than minimal, had to be stretched still more.

The summer of 1885 was spent visiting the Rio Grande pueblos, including Cochiti, where he arrived at the time of the July 14 Feast Day. On the 1st of August he returned to Cochiti and went on to the Rito de los Frijoles. The next two months were spent in the northern portion of New Mexico. Following this trip Bandelier left Santa Fe for Highland, arriving on the 24th of October, apparently for a hearing on the indictment. The case was not prosecuted, however; Bandelier was released from his bond and the family moved to establish their permanent home in Santa Fe, leaving on November 14.

---

31. In a letter to Mrs. Morgan, dated July 18, 1883, Bandelier supported his complaint of this inequality of interest and expenditures with the following figures: In 1882, the Institute received donations of $5,620 for classical research and $200 for American research. In the same year, the Institute spent $10,-266.64 in Greece as compared with $2,456.90 in America.

Trips to El Paso, Albuquerque, Peña Blanca, and Cochiti were made during the balance of the year, 1885, with intervals in Santa Fe where the first six months of 1886 were spent. During the second half of 1886, there was a short trip in July to Santa Clara, Puye, and San Juan, and a brief visit to Albuquerque in mid-December. His financial status, already precarious, received another blow when the Archaeological Institute of America, itself short of funds, found it necessary to drop him from its payroll. Bills mounted, and Bandelier desperately wrote articles for newspapers, and letters to anyone he thought might be interested in his materials, both in the United States and in Europe.[32] It was in this situation that he began work in earnest on his novel, *The Delight Makers*. It had been started in 1883 (August 24), but only two chapters had been finished by the end of 1885. He finished the novel, in German, on May 12, 1886—writing the last twenty chapters in four and a half months, all by hand.[33] In between work on the novel and other writing, Bandelier worked on the *Final Report*.

At this point, Bandelier's right arm began to trouble him, at times being virtually useless. When writing seemed impossible, he drew ground plans for the *Final Report* or painted pottery designs and ceremonial objects in watercolors. On May 23, news of the missing senior Bandelier arrived in Santa Fe. About that time in rather close succession, a number of articles were sold, and Bandelier's horizons brightened considerably.

Toward the end of June, Bandelier began the study of law, planning for himself a new profession. Mr. Eugene A. Fiske of Santa Fe was to serve as his tutor. However, the already men-

32. Among Bandelier's desperate measures at this time, Goad (p. 124fn18) said that he offered lessons to the townspeople of Santa Fe in Spanish, French, or German. This venture was not particularly successful.

33. When the German version of the novel, *Die Koshare*, met with failure, Bandelier translated it into English, finishing it in 1889. Titled, *The Koshare*, the manuscript was turned down by Harpers, Holt, and Scribner's. Dodd finally agreed to publish it under the new title, *The Delight Makers*. (Letter from Bandelier to Professor Norton from Santa Fe, dated September 18, 1889, in files of Peabody Museum, Harvard University.)

tioned trip to the Santa Clara area in July and other interests appear to have taken precedence over the aspirations toward a legal career.

On October 4, 1886, Archbishop Salpointe[34] commissioned Bandelier to do a work on the history of the missions for presentation to Pope Leo XIII. This commission removed the financial worries which had surrounded Bandelier in the preceding months. An advance from the Archbishop could be

---

34. Father Salpointe came from France to New Mexico in 1859. He succeeded Lamy as archbishop after serving a short period as coadjutor in 1885. Salpointe died in 1898.

This work for the church brings up the question of Bandelier's religion. The family seems to have been mainly Protestant (as were both of Bandelier's wives), but Bandelier, in later years, was a member of the Catholic Church. He became a formal convert to Catholicism on July 31, 1881, while on a trip to Mexico. (cf. White and Bernal 1960: 248 et seq.) Though not wishing in any way to question the sincerity of Bandelier's conversion, it should be recognized that his religion probably made it easier for him to do certain archival work in the Southwest and in Latin America. Here the present editors must echo White (1940: I, 96) who says". . . the question to what extent was Bandelier influenced by his decision to become a Catholic by professional, ethnological, considerations, we must leave to Bandelier's biographers of the future."

As further background, it is of interest to note here various bits of evidence on this phase of Bandelier's life. Hodge once wrote, "As long as I knew him, Bandelier wore a clerical collar. I have a dim recollection that he became a Catholic when he undertook the writing of the History of the Missions for the Archbishop of Santa Fe for presentation to the Pope." Before his initial departure to the Southwest, he had written Morgan on June 11, 1880 (White 1940: II, 199), suggesting that he travel in priestly garb. "Again, while I respect that church, I still am not a Catholic, and may thus hope to worm and 'wiggle' through even where a priest would be disregarded." After his arrival, Bandelier wrote again on August 31 (White 1940: II, 211), announcing his intention of visiting a Father Ribera at Peña Blanca, "who has invited me to spend a few weeks with him." He added, "The clergy here is very friendly to me, they have given me free access to their books and registers. The Indians are exclusively under their control." In a note to this letter, White pointed out that, as of that date, Bandelier had not actually become acquainted with any Indian group. "They were, and still are, far from being 'exclusively under the control' of the Roman Catholic priests." In journal entries of 1889, while in Santa Fe, Bandelier wrote on Sunday, February 3, "Did not go to mass, owing to neglect and because I did not feel like it. Still I must become different again. This life of a Heathen won't do in the long run." No great change occurred, seemingly, in the next weeks, as he wrote on an April Sunday, "Remained in bed til 9 a.m.—Did not attend mass therefore, I was too late, or rather, to tell the truth,—I preferred to stay in bed."

depended upon in case of need, and, furthermore, he was again at work on material of utmost interest to him. Three days later, on the 7th, Bandelier received additional good news—Cushing wrote that another expedition for the study of Southwestern archaeology had been financed by Mrs. Hemenway and that Bandelier could serve as Historian.[35]

Thus, in the year between December, 1885, and December, 1886, Bandelier's life took a turn from the depths of despair to a considerable degree of security and happiness. Late in December, Cushing and Hodge provided Bandelier with funds, $450.00, with which to go to Mexico City to work in the archives relevant to the Hemenway investigations. Accompanied by Joe, he arrived in Mexico City and, after some difficulties, arranged to copy documents in the National Library and Archives. García Icazbalceta also loaned him a number of rare books to copy. As funds ran out, Joe returned to Santa Fe in March, 1887; money from the Archbishop in Santa Fe and from the Hemenway Expedition enabled Bandelier to stretch his stay until May.

Aside from a brief trip to San Juan in September and a ten-day trip covering various towns between Santa Fe and Bernalillo, Bandelier was in Santa Fe for the remainder of 1877. The primary projects were work on the manuscript for the Archbishop and writing of a history of Zuñi. On the 20th of January, 1888, he completed the first project, and he helped the Archbishop pack it as a golden jubilee gift to Pope Leo XIII.[36] In

35. In a letter from Dr. Hodge to Dr. E. L. Hewett, Museum of New Mexico, dated May 3, 1938, the opinion was expressed that Cushing was essentially ignorant of Bandelier's commission from the Archbishop. Hence, when Bandelier's productivity in behalf of the Hemenway Expedition seemed to lag, Cushing complained. Hodge added that the situation almost resulted in a serious breach between the two men, but that it was eventually "patched up." (Files, Museum of New Mexico.)

36. Hodge (1932: 366) listed this item in Bandelier's bibliography as follows: *Histoire de la colonisation et des missions du Sonora, Chihuahua, Nouveau Mexique et Arizona, jusqu'a l'an 1700.* Manuscript, 1400 foolscap pages, 400 water-color drawings by the author, in four volumes, with an atlas. (This manuscript, written in 1887 and 1888, was finished at Santa Fe and presented to Pope

his spare moments during these past months, Bandelier also completed his English translation of The Delight Makers.[37]

Thus, by the end of January, he was relatively free from commitments again, and he joined Cushing and others of the Hemenway group in Tucson and Tempe where a week was spent examining ruins of the area. Returning to Santa Fe in mid-February, he was quickly away again on a short trip to Tesuque, San Juan, and Taos. At the end of March, he journeyed to El Paso and Juarez where he copied some church documents, though severely hampered by sciatica, chills, and fever. In early March, Bandelier's father had written from La Guaira, Venezuela, and on April 6 Bandelier met him in El Paso. Happy as Bandelier was with this reunion, he frequently recorded his complaints. Always domineering, the senior Bandelier apparently expected special consideration because of the hardships of recent years, paying little heed to the other family members whom he had left behind to bear the brunt of the bank failure.

For the remainder of 1888, from the time of his return from El Paso with his father on April 8, Bandelier was away almost

Leo XIII by Archbishop J. B. Salpointe of Santa Fe on the occasion of the Pontiff's Jubilee. It is now in the library of the Vatican. See Eighth Rep. Archaeol. Inst. Amer., p. 47, Cambridge, 1888. In his accompanying sketch, Hodge provided no further data (p. 358); in the letter of May 3, 1938 (cited in the previous note) Hodge wrote: "I do not see that I can offer any constructive suggestions. My bibliographical reference to which [Dr. Lansing B.] Bloom alludes was based entirely on what Bandelier told me personally as to the content of his Vatican manuscript, aside from which I am quite ignorant." In a letter of August 20, 1937, Dr. Hewett had written W. W. Postlethwaite of Colorado College, Colorado Springs, that this Vatican manuscript was "probably the most important unpublished work left by Mr. Bandelier." In line with this appraisal, Bloom spent great time and effort in the Vatican Library attempting to find this manuscript. The illustrations were found, but nothing more. Others have tried in a sequence which has become a story in itself. Perhaps most recently has been the effort on the part of the present editors, with the splendid cooperation of Reverend Lowry J. Daly, S. J., and Mr. Charles J. Ermatinger, together with their colleagues, of the Pius XII Vatican Microfilm Library, St. Louis University. Despite the renewed examination of the Vatican archives in search for items to be microfilmed for the St. Louis collections, no trace of this manuscript has as yet been found.

37. See footnote 30.

half of the time. For the most part, his travels were in the Rio Grande drainage, primarily among the Tewa villages. His last trip of the year, in October, took him westward to Zuñi and the Mount Taylor area. Undoubtedly, his travels, to a great extent on foot, were motivated by his scholarly interests and in the spirit of cooperation with his colleagues as when he visited Taos with Cushing. It is also likely that extra incentive was provided by his father whose personality continued to make life difficult at home. The year 1888 came to a generally successful end, though not completely so, as evidenced by Bandelier's closing entry.

> Another, so far, fortunate year. We have succeeded in bringing papa home, but with him we have secured a cloud on our otherwise happy sky. Well, God has so disposed, and we must take it as it comes.

The year 1889 in many respects repeated previous patterns, with days and evenings of copying documents, writing, and visiting friends. The month of February was largely spent at San Juan, with other trips to Santa Clara and elsewhere. Later, in June, he went to Albuquerque, and in August to El Paso, this time for about two weeks. The year saw the completion of the *Final Report*,[38] and the reworked English version of *The Delight Makers* accepted by a publisher in America. Also, 1889 was the year in which Bandelier became well acquainted with Charles F. Lummis, whom he had probably first met in 1888. Goad (pp. 136-137) referred to Lummis as a "fellow spirit, friend, great admirer of the historian for the rest of his life, and his eulogist after death." This characterization was essentially accurate. However, an examination of the journals and correspondence from the later years in South America (actually be-

---

38. The full bibliographic citation for this important work by Bandelier is: 1890-92. Final Report of Investigations among the Indians of the Southwestern United States, Carried on mainly in the years from 1880 to 1885, Parts I and II. *Papers of the Archaeological Institute of America*, American Series III and IV. 323 pp. and 591 pp.

yond the scope of this series of volumes) reveals devastating (and probably quite unjustified) tirades against Lummis by Bandelier. The year 1889 also witnessed a shift in the Hemenway support. Cushing, in poor health, went east in May; Mrs. Hemenway sent Dr. J. W. Fewkes west to talk with Bandelier and after a day of consultation, Bandelier noted in his journal that his proposed resumption of the Mexican investigations would not be possible. The Expedition, as a whole, was to be abandoned due to a lack of funds, but Bandelier was to continue his historical researches on New Mexico and Mexico.[39]

Actual monetary support for this work, however, was slow in coming, and Bandelier, waiting for the "Great Bostonians," spent an uncomfortable summer marking time. Near the end of the year, Fewkes sent a check for $100.00 for expenses on the El Paso trip. While the Hemenway people appear to have done all they had agreed to do, Bandelier, in typical fashion, complained, "I do not want much, but I think my wife should live." The Archaeological Institute retained Bandelier on the payroll through 1889 and 1890 though work in New Mexico was virtually at a halt due to Cushing's illness and the general shortage of funds.

Further complaints in his journal reveal his tendency to feel sorry for himself—as on his 49th birthday, August 6, 1889, he moaned, "I am now 49 years old and: —what have I done? —Nothing."

Continuing under the auspices of Mrs. Hemenway and the Archaeological Institute of America, the Bandeliers arrived in Mexico City on February 12, 1890, to do additional research in

39. From Santa Fe, on October 10, 1889, Bandelier wrote to Professor Norton, complaining. "It is a pitiable failure, this 'Hemenway Southwestern Archaeological Expedition.'—A fabulous amount of money has been spent by Cushing, and Fewkes assured me, that there was nothing to show for it but unassorted collections, and Field-notes which are completely unserviceable. The only part of the work that is in good shape is my part. But what will Mrs. Hemenway get, when she takes these documents to Boston?—Not a soul can use them or does know how to use them. They are certainly monuments of my industry, but away from me they are of little avail." (Photostat of letter in Library, University of New Mexico.)

the archives. By March 6, they were again in Santa Fe. Bandelier had acquired the idea that he had exhausted the materials in New Mexico, and he was eager for the chance to search farther afield. Funds were not forthcoming, however, and Bandelier found it necessary to remain in Santa Fe the rest of the year except for short trips to the Tewa Basin in July and September and to Peña Blanca, Cochiti, and the Rito de los Frijoles in October.

There was little change in Bandelier's routine during 1891. In March, he went to La Junta, Colorado, and at the end of September, to Denver.[40] In the meantime, there were visits to Isleta, Cochiti, San Juan, Taos, Santa Clara, and other places in the Rio Grande valley. After his return from Denver, Bandelier made a trip in October to Peña Blanca, to Jemez, Zia, Santa Ana, and Bernalillo, and in November to Isleta, for an extended visit with Lummis.

Returning to Santa Fe, January 2, 1892, Bandelier was at home only briefly before leaving, this time via Isleta and then Albuquerque, for the East—to New York. In April, on his return trip westward, he was briefly in Highland, after which time he reached Santa Fe on May 12. On the 24th of May, he and his wife left for the west coast and San Francisco, from which port they sailed on June 6 for South America, in effect, bringing to a close Bandelier's Southwestern researches.

Bandelier, prior to this time, had restlessly searched for new horizons. An opportunity came when Henry Villard[41] of New York, in collaboration with the American Museum of Natural History, sent an expedition to Bolivia and Peru. Bandelier was placed in charge, and Lummis, "also a trained archaeologist," accompanied him. This rather drastic switch in geographic area

40. Goad (p. 141fn51) stated that the various trips Bandelier made by rail were on passes from the Santa Fe Railroad but he did not know the basis for issuing these passes. Information from Mr. Dudley C. Gordon, Los Angeles City College, makes it likely that Lummis was instrumental in making arrangements with the railroad.

41. Villard was owner of the New York Evening Post, president of the Edison General Electric Company, and a railroad financier.

seems best explained simply in terms of finances. Mrs. Hemenway had withdrawn her support from the Southwestern work; his novel, *The Delight Makers*, had achieved no popularity; other plans for the support of his documentary work in Mexico failed to materialize. The Villard Expedition provided financial security though its primary interest in the collection of museum specimens was somewhat alien to Bandelier's personal interests and experience.

Arriving in Lima in July, 1892, Bandelier accomplished little, due to the poor health of his wife. Ultimately, on the 11th of December, 1892, Josephine Huegy Bandelier died. In the following year, Bandelier remained at Lima until October or November when he made one major trip, to the eastern part of Peru, a trip he described as "frightful." Aside from visits to sites near La Paz, Bolivia, his time was occupied with the study of the archives, in the course of which he concluded that, "at the time of the arrival of [the] Spaniards, the most extensive ruins on the Peruvian coast were either completely or partially abandoned." As in New Mexico and Mexico, Bandelier held that the documentary evidence pointed to a much smaller population than had been popularly thought, and also that the extensive ruins of Peru and Bolivia were successive in time.

In December, 1893, Bandelier married Fanny Ritter, in La Paz. She was the daughter of a Swiss immigrant; her widowed mother may have been the proprietor of the boarding house in which the Bandeliers had earlier stayed. Considerably younger than Bandelier, then fifty-three, Fanny was an accomplished linguist and, in time, proved herself to be almost as much a scholar as Bandelier. In addition to Spanish, she read French, Italian, German, and English. Goad (p. 149) commented,

> Vivacious and devoted, she was a worthy companion to such a man as Bandelier. Thenceforth, they were constantly together, enjoying life in times of plenty, suffering in hardships and lack, always working together, with Adolph leading and Fanny picking up the pieces. Before the death of Bandelier, Fanny translated the narration

of Cabeza de Vaca into English, and after his death, while teaching in Fisk University, she translated one volume of Sahagun into English.[42]

In the main, Bandelier's work in Peru and Bolivia paralleled what he had done in New Mexico. The archives and libraries occupied much of his time and effort, and, as he frequently wrote, he "moved in the best circles." He continued to travel, on mule or horse, by train or boat, and when these were lacking in his search for a distant ruin, he walked. As in Mexico, he had little to do with the Indians, considering them low and degenerate forms of mankind. At least three factors contributed to this dislike or contempt. In both Mexico and South America, the people with whom Bandelier associated, the scholars and upper class generally, viewed the Indian peoples as peons, or servants. Further, he felt that the Indians of these areas had degenerated through mixture with the lower classes of the conquerors. Finally, it was the philosophy of the Morgan school (later, sometimes referred to as the Bandelier school[43]) that the American aborigines were still at a rather low level of social evolution as of the time of European contact. They had no *civitas*, only tribal and family structure.

Goad (p. 151) maintained that Bandelier's aristocratic atti-

---

42. Noting that Bandelier "died in harness," leaving no fortune, Goad (p. 170) continued, "In fact, he left his widow to make her way as best she could, by translating, teaching, and clerical work. Late in her life she was appointed a member of the faculty of Fiske University, where she died in 1937."

43. In a letter to Hodge, dated September 22, 1904, New York, Bandelier wrote, "Mr. Dellenbaugh has lately been boasting that the 'Bandelier School' would have to come to him yet. He is preparing a new volume of elucubrations [elucidations] on the seven cities [of Cibola, or Zuñi], I am informed. Well, the Almighty preserved his equine prototype in the Ark, and it landed to prosper and thrive. . . . The more the fellow writes the better it is, for the better will he become known." (Frederick Samuel Dellenbaugh was a member of the Powell Expedition through the Grand Canyon, 1871-72, and the author of several popular books on the West. One was *Breaking the Wilderness*, G. P. Putnam's Sons, New York, 1905, the book to which Bandelier apparently had reference in this letter.)

tudes precluded feelings of brotherly affection for the Indians he studied. Even with the Cochiti, Goad insisted that the scholar's feeling was one of kind condescension, the very antithesis of the Romantic idea of the "noble savage." This attitude was reinforced by study of the Spanish documents and close acquaintance with the Catholic attitude of "fatherly interest toward people whom [they] considered children."[44]

Bandelier's trip of the latter part of 1893, his one venture into the Amazon drainage, was filled with hardships, but yielded data on the etymology of the Quichua language, as well as measurements and notes of ruins, and general geographical features of the region. Such matters, it seems, were of little or no interest to Mr. Villard. Consequently, arrangements were

44. In Bandelier's *Islands of Titicaca and Koati* (p. 19), one reads, "Cupidity, low cunning, and savage cruelty are unfortunate traits of these Indians' [The Aymara] character." These traits, he explained, " are peculiar to the stock and not the result of ill-treatment by the Spaniards." In sharp contrast and incompatible with Goad's evaluation of Bandelier in this particular feature, is the following excerpt from a letter written by Bandelier from Cochiti, November 27, 1880, to Norton (Wissler 1914: 8). "My relations with the Indians of this pueblo are very friendly. Sharing their food, their hardships, and their pleasures, simple as they are, a mutual attachment has formed itself, which grows into sincere affection. They begin to treat me as one of their own, and to exhibit toward me that spirit of fraternity which prevails among them in their communism. Of course, they have squabbles among themselves [Something of an understatement, in view of the controversy, still raging, about blows struck at the time of the rabbit hunt earlier the same month. See the journal entries beginning with November 6, 1880, and continuing to that of December 13, 1880.], which often reveal to me some new features of their organization; but on the whole they are the best people the sun shines upon. How long will they last? They progress slowly, but still they are progressing. God preserve them from any attempt at rapid 'Americanization.' It would be their deathblow. At night if they do not come to see me, to sit around very modestly without interruption of my work, I sometimes go to call on some of my nearest friends among them, especially the Lieutenant of the 'Capitán de la Guerra,' Victoriano, a young man with a small family. Squatting on one of their low stools, hewn out of one block, or stretched out side by side on serapes, we chat and smoke— water, out of the common tinaja, being the only refreshment offered and expected. His wife and sister go about, mingling freely in the conversation— for both sexes are on a footing of great equality. We talk Spanish, and sometimes a word in Queres. The girls tease me about my pronunciation."

made whereby Bandelier was to be employed directly by the American Museum of Natural History.[45] Bandelier had at least momentary doubts as to his ability to satisfy the Museum; however, Putnam was named Curator at about that time, and Bandelier's relations with the Museum improved.[46]

In August, 1894, the Bandeliers moved to La Paz, supposedly because of the unsettled political scene in Peru. They established their home in La Paz, and they remained there until 1903. Bandelier shifted his interests to the Lake Titicaca area and the slopes of Illimani. During this period, the Bandeliers enjoyed the social life of La Paz, and work in the civil and ecclesiastical archives continued as before. Archaeological work in the field was reduced, with the one extensive project in Bolivia being that done on the islands of Titicaca and Koati. Bandelier first visited Titicaca from January 1 to mid-April, 1895. After a short interval, the second phase of the work there was carried on until the end of August of that year.

From November, 1895, until August, 1896, the Bandeliers were in Lima again. In May, the Garcés collection was purchased for the Museum. Later that year, after their return to La Paz, the Bandeliers visited the tin mines at Huayna and

45. Goad (p. 147) noted that, as a collector of interesting and rare antiquities, Bandelier was a faithful, but not very dependable, agent. In Bandelier's first shipment, arriving in December, 1892, there was a mummy that did not stand the voyage too well. "There was much trouble in the New York customs house before the evil smelling souvenir was removed by Mr. Villard's agents." (p. 148fn 10) It seems that Mr. Villard also grew weary of Bandelier's complaints about the difficulties of obtaining collections and then of getting them out of the country once they had been purchased or collected. In regard to Bandelier's transfer to the Museum, Goad (p. 153fn18) cited "A note of President Morris K. Jessup of the Museum, on a letter from Bandelier dated Lima, Peru, 3 April, [authorizing] the engagement of the scientist from April 1, 1894, at $4,000 per year."

46. Tangible evidence of this satisfaction with Bandelier's services, aside from the fact that his employment was continued by the Museum, is demonstrated by a note initialed by President Jessup on the back of a letter from Bandelier to John W. Winser, Secretary, American Museum of Natural History, dated October 30, 1898, in Yarcachi, Bolivia. This note indicated that Bandelier was to be continued, and the wish was expressed that finances would permit an increase in his salary. (Files, American Museum of Natural History.)

conducted explorations in the province of Potosí, Bolivia. The following years passed without notable event; visits, travels, measuring ruins, watching ceremonies, and gathering collections of interest to the Museum occupied their time. Writing, of course, also continued during this period, the major accomplishment being the completion of the fourth and fifth chapters of the work at Lake Titicaca in July, 1901. It seems that the Museum showed little interest in this work insofar as publishing it was concerned. This, understandably, antagonized Bandelier; after some further negotiations, Bandelier finally withdrew the manuscript from the hands of the Museum. Ultimately, it was given to the Hispanic Society under whose auspices it was published in 1910.[47]

The Bandeliers had planned a return to the United States in 1902, but the unsettled conditions on the political scene and other events combined to delay their return until 1903. For the years remaining until Bandelier's death in 1914, his research was confined to the library and archive, the years of field exploration having been completed.

THE FINAL YEARS: 1903-1914

Bandelier's scholarly productivity declined gradually in the final years of life. His considerable age combined with the hardships of past field experiences to impose periods of poor health. Also, for almost three years, between 1909 and 1911, Bandelier suffered virtually total blindness as a result of cataracts.

Upon their return to the United States, Bandelier and his wife briefly visited Hodge and other friends in Washington before settling down in New York City. There, continuing his affiliation with the American Museum of Natural History, Bandelier busied himself with the sorting of his collections and the

---

47. Goad (pp. 155-156) considered this study to have been one of Bandelier's best works. "Increased experience enabled him to avoid the faults of the *Final Report*, and sufficient funds and time permitted him to make a thorough study of the documentary evidence, while the limits of an island prevented his indulging his exploring instinct too widely."

preparation of his South American data for publication. He remained with the Museum until 1906, giving lectures on various aspects of his research as well as continuing the research and writing. In rather typical manner, these years were marked by alternate periods of contentment and unhappiness. In July, 1905, Bandelier wrote to Hodge (Goad, p. 160),

> I am still at that unfortunate institution, but as a volunteer, so to say, and financially as good as independent from it. An entirely new perspective has opened, under distinct auspices.

In a footnote to this, Goad cautioned again that Bandelier's "animadversions against men and institutions should not be taken too seriously," as he was frequently vituperative toward those who refused to see eye to eye with him.

> He was displeased with the management of the Museum (which he sometimes facetiously referred to as the "American Museum of Unnatural Misery") on two counts. He disagreed with the director's theory that its function was primarily educational, and he was angry at their failure to publish his writing. His only publication by the Museum during this period was "On the Relative Antiquity of Peruvian Burials," . . . 1904.

In the meantime, in May, 1904, Bandelier was appointed a lecturer by Columbia University in the field of Spanish-American literature, particularly in relation to the ethnology and archaeology of the area. He was to lecture two hours a week under this arrangement; the appointment was for a year but it is uncertain how long he actually served in this capacity. (Goad, p. 161).

During this period, Bandelier stood in a rather ambiguous position. He was at the peak of his scholarly career—familiarity with the archival sources and early authors on the Conquest period, his first-hand acquaintance with innumerable archaeological sites, and his writings gave him a preeminence in the

Bandelier and his wife, Josephine Huegy Bandelier,
standing beside his father, A. E. Bandelier

Standing: Bandelier and his wife, Josephine;
seated: Josephine's sister, Amalia Huegy,
and Bandelier's father

Bandelier in mature years

Bandelier and his second wife, Fanny Ritter Bandelier

field. At the same time, he was uncertain that his work was acceptable. "The Cross of Curabuco" was sent to Hodge, then editor of the *American Anthropologist*, with fifteen pages of text and twenty-one pages of notes (a not unusual ratio for him), with the additional note, "Please read the paper carefully ere you decide about accepting. It may not suit for publication after all, and I am just as ready to take it back as not."[48] As Goad (p. 165) has pointed out, notes were "the bane of Bandelier's publishers."

Resigning from the American Museum of Natural History in 1906, Bandelier moved to the Hispanic Society of America. Having first written "The Islands of Titicaca and Koati" in La Paz and having rewritten it for the Museum, which then chose not to publish it, Bandelier began again on this manuscript. It was finally published by the Hispanic Society in 1910. Hiram Bingham (1914: 328) evaluated it in these words,

> This book is typical of his [Bandelier's] life-long crusade against tradition and for the truth. In it he shows the falsity of many historical myths for which the Spanish chroniclers and their followers are responsible. Prescott had to rely almost entirely on such sources as Garcilasso de la Vega. Yet that noble Inca left Peru when but a youth, lived forty years in Spain before he began to write, and then with pardonable pride sought to surround the empire of his ancestors with a glamour that should command the respectful admiration of the sixteenth century Europe.

Goad (p. 167) was of the opinion that Bandelier was the first historian to make significant criticism of this particular source.

In 1909, Bandelier lost his sight, and Fanny became his eyes and hands. She read his notes and manuscripts to him and wrote the notes for the *Islands of Titicaca and Koati* manuscript. So far as known, this was Bandelier's last publication.

---

48. Hodge did accept this paper; it appeared in the *American Anthropologist*, VI, 1904, pp. 599-628, under this title, "The Cross of Carabuco in Bolivia."

By 1911, however, Bandelier's eyesight had improved to the extent that he could accept an appointment as research assistant with the Carnegie Institution of Washington. In this capacity, Bandelier and his wife went to Mexico in 1912, spending several months there gathering materials. Returning to New York in the spring of 1913, they remained there until that autumn when they sailed for Spain to continue their pursuit of documentary material pertaining to New Mexico in the archives of Madrid, Seville, and Simancas.

Serious plans for this work had been made by Bandelier in 1910. Now that he was given the opportunity to achieve it, his health failed. His work in the Spanish archives could not be continued after December 18, 1913, and on March 18, 1914, Bandelier died in Seville.

Fanny Bandelier continued the work in the Spanish archives to the end of 1915. At this time, she returned and presented the manuscripts to the Carnegie Institution—one bound volume of transcripts and some nine hundred pages of unbound manuscript. Approximately half of this material consisted of copies of books, evidently for Bandelier's own use. The other half consisted of transcripts of documents from the Archivo General of Mexico. There was little unity or organization to the material as Bandelier apparently planned work with the documents following his return to the United States. Most of the documents were relevant to the provinces of New Mexico and Nueva Vizcaya and to the Rio Grande area.[49]

In bringing this sketch of Bandelier's life and career to a close, several comments are in order. Hobbs (1940: 122n1), in pointing out "a number of errors" in an earlier sketch (Bartholdi 1932), commented, "A complete and well rounded story

---

49. Together with other pertinent materials primarily from the Bancroft Library, University of California, Berkeley, these manuscripts were edited by Charles W. Hackett and published under the title, "Historical Documents Relating to New Mexico, Nueva Vizcaya, and Approaches Thereto, to 1773, Collected by Adolph F. A. Bandelier and Fanny R. Bandelier" (*Carnegie Institution of Washington*, Publication 330. I, II, III. 502 pp., 497 pp., 430 pp. 1923, 1926, 1937.).

of the life of Bandelier is yet to be written." The two interven-
ing decades have produced nothing to change the validity of
this statement, and the present sketch is not intended to be
anything more than a context within which Bandelier's journals may be better appreciated and more clearly understood.
Whether or not Hobbs, in making her statement, was aware
of Goad's unpublished dissertation, is unknown. However, despite the considerable data compiled by Goad, presenting new
and important facets of Bandelier's life, the definitive biography, in an exhaustive sense, remains to be written. It is equally
apparent that data relating to certain episodes of Bandelier's
life, in all likelihood, will never be recovered, thus making such
a definitive study exceedingly difficult.

There can be little doubt that, for most people who knew
him or have come to know of him, Bandelier was a uniquely
colorful, arresting, and dynamic personality and, at the same
time, often an exasperating one. A multitude of factors may
be recognized as having played important roles in the formu-
lation of Bandelier as an individual. In his family background,
the personality of his father particularly came to bear in a variety of ways—the elder Bandelier's broad intellectual interests;
his business ventures, especially his behavior in connection
with the bank failure; and his egotistical passion for domin-
ance in virtually every realm of activity and human relationship. In Bandelier's own life, there was an exposure to scholarly
subjects and the attraction to these developed into a career
rather than an avocation. The tremendous influence of Lewis
Henry Morgan can hardly be overemphasized, for he gave en-
couragement in the earlier years when Bandelier, had he not
been so inspired, might have abandoned his scholarly ambitions or at least might have satisfied himself with lesser goals.
Again, it was Morgan who used his considerable influence to
obtain for Bandelier an opportunity to enter the professional
circles of that time.

While throughout the journals frequent mention is made of
correspondence between Bandelier and his first wife, Joe, her

true personality and the role she played always remain rather obscure. It is certain that she never shared the professional aspects of Bandelier's life as did Fanny, the second wife, who joined her husband in his field investigations, in his examination of archival material, and in his writing.[50]

Paradoxical patterns and characteristics typify Bandelier to a highly unusual degree. Goad (pp. 171-174), in his final evaluation, explained much of Bandelier's behavior as the result of an inferiority complex, and this may well have been a factor. Strongly desirous of recognition, fame,[51] and financial security, he frequently exhibited intolerance of the work of others. Though he often depreciated his own work and its value, he was insistent upon the correctness of his conclusions and employed voluminous notes to document his position. The large number of items contained in Bandelier's bibliography stands as an enduring and respectable memorial to a scholar who pioneered in researches not greatly improved upon for several decades. These previously unpublished journals provide, half a century posthumously, voluminous and valuable eyewitness details for a time period long since closed to such original observation or recollection. Subject also to certain superficial-

---

50. At least for the earlier years White (1940: I, 84 fn) could find only one intimation that Joe ever assisted her husband in his research work. Even this was a rather ambiguous reference (in a letter to Morgan).

51. Something of this feeling is expressed in a letter from Fanny Bandelier, dated July 25, 1935, Nashville, Tennessee, to Brother Cassian Edmunds who was making a study of Bandelier at that time. "His [Bandelier's] modesty was often an outward expression of a very deep spiritual wound. It hurt him inwardly that he never received any outward sign of acknowledgment of his work and his suffering for the sake of science. Other men, within the circle of his friends and contemporaries, were given honorary degrees, etc., but he was never so honored! Why? It may partly be due to his own reticence, his shrinking from notoriety,—which he called cheap. Yet he went on and on doing his work as faithfully and as thoroughly as ever. He always rather minimized his accomplishments and people may have taken him literally, but I know it would have made him very happy if some outward honor had been bestowed on him during his lifetime; he suffered so much, off and on and not only physically—but, he went to his grave in far away Seville—unrewarded. It often makes me sad when I think of how much a little timely honor would have meant to him."

ities and errors, the journal entries offer a candidness and frequently a richness of detail which never appeared in Bandelier's publications.

In defining Bandelier's field investigations, his archival researches, and his publications, it is noteworthy that Goad, in his exposition, vacillated several times. Bandelier was referred to as an anthropologist, archaeologist, archivist, ethnologist, explorer, geographer, historian, and scientist. As pointed out at the beginning of this present discussion, the problem of properly categorizing Bandelier is less important than recognition of his varied interests. Bandelier's unique contribution was a determined attempt to combine several disciplines in an effort to reconstruct the culture history of a significant phase of America's past.[52] This spirit has been effectively captured in the simple wording of the memorial plaque in the Headquarters Building patio at Bandelier National Monument, New Mexico:

ADOLPH F. BANDELIER

ARCHAEOLOGIST ARCHIVIST HISTORIAN

BORN IN BERN SWITZERLAND

AUGUST 6 1840

DIED IN SEVILLE SPAIN

MARCH 18 1914

A GREAT AMERICAN SCHOLAR

---

52. This is not to distract in any way from the work of such Southwestern experts as Cushing, Fewkes, Mindeleff, and Holmes. As Taylor (1954: 561 et seq.) points out, those men—and Bandelier—had a number of ideas in common, one of the most important of which was to approach archaeology through ethnology. Taylor rightly characterizes this as the "Cushing-Fewkes Period," for in the Southwest alone the latter men out-produced Bandelier. We must, however, consider the wide-ranging nature of the latter's interests both in subject matter and in area. In that sense the characterization given here seems fair.

THE SOUTHWESTERN JOURNALS
OF ADOLPH F. BANDELIER

1880

AUGUST 20: Left St. Louis 9:25 P.M., Missouri Pacific.

AUGUST 21: Reached Kansas City 8:30 A.M. Left on Atchison Topeka and Santa Fe 10 A.M. Fine farming country with much rocky timber between. Walnut, oak, etc., but trees young and small. Crossed into Kansas near Kansas City. Kaw River to the left. Woods and rolling prairies. White Heron. Lawrence at 12 noon. Pretty town. Left Kaw River between Lawrence and Topeka. [Arrived] Topeka 1 P.M. State capital. Low, extensive —fine schools. Temperate. 20,000 inhabitants. From Topeka on, the timber gradually disappears, and an extensive, rolling prairie begins, poorly settled in places. Timber only along creeks—mostly cottonwood. Sunflowers, buffalo-grass appeared in whitish patches about Osage City. River Marais du Cygne, densely wooded. Emporia, 6,000 inhabitants, 4:30 P.M. Crossing of Missouri Kansas and Texas Railroad. Many good peaches and grapes raised. Large orchards between Emporia and Redding—also sugar cane. From Emporia on, prairies again. The undulations, mesa-like, are formed by strata of whitish fine limestone, covered with soil. Abrasion [erosion] and denudation.

From Florence on, the country becomes very level again, thinly settled. Dry after passing Newton, Kansas. Air cool, but dusty. Later at night the prairie lies perfectly flat, not even ridges appearing at the horizon.

AUGUST 22: Perfectly level, dreary prairie, occasional small houses, but neither shrub nor tree. Crossed into Colorado 9 P.M. Change in vegetation. Yucca cactus. Caddoa. Arkansas River. Mountains (Pike's Peak) seen indistinctly. Fort Lyon. Sage brush, yucca, *Opuntia*. Stone and mud houses in Colorado. Few trees. La Junta. 12:20 P.M. on Arkansas River, sandy. To Arkansas River 1 P.M. Beech, sycamore trees. *Opuntia*, sages. Collected two *Blaps*, two *Cicindelidae*, and one wasp. Current of river swift. At 2 P.M. started south for hills. Arid, slaty, covered sparsely with *Opuntia* and yucca. Washings. Two mountain chains in view. On the hills another species of *Blaps*, very large. At the hotel, most splendid specimen of *Mamgen denthritis*.

AUGUST 23: Left La Junta 1 A.M. Moonlight. Barren, cool. Trees become visible about 2 A.M. on high ridges. Pines. Slept till 4 A.M., when a high range appeared left, and also, with distant hazy peaks right. At the foot of the left-hand range (with prominent peak, Fishers' Peak). 9,076 feet. Trinidad, 3,000 inhabitants. Farther on, El Moro with large coke-works. Began to ascend the Ratones at 5:30 A.M. Very wild and picturesque. Ridges and tops covered with pines, slopes with pinavetitas and encina. Much more vegetation than at La Junta. Very wet. All one coal-field, seams cropping out everywhere. Occasional glimpses at the snow covered Sangre de Cristo. Padre Alex-[ander] Leone, S. J. [entrained] La Junta, New Mexico [Colorado?]. Very interesting. Out of Ratones 6 A.M. Willow Springs. High, grassy. Crossed into New Mexico 6 A.M. Fine view on Ratones left, and 8 A.M. in the high range right, fine mesas, prairie-dogs, eagles and hawks. Yucca appears after Dorsey, 8:30 A.M. Springer 9 A.M. Adobe. Fine view on the sierra to the right. The mesa formation is very prominent all forenoon. Fine pasture, chamizo, grama, and zacate. No cactus yet. Doubtful about the Sangre de Cristo range; probably seen behind the others. Snowclad. From Springer on, totally treeless except the distant mountainslope. Enormous mesas. Hawks and eagles. Near Wagon Mound, a large pond and circular mesas. Soon after, for miles along the road, fine trachytic rocks scattered. Sierra de la Gallina, left hand. Volcanic crater. Beyond Santa Clara the Sierra de Mora appeared right and in front. Are moving towards it and swinging round toward Sierra de la Gallina. Entered Cañón de Fortecito 11 A.M. Very fine. Cactus, sunflowers. La Junta 12 noon. Las Vegas 12:45 P.M., at foot of Sierra de Mora. Fort Union near Sierra de la Gallina. Fight between U. S. Government and railroad company. Fine view of the whole mountain chain from La Junta. From Springer we had the Rio Colorado [Canadian] to the left and the Rio Cimarron to the right. Small creeks there. Almost uninhabited pasture from Willow Creek to the canyon. From [beyond] the canyon much maize, large tracts of sunflowers in bloom. Mountains sloping gradually. Las Vegas two towns, and the springs of Ojos Calientes. Scenery through canyon fine, great damage through floods. Two miles from Las Vegas entered Romero Cañón, then Bernal with Starvation Point, Arroyo de Pecos, church of Pecos with ruins of pueblo in the distance. Finally, after Galisteo [Glorieta], Cañon del Apache. Very romantic, with fine granite, and fine *Opuntia arborescens*. Beautiful mountain views. Rainbows. Reached Santa Fe late (7:30 P.M.). Grand Central Hotel.

AUGUST 24: Slept until 9 A.M. with bedbugs. Went to General Wallace,[53] not at home; to Honorable L.Waldo,[54] not at home; to General Atkinson, not at home. General Wallace has the mining fever and is forty miles from here on a placita. General Atkinson is at Taos. Went to the Vicar-General, Padre Eguillon.[55] Insists upon my going to Isleta. No documents at the archbishop's. Report of Vargas stolen by an American. It be-

---

53. Lewis Wallace (1827-1905) was governor of New Mexico from 1878-81 and minister to Turkey 1881-85. He is best known for his historical novel *Ben Hur*.

54. Waldo was a well known lawyer and judge in the New Mexico of Bandelier's time.

55. Father Eguillon was originally from Clermont in France. He came to Santa Fe in 1854 at the invitation of Father Joseph Macheboeuf (Machebeuf), Lamy's Vicar-General. He was first a parish priest at Socorro and later priest of the Cathedral of Santa Fe and Vicar-General. Eguillon died in 1892.

longed to Tomás Cabeza de Vaca. Destruction of old documents at the territorial library. S. Ellison, the librarian, down with broken leg. Felsenthal out of town. Went to see two photographers. One of them, Bliss asks $5.00 per day and $2.00 per copy.

In the afternoon wrote till 2 P.M., then went up to the vicar's. Met Fathers Gasparri and Rolli. Latter spoke of Abó, Gran Quivira, etc. Also in the garden of the Archbishop met Father [Donato] Gasparri of Albuquerque, promised to show me archives. Saw chapel of Guadalupe. Very fine; made by imported French artists. Cathedral. Grapes. Concluded [decided] to go to Pecos tomorrow. Received letter of Rev. J. Bender [Bencher?] to Archbishop Lamy.[56] Wrote till 9 P.M. Very tired.

AUGUST 25: At the "cure" 7 A.M. Discouraging interview with Mrs. Tench and Father Parisis. Judge Waldo not at home. Archives locked up. Was informed by Mr. Hathaway of the General Land Office, that Major Brooks discovered and explored mounds near Fort Marcy, flint chips, agates, etc. Knows not of any ruins at Santa Fe. Bennett and Brown[57] photo offer, 5 x 8 plates. Will do the work and give twelve prints from each plate, at cost, they keeping the plates. Then went up to Fort Marcy. High on top of hills overlooking the city; view fine and extensive. Found a *Cetonia* and, on old Fort Marcy, a *Rhynchophore* (*Curculionida*). Houses all adobe, some new. Population of Santa Fe 6,500 souls.

Afternoon at parish. Discouraging. Met Mr. [Worth?] friendly. Went to see collection of Mr. Gold.[58] A lot of fine pottery,

---

56. John B. Lamy (1814-88) was born in France and came to America in 1839, after his ordainment. He arrived in New Mexico in 1851 and was made archbishop in 1875. Father Salpointe was appointed coadjutor in 1885 and Lamy retired soon afterward.

Father Lamy has been commemorated by Willa Cather in the book *Death Comes for the Archbishop*.

57. Well known photographers in Santa Fe. G. C. Bennett and Henry Brown worked with Bandelier for some years and accompanied him on trips to various pueblos.

58. Jake Gold, an early curio dealer in Santa Fe. His curiosity shop was established at the northwest corner of Burro Alley and San Francisco Street.

but all recent. Mr. Gold offers me the pottery at $4.00 per dozen. All right so far, if Professor Norton acquiesces. Saw Pueblo Indians on the streets, fine fellows, clad in white with hair tressed behind and hanging down each side. Driving a herd of burros.

Great vice here, gambling—at hotels, at Mr. Gold's, everywhere gambling places, in the form of "clubs." Meat (sheep and beef) hung out on the portales here. Not very inviting. Padre Eguillon very strong concerning the wanton destruction of the archives under Governor Pyle [Pile], says it was done on purpose to destroy Mexican claims. Cites claims of one Wilson as example.

AUGUST 26: No train. Received by Hicks, *Libro 3a de Casamientos* [Book 3a of Marriages] from Padre Eguillon. Then went up to San Miguel with Mr. J. D. Culbertson of Pennsylvania. He kindly assisted me in measuring the old so-called "pueblo" house. Two stories, at the end of each room a cut through which the upper story is ascended by a ladder. A new addition, one story high, is made and is also fully occupied. Occupants all Mexicans. Know nothing of the building, but kind. Then went to Nuestra Señora de Guadalupe. Old paintings, could not ascertain their ages, but their make very similar to the faces on pottery. Sacristán not at home, boy came after us with key; "*dos reales*" [about ten cents]. Did not beg, however. Tombstones all recent. Saw Captain D. J. Miller again and complained. He was pleasant and gave me the centennial address to read. Also letter to Dr. Thomas. [By-]passing old man Dunant, I met, at last, Mr. Felsenthal, who offered to introduce me to the Indians at Tesuque. Went to Dr. Thomas, who was sick. Indian Bureau in the hands of Presbyterians. Met Dr. Milburn and Mr. Thurston, and arranged with the latter to accompany me to Pecos.[59] Saw Dr. Thomas finally, who promised to write to Laguna for me. Disturbances there. Plan to go to

---

59. Cicuyé (probably the Tiwa name for Pecos Pueblo) was the word used by early Spanish writers to refer to Pecos.

Acoma. Isleta matters explained by Dr. Thomas. Worked at *Libro de Casamientos* till 4 P.M. Went to Padre Eguillon and returned the book. All very cordial: explained situation at Isleta. Padre Eguillon advised [me to go to] Tesuque also. Went to Mr. Felsenthal. He showed me the manuscripts of the year 1643. Previously had seen Mr. Gold, who showed manuscripts (petition and grant) of 1711 and 1712. Very important for Puaray. Kind. Mr. Felsenthal called at my room with me; read to him what I had written. Wrote upon Tiguex and Cicuyé till 11 P.M.

Called at Swope's. No conveyance to Pecos tomorrow. I hear that there is a surveying party at Pecos with photographic instruments.

AUGUST 27: After breakfast went to Swope and engaged two-horse buggy for Pecos tomorrow. $5.00 per day with feed, but no driver. To be ready at 6 A.M. tomorrow. Then saw Mr. Felsenthal, who gave me a fine pen-sketch map of New Mexico. Met several Fathers, also Governor Wallace, who is a thorough miner. Great "Powers" procession of guests of the Grand Central. Ludicrous. Saw and conversed with Padre Rómulo Ribera[60] of Peña Blanca. Invitation to stay with him next week. Good hints about Pecos by Felsenthal. Santo Domingo Indians in town. Wrote greatest part of the day. Called on General Wallace, 4 P.M. Very kind and polite; hints about Pecos. Much taken up by mining. Claims that archives were much neglected by Governor Arny,[61] his predecessor, thrown into an outhouse to rot, and that he saved them. Does not disavow the destruction of the archives by Governor Pyle, but says it was through ignorance (??).

AUGUST 28: Started with J. D. [Culbertson] and Thurston for Pecos about 7:30 A.M. with two-horse buggy. As soon as we entered the mountains, piñones appeared with encina. Vegetation increasing. Some small fields of maize, very few. About

---

60. Padre Rómulo Ribera was one of the priests added to the New Mexico church by Archbishop Lamy.

9 A.M., high ridge of coarse-grained granite with piñones. Trees all inclined to the northeast and east. Left, high rocky slopes, traversing a valley. 11 A.M., Cañoncito, fine rocks, soil getting red. Approaching Glorieta, 12 noon, in sight of the red-streaked rocks. At the tie camp overlooking Pecos valley, 1 P.M. Walls of church, north: 1 meter 50 centimeters thick, running east to west. Pueblo, north northwest from church. Adobe of church 55 x 28 centimeters; 8 centimeters thick with interstices of 5 centimeters of mud.

Found also two horns, like buffalo horns, a metate, much obsidian, flint, and pottery. Returned to "Ball's" [Baughl's]; slept there.

---

61. Because of frequent mentions of New Mexican political figures in the journals, we append here a list of governors of New Mexico from the time of Mexican independence through the Bandelier period.

Mexican Period		American Period	
1822-1823	Francisco Xavier Chavez (replaced Melgares, last ruler under Spain)	1846-1851	Control of New Mexico by the U.S. military forces. In 1851 New Mexico was made a territory and the first territorial governor took office in that year.
1823-1824	Antonio Viscarra		
1824-1825	Bartolomé Baca		
1825-1828	Antonio de Narbona, Manuel Armijo, Antonio Viscarra	1851-1852	James S. Calhoun
1828-1831	José Antonio Chavez	1852-	John Grenier, acting
1831-1833	Santiago Abreu	1852-1853	William Carr Lane
1833-1834	Francisco Sarracino, Juan Rafael Ortiz, Mariano Chavez	1853-	W. S. Messervy, acting
		1853-1856	David Merriwether
		1856-1857	W. W. H. Davis, acting
1835-1837	Albino Perez (assassinated by a rebel group in 1837)	1857-1861	Abraham Rencher
		1861-1866	Henry Connelly
1837-	Gonzales (Taos Indian, murdered by Armijo in 1837)	1866-	W. F. M. Arny, acting
		1866-1869	Robert B. Mitchell
		1869-1871	William A. Pile
		1871-1875	Marsh Giddings
1837-1844	Manuel Armijo (head of a "loyalist" faction that overthrew the rebel force)	1875-	William G. Ritch, acting
		1875-1878	Samuel B. Axtell
		1878-1881	Lew Wallace
		1881-1885	Lionel A. Sheldon
1844-1845	Martinez de Lejana	1885-1889	Edmund G. Ross
1845-1846	Armijo (resumed office)	1889-1893	L. Bradford Prince
1846-	Bautista Vigil		

August 29: John McRae and an American went with us to the ruins. On the Pecos, where the road crosses, showed us footprints, and other rock carvings; also cup-stones, and a cup-circle. Mr. Thurston surveyed the upper part of the ruins, and I surveyed the lower part, south of the church. Were also shown a fine spring on the west bank of the Pecos, nearly opposite the pueblo. Heard of a pueblo four miles south, on the Pecos River. Left the ruins at 12 noon, and arrived at Baughl's at 1 p.m. Mr. Thurston left about 2 p.m. with the horses.

Am told that deer, wolves, etc. are abundant. Thomas Munn found an old bell on the mountain about three miles from Pecos. No date on the fragment which he showed me. Says there are other buildings there. Very interesting conversation with John McRae, an old Canadian trapper. A young man from Arizona told me that a friend of his near Florence, Arizona, dug out an olla [jar] containing some human bones with a human skull on top of the olla (cremation). He also says the Casas Grandes [Casa Grande, actually][62] on the Rio Gila are higher than the church at Pecos.

August 30: Started with G. Gristman, and took straight road to the ruins, 7:30 a.m. Reached the Rio Pecos 8 a.m. On the right bank stone enclosure.*

August 31: *Started 7:30 a.m. Got through with survey about 1 p.m. and went home.

September 1: Went alone to rock inscription, found some pottery. Large flock of sheep, etc., guarded by two fine dogs. Examined the plain south of the church. No pottery in the rectangle between mound and basin; in fact, no pottery until the

---

62. The ruins referred to are of Casa Grande, a Hohokam site, on the south side of the Gila River near present day Florence, Arizona. Casas Grandes (later visited and described by Bandelier—see footnote 10) is a large archaeological site in central Chihuahua where recent excavations suggest a mixture of Southwestern and Mexican High Culture traditions. Both sites were deserted some centuries before the coming of the Spaniards.

* Asterisks are used throughout the text of the journals to indicate deletion of sketches. See Preface, pp. xi-xii.

talus before the church and the great stone enclosure south of it are reached. Pottery scarce in the enclosures. On the talus, obsidian and other [types of] arrowheads. Made a little heap of stuff on projecting ledge north of church, east slope. Dug in the center of ruined structure*.

On the north side of the house, east edge of the mesa, an opened grave, square, walled in, opening to the east. Excavated depth 1 meter, and still not at bottom. Much pottery, hard burnt. Some yellow pine wood and bones. Excavated along the wall and in the bottom, but found nothing at all. Returned home about 2 P.M. Very tired. Found wheat straw on the roof of one room.

SEPTEMBER 2: Went to Mrs. Kozlowski. Has been living here well over 22 years. Says that the Indians had all left before she came. Does not recollect having ever heard or seen anything of graves. Refers to Mariano Ruiz and met him on the plain returning from the station of Kingman. He was friendly and told me that indeed he and his family had come to Pecos from Jemez in 1837; that he had been adopted into the tribe; that in 1840, the remaining five Indians of Pecos were removed to Jemez by the three oficiales of Jemez, calling for them. He says that at the time the Indians of Jemez [Pecos?] gave him a deed for their land [at Pecos], which deed is now in hands of Major Sena at Santa Fe. He also says that the Pecos and Jemez speak the same language. The names of the five Indians of Pecos were: Antonio, Gregorio, Goya, Juan Domingo, and Francisco. Asked him about the language, but he did not remember. He, however, told me that the burial places of the ancient Pecos are on the right bank of the river, *al primer rincon* [in the first rincon]. I went after [followed] his directions but could not find the place. Shall return tomorrow. Returning home I found Mr. Bennett at Baughl's with his photographic apparatus. We walked out at 2 P.M., and worked until 6:30 P.M. when, there being no wagon in sight, we shouldered our traps [gear] and walked home with them. It was a heavy load. Confounded pen won't work again!

SEPTEMBER 3: Very fine, went out with Bennett to photograph and then to Kozlowski's and to Ruiz.* Called at Señor Mariano Ruiz. Found him after considerable trouble and search. Sat down under a tree and talked. He came in 1837 from Jemez, when there were but eighteen Indians left. Was adopted *como hijo del pueblo* [as a son of the pueblo]. In 1838, the *capitán de la guerra* [war captain] of Jemez came over, having heard that the Indians of Pecos were fast dying, as well as their flocks. The sickness was fiebre [influenza], commencing with tembladas [*chills*], and closing with calenturas [fever]. The Pecos then were not willing to leave, but in 1839 they sold the flocks and everything, and made a deed to Ruiz for the land. This deed is now in the hands of Major Sena at Santa Fe. In 1840, the gobernador, the capitán, and the cacique of Jemez, with two or three other Indians, came over again, and the Pecos, five in number, with their families, left for Jemez. Their houses were still standing, three stories high. They kept their holy embers (not fire) alive in the great room at the north wing, and met in the estufa,[63] but Ruiz was never permitted to assist. Every year an Indian was elected *para cuidar del fuego* [to care for the fire], and the tale was, that if anyone who had ever taken care of the fire left the tribe, he would die. On that account, Ruiz always refused to take charge of the fire. They were idolators, and Ruiz says that the report was that they worshipped a [large] serpent (una vivora grande) which they kept concealed. He presumed that they took both the embers and the snake to Jemez.[64] Does

63. The Spanish word *estufa* (stove) was given by the early Spanish explorers to the ceremonial rooms of the Pueblo Indians presumably because of the resemblance of the Rio Grande structures to an outside oven or, possibly, to a sweat-house. At present the Hopi word for these ceremonial buildings, *kiva*, has completely replaced *estufa* in anthropological literature.

64. The "snake worship" probably refers to the activities of a snake society. Of the sacred fire, Parsons commented:

"Accounts of such fire-making or keeping ritual have combined with White preconception to produce the legend of the perpetual fire which has been current for years among the Whites in the Southwest. The account given Simpson of the Pecos fire is in this connection of interest. 'The old man and his daughter, who at the time were tending the Sacred fire at Pecos (i.e., engaged in some

not recollect anything about their language beyond that it is the same as that of Jemez. Insisted that they understood neither those of Santo Domingo, nor those of Tesuque, but conversed with them in Spanish.[65] Therefore he did not pay any attention to it.

Says that all the officials, the gobernador, capitán, and cacique, are elected for life. The son can succeed to the father *si está bueno* [if he is competent]. The two first officers *son guerreros* [are warriors]. The capitán has charge of the lands. I asked him about the burial places, and he said that el campo santo [cemetery] of the heathen Pecos was in a barranca [canyon] on the right hand side of the creek. This is doubtful. I then went back

---

ceremonial), the enemy (Mexicans) seized and beat—the daughter at length being carried away captive, and the old man escaping by way of Galisteo to Jemez. This was the reason of the fire of Montezuma ceasing . . .' At the time of Simpson's visit the Montezuma legend was in full career as the most convenient camouflage for native ceremonial. The kivas were described to the enquiring lieutenant as the churches of Montezuma." (Parsons 1925: 75-6)

65. There are several language stocks and sub-stocks located in the Southwest. Among Pueblos in the Rio Grande drainage two such stocks are represented, Tanoan and Keresan. Tanoan is further broken down into the languages Tiwa, Tewa, and Towa, plus Tano (actually only a variant of Tewa) and Piro. Tiwa settlements include the pueblos of Taos, Picurís (now called San Lorenzo), Sandia, and Isleta. Tewa is spoken at San Ildefonso, Santa Clara, San Juan, Pojoaque, Nambé, and Tesuque with Tano, the language of the extinct Galisteo pueblos represented at Tewa village or Hano in Hopi country. Towa is spoken only by Jemez (and settlers from the town of Pecos in the Pecos drainage, now living at Jemez). Piro was the language of the pueblos in the Abó, Tibira area, and of groups along the Rio Grande south of Albuquerque.

Keresan pueblos along the Rio Grande proper include Cochiti, Santo Domingo, and San Felipe, while Zia and Santa Ana are in the Jemez drainage. Farther west and somewhat more isolated are the pueblos of Acoma and Laguna.

In addition to these stocks two others are found among the pueblos. Zuñian is represented only by the language of the Zuñi Indians of west central New Mexico. The Hopi villagers (with the exception of Hano) speak a Shoshonean language.

Non-puebloan peoples include the Navajo and Apache speaking languages of the Apachean branch of Athabascan, the Utes, Paiutes, and Comanche speaking dialects of Shoshonean, the Pima and Papago using Piman languages (related to Shoshonean and, with the latter, part of the great Uto-Aztecan stock). On the eastern edge of the Southwest the Kiowa speak a language probably related to Tanoan.

to Mrs. Kozlowski, who confirmed the veracity of the old man. She has been here for twenty-two years and saw the houses still perfect. The church was with its roof and complete. Kozlowski tore parts of it down to build stables and houses.

Examined the creek right and left from Kozlowski's up without result, except that on the left bank, below the rock-carvings, there is a mound covered with, or rather strewn over with, stones. Could not dig. Returning to the church, found Mr. Wittick with Bennett. [Wittick] is at Pecos and is a photographer. He told me that on the right bank of the creek, opposite the rock-carvings, stone walls, human bones (skulls), and charcoal have been found. We went there and found a projecting wall, and farther on, bones. A stratum of white ashes, burnt clay, and charcoal runs all along the bank for about 50 meters, evidently in line with the wall which, if continued, would run outside of the bank, across the bottom. All red clay and loam. Pottery of lower strata all ribbed. Much painted pottery above, and very extensive flat mounds and ridges on the surface.* Could take no measures nor plans. They run partly across the road and along the banks of the creek, opposite to the lowest ruins south of the church.

Ruiz told me that the great enclosure, below the pueblo, was the huerta [orchard or garden]. The enclosure on the opposite side of the river or creek, the "corral," the one opposite the church the huerta de la iglesia [church orchard and, probably, garden]. By the side of the church stood the convento. He also says that the Indians of Pecos, of Santo Domingo, of Jemez, of Tesuque, etc., claim to have taken no part in the revolt of 1680, throwing all the blame on Zuñi, Acoma, Moqui [Hopi], etc.[66] Says also that all the lands belong to the pueblos, the individuals having only rights to plots for cultivation, for as long as they cultivated them.

---

66. Since Bandelier failed to evaluate this information, it is well to note that the Pueblo Indian Revolt of 1680 was essentially the result of collaboration among the Rio Grande Pueblos. A commonly recognized leader was Popé of Taos; the roster of participants included virtually all Pueblos north of Isleta (Hackett 1942).

Concluded photographing about 4 P.M. and gathered all my objects into the church. Then hired a Mexican wagon and rode home. Hard job, very tired. Bennett left at 9 P.M. He told me the vivora story [as it appears in Taos]; he had it from Judge Joseph [Antonio?].

In the morning I had seen Capt. F. A. Blake from White Oaks, who invited me to call on him and see Gran Quivira. Gold excitement there. Mr. Hornbeck came in and confirmed Mr. Blake's sayings, fine country, but wild. No obsidian flakes on the ruins opposite the carvings. Do not believe fully in the *campo santo antiguo* [old cemetery] of Ruiz, but believe it to be pueblos of very ancient date. Vegetation to the south better, and some *Cicindelidae*. On the ruins always a very brisk wind.

SEPTEMBER 4: Collected the specimens.

Distance from buried wall to road, north, 68 meters; from buried wall to place of human bones, south, 5 meters. If wall had continued south, it would have passed inside of the bones, not enclosing them. 62 meters south-southwest from wall, another barranca. Then several seams of charcoal, ashes, and burnt clay, at the depth of 1.30 [meters], the lowest; highest seam about 0.45 centimeters high. Human bones above that and in front. No trace of remains in bluffs projecting beyond line from north-northeast to south-southwest, nor beyond to the south.*

Afternoon, very interesting conversation with F. A. Blake and Mr. Debrant. The latter told me how the flint arrowheads were indentated. By small firesticks. Therefore not chipped on the edge. At every contact with fire, if blown on, a piece flies off.[67]

SEPTEMBER 5: Walked over to Pecos, about 4 miles, crossing high ridges with cedars and piñones. Stopped with E. K. Walters and talked with a number of Mexicans. The source of the Rio Pecos is the Jicarrito, seen northeast from the ruins. Dined

---

67. This belief is still common in many parts of America. Actually flint and other fracturable material are chipped by applying pressure with a piece of wood, bone, antler, or metal. Chips are normally flaked off the core on the side opposite the application of pressure.

with Juan Baca y Salazar and his brother-in-law, Ambrosio Pino. The latter lives at Galisteo, where there are about seven Tano Indians left. They all say that where the bell was found on the mesa of Pecos were the winter-houses of the Pecos Indians, and that they carried the bell along with them when they destroyed the church in 1680.

Then called on Father León Mailluchet (from Franche-Comté, and well-known about the Jura [district]; was the vicar near Porrentruy). He lives with his brother and family, who are keeping house for him. No church records back of 1862. Has two paintings, one on buffalo-hide representing Nuestra Señora de Guadalupe, 1.75 [meters] long and 1.45 [meters] wide, the other of same size on cloth representing Nuestra Señora de los Angeles. Sells them for $60.00. Both from old Pecos church. The latter is remarkably well done. He says the grounds of the ruins of Pecos were sold by the Indians to the archbishop.

Returned on foot and met Thomas Munn. Interesting. He says that where the fragments of the bell were found, there is a circular basin (estufa)[68] and that a man named Murphy noticed the ruins of what was like an old fortification, also an oblong chamber of cut stone, containing a skeleton, looking to the east. Says also that the timber is cut in many places, like unto an opening. Train on time at 5 P.M., but missed it. Compelled to stay. Made arrangements with Thomas Munn to go to the mesa tomorrow.

At night had an interesting conversation with John D. McRae about Indian customs. He says that [to the] north the Indians will indicate, upon leaving camp, their direction and next camp by a bent stick.* If they go out in the same direction several days, they will bend their stick as many times as there are days. He insists that the carvings on the rocks[69] indicate going after turkeys, there being turkey-tracks pointing to the high mesa.

---

68. See footnote 63.

69. Petroglyphs (carvings) and pictographs (paintings) on rocks are found in many parts of the Southwest. They are ideographs but are in no sense a written script and usually cannot be interpreted with any assurance.

Says that among the northern Indians, killing is indicated by a motion of shooting the bow, and then with both hands throwing over the right shoulder. Number of days by pointing to the sun, and counting off the fingers.

SEPTEMBER 6: Rather unwell. Started for the mesa with Thomas Munn at 8 A.M. Walls of rubble sandstone run north and southeast and west; 50 yards north, a round estufa, 4 meters in diameter. Walls about 1 meter [high] around and straight up the mesa, along the tiechute. Mariano says that all along the foot of the mesa, there are stone graves and remains of buildings over them. On the slope of mesa toward the southwest in a canyon found the bell. Between it and camp, building 11 x 3 [meters]. Impossible to find out whether Indian or Mexican. No trace of other ruins, except reports. Mesa is covered with white pine and piñones. Much encina, many flowers, mountainsage, large yuccas. Slopes sometimes fertile, but no trace of ruins. Ascended to two tops. Red sandstone: on top, yellow. Splendid view beyond [to] the peak of Bernal. Descent into the valley very steep but grand. Large ruins about one-half mile from railroad. Left Baughl's 4:42 and reached Santa Fe 6 P.M. Found on top of mesa *Chamaerops*, and many beetles. At night in room, first *Capriciamia*. On slopes of mesas large *Buprestis*.

SEPTEMBER 7: At the Surveyor General's office found plat of the "Pueblo de Pecos," also grant to the Indians of Pecos, dated September 25, 1689, El Paso del Norte, and signed Domingo Jíronza Petriz de Cruzate.[70] The grant covers 18,763 33/100 acres according to report September 30, 1856.

To SEPTEMBER 13: Day for day at work on the report. Sometimes till 1 and 2 A.M. Sent off the first 24½ pages to Professor Norton Thursday, September 9; 61 pages done by 6 P.M. Sep-

---

70. Domingo Jíronza Petriz de Cruzate, Governor of New Mexico (1682-86, 1688-91) during the Pueblo Revolt period, exercising his office from the El Paso area. In 1689 he captured the Pueblo of Zia in a reconquest attempt but shortly thereafter was forced to retreat south.

Grants issued by Cruzate to various pueblos have been questioned as to authenticity.

tember 13. Wrote today to E. H. Greenleaf about membership of D. J. Miller, and also wrote historical sketch of Pecos for Bennett. Was presented, by Mr. Andrews, with a one-fourth medallion stone. Priests and everybody very friendly. D. J. Miller was over at night, 12 and 13. Many Indians from pueblos here. Sandia, Cochiti, Tesuque, Nambé—with pottery. Those [Indians] of Sandia particularly copper-colored and small. No letters from home. Spent the evening at Governor Wallace's on September 10. Costly living. Society I don't know.

SEPTEMBER 14: Visit to the Honorable S. Ellison. Very, very kind. Insists upon my going to Jemez. Informed me that Señor Vigil had a document proving the destruction of Pecos tribe by the Comanches, probably in the eighteenth century. Called on Señor Vigil at the secretary's office, who promised to show me the document at 2 P.M. Made a short call at Dr. B. M. Thomas and met Felsenthal. Sent off beetles to Maly and to Dr. Hagen. Conversation with Señor E. Vigil. Very interesting. He explained the round towers. He says they were the store-houses. In general, he confirms the plan and diagrams.

The Comanche were the greatest enemies of the Pecos, but he knows of no document in possession of his father, Donaciano Vigil, in relation to it. He knows a good deal about the Indians of Pecos; says that in 1840 there were fourteen left in all. They came before Governor Armijo and declared to him that they could not maintain themselves anymore, and that, their friends and parientes [relatives] of Jemez having invited them to live with them, they would abandon their place, and go to Jemez. They had sold most of their lands (Señor Juan Estevan Pino having bought the greatest part of them). The rest they had given to Ruiz, as hijo del pueblo [son of the tribe]. Important mention regarding the manner of making pottery. Promises to look out for documents. Evening at the Governor's till 10 P.M.

SEPTEMBER 15: After breakfast, two Indians of Tesuque came into my room, asking for matches. Heard the Tehua [Tewa] language for the first time. Does not sound unpleasant. The name of their governor is Juan Domingo. They begged, rather

decently. Finished the general plat [of Pecos, working] till
3 P.M.

Governor Wallace left for the placitas this morning—two
turquoise mines, 17 and 20 miles from Santa Fe at the Cerrillos.
At night, letter from Putnam.[71] Jewish New Year; most of the
Jewish stores closed. Serenade to ladies across the alley about
9 P.M. Good voices. Call from D. J. Miller. Interesting on
archaeological topics. He says they had a historical society at
Santa Fe previous to the year [1861] and quite a collection.
When the war broke out, it disbanded, and the collection was
lost. Efforts to gather a mineralogical collection failed. He
insists that the Taos speak the same language as the Isletas.

SEPTEMBER 16: Flies again much troublesome. Miller called
at 9 A.M. Loafed around much today. Showed Thurston the
map or plat of the ruins, and he declared them very truthful
and correct. Letters from Papa tonight, also enclosing one from
[Lewis Henry] Morgan. Wrote to folks and to Norton tonight,
sending home pages 25-61 inclusive.

SEPTEMBER 17: Called at Governor's to get Vetancurt. Then
at Secretary Ritch three times. He placed his notes at my disposal. Finished "History of Pecos." Night most magnificent,
spent with Miller at Ritch's.

SEPTEMBER 18: This morning mailed "History" and diagram A
and general plat to Papa. Cards to Norton, to Putnam, and to
R. L. Packard, Washington, D. C. Finished the text about
1 P.M., and sent it off. Evening superb. Met a Taos Indian, a
very large man, begging. Thurston left Indian bureau tonight.
Met E. B. Safford, of San Isidro, Jemez, who offers to board
me for $25.00 a month. Jemez 54 miles from Pecos. Tonight,
news that Las Vegas (lower town) is burning. Letter from
Professor Norton tonight.

---

71. Frederick Putnam (1839-1915), an early American anthropologist. His
positions include Curator of Peabody Museum, Secretary of the American Association for Advancement of Science, and Curator of Anthropology, American
Museum of Natural History. In 1903 he was named Professor of Anthropology
and Director of the Anthropological Museum at University of California.

SEPTEMBER 19: Letter from Joe, A.M. Finished "Historical Introduction" about 5 P.M. Wrote to folks at home and to Professor Norton. Began letter to Hecker.

SEPTEMBER 20: Mailed to Prof. Norton, to Joe, two cards to Gatschet[72] and Padre Ribera, also letter to Hecker. Bought pottery for Joe's birthday at Gold's. Could not get to see manuscripts there and at Felsenthal's! Both absent. Last evening, I turned over to D. J. Miller my papers, Vetancurt and Castañeda.[73] About 10 A.M., Tesuque Indian came into my room. Begged for water. His name is Juan Diego Andieta, Indian name Oqqe, also Venaka. Says that the governor, Juan Domingo, is in town. Also that they do not understand the Queres [Keres], Taos, and Jemez in their own idioms. Dirty. Gave him a red pencil. Was very friendly. Received from Gatschet, a paper, and from Greenleaf, a stylographic pen. Sent card to Bohn and a few lines to Joe, with scraps [clippings].

Called on Mr. Fickett and Monfort and was most politely received. They gave me specimens of turquoise from the Cerrillos.[74] Mr. Monfort then promised to go out and get me specimens himself. They have a specimen of turquoise, weighing 4½ pounds, solid mineral. Mr. Monfort then gave me interesting statements. At Cerrillos there are two shafts of old date. In one of these shafts he met two Indians cutting out turquoises with hatchets and carrying them up in leather bags. The turquoises are in a vein and also in pockets. This system

---

72. Albert Samuel Gatschet (1832-1907), an American ethnologist and linguist associated for many years with the Bureau of American Ethnology.

73. Probably Father Augustín de Vetancurt's *Teatro Mexicana. Descripción breve de los sucessos exemplares, historicos, politicos, militares, y religiosos del nuevo mundo occidental de las Indias*, 1694. Pedro de Castañeda de Naçera was a chronicler of the Coronado Expedition who wrote a *Relación de la jornada de Cíbola . . . 1540.*

74. Turquoise, a semi-precious stone, now much used for costume jewelry, was of a considerable ritual importance to the Pueblo Indians. It was mined in the Cerrillos area south of Santa Fe in pre-Spanish, as well as in historic times, and much of the Cerrillos turquoise is of very high quality. This same region is rich in metals; gold was discovered there in the early 18th century and the area also contains silver, lead, zinc, and copper.

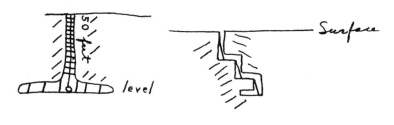

of mining is entirely different from that of today, and he illustrated it by drawings. Instead of sinking a shaft straight and then working on a level on both sides, as follows, say 50-100 feet, they go by steps, about in the following manner. Each shaft is 10-12 feet, and in each they place a ladder, leaving in every case a sufficient platform to rest it upon. Their ladders are but a round beam in which they cut notches.

He showed me a very imperfect stone hammer found there. (Mr. Bennett also has a stone hammer found at Cerrillos.) Mr. Monfort says that the Indians of Santo Domingo even wear these ornaments of turquoise in their ears and as necklaces at the present time, but he could not buy any of them. Even the boys wore them. It shows that the use of the turquoise ornaments is not lost.

Called on E. K. Walters and wife at Herlow's Hotel; he told me that they had found several images of stone south of the place where the corrugated pottery is. They were set in the ground, about 3 feet below the surface. They keep them for me. Met Mr. Wittick, the photographer. He told me he found a round tower opposite Glorieta, on the other side of the mesa; also other ruins, some 3 feet in the ground. Copied the "Deed of Uribarri to González" (October 17, 1711) from Mr. Gold's manuscript, and returned the manuscript to him in Staab's store in presence of his brother and Mr. Zimmer.[75]

Spoke to Mr. Fickett. He said the turquoise mines were on top of the mountains and formed an excavation 50 x 75 feet. Wrote cards to Valentini, Engelmann, and Conant. Also a short letter to Icazbalceta.[76]

SEPTEMBER 21: Went to see Mr. Ellison about 10 A.M., Mr. Gold not being up at that time. [Ellison] was up in bed and improving. He told me that the Indians of Laguna preserved very well the tradition of a volcanic eruption whose crater could

---

75. It is interesting that Bandelier exercised so much care in attesting the return of this document. Apparently such documents were considered valuable for reasons other than scientific curiosity. Probably they were collectors' items.

76. See footnote 24.

yet be seen, [with] streams of lava flowing out. They are also intersected by channels 40, 50, to 60 feet wide, and 40 feet deep, overgrown with grass. These channels may, I conjecture, be decayed pumice-stone. The Indians call the eruption "*el año de la lumbre*" [the year of the fire], just as they call the year of the eclipse "*el año del eclipse*." I understood Mr. Ellison to say 1806 (might be 1860?). He says that this tradition is as definite as "that of the reconquest of New Mexico." This indicates that their recollections go back further than 1680, and possibly, that this eruption took place before that time.

In regard to Peña Blanca, he refers me to an Indian of Cochiti called José Hilario,[77] as the best guide and informant, also as an instructor in their language, which I might secure. He says there are any amount of ruins in the mountains and all along. In his opinion, they may date from before the reconquest, the Indians fleeing to the mountains before the approaching Spaniards. One ruin he mentions particularly as very old, on account of the path worn in the "friable" (!) sandstone from a spring up to the pueblo. He promises to examine the documents for me at the archives, and to assort them for me.

From him, went to Dunand. He said the Indians were very reticent about communicating their language. Even the padres do not know it, and the Indians conceal it from them. He says the two boys of Mrs. Tonche, at Isleta, have learnt the language well, because they had to speak it with the Indian children with whom they were raised, and who did not speak Spanish themselves.

Carried the remainder of my books to Mr. Miller (Simpson, Emory, Holmes and Jackson, Sitgreaves, Davis, Smithsonian report containing Coronado's march). Very busy. Mr. Gold in

---

77. This reference was to José Hilario Montoya and was well advised. José Hilario was an important figure in Cochiti life during the last quarter of the nineteenth century. He served as governor for at least ten annual terms but interestingly belonged to none of the secret societies with the exception of the Kachina Cult. José Hilario was the recognized intermediary between the Cochiti and outsiders for many years.

court at 11 A.M. Sent $80.00 to Joe with two scraps, etc. About 2 P.M. went to Secretary Ritch and had long talk with him.

About 3 P.M. started for the lomas [hills]. Passed by new gasometer and conduit, just in process of erection. Loma as usual, deserted. Collected citrine, epidote, etc., all among the drift. Cactus also. Attempted to go around by the northwest, but on the north-northwest faldas [slopes] was attacked by dogs and forced to retreat. On the north-northwesterly corner of the loma, found a hexagonal structure, 4 meters each side.* Rough foundation, overlooking the city and the south. Very good as post of observation. The foundations appear to be of rough boulders or drift-pebbles. Governor Wallace returned.

Received two letters tonight. One from Mr. Greenleaf and one from Mr. Norton. Quite unexpectedly I met Colonel Stevenson and party. (Messrs. Gilbraith and Hellers.)[78] They are going [to] Rio Arriba [Tewa Basin]. Reverend Ribera also came in. Will start Thursday by conveyance. Mr. Stevenson promised [to reconnoitre] the route. Mr. Hellers also promised to photograph if necessary. Got a bug for Maly. It was in Mr. Dunand's room. Looked at a new hammer and attended to clothing.

SEPTEMBER 22: A perfect day of tribulation. Had the greatest difficulty in getting the money—$60.00. Secured it with the endorsement of Mr. D. J. Miller and General Wallace. Met an Indian of San Ildefonso at Hayt and Joy's. He told me again that the Tehua and Jemez did not understand each other, nor do the other stocks, except [for the people of] Taos, Picuris, and Isleta, who understand each other. He told me also that the name of the governor of San Ildefonso was Te-huen (French "in"), and that it signifies *cola de águila* [eagle tail]. Very busy

---

78. James Stevenson (1840-1888) made a number of collecting expeditions in the Southwest for the Bureau of American Ethnology beginning in 1879 and continuing throughout much of the 1880's. Bandelier's "Hellers" was undoubtedly J. K. Hillers, a photographer with the Stevenson 1880 expedition. "Gilbraith" was probably F. G. Galbraith, an archaeologist.

running about. Money matters troublesome. Padre Ribera in town. Promises every assistance. Had a long conversation with Mr. Stevenson, interesting for language. Gave me many illustrations from the Dakota language. Does not believe in grammar for Indian idioms.[79] Saw Mr. Gilbraith too.

SEPTEMBER 23: Left 9:30 A.M. Went off at a lively pace, west-southwest. Vast plain, small *Opuntia* appearing. Six miles from Santa Fe, the foundations of the Pueblo Quemado [Pindi Pueblo; see Stubbs and Stallings 1953.] to the left of the road. Nothing but the foundations and the small mounds remain. Farther on, the small monument where Col. Pino [Governor Albino Perez] was killed in 1837. At the Cíenaga, the lava appeared. We passed south of the Tetilla [*La Tetilla* Peak]. The entire sierra is volcanic. Dark lava, capping yellow sandstone. Very picturesque. Rounding the Tetilla by a very difficult, though grand, bajada [descent], we struck the upper mesa of the Rio Grande. As soon as the lava appeared, the *Opuntia* also made its appearance in very large shrubs. The valley of Santa Fe is 18 miles to the cienaga, and the Rio Grande plateau 9 miles. It is barren, covered with *Salvia*, sabina, and cacti. Saw many prairie dogs about. A different kind of *Opuntia*, also a *Cereus*, appeared west of the Tetilla. A second descent to the Rio Grande bottom, on whose western slope we reached Peña Blanca about 3 P.M.

I collected four lava specimens from the bajada, which is very grand.* The mountains themselves extended in full view, *the Cerrillos*, Nuevos Pláceres, and the Sierra de Sandía being very prominent. The Sandia Mountains plainly visible south as a huge mass. People say that potatoes don't grow here, but Padre Ribera has found the contrary. Soil less fertile here than at Santa Fe. To the south along the river, the Mesa de Santa Ana closed the horizon. Into the farther south [west], the Sierra del

---

79. American Indian languages, like all known languages, historic or present, have complex grammatical systems. There are, of course, not only many languages but a large number of linguistic stocks in the Americas, so to talk of "Indian language" is in itself misleading.

Valle is very rugged and bold, and in front of it, 3 miles north of
Peña Blanca, the pueblo of Cochiti is situated above the river.
Santo Domingo is 4 miles south along the river, and San Felipe,
10 miles below Peña Blanca. Cochiti has 60 to 70 escaleras, Santo Domingo about 100. By escalera they mean families [house-
holds], including grandparents and grandchildren, etc.

At Peña Blanca, the cura lives with his father and mother,
the one 70, the other 65 years old, who keep house for him. He
is 32 years old, has been educated at Montreal, etc. He showed
me the books of the Church. At night mosquitoes plenty, but
they soon disappeared, immediately after sunset. Very, very
pleasant evening.

Ate atole for the first time. Tastes very good, also the frijoles.
Both are excellent. The plaza de Peña Blanca contains about
100 families, all Mexicans. Cottonwoods, alamos, grow in the
place. Walls all of adobe, very large. Wheat also very large, grain
long. Corn mostly variegated. Opposite, the Sierra del Valle
looks rugged, bold, and very fine. To the east-northeast the
Tetilla. The Rio de Santa Fé empties into the Rio Grande 2½
miles north.*

SEPTEMBER 24: Rode over to Santo Domingo with Father
Ribera and his father. Soon [reached the Domingo fields] in the
Rio Grande bottom 4 miles from Santo Domingo. The fields,
therefore, begin about 3 miles from Peña Blanca. Corn, not
high, but large ears. Wheat, irrigation everywhere, the fields
divided into squares. The main acequia is carried from the
river, one-half mile north of Peña Blanca, and the water distributed through the fields. These are squares or rectangles,
surrounded by little embankments along which the water is
carried. The trenches are then opened when the fields are dry
and the water permitted to overflow the banks.*

Arrived at Santo Domingo about 8 P.M. Went to the church
and to the parish. Indian home. Picturesque ovens on housetops. Two churches, old, very interesting. Fine library of Do-
minicans. Bells, old and new. Remnants of wooden sculptures.
Spoke to governor and fiscal. Kind, but discreet. Visited both

churches. Saw the calix, etc., made in Mexico, massive silver. Walls of the churchyard 0.48 [meters] thick.* Churchyard strewn with fragments of pottery, also fragments of corrugated pottery, fine obsidian, moss-agate, gypsum, agates. Also, outside, west towards the Rio. Distance to eastern arm of the Rio 49 meters, then a bluff from 5 to 10 meters high.

The old men told me that this corrugated pottery was very ancient; that the oldest pueblos made it before they left Rio Abajo. Gypsum and obsidian in the hills. Twelve infants baptized today, all from 23 to 38 days old. Collected the primicias [first-fruits], every one bringing in their bundles. The name of Santo Domingo is *Ti-guame*; of San Felipe, *Qqá-chista*. The sacristán declared there was no meaning to these names.*

I remained in the pueblo, selecting the room of the priests. All the Indians gathered around me to see me write. Before, I had been to see the pozos [water holes], half-way to the Rio Grande, west of the church. They are hardly 2 meters deep. Water alkaline. The sacristán, Santiago Crispin, told me that the lands could not be sold by individuals, and that they could not even sell all their crops without the consent of the governor. The fiscal has charge of the church matters. Padre Ribera promised to send me my mattress. Thus was left all alone with the Indians. Began to form acquaintances. Met Gregorio, a young married man. [Bandelier began to gather vocabularies at this point.] Refused to give me the word for sun, at the command of the governor.

Had a very long conversation with the sacristán, Santiago, and with my friend Gregorio. We discussed the matter of the chimneys. He says positively that, anciently, they used no chimneys. The fire was in the lower story, in one room, where they cooked; they slept in another room and kept their stores in another. Now they have chimneys. He says further that this pueblo has its hunters, 40 or 50 of them now. Some are buffalo hunters, others [hunt] deer and antelope, still others hares and smaller game. Their sole business is to hunt for the tribe.

Gregorio is a deer hunter. If they kill a buffalo, they cut the [meat] into slices and dry it in the sun. When it is well sliced and dried, they pack it in the buffalohide, saddle it on their horses, mules, or even carts and bring it home, where it is divided among the Pueblo. He is very positive. Says that now they use firearms, but that anciently they had but bows and arrows. When the Navajos made their appearance, or when it became known that they would take the warpath, the lower pueblos took to arms, and each one sent from 20 to 30 men. Santo Domingo sent about 50 men, armed with bows and arrows, lances, and clubs, and protected by the round shields of buffalohide. They held the bow with the left hand, the arrow with the fingers of the right hand, thus spanning the bow.

In the year when the Americans came (1846), Santiago was at school—the school then being held in the pueblo at the cabildo*[80] by a man called Luis Benavides. He was then 12 years old. In this year the school was dissolved. The cabildo is not used any longer. (The adobe of the old church is 35 x 27 [centimeters], 8 [centimeters] thick, with 6 [centimeters] mud between. Everything with straw.) Continued towards the east. Santiago became sacristán, then, in 1848, when 14 years old in place of Luicito who died. In 1877 (*hace tres años* [three years ago]), there was an epidemic of smallpox, which took away about 20 men and nearly 100 boys. He says that, now, the lower stories of the houses are used as summer dwellings, and the upper as winter dwellings.

The pueblo very noisy, on account of the dogs which bark all night. About 7 P.M. the parties, who had been cutting wood for the roof and for a bridge, came back singing. They were heard far away, while crossing the Rio Grande. Tonight, the principales (there are about 30 or 40 of them) meet in the estufa. They discuss the matter of my admittance, and another matter

---

80. The term cabildo (or ayuntamiento) means both the local unit of government in Spanish America and also the building in which the cabildo members meet. It is used here in this latter sense.

concerning the tribe, of which I may hear tomorrow.[81] I sleep
in the room of the priest in the old convent, on a buffalohide
and covered by a quilt. For supper (which Santiago brought),
I had four tortillas and excellent pea-soup with green chile. Mosquitoes, but only a few. Room well whitewashed. Window
broken, and no panes at all. Even the frames in pieces.

During the day I was struck by the eagerness with which
Gregorio picked up a small piece of turquoise lying in the
churchyard. He also knows where the turquoises are found. I
promised him one. According to St. Iago [Santiago], the deer
and the cimarron [mountain sheep] are pretty well driven out
of the Sierra del Valle, etc., by the Apache. The antelope are
still found in the Cerrillos. Began to write to Joe, but soon went
to sleep on the floor.

I mentioned the name of Montezuma[82] to Santiago. He
nodded assent. But these Indians are very cunning and have a
way of not understanding questions when they will not answer,
which is very peculiar.

SEPTEMBER 25: I slept well, on the ground. About 7 A.M. Santiago called me, bringing water for the wash and for drinking
purposes. Breakfast, goat-milk and tortillas. About 8:30 A.M.
I heard crying at the plaza. It is done everyday, warning the
inhabitants to shut up their pigs. The casa de comunidad [com-

---

81. As Bandelier was to discover, the Santo Domingo Indians are very unfriendly to outsiders. A half century later the anthropologist, Leslie A. White, had
this comment:

"Santo Domingo is one of the most conservative of all the pueblos and is
bitterly opposed to telling white people, ethnologists above all, anything. That
great student of the southwest, Adolf Bandelier, was never able to learn anything in Santo Domingo: '[it] has closed its doors to me in consequence of
one of those errors which the novice in ethnology is liable to commit and
which I committed at the very outset.' Captain Bourke was thrown bodily out
of a kiva on the day of the feast for the Saint in 1881. An Indian agent's report
of '83 describes the Domingo people as 'filthy, fanatic, and immoral.' Their
secretiveness and militance have, if anything increased since those days, since
there are more people to pry into their affairs." (White 1935: 7)

82. Montezuma II (died 1520) was the leader of the Aztecs at the time
of Cortés. His name became legendary in the centuries following the Spanish
Conquest, reaching as far as the American Southwest.

munity house] has been abandoned two years, and is now used as an inn or staying place for travelers. I explained to the governor about the gentes [clans] of the Mexicans. He said that there were *eight* such "quarters" at Santo Domingo. Could not ascertain from him as to whether they had particular names.[83]

Wrote a long letter to Dr. Thomas about the Pueblo and the matter of Benito Tenorio and Felipe Roque. The governor also told me that there are 100 families in the pueblo all mixed up (todos revueltos). This shows that the clans do not live together, [but] are separate. The capitán de la guerra is under him and has charge of the war matters of the Pueblo. When the Apache, Navajo, Uta [Ute], Pa-Uta [Pai-ute], etc., are feared, each Pueblo sallies out with its war captain. When all are gathered, the common war captain is selected by choice. When the people proceed to an election, the principales go from man to man, from house to house, to ascertain the choice of the people, and when they know who is the favorite, they elect him to succeed in office.

About 2 P.M. I went to the pueblo with the governor to his house. It is upstairs and is the winter dwelling. I misunderstood Santiago when he said that the winter house was below, and the summer house above. It is just the reverse. The winter house with the chimney is above, and the other below. I visited the winter house of the governor, upstairs. It is airy and clean. The stove and chimney occupy the whole west end.

Very fine pottery. Two girls were grinding corn, the east end being occupied by the metates, five in number. The grain was kept in large ollas and tinajas of very beautiful make. He also showed me a fire drill with quartz-point, used for boring holes into turquoises. The windows of the lower stories are almost square and closed with plates of gypsum as panes. Two estufas, both round. When I asked the governor why two, he said be-

---

83. White listed some 21 clans for Santo Domingo. His clan group, however, shows relatively few correspondences with a list of some 18 clans made by Bourke in 1881. (White 1935: 71-72) For nearby Cochiti, Lange (1959: 376) recorded 16 clan names for the period 1947-1952.

cause there were always two parties dancing at the same time. Sacristán brought me my dinner, bean-soup and tortillas. The governor and his son, also Felipe Roque, brought me milk, tortillas, melons, and watermelons.

This trouble is very interesting; it shows the belief in witchcraft as still existing,[84] and also how the Indians hold together and stick together. It further gave me occasion to inquire into their modes of punishment. The governor said that murder never occurred, but that if it ever should occur, then the murderer would be judged by the principales of the tribe. But they would not kill him; his punishment would consist in being imprisoned and in paying for the murder—as far as I could understand—to the relatives of the dead. But, he said, such a thing can never occur. It is very singular that they have not, or do not pretend to have, any cacique. There are: the governor and his teniente, the capitán and his teniente, the fiscal and his ayudantes and teniente, ten or twelve mayores principales, but thirty to forty principales in all. The gobernador is much respected and his authority acknowledged.[85] He is very proud of it and of his vara [cane of office]. He has not yet shown me the latter.

It is very interesting to see the people go about with their children, and also very queer to see them appear upon, [and] disappear from, their housetops. The girls carry children very soon, and the boys go out with their fathers, who teach them to carry [work]. The girls wash the grain in the river, and then

84. A strong belief in witchcraft is characteristic both of the Puebloan and the Navajo-Apache groups in the Southwest. Many of the specific ideas and details of witchcraft are of Spanish origin but the belief in witches is aboriginal.

85. There are actually two sets of officers at Santo Domingo (this is a common Pueblo pattern). The "Native" group includes the cacique and his helper, two war priests (representing the twin war gods), and ten Gowatcanyi or helpers of the war priests. The "Spanish" set of officers includes the governor, lieutenant governor, six governor's helpers (fiscales), a ditch chief, a bugler, and a drummer. There is in addition a series of principales drawn from past officers of both the above groups. Bandelier seems to be talking mainly about the "Spanish" officials here. (cf. White 1935: 35-47)

grind it with the manos and metates. The former is now of lava, formerly of gneiss or granite.

Wrote to Joe, Felsenthal, and Bennett. Dance they call pinito. It appears that the fiscal is also the pregonero [crier], and that the pregón at sunrise takes place often, though not regularly. The highest housetop is used for that purpose. Santiago told me that the infants were nursed until the second year, and that afterwards they gave them to eat of the table. About 6:30 P.M. the pregonero spoke very loud. He proclaimed that a child had lost his shoe yesterday in the river, and that anyone finding it should return it, or if anyone should see it picked up, he should at once accuse the thief. The gobernador has eight alguaciles, also elected for life, two of which serve one week [in each month]. All these elections [appointments, actually] are made by the principales, and not by the Pueblo at large. The fiscal has his teniente and five fiscales for aides. The latter has but the care of the church and its property. In case of public work, like an acequia or something like it, all the principales take a hand in it, assisting in its erection. When a house is built, the Pueblo details ten men to build the walls, and also ten men to construct the roof. All the offices are gratuitous, and not salaried. The church is only cared for by unmarried men, and when the sacristán advises the fiscal mayor of anything that should be done, the latter details his fiscales for the purpose. Santiago asserts that he knows nothing of an Indian name for the children; still, he has an Indian name himself. At 7 P.M. the men came back again, singing very low.

Turquoises are frequently met here. The young men and young women wear them as pendants from necklaces. Some are very handsome ones, too. The women are small, and commonly ugly; the men taller, and not very handsome. They are a very jovial people—laugh and chat together. Their dress now consists of the shirt, leggings, gaiters, shoes, and of the tilma [blanket] or serape, as the case may be. In summer they go about naked. This morning, as it had rained, they nearly all went barefooted, and this evening nearly all in the shirt and without leggings.

SEPTEMBER 26: The leading men of the pueblo had gathered on the south porch of the convent around a fire before I awoke. The gobernador, when I came out, asked me to write a list of the names of the Indians of his pueblo. (Sent off the letters and cards to the Padre, and a few words of excuse.) At 6 A.M. the crier was heard, and again at 7 A.M. He spoke long, especially the last time. Now there are two criers. I noticed, and have been told also, that in the morning their first act is to look at the rising sun. The village formerly extended farther west, but the river washed away a part of it, and its inhabitants now build new houses to the east. There are two albañales [dykes] at the foot of the bluff to keep off the current, should the river overflow.*

The appearance of the Indians coming to church in their gaudy robes is very peculiar. The criers still continue to drive them to church. Yesterday there was a dance at Cochiti, at which a few of the young men of this pueblo assisted. Tomorrow there may be one here.[86]

At 8 A.M. was taken to the meeting house of the tribe, a large rectangular hall, very well whitewashed (gypsum), and very clean. There is a round table, and a chair was brought. A triangular chimney is close to the southwestern corner of the hall, which is indeed clean, large.* It appears to be a meeting of young men. Wood was split outside with an American axe, and a fire was built. The governor then came in. They talked lively and laughed a good deal. All in the best of humor. One Indian

---

86. The practice of people from one pueblo, or tribe, assisting with, or participating in, the ceremonies of another tribe continues to the present day. Without a high degree of familiarity with the people of the sponsoring pueblo, such interaction is likely to go undetected and, hence, unstudied. Such reciprocities and similar exchanges have apparently characterized Pueblo culture for decades and probably centuries. They have obviously been significant factors in cultural dynamics, from the viewpoints of both change and stability. They merit greater attention from students of Puebloan culture. (See Lange 1959: 350 for further comment.)

came in with a perfectly naked child, notwithstanding the bitter cold. The ceiling is supported by round beams, and composed of sawed planking. They call me amigo, compañero, whereas they themselves call each other *omo* (*u-mo*). The governor says it means "*lo mismo que tata.*" In this case it would be the same as "grandfather."

Lista de la gente del pueblo de Santo Domingo, que está para irse á tratar con los Comanches, tomada por mando del Sr. Gobernador y de la Junta de los principales del dicha pueblo. Domingo, el 26 de Septiembre, 1880: [List of the people of Santo Domingo Pueblo who are going to trade with the Comanche, recorded at the request of the governor and principales of the said pueblo. Domingo, September 26, 1880]

Santiago Tenorio
Alejandro Baylon
Bautista Gorriz
Sebastiano Aguilar
Crescencio Labato
Ignacio Chiama
Santiago Aguilar
José Santo Lozero
Francisco Catá
José Calabaza
Benito Tenorio
Ignacio Calabaza
Luis García
Reyes Aguilar
Carmen Pacheco
Benito Montoya
Victorio Melchior
Francisco Tenorio
Vito Pájaro
Reyes Tenorio
Santiago Chacón
José Pacheco
Ventura Crispin

Santiago Aguilar
Juan Pacheco
Juan Pedro Pájaro
Juan Tafoya
José Domingo Beyta
Juan Pedro Montoya
Albino Pacheco
José Atanas Herrero
Felipe Calabaza
Francisco Calabaza
Francisco Chacón
Mariano Montoya
Francisco Reaño
Ventura Melchior
Ascensio Calabaza
Francisco Zamora
Marcos Lobato
Antonio García
Juan Montoya
Juan Pedro García
Antonio Calabaza
Miguel Aguilar

Lorenzo Calabaza	(de Santa Ana)			Manuel Armijo	(de Santa Ana)		
Pedro Pino	"	"	"	Manuel Agustín	"	"	"
Salvador Barranco	"	"	"	Pedro Yanahua	"	"	"
Miguel Silva	"	"	"	Pedro Montoya	"	"	"
Miguel Tomás	"	"	"	Domingo Montoya	"	"	"
Cruz Abiel	"	"	"	Juan de Dios de Chorra		"	
Antonio Mintiego	"	"	"	José Antonio Loreto		"	"
Hilario Truxillo	(Sandía)			Vicente Truxillo	(Sandía)		
Manuel Gutierrez	"			Pedro Ysidro	"		

This meeting is one of the most interesting ones I ever saw. It was very orderly, the principales sitting near the chimney together and smoking cigarettes with maize-straw [corn-husks]. A young man brought in the "weed" and the leaves, and they, the principales, smoked, while he made the cigarettes for them. The young men sat at some distance but none of them smoked. (This explains the statement of Padre Ribera: that it would be considered highly impolite to smoke in the presence of the parent, before marriage. He himself did not smoke, up to the time of his ordination.)

I asked for each name in succession, and one of the principales, Sebastian Aguilar, gave them to me. The governor presided over the meeting, and when the young men grew too noisy and laughing, teasing each other, etc., the principales said, "sh, sh!" to hush them. There was a delegate of Santa Ana present, who had a common piece of wood in his hand, and as many cuts in it as there were young men to go from his pueblo (fourteen), and while he gave me the names, he whittled off the "recollection-notches," in succession. The people of Sandia were not present so I went home (barked at by all the dogs, as usual).

Santiago came soon afterwards, and when we were alone, I told him the names of sun and moon in Queres, and then he confessed that the principales had forbidden him to give me their language. He then told me about their fields. Everyone can select his own site, and when he has once chosen it, no other may occupy it. If he dies, leaving married children, the ground is divided among them equally. If he dies intestate, that is, without issue, the field falls back to the Pueblo, and if his children are unmarried, then one of the principales, "el más cerca" of the family, administers the field until they marry, when the field, or part of the original field, is turned over to the married ones.

(By el principal más cerca is meant, not the one from the cuartel, but the one nearest in relationship, although he might live in the opposite end of the pueblo, thus confirming the report of the governor, that the cuarteles are now todos revueltos [all intermixed] and that, as I suppose, they were formerly localized relationships—clans.)

Unmarried males are very rare, there is one in the pueblo now. A few years ago there were three or four only. They had their fields and worked them themselves. He says that the principales may have a plat of their [the Pueblo's] lands. He is reticent yet. About 1 P.M., the governor came with two Indians of Sandia; and they gave me their names, and one of them invited me to come and stay at his house. They are Tiguas [Tiwa] and acknowledge it.

After having made the papers, I had to draw up an account of Luis García against Tonio García, a Mexican, for 4½ pesos. Luis is an Indian, brother of the capitán de la guerra (Antonio García), and is amado in the latter's neighborhood (has a sweetheart). On the 24th, Padre Ribera told me that while intermarriages with other tribes occur, they are very violently resisted. An Indian of Cochiti married a Cia [Zia] girl some time ago, but under violent protests from both tribes. According to the Roman (church) law, no marriage is valid unless celebrated at the parish of the woman.

The governor is still suspicious. He promises to inform me of everything as soon as he is back from Santa Fe, for which place he will start tomorrow—but no sooner. Wrote to Prof. Norton and to Mr. Morgan today. Padre sent me cigars and whiskey. The list I made this morning will be handed to Dr. Thomas, so that he may make a copy of it, to inform the commanding officer that the Pueblos are going to trade with the Comanche. Governor says all the tribes are friendly now, even the Navajo. Pueblo not much occupied—people seem to be in the rooms. Women are about carrying water; saw two of them on the upper story, one was combing the other. Along the bluff there are also albañales. The governor brought me wood, very fine pinabete, freshly cut, and one of the young men, a watermelon. Serapes cost $3.00 to $8.00.

At 7 P.M. the crier was heard again. Santiago here again. Previously, the gobernador [had] told me that, when the Chimahuayos warred against the Rio Abajeños, he was already married. This was in 1837. He pretends that he did not take part in the murder of Pérez and others, then committed, although he perfectly recollects them, but that he stayed in his house. (This is very doubtful.) "Chimahuayos" means those of the Rio Arriba, above Cochiti; the "Rio Abajeños," those below. He mentioned the Sonoreños. It is evident that they know much more than what they care to say. Santiago told me considerable about the Comanche. It takes the people of his pueblo a month to get to the Comanche, and one month also to return. "Si son ricos" (that is, if they have many hides, etc., in their ranchos), all the trading is done in two days. They use signs to understand each other. For "buffalo" they designate horns; for "to go horseback," they designate the direction with the right hand, and then put the forefinger and the middle finger of the right hand astride the forefinger of the left. For "to kill," they span the bow, etc. He described also an instance when a Comanche ranch had lost two children, the horses having come home without them. When, after diligent search, no trace of them could be found, the two women in the ranch each took out her horse, fully saddled, and stood beside them, stripped naked to a broad girdle about their loins, and holding a knife. Each one put her hand on the saddle-bow first (or, rather, touched it); then with the knife cut off her hair, and afterwards began to cut their faces, arms, breasts, thighs, legs, etc. in token of their grief and mourning.[87]

An interesting sign was made to me to designate twenty, this morning. The fingers were counted one after another on both hands, afterwards, both hands were closed simultaneously twice. They have cats here, too, and they are rather better kept and less treacherous than the dogs. These [the dogs] are a miserably noisy and shy set of dangerous, wolf-like beasts. Santiago left me early.

The gobernador had told me that green-stones were very precious, and many of them wear turquoises. One of them had them as earrings, but there appears to be no difference as to rank in wearing them. Whoever finds or gets them uses them as ornaments. It is the same with the iridizing [iridescent] conch-shells. The largest turquoise I saw was worn by a woman during the baptism, hung to a necklace. During this baptism, it was very queer to see how few of them recollected their family name. When the governor was asked by me whether the Indians still had their Indian names, he told me "yes," but that he would speak to me about these matters after his return from Santa Fe.

Meanwhile, I can go everywhere. A good Mexican blanket here costs $3.00 to $4.00; a Navajo blanket much more. There is a man in the pueblo who makes blankets;[88] otherwise the Pueblos scarcely make them. The governor says that when they make them, they are still better and finer than those of the Navajo. Tonight, I lent my knife to Santiago to go across the

---

87. This rather "Dionysian" behavior (regardless of the correctness of detail) is in strong contrast to Puebloan "Apollonian" attitudes.

88. Among the Pueblos, men normally were the weavers though women did also occasionally weave (cf. Bandelier's journal entry for November 22, 1880). The nearby Navajo Indians were also weavers and, though this trait was clearly adopted from Pueblo models, Navajo women did most or all of the weaving. Underhill (1958:47) has pointed out that following the Pueblo Revolt (1680) and up through the De Vargas reconquest period (1692-1700) there were numbers of marriages of Navajo with Pueblo refugees. She made the intriguing suggestion that skilled Pueblo weavers, unable to teach their trade to sons (who were by custom hunters and raiders) imparted the knowledge to their Navajo wives and daughters.

river to look after his watermelons. May have been a lie. Pea-soup very fine. Prohibited further tortillas, for the present. Watermelons not ripe yet. Corn in bloom.

Padre Ribera told me that the climate here was rougher than at Santa Fe, though thermometer generally 10° F. higher. This is due to the north winds blowing down the Rio Grande, and also the dry parching south winds blowing up. This was said on the 24th, when coming from Santa Fe. On the 25th, between Peña Blanca and Santo Domingo, a horned frog ran across the road. Before sunset, Santiago told me that snow had fallen on the Sierra de Santa Fé. They gather their wood from the Sierra del Valle and from the hills and arroyos of this spur. Piñón and sabino; but pinavete and cedro are too far off. Eat the tuna, and the fruit of the yucca, which they call "natir." The natir is dried in leaves, rolled up, and thus preserved. Went to bed early, about 8 p.m.

September 27: Got up at 6 a.m. The crier was heard very early, and soon after the sound of axes, indicating the hewing of wood. It was almost dark. Santiago came at last, and we measured four blocks of houses and one estufa until 10:30 a.m., when I went home to write. During the time I was on the roofs, I noticed the houselife. The girls always sing when they grind. The people are very lively, they chat and laugh together, both sexes, and there seems to be among them a kind of sociability analogous to ours. About 10:00 a.m. the men came home across the Rio Grande bottom, singing loud, in chorus, but all the same tune. Then they went to their respective homes, and began to laugh, chat, and play with the females and children. One man slaughtered a sheep on the roof of the first story, in our presence, his wife assisting him. There is much cheerfulness among these people. As to neatness I could not say. On every roof there was the tinaja with the urine of the night, which smelt ugly. They carry it out into the fields. Santiago told me that the northern rooms were the storerooms always, and he insisted that the winter room was the one below, and not as the governor had said. He himself has but one room. For dinner, he brought me

sheep-tea, and meat. Very good. He says that the hunters, for
the first four days after their return, give away their meat, but
that afterwards they can sell it. If buffalo-hunters, then the
brother cares for the field during his absence.

In the afternoon, we surveyed. [At this time the western
portion of the pueblo contained the older houses. Floods had
destroyed buildings still farther west and new houses were being
added to the east.] [The town] is made much better and differs
very little, if any, from a Mexican town. There are only two
houses in this part of town which have two stories, and these
houses are new. Some of the houses have door openings to all
sides; still the majority has doors to the south front only. Of
the greatest number of houses, the walls are only in process of
erection, and look like courts, still, Santiago tells me, that they
are casas nuevas. Ligorio lives in one of these large rooms, he is
lame and cannot go out much. I must, tomorrow, make a better
survey of this old town, examine the construction of their
chimneys, etc. Looked down into the eastern estufa but saw
nothing else than a hearth made of huge stones, like an arm-
chair, containing ashes. It was dark inside.* The staircases, by
which they ascend to the estufa, are as follows. The ladder, by
which the descent in the estufa is effected, is very long above.
The hole is not in the middle of the top, but more to the south-

southeast. Entrance in both cases from south-southwest. Went
out after 4 P.M. into the small field east of the convent. Caught
a *Coccinella*. Apricot trees, a small grove.

This afternoon, three Indians from Jemez came on horseback.

They wore partly European clothes, like the Sandia man yesterday. They were very friendly, and while they stopped, a Mexican rode up, totally drunk, and entered the house. The woman soon after ran out, frightened, although she was old and very ugly. The Jemez Indians came out with the drunken man, who at once recognized Santiago, called him his friend, etc. He attempted to talk to me, but I refused. He finally [departed], after several unsuccessful attempts to mount his horse, and after having paid his addresses to a buxom girl standing on one of the ladders. The Indians all the while behaved very peaceably and with great meekness. There was something like compassion in their mind for the beast.* Supper: sheep's meat and tortillas; also, soup of sheep.

Asked Santiago if the girls also inherited land; he said they did, as soon as they married. If the father died alone, the lands and property all went to his wife, and she might remarry again. (This is doubtful at least.) But the girls, in every case, inherited equally with the boys. If father and mother die without issue, the agnates inherit: tios, hermanos, primos, etc.

At 6:20 P.M., drumming, crying, and singing began in the pueblo. There is evidently a dance in progress. Guns are fired, dogs bark, and the noise is generally hideous. There is particularly one shrill boyish voice which, when "let loose," pierces the air most abominably. Happily, it is rare. The song is monotonous, and the drum still more. The entire noise lasted about 10 minutes, then ceased completely. About five minutes thereafter, the drum began to beat, the song rose again, and a crier interloped occasionally. Shots were again fired. I would like to see the dance, but must wait till Santiago comes, as I do not like to go alone, on account of the dogs. After five minutes the dance again stopped. 6:35 P.M. all quiet. 6:36 the drum beats and a big shout arises, then the song, etc. 6:41 stops again. 6:42 shout, drum, and song, etc. 6:47 stops again. 6:48 shout, drum, and song, etc. again. 6:52 stops. 6:54 shout, drum, and song, etc. The noise seems to reach from my quarters. 7:02 stops. 7:04 shout, drum, etc. again. 7:12 stops. 7:15 starts again, but very far off. 7:23 stops. 7:25 starts again. 7:34 stops. From 7:50 to 8:05 very strong and rapid measure, tune different. Ceased completely, in the distance, about 8:20 P.M. Went to bed at 9 P.M. Have written home.

I remember, here (24th), that Padre Ribera told me that his receipts, all told, did not exceed $1,000 a year. In regard to their language, I notice that, when they use Spanish words, they change the "e" into "ae," for instance, paeso for peso, Paedro for Pedro, like the Swiss-German.

It is remarkable how cool this adobe structure is. Not only does it remain very cool during the day, but even the water in the tinaja keeps very fresh. Today, while measuring, I saw, in a hollow on the top of a hill overlooking the whole town, and between its two sections, two old men sitting and peeling off corn-leaves, then smoking. One of these is the old principal who gave me so much information the first day. Now he appears sullen.

Nowhere did I notice any nails. Even the sticks on the corrals are tied together with leather strips . . . about equidistant from each other, 2 to 4 inches, and on average 8 to 10 feet high.* The sticks or poles are about 10 centimeters in diameter. There are occasional sheds in the corral, and some of the corrals are of adobe, very heavy 50 x 28 x 28 centimeters. Look like square blocks of stone. It is laid differently from the other.

I forgot to mention here, in regard to the earrings, and turquoise in general, that Santiago told me the price of the work to be the same as that of the stone. For instance, a stone worth $1.00 will be $2.00 when cut.

This morning I met with a fragment of a centipede (Scolopendra) on the convent porch. Must have been tolerably large.

SEPTEMBER 28: Slept until nearly 6:30 A.M. Criers very lively about the pueblo for about thirty minutes. Went for Santiago about 8 A.M. Not at home. Afterwards called on Ligorio. He is very kind, has two children—one a baby five months old. Three rooms, all on the same floor. The east room is for the winter,

the west room for summer, and the north room for storage. The east room is also used for storage now.* Clean so far. His wife gave me two painted bowls. She makes the bowls. The paint used is yellow (ochre probably), but when burnt, it turns red. None of the pottery vitrified; the old men say that this art is totally lost.

I inquired of him about hunting, and he gives a tale different from that of Santiago. He says that when they kill a deer, it is for him and his family; but if he has a surplus, he sells it. There is not giving away like Santiago said. In general, Ligorio is the most frank of all, and the most truthful. (His leg hurts him.) He says that he has his field, but no cattle, sheep, etc. The teniente of the gobernador came at 8:30 A.M. He wanted fosforos [matches]. I asked him how it was about the baile [dance], and he replied, "Por contento [satisfactory]," and laughed when I reproached him for not having called me. Upon my asking permission to enter the estufa, he asked, "Porque?" [why?] and I told him, "Para verla" [I wanted to see it], whereupon he shrugged his shoulders with "Quien sabe?" and said it would be better to wait for the return of the gobernador, "porque el lo manda todo" [because he is a charge]. They appear to be very obedient to the governor, as long as he is such; but I cannot detect anything like a reverential salutation. They address him, umo [grandfather], and he terms them alike. There is neither in dress, nor in address, anything like a marked difference. I went with Santiago again to measure the southeastern part of the pueblo. The dogs are already more indifferent toward me; they bark less.

This portion of the pueblo is entirely new and in fact a Mexican town. It contains courts, all the houses have doors, and some porches. South of it are peach trees, and east runs the great acequia, which starts two miles above Peña Blanca and empties again into the Rio Grande at Cubero. It is used for irrigation and to bathe. Its width is about 2 meters, and its depth may be from 0.50 meter, to 1 meter. A boy waded through in my presence, and it did not reach up to his knee. The water is, of course, dirty. On both sides from it run the sangrias to irrigate the fields. About 10 A.M. the men went to work at the bridge across the Rio Grande, the criers having called them together, and the principales having gone to work. It is very evident that there is much communism.

The adobes used for construction of the new houses are 55 x 26 x 5 centimeters, . . . and those in the western part, which is the oldest section of the town, are the same size, and contain straw also. This straw is distinctly wheat straw.

Very good bean soup at noon. Sun very hot. Santiago tells me that, for the Father immediately preceding [Padre] Ribera, he made four pairs of earrings of turquoise, and the Padre paid him 25 pesos for each pair. They are very much sought for and high priced. I asked a boy, the most handsome boy I ever saw among the Pueblos, for the price of a chain composed of perhaps fifteen small stones, and he told me $10.00. For each of his earrings he asked $1.00. On the earrings of the Padre, Santiago worked four months to perforate and polish them. He showed me one, as follows. Price $2.00. It is well polished by hand. This work is done merely by rubbing. Santiago told me that the pits of the Cerrillos were made by the Indians of San Marcos, San Cristóbal, San Lázaro, to whom these turquoise mines belonged. After they were driven out, they turned over the mines to the Queres. He says that the Acoma, Zuñi, Moqui, etc., pay as much as a manta for one of these piedras verdes. In regard to the loza [pottery] he says also that the women make it.

At 2 P.M. I left on foot for Peña Blanca. Warm, still very pleasant. Found, on my way, many beetles, among which a very peculiar one. The bottom is sandy—dry, many ants, and many bees. Padre Ribera very kind, gave me his photograph. Letters from Joe, Lizzie, Dr. Bruhl, Norton, etc. Padre [Ribera] told me they had a cacique but would not tell it. I left home late, but was taken up by a Spaniard who had a Santo Domingo Indian with him. When I told the latter that they had a cacique and that I knew it, he asked: *"Quíen te lo dijo?"* [who told you?]

He then acknowledged it. But he told me afterwards, while alone, that such things ought not to be spoken of before Mexicans. Trouble about keep. Found room in perfect order. Splendid sunset. Reached home at 6:30 P.M. 7:30 P.M. drum again audible. Did not last long, however. Wrote to Joe, Annie, Schenck, and Norton. Santiago failed to bring his blankets. Very annoying.

In regard to the pottery, they first build a large fire, and when it is flaming, they extend it over the floor. Then they put in stones, and on every three stones, a vessel, cover the whole with dung, and burn it in this way. After it is well baked and cooled off, they paint it and then burn it again. For red they use a kind of earth, for black they use guaco wood [bee-weed stems]. The earth is taken from the Peña Blanca, and well ground before it is mixed and shaped. All this work is done by the women. . . . It is remarkable what honest, good, care Santiago took of my things. Even the window was closed with a board.

9 P.M. the drum seems to be heard again faintly. Padre Ribera told me that at their dances they excluded all foreigners from the pueblo and even placed guards around it to watch their approach. The "kachina,"[89] he says, is danced naked, by men and women, even in open air. But on such occasions the pueblo is always well guarded and watched from the outside.[90] The

---

89. Here, Bandelier used the term "Cachina." A number of other forms have been used by various writers, some trying to write the word phonetically. We have elected to standardize these variations (which occur within Bandelier's own writings) with the most commonly used form, "kachina." Actually, among the Keresans, such as Santo Domingo and Cochiti, the form "ka'atsina" is more common.

Only rarely do Pueblo women dance kachina; female impersonations are almost always done by men.

90. Bandelier's description and use of the term, "naked," should be qualified. To the best of our knowledge, based both on published and unpublished data, no Pueblo dancers actually perform "naked," despite such statements as Bandelier's to the contrary. "Naked" means generally that the legs, perhaps the feet, and the upper trunk and arms are bare. The lower trunk and loins are covered by either a kilt or a breechcloth, seemingly an indigenous pattern of long standing.

Padre has secured some words from the Santa Ana Indians
showing that there is a dialectical variation between the two
Pueblos, even of some importance sometimes.

The main acequia, on an average 1½ meters wide, branches
off from the river below Peña Blanca one-half mile, therefore at
the limit of the grant (3.65 miles) and runs past the pueblo to
Cubero, on the other side south of the grant. It is, therefore,
about 7.3 miles long, 1½ meters wide, and one-half to 1 meter
deep. Its current is very swift. There is a similar one on the other
side of the river.*

A field is divided into compartments by little ridges. These
plots are generally 4 to 5 meters wide. Sometimes they are 10,
sometimes 6, again 20-25 meters long. Various have onions,
Indian corn, chile, or melons.

SEPTEMBER 29: At about 5 A.M., perhaps sooner, a plaintive,
melancholy sound of a female voice was audible at the pueblo.
The song was, of course, *mole*, but the voice was sweet and clear,
without being shrill. Got up after 7 A.M. . . . Called upon Santiago. Feigned to be angry with him and the Pueblo. Asked him
for the name of beetles; [he] did not know. Santiago affirms that
the songs of the women are not understood by the men. I then
asked him if there was another language, he said, "No," but still
they did not understand their songs. I went with Santiago to see
their corrales. They are on the other side of the acequia. While
there, saw a woman with a jícara [basket] washing sheep's tripe
in the acequia. Water very turbid and dirty looking.* In the
northern one of these corrales a family had just killed a head of
cattle. They were carving it, the man cutting, and the woman
taking out the intestines, etc., and washing them in the acequia
close by. The meat is cut in strips, and the young men carry it
home in this way.

There is again a good deal of crying going on, a fresh detail of
men is sent out to the bridge, which is built over the Rio
Grande. Santiago also went out today. During the absence of
the governor, an old man is appointed as *interim*. Santiago calls

him *interim de gobernador*. He sits on a hill between both parts of the town, which looks very much like a mound, in a hollow, and this morning assisted in crying lustily from its top. But his was more like a speech than the ordinary pregón, and he seemed to command. The first time I saw him this morning, the other old man was with him again. Might it be the cacique? When I informed Santiago this morning about my knowledge of that officer, he did not deny it but asked, "*Como lo supe?*" [How did you find out?]

This morning I saw two women cleaning wheat. It was done by throwing it into the air with a jícara, and catching it again. Thus the chaff was thrown over on the floor. Previously, they had poured it out on two pieces of sack cloth lying on the ground, and sorted it with the hand. Then a small quantity was taken in the jícara and "tumbled," or "tilted." The balance is done by "washing." The fine chaff is thus floated off, and the soluble dirt is sifted through with the water.

Men nearly all at work on the bridge. I decided to go to the lomas this morning and to the bridge this afternoon. 12 noon. Instead of going to the lomas I began to measure their fields. It is very difficult work, since they are very irregular.* It is only horticulture by means of irrigation. Santiago comes with peas (albejones). I asked him about the Queres name for tortillas, and he said it was *castira-ta* (Castillapan). This is interesting and important. He says that everyone who is not sick or lame, or who is not very old, has to work on the bridge. He was excused on account of being required to assist me. Santiago tells me that his name in Queres is A-shka-a, *que quiere decir espina* [which means thorn]. Ligorio came to visit me; the poor fellow suffers much, his leg is swelling. While he was here, I shaved myself. Went very well. Then went with him to his house.

Afterwards went back and then crossed to the Rio Grande, to see the new bridge. From foot of bluff 50 meters to brazo; brazo, 3 meters; 600 meters to Rio Grande brazo. This is about 30 meters wide. The bridge is about 50 meters long. From the

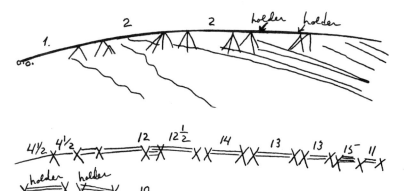

brazo to the Rio 250 meters. Height above the river about 3
meters. Width 60 meters of the Rio. Current very swift. Width
of west bottom 140 meters, then to nearest field 60 meters and
300 to west acequia, 1 meter wide and 1 meter deep. The hollow
beams are 0.55 centimeters in width, and whenever there are
two beams, they are together about of same width. [Recorded
measurements summarized in chart below.]

Measurements in Meters	Height	Chest Width	Shoulder Width	Arm Length
Cristóbal Moquino	1.60	.81	.37	.64
Santiago Tenorio	1.69	.88	.43	.72
Adolph Bandelier	" "	.83	.43	.74

Deferred further measurements for another day, although
both were very willing, chatted and laughed freely. Afterwards,
the governor came in and brought me a letter from Milburn.
After a long talk, the governor decided to gather a meeting of
the principales for tomorrow, but I could not get him to meet
in the estufa. The Mexican is here, and there may be trouble
for tomorrow. At all events, it cannot fail to be interesting.
Ligorio brought me my caxete [bowl].

The pillars of the bridge are interesting. They are of wood
selected for that purpose—forked and heavy. One is cut as fol-

lows: the other as follows: The point *b* is inserted into the square hole *a* and the two form a fork standing on four legs. On this fork the log on which the men cross, is rested. Thus the

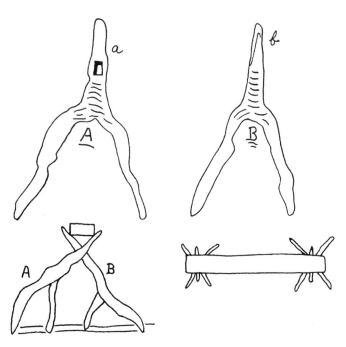

whole bridge consists, in fact, of a succession of trunks. There is not a nail in the whole construction. A few of the logs are evidently sawed; but as I have not seen a saw in the whole pueblo as yet, I presume they were bought. Nearly the entire male population was out, and the whole work of setting up the bridges was done in two days. (Bridge, *tse-shtia-wa-tsesh*, told by Cristóbal Moquino.) The timbers were dragged from the mountains by mules and oxen, therefore many have holes cut in them at the end. Similar holes are found in the timbers of the new church. How much time it took to cut and prepare the wood I cannot tell. The whole affair is, in fact, very interesting —the capitán directed it. The troughs were cut out by hand, so

Santiago tells me. At night, Santiago Tenorio came back, brought me a serape for $3.00 and two turquoises for $2.00. He also offers me four turquoises for $2.00 more. I have accepted and shall pay him Friday. The good boy came twice; he has captured me.

With the exception of the parallel ditch all the others are dry. The water in the acequia, however, runs very swiftly. Peach trees, crippled and horribly neglected, apple trees, etc., are planted in some of the gardens. In others, the peach trees line the ditches, but the trees are not cared for. In one of the fields I found a very fine dung beetle. I found corn, chile, onions, and melons in the field northeast of the acequia. The patches are very small.

SEPTEMBER 30: I rose late in the morning, and both the governor and the sacristán came. I saw at once that there was something wrong, indeed, the governor told me that there was no conveyance to be had, and acted in such a manner that I clearly saw there was something wrong. The suspicions of somebody were aroused on account of the coming of Mr. Bennett, and this irritated me to such an extent that I flew up considerably.

Went out to measure the fields.* The wife of Santiago came to bring me breakfast. Goat milk and tortillas. Am still very mad. Don't know how to get Bennett here. There are plenty of burros about, and even mules, and I saw a cart, coming in with wood, drawn by six oxen. There is a big lie, and bad intentions, suspicion, and deceit.

Went, at 10 A.M., to the south side of the pueblo, and followed the acequia south and south-southwest until the fields stopped (1.11 meters [high] scaffolds). There are no fields east of the acequia. The patches are of very irregular size.* There are 200 meters to the edge of the arable bottom-land, which is about in a line south of the church. . . . Thus, the distance between the western line of actual cultivation and the bottom is about 200 meters, but the bottom encroaches very much farther north—so much so that, while the line is almost straight toward the middle of the distance between the pueblo and the farthest point, the bottom nearly touches it. South of that point, the soil has also been cultivated; ridges running toward the bottom, 4 to 6 meters apart, and of various lengths, designate the former beds. The distribution of cultivation is irregular, but here it is mostly corn. Melons, chili, and calabashes are cultivated in outside patches. Upon my return I saw a wagon and three good carts standing idle in the middle of the pueblo. Went to meet Bennett where the train [passes] about one-half mile from Santo Domingo. Carried his things to the pueblo. Two girls of Santiago brought us pozole soup and sheep's meat.

[With Bennett] began to photograph 2:30 P.M. Took position on top of the church. As soon as we began, a drum was beat opposite. It beat constantly, and an old man came out once and went in again. During the time he was out, the drum ceased, but it began again as soon as he was in. When we withdrew the instrument from the roof, he began to sing—a wild, excited tune. Some of it sounded like wild laughter. The drum was beat in an alternately loud and low tune [tone], but scarcely any quicker. I finally went and looked into the room, whose door was open, and saw a woman, half naked, sitting near the chimney in a little room, beating a large drum which she held horizontally on her knees, while in another corner a little girl was grinding corn, to the sound of the drum and her singing. This old custom is very interesting. When I asked a young man about it, he laughed and said: "*Buena para moler!*" [It helps the grinding.] Is it to teach them how to grind? We took three views this afternoon, all from the top of the church. The people are bringing in melons and squashes in big wagonloads. Went to Ligorio, who was at home.

I also met an old man, lying on the stoop of his hut or house, and asked him about the widow's share in case of death. He says that this was very odd, and hardly ever occurred. But if the wife, upon her marriage, owned any land, then she kept it as hers in case the husband died—if not, then she shared with the family the products of the whole grounds which the husband had tilled. At night, callers, Santiago Tenorio, Santiago and his two daughters who were very lively, and two or three other Indians.

On the 29th, I was told by two boys that the men made their own clothing. On the 30th, the wife of Santiago Crispín, Reyes Herrera, told me the same thing. The mantas are called po'tsin in Queres; they are not made in the pueblo but at Acoma and at Zuñi. She had her little grandson, Santiago, on her back. He is one year old. Only one of her sons is married. The Mexican is still here.

OCTOBER 1: Santiago, fiscal, and his teniente came. Soon after, I saw a pretty scene. A woman (young) with a child on her back, came up a ladder; a young man descended it, and kissed her very affectionately, then went to mount a burro to leave. Santiago denies again the existence of the cacique. He also, by means of excuses and shifts, declines to assist us, and ran away when I wanted to take his picture with the view of the church. Took views of the bridge, and by dint of 25 cents secured Indians to be taken with them. They are very, very shy of being photographed. The people are anxiously gathering [musk] melons and sandías [watermelons]; they are afraid of frost. Ox-teams with two-wheeled carts are croaking through the bottoms; everybody hustles and bustles about.

Photographed the estufa and several street scenes, and had less trouble in getting people to be quiet, at least, if not to sit for us. Called on Juan Antonio Pacheco, who wants me to write for him next Sunday. Of course, he was very friendly. Shall see about him in future. Met the carpenter, José Lucero, who promised to be in tomorrow for boxes. An old man confirmed the report that the winter houses are below and the summer houses above. Pacheco was in his winter house (casa de invierno). Santiago Tenorio came in with a muskmelon, very good. While he was here, general public crying took place. A boy, or young man, has lost his hatchet or axe, and this is proclaimed. Very loudly, at that.

I looked down into the estufa. It appeared to be clean and entirely plain. Right beneath the top entrance is the hearth, shaped like an armchair, built of adobe, as follows: (a) fireplace. The opening of the hearth is to the north. The width of the adobe walls appeared to be at 0.40 [meter?]. On the floor was a drum (b), and a square block of wood or stone, etc. Sticks for fire were placed upright in one corner of the hearth (c). As far as I could see, the walls were daubed over gray and without ornaments.

The winter house of Pacheco is as follows: (a) trapdoor with ladder, (b) room or closet of upright planking, (c) fireplace, (d) melons and calabashes. He took a fine watermelon out of storeroom (b). There was but one story to the whole house, but the old man told me that he had another house above too, therefore, I presume that one of the upper stories adjoining his house now, must belong to him. Shall inquire further.

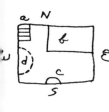

The seats, of which I have never seen more than two in one room, are cut out with the axe. They are low stools, made of one block of wood, and slightly scooped out in the middle. The beds are hides of buffalo, sheep, deer, but mostly blankets. The fire is made in the chimney. At Pacheco's the chimney is square, or rather, rectangular. In the middle of it an iron tripod is commonly placed, on which the ollas, comales, etc., are placed.* Of other implements I noticed two fire-drills hung up in one corner, and a lot of wooden crosses. I may have occasion to go there oftener. He had with him his father, his brother, and a woman.

OCTOBER 2: Had a bad night.

There are two Navajo in town, wearing very gaudy, black and red tilmas. It is remarkable how much smaller the women are [than] the men, while the latter are nearly all bony, or at least slender, the girls and women are all stout, even fat, with heavy breasts, and thick, fleshy arms and legs. This morning— beans, good. Santiago refused again to be photographed, and also to have the picture of his daughter taken. What [is the situation with] the Navajo? Santiago said yesterday that they were bound for the Comanche. Suspicious almost. This morn-

ing bell is tolling, and some few of the gente come in to rezar [pray].

Yesterday I asked a young man how deep the posts of the bridge were set into the ground, and he showed me they were about 0.75 meter. The old man yesterday told me that it was eight years since the western part of the town had been washed away. He also said that he remembered, being a boy, when the Pecos Indians passed through Cochiti on their way to Jemez. He said there was no other Indian name for Pecos than Pecos, but that Santa Ana was called *Tam-mai*, or *Tamai*. While photographing the bridge, an Indian came galloping along on a burro. He wore a bow and an arrow, in a deerskin sheath, but would not sell it. He wanted $4.00 [in coin] for change. In general, they want no paper, only silver or gold, but the silver dollars they like best. Had a great deal of trouble getting Santiago Tenorio's photo—first failed because he turned his head. His girl could not be persuaded to come. Rode over to Wallace with Miguel Montoya, who, on the way, told me that both acequias were of equal length; that is, in all probability, from the north to the south end of the limits of the grant, since it is 7 to 8 millas long. The road to Wallace is very dreary. The high top of the Sierra de Santa Fé, on which snow is still seen, is the Jicarrito, and it must be higher than "Baldy."

Many Indians are going to the depot with eggs, the governor among the rest, carrying his little tin pail with eggs to the depot. He is O.K. again, but his interim, at the depot, who had gone there with another man, thought it was muy malo that I did not leave. When I asked him why, he replied, "No lo digo" [I can't say]. This morning there are Navajo in town trading with the people. Coming from Wallace, I met a man and a woman who told me they were going to get barro for loza [pottery clay]—red clay (colorado). They also showed me the place in the hills where it is found. Hardly a mile from the pueblo.

High wind from the west, driving the sand in clouds. Very disagreeable. No beer and no dinner. Sandía and a dry tortilla—

that's all. Furthermore, no guest, so hardly any advance in information. It is getting tiresome. Yesterday I had made arrangements with José Lucero to come here after 12 noon. It is now 2:30 P.M. and he is not here yet. Wind still blowing in gusts, whirling much sand about.

I went up to the plaza which, by the way, is nothing else than an old corral, and there found the sons of the governor, Francisco and Santiago Tenorio (not my handsome boy), making iron arrows. The arrows had been cut with the axe previously (striking the axe with a heavy stone on its back) and then they were filed into shape with a common file. It went very quickly. They confessed that, though they had firearms, they still preferred to use the bow and arrow, being more skilled in it. The Navajo also made their appearance, very large men. I fooled around with the boys awhile, and finally one of them stole my wife's picture. He teased me with it a long while, until, taking him home, he gave it back to me, whereupon I presented him with my small knife. Have not learned much, still a little. Carpenter Lucero came and I talked to him about the boxes. He promised to attend to it in time.

The Indians are exceedingly suspicious, and in consequence of their ignorance, superstitious; I have already remarked on this and note it more and more every day. This forenoon, Santiago Tenorio fairly trembled while Mr. Bennett took his photograph, and frequently said: "*Malo, muy malo.*" This afternoon the other one, his namesake, the governor's son (though not related), when the train passed in sight, burst out with a threatening look: "*Carrojo del diablo!*" [devil carriage] (Probably *carruaje*). My presence among them is muy malo for the old ones, whereas the young people rather seem to like me. The wind still blowing fiercely and the sand rising in clouds; I remained indoors, although it would be my duty to see the Navajo.

The old church is certainly very old, for all the wood on it is round, the door lintels excepted, which are hewn (not sawed) square. The roof is the common pole-roof, neatly made; the crosses are coarsely hewn of wood, and without nails. In fact, the doors excepted, there is scarcely any iron in the whole building. In the apartment of the northeast, there is a roof with covering of splinters. Along the east side there are five rooms from north to south. In the middle eastern room, there is the kitchen with the great and long fireplace.

Two boys, José Tenorio and Reyes Tenorio, came in, offering me beads to sell—turquoises—and fooling around with me. Meanwhile, a grave was dug in the cemetery. The fiscal and five men (his aides) dug it in turn. The grave ran from north to south, not from east to west like ours. I asked them who had died, and what they were doing, but they simply shook their heads and replied: "Quien sabe?" The grave is dug, apparently, very deep. Everything is done very silently. Previously, an old man had come in, inquiring for the sacristán. The bell was tolled thrice, when a young man with the cross, followed by the sacristán, two aides carrying the bier, and three others after it, went out of the cemetery.

I was politely requested to go inside my room and not to look out. So I went into the old church, whence I could have a very good view, unseen. [After] about fifteen minutes the cortege returned, four men carrying on the bier a dead body, closely wrapped, mummy-like, in a white and blue serape. Prayers were said by the sacristán, while the others and four men who came dropping in, one after the other, stood around and occasionally made the sign of the cross. The bell kept tolling all the while. Finally, the body was taken from the bier, two men descending previously into the grave, where they received the body. They then, apparently, placed it at the bottom. Then earth was thrown over it, and they tramped it down very firmly over the body. At this time, one of the men came back with the bier which belongs in the old church, and I had to flee into the recess behind, thus failing to see the rest of the ceremony. When I returned again, they were filling up the grave. Those who had come last had already gone, and those who had first filled the grave were cleaning their mocassins in another part of the churchyard. I retired; when the men left the churchyard, I went out. They were still cleaning their shoes, shaking the dirt into the yard. Afterwards, the fiscal entered the church and came out again and in a subdued voice delivered a speech in Queres. The body had been placed with the head to the south, facing the church. Of course, the most interesting part of the ceremony escaped me—the ceremonies at home and in the church. Otherwise, it appears to be a "Catholic burial." During the procession, the people appeared quiet; but few were on the streets, and these appeared to take no notice of the ceremony whatever. There is, thus, at least one new scene in this apparently luckless stay here. I might have learned and done more today, by watching the Navajo in their trading with the Indians of the pueblo, but missed that by fooling around with the boys and on account of the detestable wind and sand. Have a whole string of turquoise offered me for $3.00. Shall buy it.

Had quite an unexpected call tonight from Dr. Thomas. He is going to Zuñi by wagon and stays with Bautista Calabaza. Took me home with him, and Cooper returned with me. After I had showed him the old church by night, the sacristán came and raised a big row. I told him I had permission from the Padre to go everywhere when it was not closed. I even told him about the library, but of course, as the Padre had forgotten to tell him about it, it was useless to insist. Am mad again at the old fool. He is conscientious, of course, and does his duty, but there is no need of acting the way he does. I go to bed late in the night, while they are still watching me outside. I presume they were up till midnight, from the noises I heard.

OCTOBER 3: Dr. Thomas sent for me for breakfast. Had coffee, with concentrated milk, canned butter, fried potatoes, apple-butter, and excellent bread. After breakfast, we went together to see the bridge. He stays with Bautista Calabaza, who has a fine collection of aboriginal arms, and in general a clean, neat residence. Dr. Thomas is very, very friendly and kind to me, but the governor is decidedly unkind and unfriendly. In the interview which I had with him this morning, he complained of the fact that I called him alone, and not the other principales, acknowledging that he could not do anything without the knowledge and consent of the Pueblo. Another bad complication about the license of the agent.

I went to Peña Blanca finally. Santiago [actually] misdirected me, and I travelled over and through the fields, without finding my path for a long while. Met with beautiful beetles of the *Melastoma* kind. Santiago went there also. Padre Ribera not at home. The pleasure of Santiago cannot be concealed. He is evidently a fiend and probably the worst one of the tribe. Padre Ribera returns but [not until] tomorrow evening. I made arrangements to stay here until his return. Not that I am afraid of the Pueblo, but it would look bad if now I should return without defiinite arrangements about a further stay. Consequently, I went for the books of the church, and began to abstract them. The oldest was presented on October 16, 1771, by Fray Mariano Rodriguez de la Torre, vice-custodio (the oldest book being preserved in the Archives of the Custodia does not say where). Consequently, this book and the preceding ones must still exist somewhere.

Old Mr. Ribera took pains to inform me about the trouble with the Indians. It is possible that the whole may be occasioned by the fact that before they start on the Comanche trip, they wish to celebrate their secret dances. At San Felipe, all the hares belong to the cacique. Last Sunday they had a great chase there, killing ten on foot and on horseback and they were all given to the cacique. Spoke to Señor Jesús Sena; he also told me that the Indians of Santo Domingo were the worst of all the Pueblos, and the most superstitious ones. He was in the pueblo, himself, when they celebrated their dances, but they only allowed him to do his most urgent trading. All the people were on the rooftops (azoteas) looking on, but he went on without seeing anything. Two Indians of Santo Domingo came, one of them Francisco Tenorio, evidently as a spy. Found a fine hammer of lava near the parish, and was told of a ruined pueblo which I shall go to see tomorrow. It is on the lomas above Peña Blanca.

OCTOBER 4: Rose at 7 A.M., after a good night's rest. It is so beautiful to sleep in a bed again, with the perspective of hot coffee before you. Started for the lomas. The boy, whom I had required [requested], came after me onto the Peña de la Bajada. The views from these heights are everywhere grand.

The enclosure of stone in the south-southwest of the peñol may be, from the statements of Don T. Ribera, a recent Mexican corral. I found no trace of chips, implements, or anything else, neither in climbing up, nor climbing down (south and southwest), nor in the enclosure, but on the top of the peñol, there were minute obsidian chips, chips of flint and agate—but no pottery or any other implements or traces of workmanship. The lava, especially along the furthest edge (west and south-southwest) has cleaved into very large quadrangular masses, often exposing concoidal fractures. On the top it scales off in tabular fragments, and it looks as if these tabular fragments had been used at one time for some purpose of building. When the lava decays, it forms a grayish soil, and such a soil is found on the peñol.

Those circular depressions marked on the ground plan look very much like the estufas of Pecos, but as there is not a trace of walls, I cannot determine. The fragments of flint chips, etc. are scattered over the southern half of the peñol, or rather of its top. On the road back to Peña Blanca I found a rather large fragment of obsidian. Went to Señor Sena, and a Mexican told me there that obsidian was found in round boulders (the size of a child's head) above Cochiti, in the Sierra del Valle. The top of the peñol inclines slightly to the east-northeast.

205 meters northeast of the corner of the parish of Peña Blanca, ascending through a cañada, [one comes to] the bare top of a hill, showing something of a denudation similar to the place where a building may have once stood. But there are no traces of foundations. Still, both Don T. Ribera and Señor Sena assert them to be ruins. They embrace some stone circles of four or five stones, some of which appear broken, and apparently "set"

by hand. A tuft of chaparro often grows out of their center. Without examining these any further, I proceeded first south where I found, on the edge of a barranca, a denuded surface of whitish clay, very alkaline. The same bareness appeared on almost every hill. Then I walked about one mile east of Peña Blanca to the sand lomas, where the lava overtops the clay and drift, and began to ascend the round table so conspicuous from all sides, and almost directly west [south?] of the Tetilla. Am now sitting on a rock, on which another one lay with some striae similar to carvings but doubtful. Some of the clay beneath the lava is greenish. From the round table, the view is about as follows.*

On the top of the mesa there is no vestige of ruins. On the northern edge of the round table there is a low structure of stone. Lava blocks, tabular, piled as follows.* It is rectangular. Some of the stones show very recent breakage; others less recent. The average width of the walls is 50 centimeters. I measured the largest stone, and found it to be, average thickness 6-10 centimeters. It is impossible to say if this structure is recent or not. Sheep and horses have been here, as the dung shows; several paths lead up to it. It has therefore been recently visited. The greatest height of the structure is about 80 centimeters to 1 meter, but it is broken down in many places. My little assistant tells me this is made by boys of Peña Blanca.*

Directly south-southeast of this recent structure there appears on the top the faint outline of what may formerly have been buildings.*

Everything very faint. On the south-southeast slope of the hill, a distinct enclosure appears. The walls of this enclosure appear much more like an embankment. On the descent to the cart, I found a few pieces of red clay, which Señor Sena afterwards recognized as the red clay used by the Indians for their pottery. Still, it is certainly not "cropping out" there. The enclosure is barren, hardly any chaparro even growing in it. It has recently been traversed by horses or mules, but there is no evidence of any cattle or sheep.

Went home, tired, about 11 A.M. and went to work at the books.

From the "*Libro de Casamientos*," Cochití, fol. 82
[From the "Book of Marriages"
(Marriage Register), Cochiti, fol. 82]

Notice

Notice to all the Parish Priests who may come to this Mission: On the 19th of November, 1819, I found that the Indians of this pueblo had an altar with Idols which they worshiped. I took these idols off and they were broken into pieces and burnt in the center of the public square, which fact I herewith leave as advice to my successors in order that they take utmost care, watching them (the Indians) in this matter being, as it is, of such vital importance. In order that this be duly recorded I sign it as Parish Priest.

Fray Juan Caballero Toril

After 2 P.M. went back to the place 205 meters north-north-east of the parish, on top of the first lomas, and found it covered with fragments of pottery, gray and plain (one painted). The only painted one had the following design. I also found obsidian and flint chips, moss agates and red agates. Measured the denuded space, and found it a rectangle 45 x 17 meters.* I also dug in a dozen places, to the depth of about 50 or 75 centimeters, but found nothing except, in one place, a diminutive corncob piece very near the surface. The flint, obsidian, and pottery were strewed about very promiscuously; the pottery is old and washed and worn. It is remarkable how the lava is largely conchoidal in fracture. For metates it is particularly apt. The change from the granite of former days to the lava is a progress in knowledge of the natural qualities of the material. I could not find out whether there were any more ruins about, on this side of the river. Señor T. Ribera told me they sowed their wheat in February; frijoles were planted in May; also corn, [in May, and only] rarely in April. The first snow sets in about the middle of October, but only in Decem-

ber is the ground fairly covered with it. It never remains long on the ground and never to any great depth. The climate of the valley is very disagreeable from February till June, on account of the heavy winds blowing steadily night and day. Storms are not frequent, and tornadoes unknown. Hail falls occasionally. This summer, in July, very destructive hailstorm at Jemez. One man lost six hundred sheep by it, being killed by hail. Also hail at Peña Blanca.

About 4 P.M. Santiago Tenorio came. The poor boy is honest; he knew nothing of my absence, for Santiago, the sacristán, did not tell him anything about it, thus showing himself again a scoundrel. There is not anything new at the pueblo; they are all busy at work, and the fiscal has refused to feed me although Santiago begged his father to do it.

I wrote diligently at the church-books. They are very interesting and valuable. It is my plan to copy all the aboriginal names, take the list to Cochiti, and there have them interpreted by the Indians. I am told by Don T. Ribera and J. Sena, that at Cochiti there are several Indians who can read and write. Among them is Juan José Montoya, brother of José Hilario Montoya. Cochiti is much smaller than Santo Domingo, and several Mexicans live in and around it. Thus the Indians have become somewhat civilized. My guide of this morning was three years old, Juan Eleazario Leyva, a bright little fellow. His father, José Leyva, lives at Peña Blanca.

Evening magnificent, cool, calm; sky cloudless. Fare good, especially potatoes and frijoles. Good coffee, rich milk, and eggs. Meat (sheep). Of drunkenness or rowdyism there is no trace. Everything goes on very quietly.

This morning I got letters from Dr. G. J. Engelmann and from Prof. J. L. Eaton. The latter asks for information which I can very easily give him. George Engelmann, however, asks a little too much. I cannot photograph women in childbirth.

OCTOBER 5: Don Tomás Ribera went to Santo Domingo early, to look after beans. I went to work at the books of the church. Highly important. While they cleaned the room, I went over to the acequia of Santo Domingo, which I met 1,400 meters west of the church. It runs still farther north and enters the Rio Grande about one mile above Peña Blanca. North of the line which I struck to the west, there are, inside of the acequia, small patches worked by Indians of Cochiti, whereas their ranchos of adobe are east of the acequia of Santo Domingo, and west of their own acequia, which commences higher up, and runs east of that of Santo Domingo.

There I met my first Cochiti Indian, Teodosio Cordero, principal of the tribe, who was governor two years ago. He and his wife, who live in a new rancho of adobe (uncovered) [unplastered] were very friendly to me. They explained to me the whole trouble of Santo Domingo. The people there are at loggerheads, because their cacique died suddenly sometime ago, without designating his successor. This successor is, therefore, to be named by the whole Pueblo (junto) and there are two parties.[91]

He was very frank about his own tribe. The cacique commands everything (*manda todo el pueblo*); when he is about to die, he chooses his own successor, and at this time he is also capitán de la guerra. His field (del común) lies about a mile from Peña Blanca, northwest near the river and the acequia of Santo Domingo, and tomorrow all the men of the pueblo are going to work on it. It is a public field, government land, so to say. They are cutting hay for the Padre; his lands, not the Indians'. It is the second cut, the first having been cut in July (Dia de San Juan [June 25]). Good and fair prospects so far.

---

91. This paragraph is rich in insight if not in detail. The office of cacique, head of the tribal theocracy, has long been important in the various Keresan villages. At any time the regular progression of men to this office is disrupted, it is easy to understand that keen interest should surround the installation of a successor. Further, Bandelier's comments reveal both the presence of a tendency to form factions quickly among members of a tribe and the value of asking members of one pueblo concerning affairs in another village. While full details cannot, or will not, be revealed through this kind of information, significant leads and shrewd insights are often to be gained.

The Santo Domingo Indians are acknowledged as the most backward of all the Queres.

At 1:30 P.M. the Padre returned, and I told him the whole story. He approved of my action, but advised me to go to Cochiti. He will attend to my baggage, etc. At 3 P.M. he left for Wallace, being summoned to Albuquerque, for an amount of $5.00 due him by a Mexican named Tonio Ortiz. Very pleasant indeed. I kept at work on the book. If judiciously managed, these Indian names ought to reveal:

(1) The grammatical structure of the language

(2) The social organization of the tribes (gentes, etc.)

(3) The relations between the different Pueblos[92]

I have by night, finished Santo Domingo and Santa Ana, and am now working on Cochiti. Tired out, backaches, from sitting over those very low tables.

At 5:30 P.M., T. Ribera returned without my things. He goes to Santo Domingo again Friday. The Cochiti Indian told me that the old pueblo of Santo Domingo stood on the lomas south of the actual site, and about one mile off. He also spoke of great ruins on the potreros above Cochiti, a great pueblo con tres plazas [with three plazas], built of piedras como adobe [stones coursed like adobes]. These might be the round adobes mentioned by Castañeda. Tomorrow I shall approach the Cochiti Indians about living with them. T. Ribera told me this evening that the Santo Domingo Indians worked with hoes and shovels, and had but oxen for their carts, whereas those of Cochiti used horses and mules for draught. *Son muy más castellanos, más ladinos.* [They—the Cochiti—are much more acculturated, more progressive.] Wrote cards to Dr. Bruhl and to Prof. Eaton.

OCTOBER 6: Went to Cochiti, through the fields. Opposite Cochiti, the Rio Grande is traversed by two bridges, one across the main stream, which here is [on the] east, about 70 meters

---

92. This is a somewhat optimistic idea on Bandelier's part, but he was working in the right direction.

long; the other, across the brazo to the west, is 30 meters long.
Both are made in the same manner as the bridges at Santo
Domingo, exactly alike, without a nail, only the beams seem to
be a little wider. Cochiti is much smaller than Santo Domingo,
but its people are more pleasant and kind. I called on Juan José
Montoya who received me in the most friendly manner. He
introduced me to the cacique and to the governor, Serafín.
Both appeared to be pleasant. Montoya is an instructed man,
who, although he is forty-three years old (born 1837) looks
young. He instructed himself and can read and write easily and

well. Has some books to read. He showed me a very fine shield
of his father's, double buffalo hide, with feather ornaments
suspended. It is painted yellow, but the paint appears to be
recent. In the middle of the shield is the following device
painted red and black. The drawing is not very accurate.

Juan José Montoya gave me a number of details in regard to
the tribe, talked freely about Montezuma, and said the cacique
was the representative of Montezuma, and that this was the
case all over the land. He said that at Jemez, they had the "book
of Montezuma" which he saw—a number of leaves, on which
the history of this "king" was painted. There is an evident confusion of names here. He mentioned extensive ruins, rock carvings, etc., in the neighborhood, and promised to show me
around himself. Arranged for two months in case of need. Left
highly satisfied. One mile [southwest] of Cochiti, on the lomas,
left bank, found obsidian, flint, and pottery. Denuded ridge,
but impossible to trace buildings or foundations. In the arroyo
descending from the loma northeast of parish, and where I
found the traces of a pueblo, found a piece of pottery, thus
showing plainly that this old pueblo belonged to the most
recent type. Governor of Santo Domingo here. Afternoon, unsuccessful attempt to cement windows of the Padre's room.

The faces and actions of the Cochiti people are very good.
There are much fewer houses than at Santo Domingo. As far
as stature is concerned, they appear to be smaller and of slighter
build. But they are evidently much more intelligent and civi-

lized. People are now gathering frijoles. They tear them out, pile them in heaps, and afterwards beat them out with poles. The round place at Pecos enclosed by poles appears to have been a threshing floor. There are many such floors here [Peña Blanca] and about Santo Domingo and Cochiti. Beetles, *Chrysomelas* and *Coccinellas*, frequent the chaparro. Also caught a chameleon [lizard] on the lomas.

About 5 P.M. I went to the lomas south-southeast of the peñol, and due west of the Bajada, south of the road. On the promontory I found again pottery, flint, obsidian chips, and two small obsidian arrowheads, one perfect. Slightly denuded, but no trace of ruins. May have been accidentally dropped. The reason why I have now collected from four different localities around Peña Blanca, is because although near to each other, they still are entirely disconnected. In the rooms which Juan José Montoya has rented me, there are several bows. It will be very interesting at Cochiti, if we can agree. Everybody recommends the place to me. Copied more names. The poles inside of the threshing floor are set to fasten ropes, to enclose the horses pounding on the wheat. Wrote card to Professor Norton after completing list of names.

OCTOBER 7: Before 8 A.M., Montoya sent a boy with a good mule for my things. I shall go after dinner. Wrote to G. C. Bennett and made some abstracts. Ready to go. God knows how it will be. Hope for the best.

At 9 A.M. started on foot for the lomas. At foot of Peñol de la Bajada, again found pottery and obsidian. Ascended the lava plateau, and southeast of the Peñol, saw what appeared to be a bed of yuccas. It rested on an expanse covered with gravel and boulders, pebbles, as if planted in rows at regular intervals of one meter. Seemed to form a field or rectangle. The gravel appears like a foundation of very small cells, but I could not find any pottery, although there were some flint chips and dark agates.

Farther on northeast is another small patch. The first contains about one hundred plants, some of which are dead; the other, thirty-four plants. East-southeast of the latter, 15 meters,

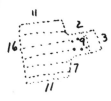

is a patch of forty, very irregular, and 30 east-southeast, a patch of about forty again, 10 meters long and 10 wide. Another 10 meters farther to east and 10 meters southeast of it, still another. I cannot make out if they are planted, or have grown there naturally. Near one I at last found a piece of obsidian. It is at all events singular that, while the yucca appears, occasionally, on nearly all the hills, there should be such a plantation-like regularity here. No other remains found, although I went clear to the Arroyo de Galisteo, where the southern limits of the lava crops out above the creek in whitish, pumice-like masses, and steep banks. The lava is arborescent, bloom-like, and pearl-white. On my return I met the stage driver, with whom I made arrangements about transfer from Santa Fe. Also letters from George Hoffmann, Annie Borchert, B. F. Bensays, and Norton. Am in trouble. Do not know what to do. What is the trouble [with] Professor Norton? His card is queer.

Left for Cochiti about 2 P.M. and reached here 2:30 P.M. Reception of people of Cochiti very friendly.

My host is just now occupied in building the chimney of my room. It is made simply of adobe, set upright. He and his boy are doing it alone. I walked about the place. It is small, the houses are closer together, and there are two small estufas outside, on the north of the pueblo. The church occupies the center, to the east. Juan José tells me that there was a school here for four or five years, but that the people of the pueblo set everything against it, so that the teacher had to leave in disgust, and the agent refused to give more funds to Cochiti for schooling purposes.

[Dimensions of room at Cochiti]
    east/west—11 meters
    north/south—5 meters
    door (south side)—7 meters from southeast corner
    door frame—1.61 x .82 meters
    door set — .17 meters inside inner [outer?] wall
    wall thickness — .49 meters
    doorsill — .16 meters below floor

window, 9 panes each — .18 x .22 meters
window set in — .27 meter recess
window — .98 x .79 meters
chimney — 1 meter west of window base facing northeast
height of room inside — 2.60 meters
height of room outside (to roof of porch)—3.40 meters
sill, lintel, frame, door, etc. of plank

Before the door there is a stepping stone of lava, an old metate set in adobe* .80 meters long, and a tinaja with water and cups to drink. Roof as at Pecos. Poles lengthwise and brush crosswise. On the north wall the beams of the other room protrude slightly; these are all rectangular. a. Heap of green chile, b. step to other room, c. bed, used as lounge, with sheepskin before it, d. heap of wheat with watermelons, e. chimney, fireplace, f. recess of doorstep, g. wheat, h. planks set against the wall, i. new window frame. The middle of the floor is empty and clean, also hard. On the east wall there is a window, .86 meters square, nearly closed, leaving only a very small opening. There is one chair and one stool. This is the winter room for the family. In front of the room, on the south side, there is a porch, six beams supporting a projection of the roof 2 meters wide. There is a step to the door.

The chimney was done by 4 P.M. and looks, indeed, very well. It is all made of adobe. I asked about the arch, and he showed me how they made it. Four adobe bricks set up together and then filled up and rounded with adobe mortar so as to form the arch.

We again went through the pueblo after sunset, just before nightfall. Called on the cacique, who was very pleasant and kind. The people are certainly good, much better than those of Santo Domingo. Juan José is very well informed. I shall gather a good many data from him. Huásh-pá (chamiza [sage]). This lineage is found at Santo Domingo and Cia also. Hiithsha-añy (cottonwood) was the apellido of the wife. (She died in 1871.) The children take the name [clan] of the mother, and not the name of the father. This is very, very important.

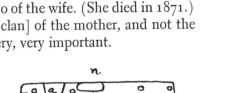

In Santo Domingo, a gens *Pahrak* (toad). In Cochiti, a gens *Shu-tsuna* (coyote), a gens *Yaqa* (maize), *Tzitz* (water),*Taña* (calabash), *Oshatch* (sun), *Ha-pañee* (encina [oak]), *Shipewe* (a kind of sage), *Shu-amo* (turquoise), *Há-kañeh* (light). These generaciones have their principales, which are tacitly acknowledged, on account of their age and experience. They have nothing to do with the government proper.

On the 26 or 27 of December each year, the governor and captain call together the people at night, and the cacique calls upon them to elect the officers. The people refuse, always, leaving it to the cacique, who then elects [designates]. If the parties chosen refuse to accept the charge, then they are imprisoned so long until they take it. The cacique himself is the father of the tribe or Pueblo; he appoints his own successor, and he has to receive at his house and entertain all strangers coming into the pueblo. Those who have been governor and captain once *se quedan principales después* [continue as principales subsequently]. But the fiscal himself is not a principal.[93]

The principales of the gentes call together their male members for the dances. Thus the gentes come in still [are involved, or function, again]. Those of the same name cannot intermarry, even if they do not live in the same pueblo. Thus, he [Juan José Montoya] said: my son cannot marry the daughter of my sister, but [he can marry] the daughter of my brother.[94] As for rules of

---

93. One wonders here if Bandelier understood his informants correctly. The cacique is and seemingly has always been the ceremonial, or religious, leader of the tribe; as such, he has very little contact with, and virtually no responsibility regarding, outsiders who may enter the community. In contrast, the governor is essentially a secular officer, and it is he who normally handles relations between the tribe and the outside world. Hospitality, then, is his responsibility.

The remainder of the paragraph is valid for Bandelier's time and even today, with the primary exception that for some years now, the fiscal and his lieutenant become principales as do the governor and war captain as well as their respective lieutenants.

94. Bandelier's discussion here was more involved than he realized. With his use of terms other than those commonly used today, the situation becomes even more confused. However, Bandelier was correct in assigning clan exogamy

inheritance, same as in Santo Domingo. If the wife had any land at the time of her marriage, it is set apart for her. The balance of land is divided equally among her and the children, each child receiving an equal share. The *cosecha* [harvest] is hers. He gave me a sketch of the manner in which he, his brother, and his sister divided his mother's estate ten days ago. The dying person can make a will, preferring child or grandchild, and it is to be respected. His mother preferred two grandchildren.

OCTOBER 8: Juan José Montoya tells me that he found [recalled], overnight, another generación of Cochiti, *Yssi* (yedra [Ivy]). The name of kin or clan is *Ha-nush*, thus *Yssi ha-nush*. Last night, he also told me about the serpent worship of the Moqui, according to what his brother saw there twice, in the estufas, at the time he went to California. During one of their bailes, an immense snake came out from behind a curtain, and when they began to dance, it coiled itself up in the middle of the estufa turning its head at the measure of the music. Another time, as the men of the tribe had been sowing [sewing?], etc., in the estufa, José Hilario Montoya went in and found them all asleep, with snakes creeping over their bodies.[95] (Juan José is well informed.)

There are three ruins—one, on the Potrero de las Vacas,

---

as a facet of ideal Cochiti marriage patterns. He failed to note (if he knew) that Juan José Montoya and his wife, María Trinidad Herrera, were both members of the Cottonwood Clan, a relatively large clan at that time. This marriage obviously violated the rule of exogamy. (See Lange 1959: Appendix 31, for other instances of this breach.) Thus, his son should not have married the daughter of his sister, but he could marry the daughter of his brother whose wife provided a different clan designation to the daughter. In typical Puebloan fashion, Juan José failed to provide a complete explanation of the situation. Bandelier, failing to obtain full genealogies (a failure also typical of many of his contemporaries and immediate successors), was unable to perceive the situation and pursue the matter with apt questions.

95. This is a somewhat garbled account of the Hopi Snake Dance held in late summer by the Snake and Antelope fraternities. A dramatic feature of the ceremony is the dancing with snakes held in the mouth and otherwise intimately handled at the public climax of this 9-day rain ceremony.

about one day's journey northwest; another, in the Rito de los Frijoles, one-half day off; and one, near, on the Potrero Largo [Potrero Viejo]. This last one, he says, contains the ruins of the pueblo of Cochiti from which Vargas had the people removed to its present site, in about 1692. Juan José Montoya says they fought hard against the Spaniards.

When they crossed the river, it was on large *huaquis* (ollas), fastened to their girdles, and thus swimming. This morning, Juan José Montoya showed me a kind of corn, steamed in the shuck, in their ovens. They are put in at night, fire being made, and the oven closed. Then water is poured in from above, and the whole allowed to steam till morning. My room, northeast corner of house [in meters]:

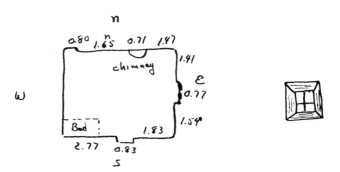

inside—.77 x .78
east window—.63 x .63
recess—.21 deep
height to top of room—.40
height of sill above floor—1.01
total height of room south—2.00
door in northwest corner—0.15 above floor
in recess—.24 deep
in recess—1.40 high
in recess—.80 wide
door itself—1.25 x .60, panelled, in wooden frame
stepping stone outside

southern door—1.00 x .66
in recess—1.17 x .83, and .13 deep
height above floor—.37

No stepping stone inside. Between my room and the southern one is the storeroom, as long as the latter, but only 3.50
meters wide. In the southeast corner of it is the kitchen fire. It
consists of a raised surface of earth .86 by .80, about, and .04
high (a) is a pole .80 supporting a wooden frame, which rests in
the wall at (b) and (c). On this frame the flue is built like a
wide quadrangular funnel. The chimney of my room is as follows. The funnel itself is made of poles resting on the frame,
fastened in the roof, and daubed with clay. Height of the fire-

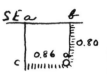

place to (a) .86. Over it, the flue itself is built of five adobes
set upright.

My breakfast consisted of fair coffee, very good cheese of cow's
milk, excellent tortillas. Tolerably clean so far. We started on
foot for the Potrero de las Casas. Juan José takes his gun along,
although he says that game is scarce. Farther north and west
even grizzly bear (*Osos platriados* [*Ursus horribilis*]) and elk
(*Venado alazán* [*Cervus canadensis*]) occur. Juan José is very
talkative. He tells me about a bird which pursues and kills snakes
[roadrunner], about the porcupine, which jumps at men and
animals to poison them with the spines, and which lately killed
one of his dogs in this manner, as the spines could not be pulled

out again. Conversation very interesting. He has read the Bible and knows it. He is an honest, strong Catholic, who speaks with fairness and still with devotion. He is one of the principales.

The trip goes to the northwest, directly toward the Sierra de la Bolsa, over a dreary plateau with *Opuntia*, and then through an equally arid cañada, formed by hills of drift and gravel, specked by sabinos. The chaparro disappears very gradually. In the sandy bottom, *Opuntia* in large specimens.

Juan José Montoya very talkative. He says that in 1853 and 1854 an old man named Antonio told him, at night in the rancho across the river, that in his time (about 1800) the corn and all fruit were much better and [ripened] earlier, and that the melons ripened by the 5th of July. He also told him that the old men (principales) prophesied that a time would come when the crops would be bad, and the corn not ripen any more. Also that if, in times to come, a nation should enter from the northwest, *vestida de colorada de guerra* (red coats!) the world would soon be at an end. But that if a nation should come from the east, white, with good, four-wheeled carts drawn by mules, then the world would last long and there would be good times. They also said that these latter people would introduce a cart which would run very swiftly. Juan José Montoya attributes this prophecy of the old men to astrological knowledge.

He then told me the story of Montezuma *in extenso*. The earlier part of it he had from Francisco Nazlé of Jemez, who was in possession of a book wherein Montezuma is painted, which book is printed in the United States; and the latter part is taken from reading. I cannot now do justice to this remarkable tale, but will reserve it for special reports.

The road is a gradual ascent through sandy lomas with sabinos and *Opuntias*, until 11 A.M. when we reached the Cañada, a chapel and five or six adobe houses, mostly inhabited by the Lucero family. Obsidian and pottery are scattered along the road and in one place a ruin is found, which Montoya says was erected by the people of Cochiti when they moved from the Peñol to the present site. The Potrero de las Casas [Potrero Viejo] is about one-half mile west-southwest [west-northwest] of La Cañada. It is a solid narrow mesa of pumice-stone, rising abruptly on three sides, to more than 500 meters elevation. Its eastern half descends in a perpendicular wall on three sides, 50 to 60 meters. On its western half are the ruins, all built of pumice-stone, with adobe earth flung in. In Queres, this pueblo is called *Haenata-catretzi* (arribas-casas); the Cañada is called *Cúahpa* [Kuapa]. The surface is covered by sabinos, cedros, chaparro, piñones (dwarf), *Opuntia* nopal or tuna. Some tall, beautiful trees stand in the center of the ruins. The ruins themselves, though large and well preserved, are still more barren than those of Pecos. Obsidian, being imbedded in the pumice, is very sparsely scattered about. There is some pottery, glazed also, but neither arrowheads nor stone implements of any kind. Juan José tells me the cause of it is that the Mexicans ransack every ruin for metates and the like, but he thinks that, by digging, much might be found. It is evident that the pueblo has been burnt, and Juan José says that after a long and unsuccessful blockade, the Spanish dragoons finally surprised the pueblo. They burnt the pueblo, thus compelling its people to abandon it. Some, however, fled to the Navajo, among them a woman, who some time after, was recognized by the people of the pueblo and who also recognized them. But she was married with the tribe and only told her people that in some place on the potrero much green-stone [turquoise?], etc. was concealed.

The potrero was a favorite lurking-place of the Navajo, and Juan José himself killed one on top of it. A fire to the north had been noticed early in the morning, so the potrero was surrounded. Two were killed on the potrero, and two more died of wounds on their way home. The Navajo usually came down through the canyons, and for years, he says, they were a terrible plague. Night and day the Pueblos had to be on their lookout. He has taken part in many frays with them. Now, he says, they are peaceable and very honest (?).

North of the potrero is a very deep gorge in which the Arroyo de la Cañada flows, past the old fields of the pueblo. There are

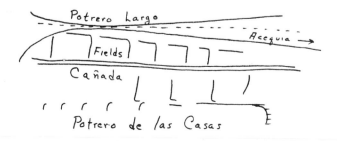

many ruined buildings of stone in this bottom, but Juan José tells me they are Mexican as after the reconquest many Spaniards settled there, but were finally driven out by the Navajo. We measured every room, not-withstanding the cacti which are superabundant in the ruins, *Opuntia arborescens* growing in them almost like trees. 210 meters east of these are a number of ruined structures very similar to the "outhouses" at Pecos, but utterly shapeless. Juan José says they may have been almacenes [store houses]. The rim of the potrero is not fortified like that of Pecos, only the four very tortuous and steep paths leading up to it—one on the north-west side, and three from the south. The following is about the shape of the surface of the potrero, (a) being the pueblo, b.b.b.b. the four places of access. These creep up through narrow gorges and on either side of their landing on the top, the Indians had erected bulwarks of stone at which sentinels and guards stood to watch any approach. It required a ruse and a feint to capture this otherwise impregnable stronghold. This survey is not complete; much is yet to be done. For example, I am told that there is water on the mesa behind the pueblo—an arroyo, and also a tank. The drainage generally is to the south. We descended at 2 P.M., very difficult and even dangerous, in the very steep and crumbling pumice. Height of potrero evidently 1,000-2,000 feet.[96]

Lucero very friendly, coffee, tortillas, and sheep's meat. Have a grant yet, from about 1694. Could not see it yet. Left at 3 P.M. and on the way talked a great deal. Conversed about the word Tihua, but Juan José could not give me any definite information in regard to its meaning. He says it is an accentuation of "man," and may be in some relation with *Tigua-yú*, from which they all claim to descend. He also says that *Yute* means "there" in *Tiguayú*. *Yu* (por allá), and *Te* as abbreviation of *Tigua*, or *Tehua*. It is evidently an old and very important utterance. There are two Piro Indians from Senecú at Cochiti who still speak their idiom. One of them is the son of a Cochiti who mar-

---

96. Bandelier's estimate here is incorrect to an extent warranting comment. Potrero Viejo actually stands about 670 feet above Spanish Cañada.

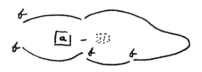

ried a Piro woman. Consequently, the child is Piro. This is important. Reached home 5 P.M. tired; 18 miles about.*

OCTOBER 9: Left for Peña Blanca at 6 A.M. Distance from church to first bridge about 800 meters; between bridges, 100 meters. Found my things at Peña Blanca. Went over to Wallace, last mile on foot. Met Padre Ribera and the Bacas. He has valise. Got shaved at Wallace.

I have forgotten to write down many items which Juan José Montoya told me. Thus, he said that before any expedition is sent out, a general meeting is held. The capitán first presents his gun, etc. to his teniente or the oldest principal, who examines the weapons. Then the capitán examines the arms of the teniente. Then each one goes around his own way in the circle of men, visiting [inspecting] the arms of each man. If any are found out of order, the man is ordered to prepare them for such and such a time. If by then he fails to be in trim, the capitán imprisons him without further delay. This he has a right to do without consulting any of the principales, for in military affairs the capitán is supreme and can act as he pleases (very important). In cases of crimes, of dispute, etc., the governor is the party to apply to, but then the council first investigates and decides upon the offense. They are the judges, and the governor is but the executive. The fiscal has nothing to do except care for the church; he is not even a principal necessarily.

Am tired. A freight train will take me up to Santa Fe. This is the windiest place I ever saw. Juan José Montoya owns thirty-seven cows, three horses, one mule, and one burro. The merced [grant] of Cochiti, is one league east, one league south, 2 leagues, 1.25 cadenas [chains of ten meters] north, and the same (2 1.25 c.) west. This is on account of the pasturage. He also told me the name of a twelfth generation [clan], but I forgot to put it down yesterday. I noticed that every morning before breakfast, the girls grind the corn for the tortillas. Therefore, the early singing.

Yesterday Juan José Montoya told me that his oldest son (Adelaido) was called Haeyiash, cloud, or rather, Haeyashtihua.

He, himself, is called Matyayatihua. The affix "*ma*" to the tribal name signifies, according to him, something like brother, thus the five tribes of the Queres would be called, and are called in fact: *Qqo-djete-ma* [Cochiti], *Tigua-ma* [Santo Domingo], *Qq'hatyista-ma* [San Felipe], *Tamai-ma* [Santa Ana], and *Tzia-ma* [Zia]. Of Cia, he says it is a very small pueblo.

His version of the Montezuma tale is highly interesting and important. It begins at *Tehuayu* which he points out to the northwest and north, and where he says, the Pueblos were all together in one. This must be coupled with what Padre Escalante says. The latter only speaks of the Tehuas, whereas Montoya now distinctly connects also the Tiguas and the Queres with *Tehuayu*. Tiguas, he says plainly, are the Sandias and those of Isleta. I also told him about the claim set up by those of Santo Domingo in regard to the turquoise mines, and he explained that when the Tanos left, some of them settled and married at Santo Domingo. Thus the people of Santo Domingo regard themselves as their heirs. This may be so (?).

Afternoon. An accident delays the train. Chilly. Wallace has very large railroad buildings. Juan José Montoya also told me that the Acoma were called *Hako-ma*. In conjunction with the *Tehuayu*, it is well to remember the Teyas of Coronado, and that they were Utes! After waiting till 4:00 P.M., I was finally told that there would be no chance to go till 7:00 P.M., when the three trains still expected would certainly come in. This would carry me no farther than Galisteo Junction tonight, so I started back to Peña Blanca. Met old man Pacheco and Juan Coriz from Santo Domingo. Tomorrow, I shall start for Santa Fe on horseback. Moon out at night. During the sandstorm [of the afternoon], the bottom of the Rio Grande appeared as if smoking, but the Indians were out working.

OCTOBER 10: Went to church. Very good. The name of the twelfth gens is Tortolita, *Hó-gogga* [Dove]. So the Padre reminds me this morning. He also says that, when a father is informed of the birth of a child, he names that child after the first object (inanimate or not) which he meets after receiving the information. I go to Santa Fe with the ambulance and both Señores Baca. Am troubled about the railroad accident at Trinidad. Dare not even think of possibilities. Left 11 A.M.

Pueblo Quemado [Pindi Pueblo] 3:00 P.M.* 25 meters north across the road another mound. Fragments of recent painted

pottery are scattered about, but no obsidian, whereas gypsum in broken pieces is found. I also collected pottery, red and black, which is much decomposed, but looks like deteriorated vitrified loza. Reception at Santa Fe very kind. At night I got invited to a singing party in the First National Bank. Pleasant evening.

OCTOBER 11: Joe's birthday. God bless her! My mail had left for Peña Blanca. Spent several hours with Mr. Ellison and Señor Vigil at the archives. Horrible condition of the papers of Diego de Vargas. Card from Norton and letter from Morgan. Bought a revolver. Began to write to Joe.

OCTOBER 12: Sent box to Professor Norton. Bought a horse. Called on General Hatch. Santo Domingo affairs with Comanche gave no trouble at all. Received box from George Hoffmann. Afternoon I shall write. Bennett is married. Among the documents at the archives there is an important census list of the Queres pueblos which I shall have copied. Very much pleased with horse. Tried to see the Archbishop, but in vain. He was not at home. Wrote balance of the afternoon, and spent evening, after 9 P.M., with D. J. Miller and General Atkinson. Photographs are very good. Card from Professor Norton.

OCTOBER 13: Sent off letter to Joe. Went to D. J. Miller and copied paper about the Rito de los Frijoles. Books very interesting. Went up to the College[97] with Felsenthal and had an interesting interview with Brother Baldwin. He gave me the fecha [date] on the beam in the church of San Miguel. All the adobes of the church and the wall around it are [made] with wheatstraw. The foundations are of rubble-stone. In the afternoon, went with Mr. Ellison to Gold and copied the documents relative to Puaray. Sent them to Professor Norton. Juan José in with horse and mule at 3 P.M.

Inscription on first beam inside of the chapel of San Miguel, as given to me by Brother Baldwin, "*El Sr. Marquez de la Peñuela hizo esta fabrica, El Alferez Real, Don Agustín Flo[s] Vengara, su Criado, Año de 1710.*" [The Marquis of Peñuela built this structure, the chief ensign Don Agustín Flores Vengara, his servant, in the year 1710.] It appears, however, that in 1703, Diego de Vargas sent men to cut timbers for the roof of the chapel, whose walls were still standing, after the outbreak of 1680. Grant of Cochiti is dated 1689. From a paper relating to Sandia it seems that this pueblo was rebuilt after 1748. Socorro destroyed by the Apaches in 1680. (This is unlikely.) Evening fine, copied and sent off the Bernalillo manuscript of Gold.

Rito de los Frijoles. Papers at the General Surveyors Office, Santa Fe.

1. Letter of Fray Antonio Cavallero, Cust. 1807. Stating that, in 1780, Don Juan Bautista de Anza, Governor of New Mexico,

---

97. Probably St. Michael's College, established in 1859 under the auspices of Father Lamy.

confirmed to Andrés Montoya a grant of that tract, executed to him by D. Tomás Valez Gachupín (governor from 1749 to 1754, and 1762 to 1766, also in 1773).

2. Petition of José Antonio Salas, February 28, 1802, confirming above.

3. Decision of Governor Manrique.

4. Manuel Hurtado, deposition, November 26, 1872. During the lifetime of José Antonio Salas, he and all the inhabitants of the Rito abandoned it, owing to the terrible depredations of the Navajo. In 1869, one returned, but was killed by lightning. No other attempt to occupy it since.

OCTOBER 14: Before I left, I met Mr. Stevenson, who told me about his remarkable discoveries in the Santa Clara Canyon. Left with Juan José at 10 A.M. Crossed north of the Tetilla. Barren, sabinos, but not as destitute of vegetation as below the Tetilla. The descent is twice as bad as the Bajada, and three times as great. The whole road is much longer than the stage-road. (Name of the Tetilla, *Qqah-sishcotsha.*) Between the point where he changed the load from the mule to the horse and the Tetilla, there is a very deep lake.

At night, letter from Papa at Peña Blanca. Padre Ribera told me about the *guerra de los Gachupines* [war of the Spaniards], when the Franciscan monks were kicked out of New Mexico into the United States. From the descent I took the road alone, southwest to Peña Blanca. Crossed the Río de Santa Fe in the cañada and got astray on the lava. Thanks to my safe horse, I got down the cuesta [cliff], and at sunset reached Peña Blanca. Very tired. Laguna trouble discussed.

OCTOBER 15: Left Peña Blanca at 9 A.M. with valise and bundle. Kindest reception. Room fixed and whitewashed. Agustín called on me. He was at Laguna when the Protestants and Catholics had their trouble. All the Pueblos sent delegates, but the Protestants ill-treated them and drove them out. Started for the Cañada about 12 noon. Don Agustín gave me some valuable information. He is of the maize gens: *Yaqqa.* He fully confirms the statements of Juan José and says that there are gentes of the [mountain] lion, bear, wolf, and others. They are not limited to one Pueblo, but belong to the Queres in general.

When I returned, I found the whole house full of guests. Nearly the entire Lucero family had assembled. They state that this is but the second pueblo of Cochiti and that the first one is six or seven miles to the north on the Potrero de la Casita, another one on the Potrera de la Cuesta Blanca.[98] They told me much about the Navajo war, how they suffered, and how they finally resisted and, under the United States Government, almost destroyed the Navajo. The Luceros had to abandon the Cañada for two or three years, but they came back every year to sow and reap, though always well-armed.

Señor Lucero tells me about rock-crystals found in the neighborhood of the puerta of the cañón. One is also showed to me. They speak of yellow sulphur, of gypsum. The latir is the fruit of the yucca, a large variety, found mostly on the mountain-tops. Quiet. Bed fair.

I reached La Cañada at 2:30 P.M. Horseback, and by a road more to the south, through a cañada [probably Peralta Canyon]

---

98. Bandelier, unfortunately and yet understandably, never succeeded in obtaining a proper sequence of sites formerly occupied by the Cochiti, other Keresans, or, in fact, other Puebloan tribes. Eighty years later, despite extensive and intensive excavations, the story remains obscure. At present, several Pueblos have permitted stratigraphic or even more complete archaeological excavations, but for the majority of the tribes, such collaboration remains for the future. Until stratigraphic sequences are demonstrated between the lower levels of historic village deposits and the deposits of strictly prehistoric sites, Puebloan culture history remains essentially hypothetical.

The large ruin on Potrero Viejo, known both as Pueblo Viejo and Kotyiti (L. A. 295), was occupied by the Cochiti and their allies during the years of the Pueblo Revolt and Reconquest, 1680-1692. It was excavated by Dr. Nels C. Nelson of the American Museum of Natural History in 1912. A short distance outside and east of this large block-8 shaped ruin are other scattered remains which Nelson and Mera considered distinct. (See entry of October 8, 1880.) However, despite the separate site designation (L. A. 84), all the glaze-paint forms are of Group F, and it would seem well justified to look upon these structures as the work of late arrivals after the double plazas had been enclosed or to consider them merely detached portions of the main ruin. (For historic details pertaining to Pueblo Viejo, see Hackett 1942, Espinosa 1940, and Leonard 1932.)

where the volcanic tuff and sandstone are eroded into singular, tower-like forms. As usual, I lost my way, and wandered about in sight of the Potrero Viejo and of the Sierra, till I finally reached the Cañada, where my reception at the house of Señor Luis Lucero was very hospitable. His son, Juan Luis, accompanied me to the Cañada and to the puerta of the Cañón de las Casas. The scenery is very grand and wild. The Potrero [Viejo] rises to the left about 2,000 feet,[99] in two and three tiers of vertical rocks of pumice stone. Between it and the Potrero Largo opposite there lies the valley, one-half mile wide, with the clear brook of the Cañada between, rippling down under sabinos, piñones, and alamos. The trees are large and fine. In this bottom, on both sides of the brook lie the ruins of Spanish houses, and the fields of ancient and modern date. A very old acequia, purported to be of Indian origin, takes from the very start of the Cañada [de Cochiti], below the puerta and runs along the north side of it, along the lomas made by the mountain streams, which here have accumulated enormous heaps, embankments of drift. The puerta of the canyon itself is very grand. Narrow, shut in by high rocks and steep walls, the bottom is still covered with a fair growth of trees of various kinds, and the clear water ripples through it, while an icy blast of wind always issues from the mouth of the canyon. At the place where the acequia starts off from the brook, the Indians of the Potrero used to descend for their water, and there also the path (the only one on the north side), descends from the Potrero. It is impossible now to determine which were the Indian fields, and which were those of the whites alone. The latter have evidently taken the place of the former. Still, in one field, very near the mouth of the canyon, we found Indian pottery, both ordinary and painted. The drift of the Cañada consists of argillitic trap, basalt, pumice, lava, diorite, limestone, and flint.

OCTOBER 16: Rose about 5:30 A.M. Luis Lucero told me that the pueblos farther north were those occupied by the Queres,

99. Bandelier repeated his exaggerated estimate here. It is about 670 feet above Spanish Cañada (See footnote 96).

and that the Tehuas drove them out, farther to the south, in
the course of intertribal wars. From the Rito de los Frijoles,
etc., they migrated to a now ruined pueblo [probably San
Miguel, L.A. 370] one mile east-northeast of the settlement of
the Cañada. Thence they went to the river, and from the river
up to the Potrero Viejo.

At 8 A.M., I went with José Lucero two miles east along the
Cañada, to its confluence with a deep barranca. There, on a
bluff, are the old pueblo ruins [Kuapa]. They are scattered over

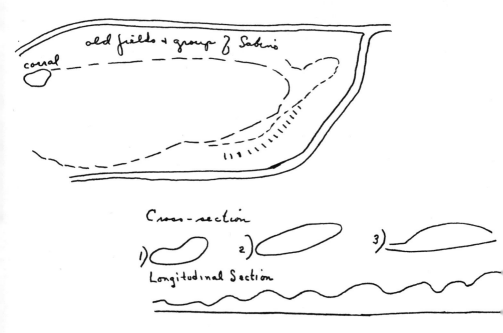

with pottery and obsidian. The pottery is plain and recent,
glazed and old, and corrugated and indented. Ruins very extensive.* Thus the ruins form, in fact, nine ribs or elevations,
transverse to the longitudinal axis of the entire loma. There is
a wall of circumvallation or rather short defensive embankment,
of about 75 meters in length, to the south of the largest estufa.

On the west of the ruins, there stand considerable Mexican structures, distinctly of stone, with very thick walls. The loma rises to the southwest and widens to the west, and the buildings almost touch the rim both north and south. The slope is not very steep, except on the south, where but few sabinos grow. It is everywhere very gravelly; so is the bottom. No fields can be made out with any certainty. Some excavations have been made already, exhuming and removing metates. Fragments of a hearthstone found.*

This is about the form of the mesa occupied by the pueblo. My measurements are not very accurate, since the whole is in a state of complete ruin with not a single wall standing. (At this moment it recurs to me that Juan José Montoya told me that the name of the youngest boy, used now in the Spanish language, is *Shocoyote*. This is the *Xocoyotl* of the Mexicans!)

Returned to the village at 11 A.M. Had to pay damage to Telisfero Lucero (50 cents) for the horse. Had to write also until 12 noon, during which time T. Lucero told me all about the different pueblos of the Cochiti. It appears that indeed the old pueblos of the Cochiti were on the mesas north near the Tehuas and that the latter made war upon the former and drove them to the south. But the version is so far different, that T. Lucero says the wars between the tribes took place after the year 1680, and not before the advent of the whites.

Left for the potrero 12 noon. Lost my way and had to go back; finally on top 12:40, [via the] eastern ascent.* . . . It appears now as if there was an old ruin, large buildings, instead of the several small ones. Descending, I found shapeless mound with oven on the eastern apron. Old pottery, glazed and recent pottery, also obsidian. Left La Cañada at 3:30 P.M. and reached Cochiti at 5 P.M., by another road, mostly over the crest of hills. [Probably via the "Long Arroyo."] Reception most friendly. [Juan José's] son, Pedro, has just returned from the Sierra with two fine horses, white, a horse and a mare, both of which Adelaido and José Hilario brought from California. Pedro

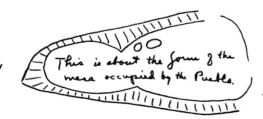

This is about the form of the mesa occupied by the Pueblo.

Rise of the Loma to the SW

brought news that turkeys (*Tzi-na*) were very abundant in the mountains. They go now in troops of forty and fifty males and females, until April, when the sexes separate.

We discussed the matter of teaching, and agreed that he should write English and Spanish, while I should write Queres. José Hilario came in, and complained that I did not take him as a guide. Explained matters to him. Then came Agustín, Yaq'qa. We had a long talk. Both agreed that in the fierce wars which the Queres and the Tehuas had [in the vicinity of] the Cañada, the Cochiti retired first to the Potrero Viejo in consequence of these wars. This was a tacit acknowledgement of the fact that the large pueblo of the Cañada was, indeed, old Cochiti.

Then we discussed the point of adoption into the tribe, and both appeared favorably disposed.[100] They denied the existence of the sacred fire in the pueblo, but said that it existed at Pecos, and that there was a proverbial response to anyone begging for fire in any house. "*Adonde hay lumbre?*" "*A Pecos*" ["Where can fire be obtained?"—"At Pecos."] Their councils are held at the house of the cacique and not in the estufas. The latter are used for preparation and rehearsal of their dances. There are always two in each pueblo—now! Each pueblo is divided into two partidos, each estufa belonging to a certain number of gentes, who congregate there for their dances. This clearly establishes the phratry, and leads to the inference that the number of phratries is indicated by the number of estufas in each pueblo. (Possible, but not yet proven.)

OCTOBER 17: The old pueblo of La Cañada is *Cuah-pa*. Left for Peña Blanca at 8:30 P.M., but since all the fields had been freshly watered and moist, I didn't reach church until 9:30 P.M. Last evening, both Agustín and Juan José assured me that the Navajo formerly used poison for their arrows, and that they ad-

---

100. This quite clearly suggests that Bandelier's adoption by the Cochiti was at least contemplated at one time and not only by Bandelier himself. However, no subsequent journal entries mention such adoption, though Hodge (1914: 350) states that Bandelier became "a member of the tribe."

mitted it. This poison is made from the blood of menstruating women,[101] boiled with a certain herb whose name they could not give me. They also use snake poison or snake blood.

We went to see [Padre Ribera's] garden, and he explained to me the manner of culture. For corn, they irrigate before they break the ground, then they irrigate after planting, and finally they irrigate once or twice during the time of growth. For wheat, they irrigate when it spreads, again when it gets into the ears, and finally when it blossoms. Some irrigate for wheat eight to ten times. It is impossible to break the ground unless it has been first irrigated. In irrigating, the water is permitted to enter, and as soon as it is equally distributed over the ground, the taparico [gate] is closed, and the ground is allowed to become soaked thoroughly. [To assure] equal distribution, the fields are small, and the bulwarks are little.

José Hilario was godfather to a child about 12 noon. Returned to Cochiti after 2 P.M. Indians mostly at work in the fields, gathering corn. Many on horseback. Juan José is tying up chile (green). He says that they also make pozole of maize, but use beef for it. In the spring they also cook the green-chile with lard or fat.

At night, José Hilario and the brother-in-law, Luis Montoya, came into my room and talked for a long while. Tomorrow, there will be a Mexican wedding and dance to which Juan José is invited. I advised him to go, and José Hilario will go with me to the Peralta, where there are other ruins, probably those of the old pueblo of Santo Domingo.

I drew up the plan of the pueblo of Old Cochiti, on the Potrero Viejo. Measures agreed very well, showing accuracy. Juan José is of the opinion that it had as many as three stories. He confirms the tale of Padre Ribera about the irrigation of corn (three times after planting). The corn is hoed, then ploughed. But before breaking ground, it is irrigated, then broken and

---

101. The special power, or qualities of inherent danger, here attributed to menstrual blood is a widespread concept; it extends far beyond the Puebloan cultures in not only the New World but the Old World as well.

pulverized. That is, the sod is crumbled with hoes. Soil is not cheap, $1.00 to $3.00 the vara, according to the length.

OCTOBER 18: The bridges over the Rio Grande are carried away every spring, and then renewed. Agustín Herrera called early (9 A.M.). He says that the Indian names are given by the fathers and mothers, after the birth. Juan José told me he had spoken with the cacique about leaving the pueblo with me, and the cacique had told him there was nothing in the way, but that if anything should transpire calling for his stay, one of his sons might go with me. This shows that they (at least the principales) are careful to inform the cacique of their actions, and it may even prove that they need his consent (?). Juan José is invited (in writing) to a Mexican wedding to be celebrated in the pueblo today. They will have a dance. Possibly in his own house, as they have asked for it. Went over to Peña Blanca reaching there 11 A.M. The mail had not yet arrived. Yesterday I wrote to Gatschet, to Greenleaf, and home—only cards. I asked for rye-seed, for a map, and for sugar cane plants. They will try them in the valley.

On my way to Peña Blanca I was stopped at the upper town by Benigno Ortiz who inquired about a remedy for his son, twenty-one years old. Three years ago a horse broke his skull on the right side very near the temple. Since then he is epileptic, the fits returning every two or three weeks, and with much violence. I told him that nothing could be done, but that it would disappear in time. Mail not in at 11:30 A.M. No letters. Returned to Cochiti about 1 P.M.

Juan José told me that there were two ruins: one left and one right. The one on the right is on the Potrero Medio and is called in Queres, *q'qe-qanyé q'qama-tsishuma* (*q'qe-quanyé*, colorado [red], *q'qama-tsishuma*, ruins). The one to the left is on the Potrero de la Cañada Quemada, and is called *Punihaenat-q'qama-tsishuma* (*puni*, por el poniente [west]; *haenat*, sobre, ó arriba [above]). The little girl is making dough before the chimney with a little salt in it for biscuit, for our trip. This biscuit they call *ya-shpa*.

We left about 3 p.m., José Hilario and I, on horseback. Route in the main west-northwest. About three miles from Cochiti the high lomas to the north merge into a cañada. This is the Cañada de la Peralta. It is well-timbered, pinabetes, piñones, fine alamos, and a rather thick undergrowth of sabinos, cedros, and encinas. As we go farther west, the vegetation increases and becomes very fine. For nearly a mile the Barranca Blanca with its splendid white cones, accompanies us on the left. The Cañada there is about one mile wide. Then a grand puerta with towering cliffs and a clear mountain-streamlet, very cold, running through it. Then the Cañada widens out to a valley about one-half mile wide. This is the Cañón Quemado, and we are seven miles west from Cochiti.

Here a fire is built; coffee, sheep meat, and blue-corn tortillas are eaten about 7 p.m. Horse and mule tied and left to pasture. The rippling of the stream is very distinctly heard. In the Barranca Blanca there are several caves, also two at the entrance of the puerta of the Cañón Quemado. It is one of the finest sceneries I ever saw. There is a discrepancy here between the sayings of the brothers [in respect to vocabulary].

OCTOBER 19: Very cold, tin-cup full of water frozen hard in the morning. Slept but little. After breakfast (coffee and eggs) saddled and rode up the Cañón Quemado. All white volcanic tuff, with erosion cones. Very picturesque. Trees fine. After about three-quarters of a mile, we began to ascend the cuesta. Steep and high, grand view into the canyon from above. Then to the head of the canyon where the Potrero Quemado shuts it to the west. There we left our horses under beautiful trees (pinabetes) and ascended, on foot, the very steep eastern brow. Short, but hard climbing. Reached top about 8 a.m. The potrero is covered with trees, some very tall piñones, cedars, sabinos.

The ruins [known to present-day Cochiti as Pueblo Quemado, also as Pueblito, L.A. 3654] appear to be extensive; they are of the same stone as the potrero; namely, a light, white volcanic tuff, enclosing feldspar and pumice fragments. It is friable and breaks in any manner to suit. The walls are about 22 centimeters thick and laid regularly in courses, with adobe mud and small stones filling the interstices as mortar. The stones are of various sizes but all are broken so as to form rectangular blocks. I commenced at the northwest corner, but soon found that it was almost impossible to measure. Estufa, 4.90 meters in diameter.

There is much pottery strewn around the buildings, and comparatively little pottery over the ruins themselves. The eastern slope is particularly rich. The corrugated and indented pottery is almost more abundant than any other. The glazed pottery is very scarce, and appears to be only red, with narrow black stripes. Then there is much gray and black pottery, and gray pottery with black ornaments unglazed. Obsidian is ever present, also red agate, white flint, and moss agate. But I could not find even an arrowhead. José Hilario tells me that many stone hammers and hatchets were found and sold by the people of Cochiti to visitors from Santa Fe. About two miles northeast from this ruin, on the Potrero de en Medio, is another ruin, which José Hilario describes as follows. He says: "No hay más de un cuartel," ["There is nothing more than the one section."] but some of the walls are still standing, if not all of them. There is no estufa, and the whole may be, according to him, about 150 feet long.

We descended from the Potrero Quemado at 12 noon and found our horses gone. José Hilario went after them, while I built a fire. Splendid, under these big pine trees, but I feel [remember] last night and do not think of seeing the other ruin. It must be more recent than this one, else it would be more obliterated. José Hilario is cooking dinner; coffee, sheep-ribs broiled on a stick, and three eggs in a pan are waiting for him. Both mule and horse are grazing, for the grass beneath the pinabetes, although sparse, is very good. Not being tied, they soon made tracks down the canyon and I had trouble in catching up with my horse. It pulled me down and nearly broke my right arm. Dinner was over by 1 P.M., and, as it would be 4 P.M. ere we could reach the Potrero de en Medio, I decided to abandon

it this time. I am really tired and need a day's rest and also need to fix up my plans and diagrams.

The two pueblos on the other side of the Rio are called, according to Agustín, *Qq'ityé-haenat-qq'ama-tsishuma* [Eastern upper ruins]. Recollects having heard of the eclipse, but was not alive yet at the time.

Agustín was very communicative. He told me that the people of the pueblo of the Potrero Quemado (which he also calls the old pueblo of Santo Domingo) had no fields, but lived on game and by hunting exclusively; that they were fierce and plundered and robbed their neighbors. (This confirms the report of José Hilario.) He also said that the pueblos of the Rio Chaco, etc., were not built by the Pueblos, but by Montezuma, and he calls them *Q-ash-catretji*, Pueblo Blanco. He believes in witches and sorcerers, both of Pueblos and of Mexicans, and says they change themselves into snakes, toads, frogs, etc. He says that they have the mal-ochio [mal ojo] (evil eye). They have superstition of a cat crossing the path, and also of Friday. Indian doctors—some of them live in the pueblo.

On the road, José Hilario told me a good deal about the Navajo wars—"Where we slept, a man was killed by them." In the cells [rooms] of the Potrero Quemado, there were cedars shooting up, 6 to 8 inches in diameter. Reached Cochiti 4 p.m. Juan José had fixed a plank in my room. Very kind, all. Made diagram of Santo Domingo houses, in part. Tomorrow, will go with José Hilario to see ruins across the river.

OCTOBER 20: Started for the left bank of the Rio Grande with José Hilario after 10 A.M. and reached ruins at 12 noon. They are near the river nearly at the entrance of the Cañón del Norte, or Cajanito, and directly opposite the last roadbed made to date of the railroad along the Rio Grande. Going there, we first traversed the northern group of splendid cottonwoods opposite Cochiti, with a thick undergrowth of jarras,[102] then fields, and

---

102. In Latin American Spanish a number of plants are known as Jarros, Jarritos, or Jarillas. The exact type of vegetation cannot be identified from the context of the journals.

then entered the lomas, which run almost along the river. Current very swift. The lomas are a volcanic tuff, grayish brown, and form a huge natural staircase. The bluff of the pueblo is formed as the head of a semi-circle. This semi-circle is sand and gravel.

On (a) much pottery is found, and there may be buildings, although I did not find any. The pueblo must have been large. It is called Encierro by the Mexicans; I therefore call it Pueblo del Encierro [L.A. 70].* The rooms, where foundations exist, were small. The foundations show walls of 0.30 meters to 0.40 meters with upright stones on both sides.* The upright stones are broken plates, mostly of black lava. Obsidian, moss agates, red agates, flint, and much finely glazed pottery. Of the corrugated and indented pottery there was—perhaps—one fragment. A number of metates and handles (manos) were found. José Hilario will get them tomorrow with a burro. They use three manos successively. (At the house of Juan José there are only two.) One of black lava is to break the corn; one of gneiss, equally large, to crush it; and the other, smaller and triangular in cross-section,* to pulverize it. The last is polished. They "pick" the surface of the mano to make it smooth. This is done with flint.[103]

The round structure is called an estufa by José Hilario, but I doubt it, although he says that the estufas are sometimes outside of the pueblo. I rather think it to be a round tower of observation, as at Pecos. The pottery resembles that of Pecos very much, in kind and quantity. There is some charred pottery, like that of the tinajas used for chimneys. The same pottery was also found on the Potrero Quemado! There is no trace of the fields, but two acequias are there, lined with embankments

---

103. Bandelier most probably slipped in his notes; "picking" the mano was done to make the surface rough, not smooth. Flint hammerstones were commonly used for this purpose, and their profusion on virtually all Puebloan archaeological sites testifies to the constant "sharpening" of these manos. Even today as the women grind in preparation for feast day or other baking, the ringing sound of mano picking is common in a pueblo.

of high gravel, thus showing that the gravel was already there
when the acequia was built. The arroyos have eaten into the
acequia, but the re-entering angles of the latter show, that they

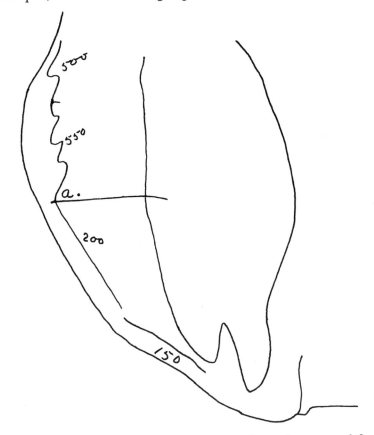

were made in order to suit the arroyos, and not the curve of the
river. It is evident that the main acequia was opened immediately below the mouth of the Cañón del Norte, from which
the river issues with great swiftness. There are some rapids, but
rather minor. No water on the bluff, nor are there any walls of
circumvallation. Ruins opposite Cochiti. They are almost
directly opposite the more northerly cluster of cottonwoods,
and on the loma, about one-half mile from the river. Pottery,

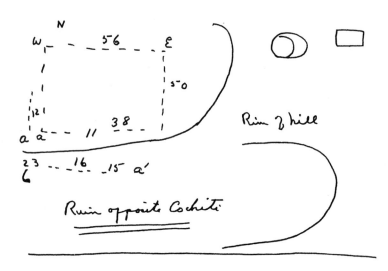

Rim of hill

Ruin opposite Cochiti

obsidian, metates, etc., for the most part similar to those found
in the ruins higher up. Ruin smaller. Found also a fragment of
lava hammer. José Hilario and Juan José told me that higher
up, in the Caja del Rio, there is, on the same side of the river, a
still larger ruin. Conversation with José Hilario. He knows
nothing concerning these ruins, but says that they are without
connection with Cochiti. (Agustín and Juan José say the
same.) They are evidently older than Cochiti, but not as old
as those of the Potrero Quemado, whereas they greatly resemble
those of the Cañada, also, in the round towers.

José Hilario told me that, about forty years ago, the Pueblos
of the Rio Grande made an expedition against the Comanche,
and, near the Ojo de Vermeja, inflicted such a terrible defeat,
that since that time the Comanche have made peace with them,
whereas they annually come up to fight the Navajo. (So do the
Shawnee.)[104] Juan José says it is less than forty years ago. José
Hilario also says the Navajo are afraid of the Cochiti, and sel-

---

104. Bandelier here probably means the Caddoan-speaking Pawnee, an Eastern Plains group.

dom come down to the pueblo. Juan José expects them next month. José Hilario says they call Cochiti, *To'ka*. He says that they are treacherous and cowardly. One night one hundred and fifty of them came down in order to attack the pueblo, but returned to the Cañada, where they destroyed everything, even cutting trees. The next morning the Pueblos followed them, but without avail. He confirms that the people of Cochiti are of slighter build and smaller than those of Santo Domingo, and that at the time he was born the people were larger.

Last night Agustín told me that the people of Cochiti formerly adored piedras, and that there are, opposite the Cañada pueblo on the loma, two stone figures which they worshipped. He finally acknowledged that they worshipped the sun also.

Juan José is preparing to go to Bernalillo tomorrow with his oldest boy, Adelaido, who is going to the Navajo country to herd for Mariano Otero until next February. We called on the cacique, but he was not at home. Finished ground plans. I lent my revolver to Juan José for tomorrow. Excellent tortillas tonight. Always coffee. The little girl is a sprightly little imp, always merry, and very active. This morning a Mexican boy named Pacífico, from the pueblo, visited her. He read aloud in the Bible. Last night the boys were very loud in the pueblo. The little girl, Ignacia, keeps my room very well. Juan José told bear stories tonight. Also about the eagles fishing. He insists that the puma is very dangerous and strong, but never attacks. Tomorrow I shall go to Peña Blanca for the mail. The day has been very valuable to me in many respects, but I am tired and feel abandoned for want of letters. All the people are very friendly.

OCTOBER 21: Rose about 7 A.M., after Agustín had already called at my door. Juan José and Adelaido gone early. Pedro is making a moccasin. Juan de Jesús Pancho, brother-in-law of Juan José, took me over to his house, opposite (south of) that of Juan José. He inhabits the upper story, where he has two rooms. Below is the store room. In one room he sleeps. *a.* is an ordinary fireplace and chimney; *b.* a large cooking-chimney; *c.*,

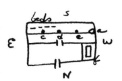
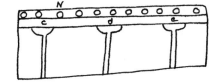

d., and *e.*, three posts, whitewashed, supporting a beam which extends lengthwise across the room-ceiling. I left for Peña Blanca at 10 A.M., arrived at 11 A.M. (Agustín called on me again. Shall see him this afternoon.) No letters. It is getting very disagreeable.

At Peña Blanca, pleasant stay at the Padre's. He tells me that there is a superstition among the Indians, that if anyone wants to injure any other one, he makes a mono, that is, an image of earth or clay, of the one whom he wishes to hurt (selecting, if possible, earth on which he has urinated), and pierces this image with thorns of the tuna at the places where he wants to hurt him. In one instance, he heard of a Navajo boy who did this trick to his master, piercing the image through the temple. The Navajo had been taken prisoner and had quarrelled with his master, and did it out of revenge. Another boy, who was with him, saw it, and accused him of it.[105]

Reached home at 3 P.M. Everybody out, but Ignacia came back and wanted to cook dinner, which I did not accept. Padre Ribera told me again that the ruins on the Potrero Quemado were those of the old pueblo of Santo Domingo. Today, the report of the Archaeological Institute of America from Mr. Greenleaf reached Padre Ribera. Pleased him much.

José Hilario came with the metates and the manos. Then Pacífico Baca came in; he told me that the Indians still had small idols of white stone, also of brown stones. He saw one with turquoises pending from the ears, and a small coral at the end of the pendant. There are male figures, *tzi-come*, and female figures, *ji-yanna*; also dogs, or similar forms. They are small. He pretends that they [the Cochiti] do not adore God, but that when asked about these idols, they reply that they pray to them for all things. In the estufas they prepare for dances, but do not have their meetings—which are held at the house of the caci-

---

105. Such practices of witchcraft were well known in Bandelier's time, and they have continued to the present day. Failure to mention them often signifies a reluctance to discuss the fearful topic rather than an absence or lack of knowledge concerning these beliefs and practices.

que. In the estufas they also hang up the scalps, for they cut off the scalp with the ears, and suspend it on the rim of a shield, which rests in the estufa, on a pole painted red. When they dance (he calls it kachina), they mask and dance with a woman (ten pairs), and then wear the scalps. He offers to guide me to the Rio Chaco.

There is an evident feeling of mistrust and jealousy existing between the Indians and the Mexicans. Thus Pacífico is not looked upon with kindness. He, however, speaks with praise of the women of the Pueblos and says they are chaste and virtuous—more so than the Mexican women. He also assures me that the holy fire is not kept up any more, neither here nor at Santo Domingo. Of Pecos, he says that they were sorcerers and kept a large serpent, to which they gave children to eat, for which reason they finally were extinct. The serpent ate them up.

The brother-in-law of Juan José, Luis Montoya, also gave me much information. He said that the yeso, used as window glass, is found near San Felipe, and the jaspe, which they use for white-washing, in the arroyos.[106] They burn the latter in their ovens, then grind it on the metate; afterwards they mix it with water and beat it. He confirms the reports of Pacífico about the estufa and the scalps being deposited there. He says that there are four stallions in the herd of the Pueblo, which belong, not to a single individual, but to the Pueblo. Every week in turn, the capitán de la guerra delegates four men to attend to the herd, for it is the capitán who has charge of public works.

Juan José returned from Bernalillo late at night, very well pleased with my horse. He answered evasively in regard to the scalps, and said that, while such a custom evidently existed, it had not been practiced for sometime, as there was no war. He then spoke about the wars with the Comanche. More than one hundred year ago, he says, the Comanche came down the river from the north and, overnight, stopped up the acequia with

---

106. Presumably yeso and jaspe here literally mean window glass and white-wash.

grass. The next morning, the man whose field was watered by this channel, went to open it and was shot with arrows and killed. The Comanche then crossed the river to the west and were pursued to the Cañón de Colle where they were overtaken on the potrero and most of them killed. A few escaped by sliding down a pino real, but many were thrown on the rocks. This appears to have been the last attack from the Comanche on this side of the river, but wars with them continued until the Pueblo Indians, together with the Mexicans, made that attack upon them of which José Hilario spoke, and which resulted in a treaty of peace, very faithfully kept. No wampum, has no idea of what it is.

But the Kaihuas [Kiowa] are treacherous, and he told me how, about sixteen or eighteen years ago, they attacked a party of forty from San Juan Pueblo (Teguas) but were repulsed after a fight which lasted from midnight till after 3 P.M. The Pueblos had one man killed and one wounded, and their entire stock was run off, so that they had to return on foot. The captain of the Kaihuas was killed, and they fled, leaving many dead behind them. The Comanche witnessed the engagement from the neighboring hills, but remained neutral. On another occasion, when his father was leading a trading-party to the Comanche, he was stopped by the Kaihuas on the way, with the request to trade with them. Although he had been cited by the Comanche for a certain day and to a certain date, he still complied with the request. After trading, the Kaihuas surrounded the camp at night, and under pretext that the Queres had introduced Texans who had killed Kaihuas, demanded return of the goods in expiation of the murder. This the Queres refused, and while they were disputing about it, even ready to come to blows, the Comanche dashed into the camp. The chief, ascertaining the cause of the trouble, had the Kaihuas whipped out, and thus delivered the Pueblos.

His statements in regard to the manner and mode of trading are interesting. The Comanche fix a certain day and place, at which the Pueblos appear, and the trading is preceded by a council and presents. The rules of trading are fixed then.

There are Navajo in the pueblo. I offered to trade beads, etc., for tilmas, but they sent me word through José Hilario that they did not care for any beads. Many callers at my room tonight. Segars [cigars]gave out at last.

OCTOBER 22: No more segars. Juan José went to Peña Blanca this morning with my horse. About 10 A.M., went with Agustín to the estufas. They are perfectly plain inside and just like those of Santo Domingo.* On the south side there is the hearth, immediately below the roof opening. Made of adobe. Two large posts support the roof, and hold simple boards for candles. Walls perfectly plain, except wooden nails to hang scalps on, and for the support of the long poles, on which the scalps are worn. When a war party returns, they appear in front of Juan José's house. The man who does the first killing, not the one who kills the most, leads the file; the war captain goes by his side. Then they deposit the scalps at the cemetery entrance and enter the church to pay their devotion to San Buenaventura. Afterwards, they go around the pueblo singing, and finally into the estufa, where they report to all the people about the campaign. Finally, the war dance and war song are performed, and the crowd disperses. The scalps are preserved by the cacique at his own house, hung to a round shield.

While [we were discussing the above], the principales had been sitting all night at the house of the capitán de la guerra about the case of a man and woman who have been living separately, and whom they want to live together again. Divorce unknown.

Juan José told me that the fever, in the early years of his mother's life, fearfully decimated the Cochiteños, twice, and it is true, indeed, that there are, at present, no old men at the pueblo; there is hardly anyone older than fifty years. This may also account for the small stature of the men. I am not well, always sleepy, sore head, and chilly. Perhaps fever? The daughter, today, has been busy washing her father's head, and now is picking the lice from it. Luis Montoya, brother-in-law of Juan José, sits beside me and sings while I am writing to Mr. Morgan. The dogs, as well as the coyotes, steal and eat maize. Dogs steal maize out of the fields at night. Coyotes also steal and eat watermelons.

At night, much trouble making fire. Agustín came. He had inquired about the pueblos on the left bank of the river, and an old principal told him that they were of the *Tanos*. This would be important. (Tonight I wrote cards to Mr. Hebler, Ellison, Will Roulet [?], and Geo. Hoffmann.) Agustín brought the news, that tonight there is to be a council meeting about a great military festival next week. My secretaryship will be needed. He will advise us of it tomorrow early. This changes my plans, and I shall be back early. Wrote to Joe.

OCTOBER 23: Nothing definite as to the feast yet. Wrote to Bennett, and sent off two letters and seven post cards with Agustín, who goes to Peña Blanca this morning. Left about 7 A.M. Road toward the Cañada, then to the left, crossing the Cañada about four miles below. Conversation important. The path crosses the canyon, leaving to the left successively: Potrero de los Idolos, Potrero Largo, Potrero del Ojito, Potrero Chiato. In some places the descents are terrible and cannot be made on horseback. The lava is reached north of the Potrero Chiato, and thence on to the banks of the Cañón del Norte which is reached by a horrible descent. [The descent here is through] ugly, black, cutting, ringing lava blocks. Reached the Rio Grande in the canyon about 12 noon. Towering cliffs on all sides. River rushing down rapidly. In the north the Potrero del Alamo.* Current of river very swift and very distinctly audible. Water turbid but not bad. We unsaddled and made coffee. The capitán de la guerra joined our dinner, which consisted of coffee, tortillas, and fine cheese. We entered the Cañón del Chapero. Exceedingly grand. Then ascended, leading our horses, rounding the Chapero. The Potrero del Alamo presented a grand sight. The crest, which we followed from south to north, is overgrown with fine sabinos, cedars, and lower down with splendid pina-betes. Turkey tracks, but hardly a living animal.[107]

About 4 P.M. the border of the almost precipitous descent into the Cañón de los Frijoles was reached, and it took one-half hour to descend—on foot, of course. The grandest thing I ever saw. A magnificent growth of pines, encina, alamos, and tower-ing cliffs, of pumice or volcanic tuff, exceedingly friable. The cliffs are vertical on the north side, and their bases are, for a length as yet unknown to me, used as dwellings both from the inside, and by inserting the roof poles for stories outside. It is of the highest interest. There are some of one, two, and three sto-ries. In most cases the plaster is still in the rooms. Some are walled in; others are mere holes in the rocks. Much pottery of the older, painted sort, but as yet no corrugated ones. I found entire chimneys, metates, manos, and a stone-axe.

Aside from the caves, there are ruins of a large pueblo, im-mense estufas, round towers of two stories, etc. But there is not as yet, any sign of horticulture, no acequias, etc. The valley is almost fully closed on the east, where it enters the Rio Grande which flows through a fearful dark canyon. The Rito is a splen-did clear brook. Vegetation around it splendid, showing very good soil.

The stories told me by Juan José run as follows: More than one hundred years ago, the pueblo of Cochiti was very large, and the Navajo, although at war with them, came in at night fre-quently, mingling with the young men, without being recog-nized. In this manner they succeeded once in seizing and capturing a girl, who had gone outdoors at night. The girl was taken to the Navajo village and there well treated, and remained for six or seven months in the cabin of another man. When she

---

107. Here, and often elsewhere in the journals, it is difficult to follow precisely the route of Bandelier. Without the aid of present-day United States Geological Survey or other topographic maps or air photos of this rough and broken terrain, it is not surprising that mesas, potreros, and their spurs or that major canyons and their principal branches become confused or defy accurate description. Further complications arise from the use of Indian or Spanish designations which have not been perpetuated on the USGS or other modern maps.

had gained the full confidence of the Navajo, she once went out with a Navajo girl to gather piñones. While in the woods, the other girl laid her head on her lap, to have her hair searched for lice. In this attitude she fell asleep and the Cochiti girl killed her and took her scalp, left the horses, etc. with the body, and fled home, the scalp speaking to her and advising her finally, when the pursuing Navajo came up, to creep into a rabbit hole, which she succeeded in doing. A pretty tale. The scalp spoke to her from time to time, advising her of the movements of the Navajo who, upon noticing the disappearance of the fugitive, went after her, found the bleeding body, and then tracked her to nearly the entrance of the Pueblo of Cochiti. (About twenty years ago, a Cochiti man going for wood in the lomas near the pueblo, met two Navajo asleep, and killed them both with the butt end of his axe.)

OCTOBER 24: I went 400 meters east of the arroyo, then up the steep slope to the north, but found no cave dwellings. They begin about 300 meters north of it. A solitary cave 4.30 [meters] in diameter, open to the southwest.

Juan José is also of the opinion that the round towers were made by the Spaniards. From the place C. to opposite the northwest corner of the Great Ruin, there are three clusters of rooms or caves, each high above on a talus or steep declivity. They are mostly two stories high. The floor in each case is about 0.30 [meter?] thick. The upper crust is black, and Juan José tells me that this upper crust, which appears like asphalt, is made by rubbing fresh blood over it, which makes it even and hard. Still done and used as such among the Pueblos. The women do it, as often as they have fresh blood of cattle. The great similarity in custom in every detail with the Pueblos is acknowledged by Juan José. Thus in the yellow plastering which appears like unto panelling, the same is recognized here in the caves. The pottery is all painted, and the same kind of pottery prevails in the pueblo and the caves. After dinner, went up to examine rooms.*

. . . This room is north of our quarters, . . . and is evidently untouched. The south side is all walled in. The wooden lintel is composed of three round sticks; the upper, for ventilation, of two strips. Chimney.* Other chimney much ruined in the southeast corner of this room exactly similar.*

I omitted to state that, yesterday, tracks of deer, mountain sheep, and turkeys were seen in the valley. Juan José told me that all this game was formerly very common. On the Chapero the Indians surrounded their game, driving it to the summit, and then killed what did not escape. (*Chacu* of Peru.)[108] At noon, a drove of wild turkeys were followed by Juan José but I scared them unknowingly, and so they ascended the southern slope instead of treeing. In the afternoon, he followed them again.

Juan José knew all about the destruction of the idols, but says that at that time (1819) there were two parties in the pueblo. One of these, infected by the uprising of the Mexicans against Spain, sought the rights of citizenship and sold many of their lands to Mexicans; [thus he explains] Mexican population of Cochiti. Three years previous, the first fever epidemic had occurred, and there was great strife in the pueblo. Both parties sent delegates to Guadalajara, where the matter was settled.

In the year after 1819, the second fever broke out. These two epidemics destroyed the Pueblo. From 1873 on, horses were kept; before that time there had been but one horse in the whole pueblo. [The tribe was] very poor. About sunset, Juan José returned with a young turkey. He shot him near the entrance of the canyon below. He told me that, still higher up, there were two pueblos of cave-dwellers, but small ones. I shall spare this for Mr. Bennett's return. He also says that twenty-eight or thirty years ago he was told that in a cave higher up, there were figures representing kachinas, or a dance, painted on the walls.

This morning at sunrise Juan José called my attention to the loud song of a little bird (called *shiuote*) which he says, is "*la buena señal de los cazadores*" [the good sign for the hunters]. Indeed, he killed and brought home his turkey.

---

108. Bandelier is probably referring here to the communal hunting drives of various Indian tribes of the Gran Chaco of South America.

The war dance is very costly. There are but few men in the pueblo who dance it. He calls them matalotes, but it should be matadores [sic]. It costs at least $20.00 for each one. The capitán de la guerra decides when the dance shall take place, but if, for some cause whatever, one of the heroes cannot accumulate enough for the costs of the dance during spring and summer, it is deferred until another year. Eight days previous, both the matalote (there are fourteen in the pueblo) and the malinche (the woman who is to dance with him, and who is selected by the capitán) become abstemious. For the first four days, the man keeps only apart from his wife, but on the fifth day he only eats a little in the morning and nothing until noon of the next day, then nothing till evening of the seventh day, then nothing until close of the dance, [which] lasts two days. The close of the dance is made by a virgin malinche, and when she stops, the bell is tolled from the church, and while the matalote and his malinche go home to eat, the remainder go to prayer on their knees.

Juan José has gathered ocote and made a terrible fire. The dog is uneasy outside. Stomach of turkey is a peculiar dish, particularly if not well cleaned. This canyon shows no traces of agriculture, although very fertile with many weeds. Night splendid, after a very hot and hard day. It is Sunday but how different.

OCTOBER 25: Juan José went for the horses. I leave the metate and everything else here, like pottery, manos, etc. The hunter's bird again sings lively. Cooking coffee. There are, higher up, two other pueblos in the rock. Some twenty or thirty years ago, the walls of the buildings outside of the rocks were still standing. Left 8 A.M. Reached Cañón de los Frijoles 10:30 A.M. On hill, foot of Potrero del Alamo, ruin. Pumice stone.*

Reached the Rio Grande 11:30 A.M. Started 11:45 A.M. up the Mesa Prieta. Reached the top of the mesa 12:15, and the top of the Potrero de las Vacas at 12:30. All pumice stone. The potrero extends between the Cañón del Alamo to the northeast and the Cañada Honda to the southwest, in a direction from southeast to northwest generally. It is covered with the same vegetation as the other potreros, and many tracks of deer, fowl, finally distinct and fresh bear-tracks, also the place where they had newly plundered pine trees.

Reached the ruins on the Potrero de las Vacas at 2 P.M. The view from the potrero into the Cañón del Alamo, and later on into the Cañón del Rito is very grand. From the ruins, which lie very high, an immense view is commanded. The potrero is very narrow; its highest side is along the edge of the precipice towards the Cañón del Alamo. The ruins are on the highest point; no brush, not even sabinos. The material of the pueblo is again pumice-stone or tuff. In southern wing, the walls are continuous from east to west, those from north to south are inserted. In the eastern wing there is the reverse. Those of the north wing generally longitudinal, but sometimes cross-wise. Some of the estufas evidently cut in the rock to the depth of 1 meter.

Yielding to the advice of Juan José, abandoned measuring for this time. Riding to the west we met three other Indians from Cochiti, and finally Adelaido himself came up from the Cañada Honda. They all had been gathering long zacate for brooms (a-yash-iañe). On the west side, the potrero extends as a narrow rocky plateau, which, at the distance of about one-half mile, drops abruptly into the Barranca de la Cuesta Colorada. The plateau is covered with a thicket of encina, sabinos, etc. It even spreads out like a "T."*

Nearly at the end of the plateau, around a young pine, there is a strong stone circle, with an entrance to the southeast. This circle is made of upright stones in part. Some of them are like staked palisades. In the center of the circle there are two figures of crouching pumas (mountain lions) carved out of the rock (says Juan José) natural size, but unfortunately the heads badly mutilated (by Mexicans). The heads are turned to the east. There is no doubt (and this is also the opinion of Juan José) that they are idols. We descended into the barranca and to the Rio de la Cuesta Colorada, a limpid, murmuring stream. Our resting place is on the left bank in the narrow cañada, under magnificent pinabetes behind a huge rock, and before a big fire

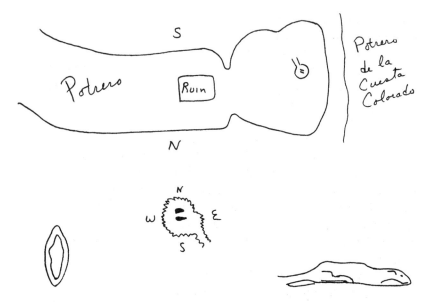

of ocote. To the left is the high Potrero de las Vacas; to the right, the Potrero de las Casas with ruins on the top. The horses are across the river, in a ruin of a rectangular pueblo (—with square [plaza]—which I also forbear to measure to-day).[109] Behind us (north), the Potrero de la Cuesta Colorada (so named for its light and dark red porphyries and volcanic rock), and southeast the cañada opens to a narrow gap.

At this time many people of Cochiti circulate among these mountains (which belong to the Sierra de San Miguel), cutting zacate for brooms, and gathering piñones. Many women and children are over in the woods, even unarmed, though it is very unsafe. In this they are competitors to the bears. The latter are frequent. They go about all night, but the horses are safe, more so than man. Game of all kinds is abundant. It is curious how the former inhabitants of these parts always selected rock when

---

109. At this point, Bandelier was in present-day Capulin Canyon, a quarter of a mile below (east of) the National Park Service Fire Cabin. In the archaeo-logical survey conducted by Lange during the summer of 1959, this relatively large ruin, now almost obliterated by underbrush, was designated L. A. 3840.

pumice or tuff was *in situ*. In the Cañada Honda, opposite the great pueblo of the Potrero de las Vacas, there are some cave and cliff dwellings. (The whole story about the military fortress turns out to be a hoax of Agustín.)

There is a very large estanque [reservoir] southeast of the pueblo on the Potrero de las Vacas, and out of it, in its very center, a very large piñon shoots up.[110] Juan José says they grow very slowly. It is best to examine this place thoroughly, for Juan José says there are many ruins also on the Potrero del Alamo. All these arroyos, from the Rito de los Frijoles to the Cañada de Cochiti, issue from the Sierra del Valle. It is a very laborious work, to gather zacate on these rocks, and very often it is fruitless. We had a very good supper—wild turkey, its meat is white and tender. Everywhere, at present, the piñones are plundered of their nuts. He says that this is the name of the Potrero de las Vacas, and that this ruin, from popular saying of the Mexicans, was the first pueblo of Cochiti.[111] The night splendid but, feeling cold, I moved to the fire and succeeded in burning a big hole through the middle of my serape. Quiet, the dog as usual, nestling close to me. He is very quiet. The trees are splendid overhead, straight as an arrow.

The sierra is full of people from the pueblo gathering zacate

---

110. This large piñon continues to flourish at the present time, apparently benefiting from the additional moisture available to its root system. Outlines of the large estanque remain visible and might be interpreted as the remains of a subterranean kiva were it not for the strategic location downgrade from the large plaza area and surrounding area from which an appreciable amount of run-off could be collected for the people of *Yapashi* (L. A. 250).

111. The data here obviously contradict the account recorded by Bandelier in an earlier entry (October 15). Obtained at a later date and after additional exploration and increased familiarity with the region, the discussion in the entry of October 25 must be given preference. The precise relationship of these sites, however, to present-day Cochiti, to other Keresan tribes, or to other Pueblo tribes, remains to be worked out through careful excavation. Pertinent to the problem of regional culture history are the large sites of the Bandelier Monument area as well as Kuapa and Pueblo Cañada to the south on the Rancho de la Cañada. Throughout the same area are innumerable small sites which must also be reckoned with in the reconstruction of the culture history of the Middle Rio Grande.

and piñones. The zacate is cut with iron sickles and gathered in bunches to be sold farther south (Santo Domingo, etc.) where it does not grow. Three bundles are worth a string of green chile two meters long. One string (ristra) of green equals one-half string of red chile.

There is no doubt but that the Potrero de las Vacas was an excellent spot for occupation. The view is splendid beyond all description. It is also insisted upon that there are estufas outside of the courts of the pueblos. This is possible, still I doubt it. It appears possible, however, from what I saw at the Rito de los Frijoles.[112] On the Potrero del Alamo there are other ruins of pueblos, but no inhabited caves.

OCTOBER 26: The horses again have gone far. Splendid growth of timber down to the valley. The Potrero de las Casas stops abruptly to the right; to the left, perpendicular cliffs of volcanic tuff, in them the signs of a two-story house, poles in the rock. Then the Cueva Pintada [Painted Cave]. It is a grand portal, of volcanic tuff; below are the signs of cave-houses. Width across entrance 17 meters from southwest [southeast] to northeast [northwest]. Depth southeast [southwest] to northwest [northeast], 14 meters. At a height of 10 meters are the paintings, red, in a semi-circle. Hands and many with the cross.* Juan José tells me that these were made by shepherds, who dwelt frequently in this cave. In it there are also remains of cave dwellings and holes for beams. The cave dwellings extend from the cave, west for about 100 meters, thus showing that there was a settlement about the cave.

On the Potrero de los Idolos, on the eastern slope of the top, a stone-circle, much destroyed, with two pumas facing south-southwest and two stone columns on the western end, facing east.* Beneath it the soil is broken up, [making] a small cavity

---

112. Bandelier's shift from outright doubt to some degree of credulity was justified. Apparently, the desire for seclusion outweighed fears of attack from enemies as innumerable pueblo sites, large, medium, and small, have kivas outside the enclosure or house block. In some instances, there is more than one such kiva, and some of these are at a considerable distance from the pueblo.

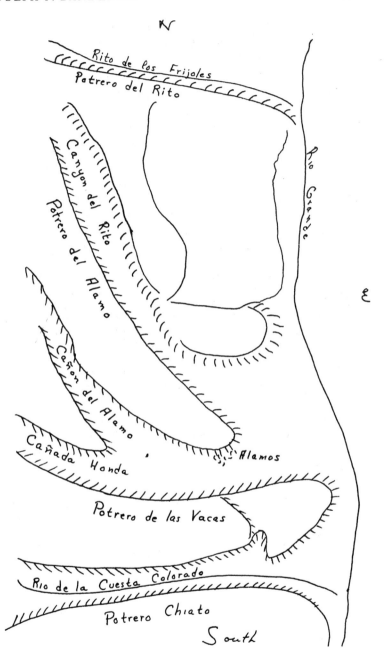

into which I entered but found nothing but the solid rock broken up by senseless treasure seekers. One column, 1.32 meters high, 1.48 circumference. The other, which is fallen and the head broken off is 1.82 meters high and a little less wide. Both are worked, but no figures can be detected. The south rim of circle is 38 meters from east point of the potrero, and about halfway between its north and south rims.[113]

The ascent of the potrero is very difficult, and demands tall climbing. The rock on top is hard grey volcanic, looks like very hard limestone or sandstone, and the image is carved out of it. So also are the standing pillars. There is no sign of an entrance as on the Potrero de las Vacas. The top of the potrero is rather barren on account of the rocky surface. Only sabinos, stunted in growth. It may have been in connection with the old pueblo

---

113. This description by Bandelier remains accurate to this day. It is interesting that this prominent elevation, actually a fine example of a mesa, according to Bandelier, called *Shkor-e Ka-uash*, or round mesa (Bandelier 1890-92: II, 158), continues to be referred to as a potrero. Of greater significance, however, is the fact that this particular shrine, the stone lion and the surrounding circle of large stones, became "lost" to the Cochiti until one of the tribe accompanied Lange to the remains in the summer of 1952.

The visit followed several seasons of futile questioning of tribal elders (accompanied by their own fruitless questioning of other tribal and Spanish elders). Finally, following the description in Bandelier (1890-92: II, 158 fn.), the Potrero de los Idolos was identified tentatively (the designation no longer being familiar to anyone consulted). Once on top of the elevation, the shrine was readily located—a convincing demonstration to the Cochiti of the value of written records.

The potrero is limited in area and vegetation, and game is scarce. Consequently hunters and others abandoned the top, with the result that it passed from tribal awareness. It was, of course, known to others, such as the owner of the Rancho de la Cañada, Mr. James Webb Young. But when one does not suspect, one does not ask—particularly outsiders and especially in regard to esoteric or ritual matters.

As a final comment, it is noteworthy that evidence for a second stone lion is largely a matter of inference. In a number of respects, this shrine duplicates that on the Potrero de las Vacas, a few miles to the north. While there is no good reason to challenge the claim of two lions, as it was recorded by Bandelier and others and as it persists to the present-day, it is somewhat strange that no worked fragment of the allegedly destroyed lion is actually described by Bandelier or any other writer. No such recognizable trace or fragment was found by Lange in two visits to the shrine (1952 and 1957).

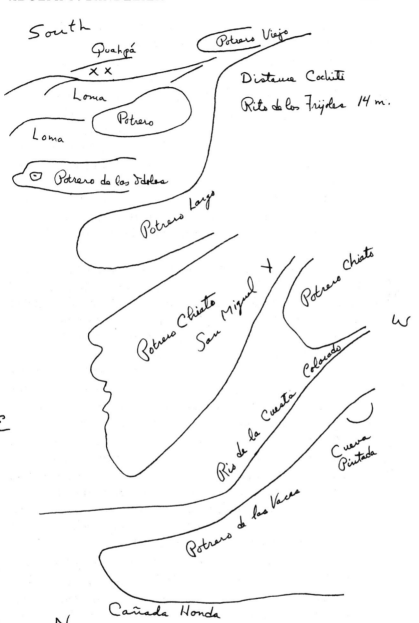

South

Quahpá
X X

Loma

Potrero

Loma

Potrero de los Idolos

Distance Cochiti
Rito de los Frijoles 14 m.

Potrero Viejo

Potrero Largo

Potrero Chisto
San Miguel

Potrero Chisto

Rio de la Cuesta Colorado

Cueva
Pintada

Potrero de las Vacas

Cañada Honda

N

of *Quah'pa*, but as [the pueblo] lies about one mile, at least, to the southwest of the idols, it is not certain.*

The puma was painted with streaks of red at the toes and in the face (head). This is done yet by the hunters, to propitiate the idol, to favor them while hunting. The same was seen at the Potrero de las Vacas. Juan José says that as the puma is the best hunter of the animal kingdom in the sierra, they still make these offerings to it, anointing the eyes to secure good eyesight, and the claws and feet for strength and agility. Juan José anointed his own eyes with almagre in my presence, stating that it improved his vision for shooting. The almagre is oxide of iron, and still contains, though pulverized, speculas of crystals of hematite. It is carried in a little leather bag, tied up with a leather string.

Reached home at 1:00 P.M. Started on foot for Peña Blanca at 3:00 P.M. Padre Ribera playing cards. Letter from Joe and Papa. Gatschet speech from Washington, and Landa's alphabet from Valentini. When I started home a furious storm broke out. The darkness was almost complete, the sand and dust terrible. Some thunder and very little rain. The wind blew down the big new door of the Padre's corral and we could not replace it. A perfect shower of gravel and sand blew into our faces, the sand clouds occasionally showing a yellowish gleam. Finally we closed the corral by bracing a wagon against the entrance, and the door against it on the other side. For two hours the storm raged terribly, but the adobe house did not quiver. At last a short gentle rain fell, and it grew calm. At 7 P.M. everything was quiet and the sky starry and serene. No damage, even to trees. Wind came from northwest, and it was very cold. Padre says that although the winds are very fierce in the spring, such a storm is of very rare occurrence. It was simply awful.

OCTOBER 27: Splendid morning. No trace recalling the storm. Padre told me about temperature. In July, 1877, it rose to 88°F. and on the 13th to 90°. The extremes of seven years are 95° and 0°, but both are very rare. Snow never lasts long. Some little

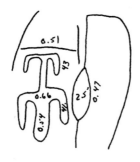

snow fell, last night, on the Sierra de la Jarra and on the Sierra de Toledo, but only a few streaks.

Returned to Cochiti about 9 A.M. Juan José making saddle braces for burro saddles out of cottonwood. The Misa de los Muertos [Mass for the Dead] is to be next Friday at Cochiti, as the Padre is going to the other places first. (Bought two serapes from the Padre.) Went to inform the gobernador. Afterwards called on the cacique. Very friendly. It appears Agustín is a liar. The cacique affirms that absolutely nothing is known about the people once inhabiting the ruins, the Tano story is a lie. The Tano were southeast toward Galisteo, and then moved to the Moqui, passing through Cubero and Santo Domingo. The Potrero Viejo is the only pueblo about which anything positive can be said, and he is not certain if they were brought down from it (bajados) two or three times. About Quah'pa, "es posible, pero no está seguro" [It is possible, but not certain]. The caza de liebres [rabbit hunt] may take place next week. This time it will be for the muchachas, who have to pick up the game.

[In the cacique's room] there are six metates. The room is clean; there are many pictures of saints, glaringly colored, hung on the southwest wall. [The governor's room is] tolerably clean also. We went to see the woman who makes loza. She was in the piñones. Many people are gone, so is José Hilario with his whole family. This evening Pedro brought news that six Americans had reached Cochiti. Visit from Juan de Jesús and Pacífico Baca. Nothing very important. José Hilario also came in, carrying his baby on his back in the serape. Agustín sat by the fire for a while. [I] was rather cool to him. Today I made a groundplan of part of the Rito de los Frijoles, and of the houses in Santo Domingo. Tomorrow Juan José goes to Santa Fe. All evening late, a woman is rattling away in Spanish next door.

This evening Ignacia cooked pozole of maize, which is very fair also, though not as good as the wheat pozole. Juan José promises me that he will show me and let me taste all the original dishes of the Pueblos, before they changed their mode of

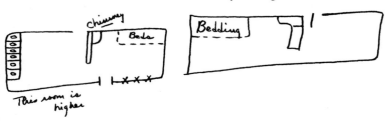

life. This indicates that, previous to the advent of the Spaniards, they lived differently from now, that is, ate other food.

There was a meeting of the council last night, at which the caza de liebres was postponed till Saturday of next week. This will give Bennett time to come over. Juan José was at the council late, and returned about 10:00 P.M. There was some talk about the función del caballo [use of the horse] but nothing was decided about it. All a lie of Agustín.

OCTOBER 28: Swept my room with one of these little brooms of theirs. Very unhandy. My horse is gone, with one of Juan José's. The boys went after them. Packed up bugs for Maly. José Hilario came. God has but the Spanish name Dios.

About 9 A.M.. Stevenson, etc. arrived in two buggies. Went to the houses of the cacique and governor. Then called on me with his wife. Very pleasant visit. Hellers and Moranay are with him. They took photographs of the pueblo. Bought many things. Old stone axes fastened with the handles, stones to cook the upper parts of tortillas with, arrowheads. Also a musical instrument which is used by a Mexican veteran. The stem is put in the mouth, the cord wound to desired stiffness (tuned) at ab., and then it is played with the fingers. A long jew's harp.* It gives but one sound, which can be varied by loosening and tightening the cord. Have learned a good deal. Some of the stone implements were originally found here, thus showing that the first inhabitants of this pueblo used stone axes. This explains the occurrence of glazed pottery about the pueblo. They took a photograph of the governor also.

Luis Montoya tells me that the round cave in the Rito de los Frijoles was the casa del común [community house] where they met as now in the house of the cacique, para platicar [to talk]. The Rito is called Stiu-oñi [Tyuonyi].

Went over to Peña Blanca and took supper with Stevenson. Butter again for the first time in two weeks. Went and returned with José Hilario. At night, call from Luis Montoya. Arranged to go to the Potrero de en Medio early tomorrow. He brought me two stone axes. Letter from Papa and card from Valentini. Wrote to home and to Norton.

OCTOBER 29: It is remarkably quiet, even for this pueblo. I rather squandered the day. Felt not at all like working. Went to Peña Blanca in the forenoon (to get rid of Agustín). Luis Montoya did not come as promised. I presume the Friday [celebration] has something to do with it. He came later and excused himself. Juan de Jesús Pancho showed me his shield, which he uses in the dances, and promised me a similar one. Both boys were here until 10:00 P.M. They explained to me their games—patol,[114] and others. We played little games, the two Juan de Jesús, la chiquita, and I. (Juan de Jesús # 2 appeared to make love to the chiquita.) I asked them about their customs of proposal. It is the father or some other male relative who proposes. They confessed to me about their dances. The women are dressed well, but the men sometimes are naked up to the maxtlatl [kilt] and their weapons and ornaments. This, however, is only in the daytime. At night, they are always in dress, both sexes.

OCTOBER 30: Juan José talked long about the cacique. If the cacique shows unfavorable character, is not peaceable, quiet, or is ambitious, then the capitán de la guerra calls a meeting at the estufa, which meeting is attended by all those who are regarded as capable of understanding the matter and worthy of participation in it, while others are strictly excluded. There, two new caciques are elected in place of the old one. Juan José affirms again that the cacique is an old institution from the pueblo of Teguayú, where the first one was elected. He compares him distinctly to the Pope, saying that, [as] the Pope is the representative of St. Peter upon earth, so is the cacique the substitute for Montezuma. He does not meddle in the affairs of the Pueblo at all.

---

114. Cf. the Mexican Patolli. For discussion of Patolli-type games in aboriginal America see Erasmus (1950).

Started for Santa Fe on horseback at 10 A.M. Ascending the Bajada I was overtaken by a Mexican boy on a pony, who had come from Bernalillo today. Almost frozen. He showed me a nearer road and a better one, down the Bajada and crossing the Santa Fe wagon road near the Pueblo Quemado. I finally reached Santa Fe at 5 P.M., thoroughly shaken and frozen, and was met by a very disagreeable announcement [an overdraft, perhaps]. The bank office finally made it right; Mr. Griffin, the cashier, acting very gentlemanly. Tired, but still nervous, I finally went to bed after midnight, but could not sleep for a long time. No letter from Norton. Don't know what to think of it. Shall probably change my quarters. No accomodations here.

OCTOBER 31: Tired and weary. Bought a cravat. Saw Ellison. He told me that one-fourth of a mile from the Bajada there is a large ruin. He also told me that the Pueblo of Sandia had once deposed their cacique for misbehavior. Called on Bennett. Arrangements for photographic trip must be different. He will probably not be able to leave before week after next. Mr. Brown is unwell too. Afternoon spent with Adamson, and went to Governor Ritch. At night, letters from Norton and Joe. Thanks. Wrote to Prof. Norton, four pages.

NOVEMBER 1: Paid my debts. Went to the Surveyor General's office and saw the Grant of the Cañada de Cochiti, August 2, 1728. Given to Antonio Lucero, "citizen of the town of Albuquerque a piece of unappropriated land [which is situated on the Mesa de Cochiti where the rebel Indians had withdrawn] in order to plant and cultivate on said piece of land 10 anegas [fanegas, 16 acres] of wheat and 2 [fanegas, 3.2 acres] of maize and to assist at the lambing of my sheep [and/or goats] and the foaling of my mares. The said land with its accesses is bounded on the north by the old village of Cochiti, on the east by the Rio del Norte, on the south by lands of natives of said village and on the west by the Jemez Mountains. Executed August 6, 1728."

Called at headquarters, but no time. Went into the archives. Journal of Otermín there in part; other papers. Afternoon, wrote

to Joe, to Conant, and to Putnam. Went to see Brother Baldwin, but he was sick. Evening very lonely. The city is full of
excitement about politics; everybody has his head full of it. Met
Governor Arny and shall call on him next Wednesday. Afterwards went to see Mr. Albert Call. He has fragments of corrugated pottery different from those I saw. They are about as
follows, natural size: It is light gray. He also showed me fine
garnets, chrysoberyls, and corundum from the Navajo. He has
stone hammers from the Cerrillos, which he sells at three for
$1.00. A tile from a church floor dug out below the house built
by Ilfeld and Company. It is very hard and smooth. The native
tradition is that it was made by the Franciscans. Shall trace the
matter further. It is extremely annoying that Mr. Brown is so
sick, and that Bennett has the engagement about his mine. It
is likely that, in consequence of it, all photographic arrangements may yet fall through.

Also met Señor Chavez. He has found and laid aside for me
the Merced of Bernalillo of 1701. Am bad off about this photographic failure. I do not venture to begin to copy from the
archives because I have not time; neither do I venture to leave
yet until this photographic case is settled. Wrote to Dr. Bruhl
about the Documentos and the Archivos de Indias. Really
don't know what to do. All may turn out better yet tomorrow.
While I am sitting here and writing (in the upper parlor), ugly
music is going on in a newly opened saloon across the street. I
find that Stevenson has bought nearly all the stone axes in
town. Easy manner of collecting for the Smithsonian Institute!
Had a pleasant chat with Dr. [Sieber?] at noon. He says that
the Navajo are nearly all syphilitic and that the disease is constitutional with them. Among the Pueblos I know of nothing
similar as yet. He is writing upon the mineral springs of New
Mexico. Very sensible, too.

NOVEMBER 2: Señor Chavez not in, so that I could not copy the
Bernalillo grant. Election, though not so very excited as I sup-
posed it would be. I called on Mr. Ellison and again drew information from him. He tells me that there was at Cia an old

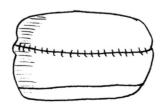

man who knew much about the Pueblos, and who also had documents to show which would be of interest. Spoke about the papers. Among them there is one establishing the foundation of the cathedral in 1721. The tiles found at Ilfeld and Company's place he says were made in Mexico, and the chapel was the castruenza, or military chapel. He also told me the story of a priest of San Juan who, saying Mass one time, noticed under the table an enormous rattlesnake coiled up.

Went to call on Father Eguillon. Reception charming. Invitation to dinner which I refused. He says that the Pueblo Indians are always non-committal, and try to please all parties if possible. Spoke about the winds, and this explains the destruction of the ruins in the Rio Grande valley, and why their walls have been so completely destroyed. He still believes in the snake story. It is singular to see these people driving the voters to the polls in carriages. The polls are outside the city, in the suburbs.

Called on Surveyor White, and he very kindly gave me information in regard to the drawing of maps and charts. Also lent me a book on the subject. Father Eguillon told me a good deal about the relations of the Indians to the Church. He also mentioned a cave on the mesa above the Cañón del Apache, which cave contained paintings, rudely made, of toads, serpents, etc. in clay, which he believes to have been the images of the Apaches. Afternoon, no improvement. Mrs. B[ennett?] is sick, if not worse. Amado Baca goes out next Thursday, and it would be very well if Bennett could join him. Met a San Ildefonso Indian again and asked him about the origin of the ruins on the left bank of the Rio Grande. He affirms that they were built by Pueblos, but that the old men knew nothing of the particular tribe by which they were constructed.

Put an advertisement into the paper about a photographer. Have found a photographer. Formed the acquaintance of Mr. McLean. Archbishop informed me of dried-up sources [of water] in ruined pueblos, also of ruins east of Anton Chico and Las Vegas. He says that in several ruins, where absolutely no water had been noticed, springs were found by digging at consi-

derable depth, and it appeared as if those springs had been artificially closed by the Indians, and even [seemed almost] ce-
mented. This was especially the case near Anton Chico where,
for twenty miles in the Cañón Largo, no water is found on the
surface.

At night there is much excitement about the election. Got a
letter from Professor Norton about Rev. E. M. Porter, and replied to it at once. I cannot use him at all; Protestant ministers
don't work in the pueblos. Met young man Vigil and Amado
Baca. Not all Americans are as bad as the authorities;
found many with very equitable feelings towards the Mexicans,
and who strongly disclaim any connection with the offensive
conduct of some big men here. Night fine, but chilly. I do not
make any advance here, apparently, at all; still, I must wait for
the photographic question to be decided. In conversation with
traders, etc., I secure confirmation of my impressions of the
honesty and reliability of the Pueblos in regard to promises and
to security of articles left in their care. But this photographic
business annoys me very much and almost disheartens me.
Everything is going against me.

November 3: Went to the Land Office.

Called to see Governor Avery [Arny?]; not at home. Another
photographer here from the railroad, but he can't come. Galbraith in from the Cañón de Santa Clara. Visionary. Mound-
builders, etc. He has witnessed, at the pueblo of Santo Domingo
near Santa Clara (?) a cremation in daytime. A principal having
died, his body was cut up (in his own house) in twenty-three
pieces, each piece placed in a vessel, and cremated in one of the
ovens of the pueblo. He secured several of these vessels with the
ashes and bones, also the vessels containing food, etc.[115] The Indians of Tehua stock do not paint their pottery; they only make
it of two colors. (This latter is a fact.)

Afternoon splendid, but very lonesome. The photographing

---

115. Having duly recorded these morbid details, Bandelier, a few lines later,
realized they were nonsense.

falls through completely. At night was informed that an official letter was in for me but had been mislaid. This is a nice business! On the whole, this visit has proven unsatisfactory. Galbraith tells me that the round stones grooved in the middle, heretofore classed as hatchets or hammers, are frog traps.[116] This is also singular [peculiar], like his statement that there is but one cacique for all the pueblos north of Santa Fe, and that he resides at Taos, also that he is invariably the oldest man in the pueblo. Such statements are transparent. He claims that there are no estufas outside of Taos, but that they are highly ornamented inside.

NOVEMBER 4: Started 11 A.M. with E. J. McLean on horseback for Cochiti. Previously, I got a long letter from A. S. Gatschet about linguistics. [At Peña Blanca], Mr. McLean left me, going across the river. [Later] I rode over to Cochiti with Juan de Jesús Herrera, whom I had met at Sena's store. (The old man Sena was beastly drunk!) We rode along in the darkness. Reached Cochiti about 6 P.M.

Glad to be home again, well received and treated, thirsty and hungry like a wolf. Juan José utterly disclaims the cremation of Galbraith and knows nothing of such a custom. He knows nothing of a pueblo of Santo Domingo [near Santa Clara] either. The bell is tolling at regular intervals. Tomorrow there will be Mass. Wind still blowing fiercely. In my absence, they have made me a good mattress of zacate. The frog traps in question are as follows. Juan José says it might be possible. He complains about the high price of zacate, $2.00 for 150 lbs. The vellotas [berries] of the cedar [juniper] are gathered now. They take one year to ripen, and they are used for tea in case of colds. The coyotes and the bears eat them. This afternoon I noticed

---

116. No ethnological confirmation of this explanation is known, although specific inquiry of older tribesmen might reveal some recollection or awareness. The most sensible use would be as a weight for a snare or trapping device. If true, however, it would hardly have been necessary to groove the stones so carefully, if at all. It seems most likely that Galbraith, or Bandelier, was the naive butt of a joke.

the ruins near the Bajada. They appear very large, with a large court and several estufas. But the whole is much ruined, and no detailed measurements can be secured any more. Shall return.

NOVEMBER 5: Bell tolling every hour, almost, at night. Early Mass. Padre here. Went to see the church. Fair paintings over the altar. Found corrugated pottery in the churchyard, and secured, in the house, an almost complete specimen of a caxete, glazed, dug out in the bank of the arroyo near this pueblo. It is a very fine specimen. We went to the house of the sacristán, where the Padre ate.

In Santo Domingo 113 escaleras, paying primicias: in Cochiti 63: in San Felipe 73-75. They raise cotton at Santo Domingo. They all raise maize. I witnessed a very interesting case at the sacristán's house, which I shall relate on the sheet following.

Occupation of the People

January. House work. Light work, carrying work. Make chiquihuites (*quish-te*) [baskets]. Hunt rabbits whenever there is fresh snow (also deer).

February. Hunt also. About middle of February begin to sow wheat. Sometimes irrigate before sowing, but not always, and only if the ground is very dry.

March. Sow wheat. The boys go out to gain money by hiring out as herders.

April. After the 20th of April, the planting of corn is commenced. The ground is invariably irrigated seven or eight days before the breaking. The breaking is done with ploughs and oxen. There are about thirty or forty ploughs in the pueblo, of which three or four belong to the Indians. They are borrowed from one another. The corn is covered with the plough again. It is not irrigated more for two months, but the ground is pulverized with the shovel or hoe, now of iron.

May to 10th of June. The maize is planted fully. In June and July they pulverize the ground in the cornfields.

July. They make the last weeding, with the plough, and then throw up their embankments and let the water in, irrigating thereafter almost every week.

From the 25th of April to the middle of May the chile is planted. In each of the crosses, a grain is planted, then covered with the foot, then frequently irrigated. It blooms about the 20th of July, and is irrigated afterwards every seven or eight days. Melons and watermelons are planted in late April. The breaking and planting is made with the aid of the plough, but the weeding, etc. is done with hoes. In July, maize begins to bloom and to throw out ears (espigas). Wheat begins to show ears in June. It is cut (the sonoreno [winter wheat?]) about the 10th to the 25th of July, and the common wheat about August 5-10. It is threshed (with horses) in July, August, and September. (No garbanzas?) Change [rotation] about every year, wheat lands being changed to corn, etc. and the same takes place with other fruit or crops. The punche [tobacco] is sown in May, and, if it grows, [trans-]planted in the same month. Frequently irrigated.

[The Padre] confirms the report of Santo Domingo about building. The capitán de la guerra directs and calls whatever aid is needed. The women carry the water, and the men make the adobes, wood-work, etc. The inhabitant of the future house furnishes the victuals. In other instances, the ha-nush [clan] assists.

This morning an old man came to complain to the Padre, while we were at the house of the sacristán, that a certain Teodosio Cordero had taken a field on the left bank of the Rio for himself, which he [the old man] had first broken. The Padre sent for the governor, who explained the case as follows: The old man, while indeed being the first one to break the ground, abandoned his crops after sowing them. The other worked the field afterwards, and so, when the old man complained about it, they sent out two arbiters who divided the field equally between them. Against this the old man complained, but the governor was firm notwithstanding the Padre's intercession. I did not witness the end of the dispute, but spoke to Juan José afterwards, who said the governor was right. Although the old man had broken the ground first and sowed or planted in it for two years, he had every year abandoned the crops. So they decided to divide the ground by a line from east to west, leaving the old man to cultivate the southern half and as much beyond it as he pleases, and Cordero the northern half with as much beyond as he wishes. He adds: that anyone who fails to cultivate his land for five years loses the claim to it.

There is, at present, considerable disturbance about the new railroad. Padre Ribera offers to secure compensation for any damage done. The damage to communal lands would be distributed among all, but that to cultivated plots would be paid to the individual tillers, which is perfectly correct.

At the fourth day after childbirth, the mother rising for the first time, an Indian name is given to the child, which name lasts during all lifetime.

The customs of marriage are: the young man gathers clothing, furs, food, etc. for his bride, who prepares a feast for the entire pueblo without exception (strangers included). They start from the house of the bride to church, and go back to the house of the bride, where the whole feast is celebrated. Sometimes the friends of the married man get up a complimentary dance in front of the house, where they are rewarded with food, which they go and eat at the house where they first met, or if they choose to enter, they can eat inside. Wedding presents are not the rule, but accepted. When he was asked to give away his daughter, he refused three times, and finally acceded, even giving the feast himself, because the bridegroom was a very poor orphan. (Sexual intercourse before marriage is strictly prohibited.)[117] When the girl is asked for, the relatives, male and female, give the reply. (Juan José consulted with his mother and mother-in-law.) If they are not satisfied, the reply is negative. The bridegroom makes the house.

---

117. As Bandelier's own comments in later entries of his journal indicate, this alleged rigidity in sex tabus was simply not true. Birth data from 1875 through 1947 in Lange's study of the Cochiti (1959: 534-535) clearly demonstrate this fact.

Inquired about the punishments. They never punish with death, but if anyone should kill another, or should commit rape, he may be flogged or shut up for as much as a month, also banished from the tribe. The murders, etc. . . . are turned over to the courts; the council decides the case, and then the alguaciles seize him. One is selected to flog him, and if he refuses to inflict the punishment required, he receives the same himself. The capitán de la guerra is criminal executor; the governor has civil cases; and the cacique attends only when he is called upon—otherwise, he takes no part in such things.

First English lesson with Juan José. He is very attentive and takes great pains but writes badly. The two boys came in and afterwards two Indians of Jemez, the oldest [sic] one the son of Francisco Nazlé, or Hosti. They [the Jemez] are very provident, and if the crop of one year is not exhausted, they do not touch the new crop. They also help each other among the tribes and within the same tribe. In the pueblo they very seldom sell to each other, but merely give or exchange. They were friendly but rather ignorant. It is not true that Hosti was ever cacique of Jemez. He was governor and capitán, but nothing else. They, after a certain time, finally understood the question about the gentes and I ascertained from them that they had them. They mentioned, incidentally, such names as sun, bear, wolf, maize, calabash, etc. But I could not ascertain their rules of marriage. Finally, Juan José got out of Juan de Jesús Nazlé that they intermarried in the same gens, but only when the parentage is very distant.

NOVEMBER 6: Everybody preparing for the rabbit hunt. Public crying early. Gave English [lesson] to Juan José. Finally, about 11:00 A.M., the horses were brought in. The public crier started, accompanied by six men carrying rattles, the faces painted white, and on the head, leaning forward, a tuft of split corn leaves. They, marched (or rather, tramped) through the whole place singing; came back across the plaza in the middle of which two of them left. Then the other four tramped to the northeast corner of the plaza, when they slowly tramped out. Soon after,

these four again started from the cross[118] in the middle of the
plaza, singing in a slow measured tone, and again went around
town. The boys, in their best clothes and on horseback, finally
gathered about one-quarter of a mile from the pueblo on the
lomas, with some of the old men along with them. A fire was
built, and when the girls began to arrive, mostly on foot, some
of the old men gathered around the fire and one of them spoke
for a long while in their tongue. It was done and listened to in
an attitude of prayer.

At the close of it, a short dialogue ensued between the man
praying and the teniente of the war captain. (The captain is
sick.) Then they presented themselves in rows of two, three,
four, and five to the speaker, with arms upheld, and he switched
them all right and left. Thereupon, they mounted their horses
and dispersed over the bosque, etc., the women and girls following them on foot. I soon heard their shouts as they scoured the
fields. But few rabbits appeared. Went home to eat dinner and
write up my notes. They were partly in the bosque near the
river and partly above. The sight of their galloping to and fro
on their horses, and in their gaudy dresses, was very fine. Shouts
and yelling, howling like wolves, were heard. All at once the
horsemen broke from the grove, a hare having been chased that
way. The whole band chased around, clear around the pueblo,
and it was only on the other side in the bosque that Adelaido
Montoya killed the hare with his club.

Meanwhile, I discovered an old estufa on the other side of
the arroyo north of the pueblo, and in its partly excavated ruin,
filled with sand and gravel, I found the finest specimens of
corrugated pottery.

There is also some very old pottery, a stone axe, manos, etc.
Without excavating, there is no way of getting more.

About 4 P.M. the horsemen assembled in the plain northwest

---

118. This cross is no longer present in the Cochiti plaza. The date of its
removal is unknown. Lange, in his study at Cochiti, was not told of it, nor
is there a known photograph of it (Lange 1959: 46-48). A similar cross has
been in the plaza at Zia Pueblo for many years (Lange 1952: 20).

of the pueblo and soon came galloping back, many of them having a girl or a woman sitting up behind "sidlings." I met Agustín and paid him the $12.00. He was very much excited. It appears that some of the boys had gone to the pueblo to drink water, and that there several men (young and old) chased them back, beating them with rods. Adelaido was beaten, and when Juan José interfered, to stop them, the son-in-law of Agustín turned upon him, striking him in the face and neck rather severely. Juan José then struck him with his hunting club, inflicting a rather painful though not dangerous wound on the left side of the skull.

At the instance of Agustín, I went to see him [the son-in-law]. He was sitting on a stool, bleeding profusely. Women and children were standing about and shouting, crying, and yelling. Agustín called in two Mexicans, as witnesses, as he was going to accuse Juan José. I was frightened, and after talking awhile with Victoriano, the war lieutenant, I went home. Found Juan José much dejected although, from all appearances, he had but acted in self defense.

I offered to mediate in order to prevent recourse to the laws and courts. My mediation was thankfully accepted. So I went again to the house of the patient but found his head bound up, and he himself talking and smiling fairly. All is well. Looked for the cacique, but in vain. Juan José requested me to offer to Agustín $2.00 for damages, and I did so in presence of Zashua and Juan de Jesús Pancho. Agustín refused, stating that he wanted no money, but revenge of some other kind. At night, after returning from Peña Blanca, where he had gone in quest of boys who had this afternoon broken the tinaja of Ignacia, Juan José was summoned before the council. The boys came in, and I gave them English lessons. Very pleasant.

NOVEMBER 7: Zashua came early to get my card for Bennett, etc. The council at the house of the governor lasted all night and things looked bad. Agustín demands expulsion of Juan José from the Pueblo, and the latter said that if the principales would not agree upon a compensation, he would simply accept the conditions of Agustín. Thus the case rests, but meanwhile, there are two parties forming in the pueblo. Juan José is quiet but suffers from headache in consequence of the strokes he received. I went to see the governor and the cacique; the latter was invisible.[119] The governor said that the principales were not disposed to banish Juan José (that in all events they could not force him to leave his house, etc.) nor to deprive him of his rights as member of the tribe. If Juan José made any offer of compensation suitable to their understanding of the case, he, the governor, had the power to compel Agustín to accept it.

Then in order to protect Juan José, I felt it my duty to call him in and showed him the ornaments which I had purchased from Agustín for Stevenson. He was thunderstruck. I easily ascertained, then, that these are indeed sacred objects, never to be sold. It is a great crime to sell them, and they are distributed among the "braves" without their knowing even who manufactures them. It surprised them greatly when I told them that the cacique made them. Even Ventura, who is one of the entremeseros (what that is, I do not know, but they are the dancers) [Koshare] and whom Juan José thinks is well informed, was perfectly thunderstruck and inquired all about it.[120]

---

119. This is a fascinating example of Bandelier's literally correct but unorthodox choice of words. The cacique was quite obviously "not to be seen" or "unavailable." On the other hand, it is somewhat intriguing to think of a cacique of Bandelier's time having sufficient occult powers to make himself actually disappear.

120. Here, and in preceding and subsequent entries, Bandelier provided a detailed eyewitness's and participant observer's account of a specific case in tribal jurisprudence. Recent issues of *Human Organization*, the journal of the Society for Applied Anthropology, have contained accounts of somewhat similar involvement between a field-worker and the people with whom he is working. There is considerable debate over the propriety of the field-worker's becoming involved, either as a mediator or as a sympathizer of any faction. While Bandelier originally offered to mediate, it is clear that his sympathies lay with Juan José. Many a more experienced field-worker has found that it may be sound theory to remain aloof, but this may result merely in antagonizing all factions—forcing on the field-worker the alternatives of taking a stand or leaving the community.

I shall now wait, but if Agustín does not stop, I shall finally accuse him of the transaction. (Called on José Hilario, paid him $5.00 and arranged for the Caja del Rio tomorrow.)

Pacífico Baca visited me and told me that he had one of the idols for me now. He also told me that once, following a she-bear into her den, he had found there an entire vase, painted, of the old sort, which however crumbled soon. (Maybe?) The boys told me last evening, that there was a woman in the pueblo, an old one, affected with syphilis. She had been a prostitute in the pueblo.

Afternoon, Agustín goes to Peña Blanca with a letter, probably to bring suit. I finally spoke to the governor in my room. He was perfectly surprised. These ornaments belong to the tribe, and not to the individual who wears them, and they cannot be sold without permission of the tribe. Therefore, I concluded to return them to Agustín, who evidently is very mad at it—but in doing so I avoided his punishment, which otherwise would have been severe. The governor immediately went to the war captain, who fortunately was not at home. Otherwise Agustín would have been seized and severely punished. This gives me a deep insight into their customs.

At my intercession, the governor was quiet, but if Agustín should do any harm, he will be immediately seized and badly punished. It appears that the war captain has this duty. Notwithstanding this, Agustín has brought suit.

At night, the boys came in, eager for lessons. They brought me many stone hatchets. *Shyayaq* is the name given to the puma sculptures, according to Juan de Jesús Pancho. It is the god of the chase, and the adoration of it is conceded. He also concedes that they go every morning, at sunrise, to wash themselves at the river and to look to the east in token of adoration of the sun. About the perpetual fire, he is non-committal, but the serpent story he strenuously denies. The boys are rather well educated, owing to [because of] the short time they have been at school, and they are very eager to learn. This evening I had blue guayaves [paper bread] for the first time, ma-atze. They are very good.

Juan José is suffering from his whipping. Stevenson and party have arrived [at Peña Blanca], but my horse is not here, and I shall not go to see him today, as it is too risky on account of the river-passage at night. The axes I got are all granite, the green coating being epidote.

NOVEMBER 8: Went to Peña Blanca about 9 A.M. on foot. Stevenson not there; had left for Santa Fe. Letters from Bohn, Morgan, George Wittick; cards from Annie Borchert and Norton. Replied to Bohn on card. Can't do else. Padre told me about 1852 there was still a priest at Cochiti; then he moved to Peña Blanca. Church at Peña Blanca consecrated December 12, 1869, but commenced in 1867. About noon a sandstorm from the west; [I]crossed the bridges in the face of it. Quiet at Cochiti at 1 P.M. while the valley and the mountains east were all covered with sand-clouds. Agustín paid me $10.00 and I gave them to Jesús Sena. Met Pacífico Baca, and he sold me a small idol of alabaster, found in one of the houses of the pueblo, and still worn like amulets in little leather bags. Also a fine axe from the Potrero Viejo. He says that they strew or throw corn to the east early in the morning (when they go to the river) to call Montezuma. On [New Year's Day] they cook a stew composed of all herbs which they feed on during the year. Sometimes they put meat into it. With thin tortillas.

NOVEMBER 9: Juan José's sister brought me panocha, Hua-hua-tzi [wheat sprout pudding]. Excellent, sweet. Reached the northeasterly ruin about 12 noon.

The condition of the ruin is such that I could not trace any walls nor compartments. . . . There are hardly anything else but mounds, and no trace of the superstructure is left. Large and small boulders, slabs of lava, etc. are scattered about and a great number of broken metates, manos, also much pottery, of three or four different kinds. Some fragments of very old, corrugated pottery; much glazed pottery; some plain grey; and some thin red; which look like recent.

José Hilario also distinctly identified some of the black, smoked fragments pertaining to chimneys. I have rarely seen such large fragments of glazed pottery. In the interior of the court, I saw no estufa; still, they may have existed, although there are none visible. The ruins are overgrown with a perfect forest of *Opuntia*, forming, in some places, shrubby thickets.

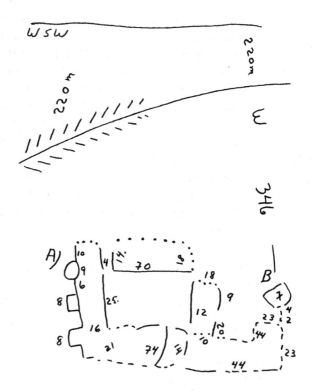

The plateau itself drains to the south-southeast; its soil is sandy; the other vegetation, grass and chaparro, also sabinos. From its top, the huge potreros opposite appear in majestic fronts, with their canyons wide open and beaming, and the

Sierra San Miguel above. The sight is grand. From the western end of the plateau, the rock juts down abruptly into the river, which here hugs the western wall, leaving some space on the east side for, possibly, the fields of the pueblo. For they cannot have cultivated on the plateau, as there is no water, while there are paths leading up to the ruins from the river below. The plateau is easily defensible, but there is no trace of fortification. Distance from Cochiti, about six miles. The river is forded above the ruins three miles north of the pueblo, and there also, the lava crosses over to the west side, and the Cañón del Norte begins. At the ruins, the chain of the Tetilla, running up from the southeast, nearly touches the river.* Return very cold, against the cutting southerly wind. Full of specimens, among them a door-plate.

José Hilario tells me that the Mexicans burn lime and the Indians buy it from them, as they do not know how to burn it. Last evening, Zashua told me that, when they want to prepare the gypsum plates for their windows, they boil them in hot water, so as to further the cleavage. This morning I saw an old man beating hide with a stone (mashing it) in order to prepare it for moccasins. Juan José has been summoned to Peña Blanca before the Justice of the Peace by Agustín. (Pacífico Baca annoyed me in my room for a long time.) Juan José has settled his affair by paying the costs $18.50. This was foolish on his part.

There is another trouble in the pueblo tonight—a squabble between one of the boys and a Mexican. All the boys are cited before the governor. They came to see me, each carrying a stick of firewood. They go begging for it from house to house. Soon after, a drum was heard, and José Hilario not being here, I went to his house. There was a whole crowd of boys and women, all in serapes, tramping about in the plaza, singing to the sound of a drum. Suddenly they would all together cower down to the ground, and thus remain for a while, during which time the leader kept on singing at a slow measure and occasionally touching his drum. Suddenly they all arose with a yell and peals of laughter, and went farther, singing at the top of their voices, and with regular tripping or trampling. (It reminded me much of the New Zealand dances.)[121] Thus they went, in the moonlight, around the pueblo, and this is the introduction for tomorrow's Baile de los Entremeseros.

Juan José tells me that these entremeseros when they dance in summer, and also when they go out as messengers to gather the people for a public work like at the acequia, etc., are dressed in black mantles, with their hair very long, their faces blackened, and white circles painted around their eyes and mouth. Just the costume of the Mexican *tlamacazqui.* Very remarkable, if true.

Tonight, a Jemez Indian sleeps in the house of Juan José. He appears very sullen, and there is a great difference between him and the boys. Have been fixing up my treasures. There is already quite a collection of stone implements, etc. Completed ground plans tonight, etc. Tomorrow must be ready for the great dance, which will last all day long. Day after tomorrow, Juan José and the chiquita go to Jemez, and want me to go along, but I can't. Have an abominable cold, and, besides, am waiting on Bennett. Without the photographs, can do nothing. The circle of the Caja del Rio has several stones which were hewn evidently. Very large ones. . . .*

NOVEMBER 10: Dance in full play. Call from two Indians of Cia, who wanted me to explain to them the proclamation of Governor Ritch. Their language appears to be the same as that of Cochiti, as I could easily distinguish and ascertain while they conversed with José Hilario in my room. The governor, Mariano Garbal, is a fine young man, good size, and fine face.

Went, about 11A.M., to see the dance with Zashua. Returned at 12 noon, during an *intermezzo* [intermission]. I went several times during the day to witness the performance, which is nothing else than a theatrical performance, accompanied by and

---

121. Presumably those of the Maori. As far as is known Bandelier never visited New Zealand, as the statement would seem to imply, so his information must have come from ethnological reports or travelers' accounts.

intermingled with dancing. The men are all naked except the *maxtlatl* [kilt], bracelets on their ankles, wrists, and collars. These ornaments are nearly all dark. The hair is tied back, and a tuft of corn leaves, sliced, is tied on the top of the head. They are painted variously: white, black, and brown or copper-colored, and look really like devils, or like the Mingo Indians in the German translation (by Hoffmann) of Fenimore Cooper's *Deerslayer*.

Some have figures painted on their body, among which I noticed, on one particularly ugly devil, a large open hand, on one side of the body, painted dark on the ashy-gray surface. The faces are particularly ugly. If the body is black, the face is white, or the reverse, but in all cases white is the prevailing tinge of the face, so that it looks like that of a clown.

It is the one with the painted hand who beats the drum. The drum is painted light brown all over, and, as far as I could see, about 0.75 meter long, and 0.30 meter in diameter. It is not suspended from the shoulder, but held in the left hand near the top, against the knee, slightly bent, and thus beaten with one stick with a round big knob. The women are also painted but dressed, and all the women wear their serapes like shawls to their knees on their backs. Some of them carried children of eight to ten years on their backs. One of the women was painted yellow in the face; others blue, white, or black. The aspect of all is simply hideous. They came in a body, singing and rattling. The rattles, of deer hoofs and tortoise shells, are suspended from the wrists, others on the ankles, others to the belts. Hands are free, and they hold sometimes guayaves, tortillas, etc.

The gait is a very light trot and therefore slow. They went around the pueblo, entering the plaza from the northeast corner, and returning by the southwest corner, around the eastern row of houses, passing that of the cacique. For a while they remained in the plaza, and while a part of them stood in a body looking quietly, others, principally men, performed all sorts of tricks—not always graceful—chasing each other, dragging each other through the dust, climbing house tops, men and women, some with children who were freely bundled about very roughly. The roof of the houses in the rear (west) of the cacique's was particularly the scene of exploits.

One woman went into an oven on top of it, and was afterwards dragged from it by the man, and her child (eight or ten years old) handed down very unceremoniously from the roof. About an hour after, I heard the drum and went to the plaza again. The malinche was with him. She is an exceptional figure. A jacket of deerskin, a large conch shell, painted brilliant rose, with green hinge irridescent, as breastpin. Around the waist, and high enough to support the breasts, a woollen garment, wound around, with two scarflike pendants to below the knees, hanging down behind as far as the dress or petticoat. This garment is peculiar.* Color is dark green, with patterns, green and yellow. It has been worn, evidently, but is otherwise in good condition. Her headdress is peculiar. The bows were green, and the upper one had, in the middle, a dark band; still, I could not distinguish as to whether it was brown or black.

They soon formed in two rows, the women on the south side, and the men on the north, single file, some of the men continuing to chase and swarm around them as clowns. They teased the bystanders, now very numerous (many Mexicans), entered the houses, took out lines, vases, skins, tortillas, pelted each other. This headdress is called *O-ta-tiushti*, and Juan José says that it signifies crown. On each side there are eagle feathers, the tuft behind of parrots, guacamayos, shia-uat. Behind is a tress of resplendent green feathers of shia-uat also. The feathers of owls and of crows are regarded as fieros [terrible] and are used by brujos [witches] in the Baile de los Comanches. This baile is called, peshari-pashca.

The manta is called tzi-ma-ti. The pattern is a standing one, and if one is used up, the new one has to be made after the same pattern. There are always two in each pueblo, one for each estufa, as for the Baile de Caballeros, two are used. It is of black wool, and the designs are needlework, in this case made by the mother of Juan José whose property also was the conch shell. Both are now in possession of the sister of Juan José, the wife of Luis Montoya. Formerly the sack was of white cotton, but there is no cotton cloth in the pueblo any more. The legs and feet were in the ordinary deerskin, but nice.

At the sound of the drum, which was beaten by the black fellow, standing outside of the northern row, while the children were mixed according to sexes, the two lines began to hop (with both feet), turning about in sections, the eastern section being last. Could not dare to count them, but there may have been forty, perhaps thirty-five, in all. Then the malinche, while the others were hopping on the spot, hopped slowly and not un-gracefully sideways up and down through the lines, blessing or fanning them alternately with a tuft of eagle feathers which she held in each hand. Finally both rows went down on their knees, all the while clapping their hands so as to keep the rattles going, and the malinche kept on hopping back and forth and blessing them between the lines.

During this time the skirmishers kept acting around them. One of them, who was particularly fond of rolling in the dust, was at last dragged about and through the lines by his com-panions till he was completely naked. There an exhibition of obscenity hard to describe took place. Sodomy, coitus, mastur-bation, etc., were performed to greatest perfection, men ac-coupling with each other on the ground or standing, and to the greatest delight of the spectators (certainly over one hun-

dred), men, women, girls and boys, Mexicans and Indians, looking on with greatest ingenuity and innocence, not the slightest
indecent look on the part of the women, and applauding the
vilest motions. I was terribly ashamed, but nobody seemed to
take any concern about it.

The malinche slowly withdrew, followed by the drummer
and the crowd, but without anything like an exhibition of shame
and haste. The dance was ended, and so she went. The clowns
followed them with their abominable gestures, and actually
carried back one girl, threw her down, and while one was performing the coitus from behind, another was doing it against
her head. Of course, all was simulated, and not the real act, as
the women were dressed. The naked fellow performed mastur-
bation in or very near the center of the plaza, alternately with
a black rug and with his hand. Everybody laughed. I went home.

About 3 P.M., hearing the drum again, I found them in a
cluster around the malinche, forming a round group (not a
ring), and hopping around her. Afterward they again formed in
a row of two, as before, and also knelt down, with the malinche
hopping between. The clowns, outside, imitated drunkenness
perfectly; one had a shield, bow and arrow, and they went about
as usual, cracking jokes, teasing each other and the people, pelt-
ing tortillas and guayaves, etc. The exit was always to the southeast, but not to the estufas. I heard the drum last at about 4
o'clock. The clowns remained in the plaza all the while for the
diversion of the people.

Juan José tells me that, early on the morning of Christmas,
another baile is held in the church, despues de rezar [after
praying]. They dress in the estufas and then dance in the
church. Four days thereafter, there is dancing in the pueblo,
in the plaza, and at night the men go about to the houses, to
dance and divert the people. They are naked, and the people
regale them with food.

On the first of January the election of officers is held, and on
the second of January another great baile is held, qqashatimae-

pashqa, in the plaza. And another one on the sixth of January (Dia de los Reyes [Kings' Day]), called, *rey-pashqa*.

I then went to the governor, who received me kindly, although his wife lay on the floor with a newly born baby, wrapped up in a serape, by her side. She was wrapped in serapes to her chin, face flushed, but healthy and smiling. The baby was one day old. Ball-play (*kua-ma-ta-shi*) is played by the boys in the spring, after the communal work at the great acequia is finished (cleaning and mending—in March or April, it takes three or four days to clean up each acequia, the eastern one often five days). No division by gentes, but a selection by two chosen ones, and if the division appears unfair, then the sticks of all the boys are piled up under a serape, and the two leaders draw them out without seeing them.

Juan José this evening confesses to me that the Indians believe in a return to this earth of the spirits of the deceased and of a steady communication of these with the living. Also of a punishment of the dead on this earth, and that those spirits who come to weep and make noises in the houses, etc., do it to instigate the living to pray for them. Therefore the custom to strew crumbs of tortillas, etc., at night and in the morning before sunrise, when the boys get up and go to the river to wash themselves, and to scatter crumbs for the spirits of the dead. They pray to God for them and have their own prayers in Queres, some of which he knows and will tell me. He confessed to me the adoration of the sun, every morning on the housetops, of the moon, stars, and earth, as still extant; he says that the puma was not their principal god, but that the sun was it in all probability; that the spirits are in the winds, and that they pray to them also, and not merely for them. He is a dreamer and a perfect spiritist. Disclaims the existence of images. Most valuable day. Juan José says that this dance is from *Teguayo!*

NOVEMBER 11: Juan José and the whole family went to Jemez, all four on horseback. Left for Peña Blanca and stopped there.

My pen broken. Shall not go to the Bajada. José Hilario at Peña Blanca. It is an unlucky day, although most splendid. Everything works against me. The boys, going to Jemez, have taken my revolver along. It is already very late in the day, 3:00 P.M., and it will be 4:00 P.M. before we can leave. What may happen yet? Don't know.

[House] foundations are [commonly] about 0.75 meter underground, of stones (rubble) with adobe flung in between. When this wall reaches the surface of the soil, then they begin to lay adobe.

We started at last, crossing successively the Arroyo del Cañón de Pino (dry), the cañada (little water) passing east of the Potrero de los Idolos, into the Cañón de José Sanchez east of the Potrero Largo, into the Cañón de la Bolsa, near the Potrero Chiato, where we built a fire between two sabinos and on the sand. Infernal pen won't work. No water. Nothing but stunted sabinos.

NOVEMBER 12: This canyon is a sack, closed to the west. The potreros are pumice stone, but in front (east), black lava appears. It has crossed the river, and neither caps nor underlies, but simply faces the pumice and volcanic tuff. Left at about 8 A.M. for the Potrero Chiato. Very cold day—almost impossible to do work. Therefore, this journal is only fragmentary, and I write most of it on the 14th at Cochiti. It was not possible to hold the pen, or even to measure with the line. All pumice stone badly ruined, at least no standing walls.* No water on the potrero; still isolated ranchos similar to those outside in the fields. These ranchos were evidently of the same stone and are generally 2 or 3 x 4 meters. They are scattered irregularly. The soil of the potrero is sandy, but evidently not poor; the vegetation consists, as usual, of sabinos, tunas, *Opuntias*, some chaparro, and occasional zacate. But the question as to where the water came from is undecided.[122] The Potrero Chi-

---

122. An answer to the problem of where water was obtained for various upland farming tracts may be found in observations first reported by Charles R. Steen and Gordon Vivian of the National Park Service. Hundreds of acres

ato forms a double-tongued projection, the central part being
that wherever the other two sides are drained. But this middle
part is almost naked volcanic tuff, merging into pumice. The
canyons at the bottom are dry and impossible to cultivate.
Still, they must have had fields, for they had corn!

NOVEMBER 13: Ruins on the loma,* foot of Potrero de las
Casas, one half-mile west of the Cueva Pintada, right bank of
the Arroyo de la Cuesta Colorada. We left the Cueva about
noon and reached Cochiti at 3:00 P.M. Juan José returned after
sunset. I set to work at once on the drawings and maps, before
everything would have disappeared [been forgotten]. The journal for the past two days will, therefore, be written tomorrow.
Finished the plats about 10:00 P.M., and then went to bed—
tired.

NOVEMBER 14: I begin thus with the morning of the 12th, writing more from recollection than anything else. Very cold day.
As soon as we reached the surface of the Potrero Chiato (about
9:00 A.M.), ascending round by the northeast corner, and winding back to the southeast side, a few coyotes on the opposite
potrero (north) set up a dismal, but nevertheless most lud-
icrous, wail and howl. It appears that this is regarded as a very
bad sign, a presage of bad weather, cold, also of ill luck.

The potrero has a fair vegetation. The trail which we had
taken to ascend was deeply indented and worn, showing that
it had been used a good deal and for a long time past. It led
directly to the first ruin, which is near the northern rim of the
southern branch overlooking the middle part of the potrero. It

---

located on the tops of spurs from the Jemez Range, Mount Taylor, and other
mountainous areas of west central New Mexico are covered by grids of loosely
piled stones, no more than a foot high. These walls, or borders, enclose rectangular plots ranging from eight to twenty feet on a side. From the air, many
appear similar to pueblo rooms, but close observation reveals none of the usual
occupational debris. Such basins, located where no run-off, or flood-waters,
could reach them, may well have trapped enough dew during a season to provide
sufficient moisture to mature a crop. Herbert W. Dick has reported observations
from the El Rito area, north of the Bandelier-Cochiti region, which tend to
support such a hypothesis.

is not 50 meters from the declivity. To the east the view is or rather would be splendid, but the clouds hang low down all over. It is very cold, and the Sierra de San Miguel, which is in full sight, is covered with a thin veil of mist. After stepping off the ruins, I collected pottery. It is all of the whitish-gray kind, striped and ornamented black. No glazed one found, but many lava chips, which here are certainly artificial, since there is not lava nearer than the right shore of the Rio Grande. Obsidian is very scarce, and appears to be replaced by lava. Corrugated and indented pottery is very frequent along with the other kind. We left, taking the very straight and plain trail, and traveling almost due west.

The next ruin shows glazed pottery, but only cream colored and black, no red pottery. Black and white striped is very fine. Followed the trail again west to the first small cuartel, called San Miguel, about two miles off. Here the character of the pottery changes in so far as to be red principally, and all glazed. But the ruin otherwise is in the same condition as the other, and about as large—without a court. There are also one or two ranchos on the way, but no trace of water or fields.

Across a barranca, and on a high round eminence which it occupies almost exclusively, is the pueblo of San Miguel. Of volcanic tuff, its walls are exactly similar to those of the pueblo on the Potrero de las Vacas, the slab regularly laid, the adobe flung in between the crevices, and little stones inserted to stop the larger holes and to keep the slabs in position.* The stonework is really beautiful, and also well preserved. While they evidently built their walls as those of the Potrero de las Vacas, Potrero Viejo, and Potrero Quemado, still, it looks finer here. But there is no trace of estufas inside of the court. The depressions are all outside. In [one] wing . . . there is, in one of the corners, a little door very low down like an air hole. Some, but very few, doors are visible also. Like all the others. Some very heavy metates, of boulders, manos of lava, door plates or steps, and much pottery is lying about. Pottery, principally glazed and colored. Fine arrowheads of obsidian are also to be found; at

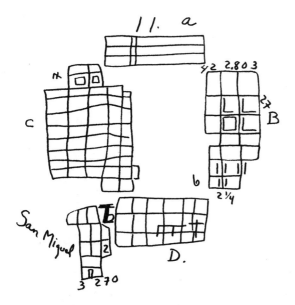

least I found one very perfect, and fragments of others. Red oxide of iron in lumps is strewn about.

The stone circle already noted is very singular. It is not very high—about 1 meter at most—but the stones (very large) are so closely fitted together that I suspect it to have been a tank, as there is no water about. North of it, and within reach of the other side of the circle (if it ever existed), the bare rock protrudes.* The ground between the stones and the rock has evidently been swept in by wind or water, as the circle is lower than the ruin. In fact, the hill on which this stands slopes on all sides from the pueblo, the latter crowns its summit.*

After taking some coffee and meat in a sheltered place (the slopes are covered with sabinos), we endeavored to measure the pueblo in detail, but the cold was so intense that we could not stand it long. So, after doing the best we could we started again about 2:30 P.M. The Sierra de San Miguel was magnificent in its bold, picturesque, outlines, the slopes showing streaks of gigantic pines, and on the base the seam of blood-red ochre, very plain, from which the Cuesta Colorada takes its name. We went to get some water in a timbered gorge in the Sierra; the drift was full of chunks of ochre. Water excellent; then re-ascended to the ruins and thence east along the northern branch of the Potrero Chiato to opposite (nearly) the Cueva Pintada, always in sight of a splendid view of the Sierra de Santa Fé.

We descended an old trail, deeply worn into the volcanic tuff, dismounting from our beasts, and reached the Cueva about 4:30 P.M. The horses were put about one half-mile farther west, on the loma of the Potrero de las Casas, and we built a fire in the cave itself. I measured the cave houses west adjoining the cave, and collected pottery, etc. This pottery is not very frequent; it is corrugated and indented, gray pottery with black stripes (finely striated), and only one small piece of red glazed.

Door plates of diorite, manos of black lava, etc. and fragments of stone hammers, metates, but principally obsidian in frag-ments and splinters used for knives and scrapers. It is difficult to ascertain what is old and [what is] not, as the cave has been the resort of shepherds so many, many years. Enormous blocks of rock have fallen right in front of the ruins of the cliff houses, and I suppose that this decay has taken place since the village was abandoned or that it was perhaps one of the causes of its destruction. All during the day, tracks of deer and turkey were extremely abundant, but I saw none of the animals themselves.

[Events of] NOVEMBER 13: I climbed up to the paintings by means of the cuts in the rock, which I enlarged with my ham-mer. The height to the lower chamber is 15 meters, and the cycle of paintings is about 2 meters higher, and 2 meters farther off. There can be no doubt but that the paintings are of more recent date than the cave houses. The ascent to them is right over the remains of a cave, and the great cavern itself has fallen in and been disfigured to a great extent.

Juan José tells me that whenever the Indians abandoned a place, they painted their dances in caves. The figures, he says, are dancers and dancing ornaments, and not houses, as I sup-posed. The crosses are of Mexican make. In general, there are

many recent carvings, mostly crosses, and the paintings themselves have suffered severely. Juan José further asserts: that the
figure of the serpent is no snake, but stands for sheet-lightning
(relámpago), and distinctly says that a vívora is painted differently. The plastering is gone from the walls of the room or
cell above, and the figures have been painted over it.

Profile of the cave: The lower part is abominably ruined, and
it is impossible to say if the great semi-circle (10 meters in diameter) was originally one or not, or if it is the product of decay.
The soil is half gravel, half dung. In front of the cave, a high
rubble enclosure has been erected. We left the cave at 12:00
noon, after having also measured the much ruined pueblo one
half-mile farther north on the loma. It is so mixed up with gravel
and drift that it is almost impossible to define it. Pottery, etc.
same as at the cave. The paintings are made with red ochre,
which, as José Hilario asserts, is also used to paint pottery. On
returning, I noticed that the lava goes under the tuff. Reached
Cochiti 3:00 P.M.—very cold and tired. Juan José came about
sunset. Drew maps all evening.

[NOVEMBER 14:] Today I wrote up my diaries for the past two
days and cultivated my very sore nose, which the late exposure
has not improved. Juan José is at Peña Blanca and came home to
slaughter two sheep, which he did in the afternoon in front of
the house. I was left quite alone all day; the boys did not show
themselves. Zashua scarcely knows me any more! I wrote and
wrote all day. About sunset, I went to the old estufa north of
the pueblo (Juan José says it is not an estufa) and gathered
some pottery. It is gray and black, finely striped, dotted, and
in squares. In this respect the pueblo on the Potrero Quemado,
on the Potrero Chiato, and that of this old Cochiti, are identical, and it is always associated with much of the corrugated and
indented pottery. The ornamentation with dots is also found
among the glazed pottery, as a fragment from San Miguel
shows.

By the way, in nearly all the ruins I found the smoked and
charred pottery indicating chimneys, and yesterday, in the room

of Luis Montoya, I saw at least one of those flues made of perforated and smoked ollas. It was facing the room straight (not at an angle like all the others), and had quite a wide arched opening. The flue was also whitewashed. The metates in his house were exceedingly large and heavy, but they could not tell whence they came. They were de cuanto hay [from time immemorial].

I also bought from Victoriano Lucero, the teniente capitán (a fine young man, married), a splendid old tinaja, very well painted, with a very artistic design, such as I have not seen here yet, for $3.00. It has been in his family "cuanto hay," is not glazed, but may not have been made here. Juan José says that the boys' grandmother used to be muy curiosa [very odd], and that the finding of old pottery there is not surprising. Shall go to the Bajada tomorrow, on one of Juan José's white horses. José Hilario has my horse for sale.

NOVEMBER 15: Left for the Bajada. I collected but few specimens—flint flakes, very little obsidian, and the pottery is so old and dirty that hardly any patterns can be made out. The southern border of the mesa is almost vertical rock, especially by the corral. The corral may be recent work. It is walled in by huge blocks.* . . . The trail to the Bajada passes north of the pueblo

ruins.* The outer walls are triple, 0.75 meter wide, three rows of lava. The inner walls of one row of stone. Pottery painted and plain; glazed.

I did not go down into the corral. Built of very large rocks. River bottom west broad and almost traces of acequia.* The ground from the mesa to the Bajada is level, though undulating. The Rio is frozen and very small, nothing but a fillet of water. The strewn stones are black lava, and the ruins nothing but mounds of earth. Collected manos, saw fragments of metates,

etc. The location is sunny and pleasant. Pottery glazed and colored. Very little obsidian. Some white flint.* Also smoked pottery from chimneys, and an unfinished hammer. Also ribbed pottery, but scarce—glazed prevailing.

This last pueblo has more fragments of all things than the two first ones; it is also larger, and it looks as if the depredations of the Mexicans had been less effective there than in the others.* It is strewn over with glazed pottery and stones (lava) used by the Mexicans for small corrales on the ruins themselves. Broken metates, manos of lava and gneiss, also of dark quartzite and diorite. Smoked pottery indicating chimneys. Pottery in large fragments. Some largely ribbed pottery also.

But in all the ruins of this day, the gray, finely painted (black) pieces on the Potrero Chiato are lacking, also the corrugated pottery. Some plain (perhaps recent) red outside and dark inside. A fragment of red ochre stone, like that of the Cuesta Colorada, was picked up. It is evidently, however, broken by hand. This would indicate that they brought it from there and had regular intercourse with that part of the country.

It also appears clear to me that the Indians formerly passed from the cañada or by way of the cañada to the Caja del Rio, and down the Peralta to the Rio de Santa Fé, and thence up the river. This was a slow migration, not a journey or travel. Juan José is of the same opinion. He also tells me that the ruins on the Potrero Chiato, Potrero Quemado, were originally not at all dependent upon irrigation for their crops. It is the same story; formerly there was more rain. He recollects that within his time there were very rainy years, while the last years were even exceptionally dry. He also adds that originally they only raised maize, for which, he says, irrigation is not indispensable. He claims to have seen crops of maize gathered in places where there was no irrigation, which exceeded those from the acequias.

Cheerful letters today—one from Gustav. I immediately spoke to Juan José about the petition to Congress. He advised me to inform the governor of it, which I did. He appeared highly satisfied.

Spent the evening with Victoriano and bought his tinaja. It is a splendid old thing, and in its ornamentation recalls the coast of Peru. Juan José is a little nettled. He says it is a very

old thing, but that there are older ones in the pueblo yet, and "más bonitas" [prettier]. José Hilario also tells me that their mother used to make very beautiful tinajas, and that they still have one of them broken, but bound together so as to hold wheat, which he will "enseñarme" [show me]. With the women making these traps, there is consequently great rivalry among the families. Victoriano showed me two shields "de cuanto hay." The larger one is of double buffalo hide, and bears in the center a bull's head on a half-moon. The smaller one is of single hide, but very thick, and also finely painted. It is enclosed in a cover of deerskin, painted with stars. He showed me how they used them.

Juan José tells me that December, January, February, and March are the coldest months of the year. It strikes me that continually dry years may have much to do with the migration of the Pueblos into the Rio Grande bottom, and Juan José intimates similar facts. It is very possible. Have work again for two days. Bennett may come any time, also. Victoriano is affectionate and calls me brother. He is a cousin to Juan José. His gens is Yssi(?).

NOVEMBER 16: Juan José left for Cia this morning. The day continues awful. The opposite side is one cloud of sand, and all the mountains are covered to their bottoms. My fire avails nothing. The wind, blowing in through the white domestic [sheet?] of the window, keeps it down. I am alone in the house with Ignacia. Juan José is very anxious about Adelaido. The boy went to Cia and should have returned Saturday. He says the highways are very unsafe from robbers, and so he took my revolver along.

At noon we had meat with chile. Terribly strong. This morning I drew the ground plans of the pueblos of yesterday. There is scarcely anybody outdoors. My hands are so stiff that I can scarcely use them. As it was utterly impossible to write, I took the rickety old working-bench of Juan José into the front room where it is relatively warm. Thus I wrote all afternoon. Juan José returned at sunset with Adelaido: he had met him on the road. The wind, which had abated a little, begins again furiously, and the cold is terrible.

This evening suddenly a woman and a girl came in; the woman asked for a candle and then inquired for a remedy against toothache. I told her the only remedy was to pull out the tooth, and she asked me whether I could do it, to which I, of course, replied negatively and then looked at the delinquent. It was an upper molar, or rather, the root of one only, rotted down to the lowest point. After giving her the candle she went out thanking me (she is lame and sickly). Then her husband came in and brought me a big armful of excellent ocote [pitch-pine]. This was a true godsend, as now I can write again. This ocote is an excellent wood; it not only heats but it even lights up. I can write with it perfectly and without a candle. Juan José has again filled me with tales of his smartness. Still he is too valuable an auxiliary to slight, but he is at all events a man who is bought and sold by flattery. Visit from Juan Chavez.

NOVEMBER 17: Fox skins sell at from $1.00 to $1.25 apiece in the pueblo. Victoriano came; he had been here last night, but I was out. He is going to Peña Blanca. Juan José's neighbor is shoveling the snow off the roof and from the sides of the house. He is kinder than Juan José himself. Have had no coffee now since the 13th afternoon. Victoriano is back, but has forgotten the envelopes. *Hi-pipi* whistle of carrizo and filled with wood. This whistle, which is the same as the one used by boys, is carried in war. When anyone kills an enemy or takes his scalp, he can mount on his horse and make the circuit of the people, whistling. This whistle is an instrument of war and dates back from before the time of Montezuma, since he used it as the story tells.

Juan José began to dictate this story to me in his language, translating it into Spanish. When I asked him as to whether the cacique would tell it the same way, he replied: "Quizas" [perhaps]. This cacique is still an enigma to me.

I spent the evening with Victoriano very pleasantly. His wife and sister-in-law were there. He showed me rattles (q'atzani), made of fibrous stones like petrified wood, found in the old ruins north adjoining Cochiti and an axe of lava from *Haenata-qodjiti* (Potrero Viejo) and promised to keep them for me. He goes to hunt rabbits tomorrow, and I am invited to take supper with him of rabbit meat. Shall go. Juan José also goes out tomorrow to hunt.

The boys go to dig up skunks. They dig up the hole on the north side, stopping the entrance as they proceed. When the animal sticks out his head, they knock him in the head.

Further details in regard to the rabbit hunt. The speech is no prayer, but instruction. If a boy and a girl run for the same rabbit, and the girl is first, then they change garments; the girl rides, and the boy in women's dress goes on foot until he kills a rabbit. Then he pays it to the woman for his clothes; or, if he fails to kill one, then, after sunset he takes a load of wood and fetches it to the girl. Feast on fourth day, after which the boys present the girls with a jícara of flour. Should the hunt be impossible on account of bad weather, then the women have the right, all winter, as often as the men go hunting, to take the game from them, but must invite them on the fourth day. Each girl invites the man whose rabbit or game she took away.

NOVEMBER 18: Rio Grande frozen to a small fillet. Juan José went out hunting. Secured amole. It is simply crushed (pounded), and then beaten in water (hot for the large species, cold for the smaller) to foam. Still they use soap in addition to it. (Gave out my washing to a Mexican woman.)

When, on the 16th at night, I mentioned to Juan Chavez the pumas and named shyayaq, asking him whether this was his name, he replied, "Es su oficio!" [It is his office.] Attempted to begin a vocabulary, arranged grammatically, but found it was too early yet. Made [a map of] the fields of Santo Domingo. Juan José came home with but one rabbit.

I went to the cacique. Very friendly. He belongs to the Hanutsh [clan] of Tzitz (water). His father was Yssi (Ivy); his children are shumute[?]. He says that there are many of his gens in Taos, and some in Nambé. Everything tends to the belief that all the Pueblos are of the same original stock, for he distinctly intimates that the same gentes are found in all the Pueblos. He further says that the eastern estufa belongs to the Shu-amo, and the western to the Tañi, and then all together go back to the Shuamo. He intimates, however, that they do not separate by gentes, but are "todos revueltos." Juan José informs me that the estufas do not belong to these two gentes but that they are thus called. Probably an old and valuable recollection. The cacique further says that in every pueblo there are now two estufas, but that formerly there were more. Took supper at Victoriano's; he is the grandson of Manuelito who killed Perez. Sat down to write to Mr. Norton.

Juan José came in. According to him, it is supposed that in the Teguayu, all the Pueblos were united under one cacique. It appears that, until about fifteen years ago, there was at Cochiti a special tract of land whose crops were gathered separately and kept by the gobernador for the relief of needy members of the Pueblo only. This tract was, however, sold. The tract of the cacique only remains, and this is never attended first, but neither last. What the "secret of the cacique" is, he alone knows. It must be a weighty one, since Juan José says the caciques hardly last longer than twenty years in office. At the rebellion of Taos the people of Cochiti were also called upon to assist, and were ready, but held back expecting an attack upon them.

Juan José's shield is about fifty-three years old. His father pounded the hide with a smooth stone in a pozo in the ground, twice, until it was perfectly smooth on both sides, and can be turned about both ways.

November 19: I went to Peña Blanca. There is only a small fillet of water running in the Brazo, and it is very low also. The bridge is broken, the beavers having eaten the beams. They are very frequent in the river and very large. There are also otters though they are not frequent in the river, but more so in the Valle [Grande]. The Mexicans call them "perritos de agua" (little water dogs).

On the 17th, the thermometer at Padre Ribera's stood at 0.0° again. At 11 A.M. it was 29½°F. within the entrance to the court, therefore inside the door. Padre Ribera tells me that in seven years he has never witnessed such a cold. Letters from Professor Norton and from Papa and Joe.

Went home about 2:30 P.M. and called on several parties, among them, on an old man called Bautista, in whose house there were not less than ten drums, variously painted, nine of which were suspended from the ceiling. I tried in vain to get him to make boxes for me; he scarcely listened. Saw them make chiquihuites and bartered for two. No fire in my room. I tried to close the window with paper. It is very dark now. My washing is done. At Bautista's I also saw pottery newly made, unpainted. Shall buy some if I can. Can hardly stand the cold any longer.

About 8:00 P.M. I was surprised again by the call of my neighbor's wife. She is better and came to have a chat. She spoke of old tepalcates [potsherds] in her possession, and so I went over to see her family. The whole [family] was acostado [had retired] and the room was dimly lighted by the glowing embers. There were two cuartos [rooms], a westerly storeroom and an easterly dwelling room; the latter was very warm and the former correspondingly cold. The outer door was, besides, hung within by a great sheet of heavy white domestic, and the communication between the two (through a thick wall) was by an elliptical doorway, very narrow and low, so that I had to squeeze through with much stooping.

They all got up, and we had a pleasant talk. The tepalcate is a broken piece of Acoma pottery. She says that, even now, the thumbnail is allowed to grow, to make the indentations of the rim in their pottery. The man said that those who came from *Teguayu* and went south are still living at El Paso (the Piros), and that they made the glazed pottery. He also confirms that the fire is kept up in the house of the cacique, but discards the snake story, though perhaps with some embarrassment. Shall return to my neighbor. It appears that Juan Chavez is courting our girl against Juan José's will!

NOVEMBER 20: The day has been spent at home and drawing. Finished letter to Professor Norton. Drew shield of Juan José. Shall send him to Santa Fe tomorrow. It is cheaper than to go myself. Call from Juan de Jesús Pancho. He spent nearly a week in Santa Fe, grinding his wheat at the water-mill; he pays $3.00 for six fanegas. Called at Victoriano's. The good fellow is all heart. Have arranged to copy his shields tomorrow. Victoriano also tells me that they divide into squads of ten when they go to war, the capitán naming the leaders. This is possibly a misunderstanding. Juan Chavez and José Francisco Chavez called on me late. Missed my pen!

NOVEMBER 21: Juan José went to Santa Fe at 10:00 A.M. There is much jealousy about me in the pueblo. I go to Victoriano to paint his two shields.

I did not do much more than copy the shield of Victoriano, and he lent me vermillion and almagre [Indian red]. The wife of Victoriano made a paint brush for me out of the palmillo (*hash-tshya, P. chiquito; ha-tyoni, P. ancho*), cutting it fine, and then pounding its end with a stone, so as to form a brush. The vermillion was but mixed with water, but afterwards José Hilario told me that if used with foam of amole it would stick. Adelaido brought me some amole at home, and indeed, it proved to stick. But the amole had no effect on pencil. The green paint used by them is malachite or copper stain, which they get from the Nuevos Placeres, and then burn with turpentine (so says Juan Chavez?). It is true that Victoriano also tells something similar. The painting and drawing now goes so well that I intend to draw and paint all the implements I can get hold of. It is cheaper than buying.

At night, there were no less than four boys in my room, Hayohua, his brother-in-law Gervasio, Juan Chavez, and José Francisco Pancho. The latter two stayed long again but are very free with their information. I have plenty of fire wood. Hayohua goes to Santa Fe tomorrow and he will return with the box, that is, if he secures a wagon. He suffers from backache. Next Sunday it is the turn of Victoriano to attend to the horses, and they will pasture them about the Potrero de las Vacas and Rito de los Frijoles, sleeping in the Cueva Pintada. On close examination, the vocabulary becomes more simple. Although in reality I have not done much, I am still very tired tonight.

NOVEMBER 22: I copied the second shield of Victoriano.* No letters.* In the afternoon, after finishing my shields at last, I went to call on old man Chavez, and found him and his wife weaving. They were making serapes, and when he sat down to talk, she took his place. They were very communicative.

They all state that the glazed pottery was made by those "pasaron por abajo" [that went south], and that the Pueblo Indians of Chihuahua (they mean the Piros) make it yet. This is an error. But the tradition of a southerly migration is very firmly implanted, and the Piros of Senecu are well known and still recognized as Pueblos. The old man threw out the suggestion that the glazing might be made by burning with turpentine! I strongly urged them to try it next spring. He also says that wooden hoes (cavadores) were used formerly, and also the round pounding stone in place of the metate [mano?]. At night a long call from Luis Montoya and from his wife. Spoke to him about the dress of the malinche, but he referred me to the cacique for the permission to copy them. After them came two boys and Juan Chavez. The latter stayed late, and assisted, or rather guided, me in drawing the weaving stand, which was

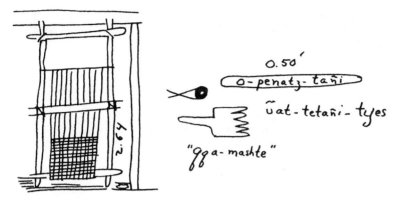

very useful to me. Although I have not done much, still I am satisfied with the day. The discovery that I can draw somewhat is a great relief to me, and I hope now to go ahead better and with greater results.

NOVEMBER 23: Juan José came back early in the morning. He brought all my things and also a long letter from Dr. Thomas requesting me to take the census, if Don Andrés Cabeza de Vaca could not do it. We accordingly went to Peña Blanca at once and on the road met August Wilcken, Mormon Elder, with whom José Hilario had stayed three years ago when he went to California. He was going to Cochiti to preach and convert. Don Andrés said that he would take the census at once, of which I was very glad. So I wrote to Dr. Thomas, and Bennett writes that he may come Friday or Saturday.

Stayed [at Peña Blanca] to dinner with Don Andrés. He told me that, at the Pueblo Quemado, at six feet below the ground, an entire room had once been opened, in which a large tinaja was found filled with flour, which tinaja was, and still may be, in possession of Alejandro Montoya of Cieneguilla. He also has a *chalchihuitl* [turquoise] which came from the ruins, perforated and polished, and he will give it to me if he finds it. He says that the ants often disinter such things. He also assures me that the Indians of Santo Domingo twice sent him back from their village, not allowing him to enter while they were performing their dances. (Obscene?)

Upon our return, met Wilcken on horseback with José Hilario. He may return day after tomorrow. Juan José goes to Santa Fe early in the morning to take our replies to Dr. Thomas. Went to Romero Chavez.* Painted the malacate [windlass] of Juan José. Visit at Romero Chavez very pleasant—they take all possible pains to teach me the language.

I asked the cacique for permission to paint the ornaments of the malinche, and he most graciously consented. So I am going to work tomorrow. As soon as I said that the cacique had given the permission, everything was all right. Ventura offered to bring me the headdress of the malinche, and Juan José will show me the ornaments of the matalote.

November 24: I spent the whole day in painting and sketching the manta of the malinche, but did not get very far, as it is a very complicated pattern. They allowed me to carry it home, where, with the assistance of the governor, I suspended it from the wall. Luis came, evidently to watch me, and was well satisfied when he saw that I appeared successful.

At sunset I took a walk into the plaza where I found boys and young men shooting with bows and arrows. They shoot at a cornstalk and the one whose arrows hit the stalk and remain in it, takes it and inters it unseen by the others. Afterwards, all shoot into the sand heap at short range, and as often as one misses, the one who has interred the stalk takes his arrow from him, until one hits. Afterwards, I set up a twenty-five cent piece on a stick of about one foot in height, and they shot at it at a distance of ten paces. Although it was dusky, the shots were fair, and Adelaido Montoya finally hit it. I placed another twenty-five cents in the hands of Victoriano, to be shot for tomorrow evening.

At night it was very dark. Still I went to see Victoriano who had killed an ox today and the whole animal was lying, spread out in pieces, on the floor. We talked for awhile and I went home, but it was so dark that I scarcely found my way and had trouble in getting down the ladders. At night, Juan Chavez and José Francisco Pancho came, and stayed till 10:00 P.M. Tonight, I am sleeping with two dogs, Amate and a little black and white pup having come in. Wind from the east. Bad omen.

NOVEMBER 25: Pen appears to work badly. Still, she [i.e., die Feder] may improve after a while. The mode of sticking the cleaner inside, is a very bad one. Ignacio began to tell me the mode of their songs but we were interrupted.

I worked the whole day at the manta of the malinche. It is very difficult, but the privilege of copying it is such a great one that I will do the utmost in my power. In the evening, the boys again practiced with the bow, and twice, at a distance of thirty-six feet, the quarter was carried off. In the afternoon both boys came back, each one with a piece of límita, a stick with a knot or notch in the middle of the length with which they are going to make my two bows for Oscar and Charlie. (The bow gives the bend of the bow.) They began to whittle at once. At sunset, Adelaido fixed a string to his bow, by splitting simply a strip of gamuza [antelope skin] and tying it. It made a fair cord. Juan José returned after sunset, with a pleasant letter from Dr. Thomas and one from Bennett. The latter will come tomorrow. José Hilario also brought my mail from Peña Blanca: letter from Professor Norton and one from Dr. Bruhl.

Tomorrow I will finish, if possible, with the dress of the malinche. Dr. Thomas sent me two erasers. This dress of the malinche is regarded as a very valuable piece. Juan José says that his mother made it about thirty years ago, and that while there used to be two in the Pueblo, this is the only one now extant. In every Pueblo there are similar patterns, though not identical. The pattern in each Pueblo is, however, consecrated, and if one manta is used up, it is faithfully copied. The manta is the property of Juan José's sister, or rather, she has it in trust, but her father bought the cloth, or rather had it woven.

NOVEMBER 26: Andrés Cabeza de Vaca took the census with José Hilario. They were through by 2:00 P.M. with only one family having refused to give its name. Result: 268 Indians, 54 houses (casas), and 68 families. He had much trouble at Santo Domingo, although the governor went with him; 1,135 Indians, besides 7 families who refused to give their names. Bautista Calabaza refused to allow him to take the measure of his shield for me, on the ground that I would only make fun of it. I asked Juan José if there was a compact or league between the five Pueblos of Queres, and he said yes—that if one called for help the others had to assist. In case of war, it is the war captain of the endangered pueblo who commands the forces.

All day, the floor of my room was being fixed by filling it up with adobe earth mixed with straw. Juan José carried the earth, etc., and Luisa Montoya spread it. It is still wet tonight, but they have been careful to spread skins and old serapes. I worked all day at the manta of the malinche, and hope to be through in three days.

At night Juan José finally told me the secret of the paintings on the manta. The upper zigzag lines signify lightning (el rayo, not el relámpago); the lower, the cloud which brings rain and thus fructifies the earth, symbol of good times. It is also the clouds dropping rain, and the outer figures are rain clouds—raindrops, too. The crown signifies the rainbow. The whole also belongs to the Kachinas. What these are I do not know as yet. He also says that in such paintings there is no red tolerated, as red is the color of hail, epidemics, war, and starvation, and if, for a Baile del Caballero [War Dance] there is no such manta in any pueblo, they go to borrow one for that purpose. There is, consequently, great superstition attached to it. At the same time he justified their adoration "despues de Dios" [after God] of the sun, moon, stars, and earth, remarking that we would be nowhere without them. (I have constant trouble with my stylographic pens. The new one even refuses to work sometimes. It is very sad that Bennett has not come.)

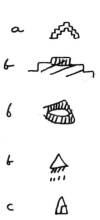

NOVEMBER 27: The result of the census for Cochiti appears doubtful. Juan José says that there are 70 hombres de armas [warriors]. He also told me that, at *Teguayo*, everything was

clear which now is hidden, speaking of the secrets of nature. I decided to go to Peña Blanca. Manuel Montoya had not yet made my slippers, having been ill. Don Jesús again drunk. Had to take dinner with him and Mr. Whitney of Santa Fe, and George. Padre Rómulo returned from Santa Fe about 2 P.M. My box is there, but Hayohua had called for it already. Zashua returned from the south today, whither he had gone to sell brooms. On Sunday the poor boy had received a note to me from Padre Ribera but had forgotten to deliver it. He was very sorry, and I, too. Don Tomasito sold me his saltillero [pistol?] (at the pueblo they call them artilleros) for $15.00.

Result of the census at Cia, 58 souls; at Santa Ana, 493. But the count of Cia is doubtful, as there are only 13 able-bodied men. José Hilario found out "que se los corrieron" [that they ran away?]. Juan José, however, thinks it may be correct. Called on Victoriano, who is going with the caballada (horseherd) tomorrow for a whole week at the Cuesta Colorada.

Met Telisfero Lucero, who informed me that there was a vereda [trail] leading up to the Potrero de los Idolos from the north side. As it is, I have to wait for Bennett till Monday. If then he does not come, I shall go and try to draw the lions myself. (Commenced a letter to Professor Norton tonight.)

NOVEMBER 28: Was at work all day at the manta, and by 11:00 P.M. can at last lay it aside. The embroidery is all sketched at last. Juan José told me that everything in the house, even all the food, belongs to the housewife. He can sell no corn without the consent of his girl [daughter], and no one is allowed to touch the contents of the ollas.

Met a Jemez Indian. Their name for Jemez, Tu-hoa; and for Pecos, Aquiu. The Queres called the Pecos, Paēqo. This explains, at last, the origin of the name, as the latter first appears on record in 1598, at the junta of Santo Domingo. Told Juan José to find out what the Tigua called Pecos.

My eyes swim, I must go to bed (11:30 P.M.). Very tired. Luis Montoya told me today that the round towers at the Rito de los Frijoles were Spanish work. Juan José also told me about

the Kachinas. He represents them as good, not bad, and as intercession *"por el bien del pueblo"* [for the welfare of the tribe],
but that the Mexicans are strictly forbidden to see them. They
are held in the timber. A few years ago Telisfero Lucero was
nearly killed by the Indians of Cochiti on that account.

NOVEMBER 29: Returned the mantle of the malinche this morning, and then went to Peña Blanca. Previous to leaving, had
talked with Don Felipe Sandoval. He told me that the proper
Merced of the Rito de los Frijoles was in the hands of Pedro
Montoya at Cieneguilla, and that it was to the Montoya [fam-
ily] originally, and not to the Salas [family]. He also says that
the Merced of the Bajada is the oldest one in the country.
Juan José informs me that the name of Bajada was originally
Majada [sheep fold] and that Padre Chavez changed it.

Bennett came, and we went to Cochiti in the wagon of Jesús
Sena. But it being Tuesday tomorrow, no one will leave on that
day, and so we shall start Wednesday. The Santo Domingo
dialect has no "r." José Hilario married from Cia, and there appears to be little opposition to intermarriage between other
Pueblos. Juan José told us two stories about coyotes pursuing
him once, one of them near the Bajada, and he firmly believes
it to have been a brujo. He also told about a tall deer pursuing
him in the Cuesta Colorada, which he shot and killed finally.

NOVEMBER 30: Photographed all day but secured only two sets
of pictures, one of Juan José, Ignacia, and Adelaido with arms
and implements, and one of the pueblo looking northwest from
the church top. Both first-class, but Ignacia got after the pictures and scratched the first set badly. Still they are serviceable.
On top of the church I gathered many specimens of pottery,
recent—painted, glazed, and corrugated. Also lava and obsidian,
moss agates, flint, etc., showing that the soil was taken from
the vicinity. Some of the flues and chimneys are very wide, and
made of wood daubed over.

DECEMBER 1: Pedro went to Peña Blanca first to get some

whiskey for me. Felt very ill in my bowels. Started finally, about
10:00 A.M., Adelaido, José Hilario, Bennett, four horses, one
mule, and I. Reached the Cueva Pintada at 2 P.M. (and caught
a live water-beetle). Took good views of the cave. Arroyo
frozen, but current running beneath. Reached ruin in the canyon at sunset and made fire at the same place where I stopped
with Juan José. Saw bear tracks. There is quite a cliff pueblo
east of the Cueva. Met Victoriano at the cave. Found fragments of a stone-hammer at the rim of the Cuesta.

DECEMBER 2: (Cuesta Colorada.) Very cold. Almost impossible to measure. Ink froze on the body [in my pocket]; very
little pottery—some glazed. Started 9 A.M.* This ruin is on the
right bank of the arroyo, and beneath the Potrero de las Casas.
In the canyon itself the trees are good, and there is considerable
vegetation. This end has nine rooms of equal size almost, and
some of the lower walls are still standing. It is built of the usual
blocks of tuff. [This ruin is designated as L. A. 3840.]

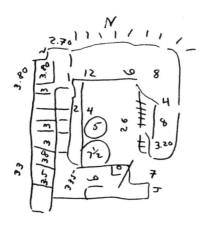

We reached only the rear part of the Potrero de las Vacas.
It still has snow on the top, but fair grass, and the caballada is
up here. On the Potrero de las Casas, one half-mile south of the
ruin, there is also a painted cave. This is the cave which Juan

José has told me of, remarking that the aborigines, when they abandoned a pueblo, painted the Kachinas in these caves nearby. Both [the stone lions of the Potrero de las Vacas]

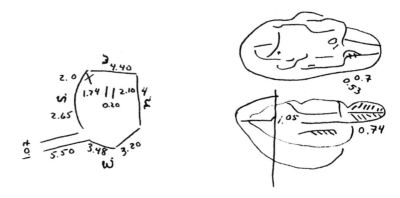

otherwise alike, and cut out of the rock, a volcanic tuff, not very hard. The sabino in the southwest corner is about 14 feet high and 15 inches in diameter. The slabs are of various sizes. The upright one in the northwest corner is 1.25 meters high, 0.48 meter wide, 0.25 meter thick, but the one lying on the edge in the southeast corner is 1.58 meters long, 0.58 meter wide, and 0.12 meter thick. The enclosure has been formed of large blocks piled against each other. José Hilario anointed the idols with almagre in my presence.

About 100 yards south of the lions, we found a square opening in the top-rock about 0.25 meter deep, and 0.50 x 0.30. What for? In the enclosure of the lions, there was some obsidian, lava and glazed pottery, which I mixed with those of the potrero. The distance from the lions to the pueblo is about one half-mile and the lions occupy the highest part of the potrero, right above the ravine beneath the Potrero de la Cuesta Colorada. We thus secured four views today, but when at night Bennett went to fix the plates, both views of the lions peeled off, and he swore tall. So we shall have to return to the statues tomorrow again.

It won't be very easy, as the path up is horrible and even dangerous. And then it will be difficult to reach the Rito in time tomorrow. We sleep in a cave 2¼ meters high, which forms a part of a suite of three rooms. It is very pleasant, after last night's sufferings. Potrero de las Vacas.* Much obsidian. Pottery glazed, and black and white, also corrugated. Lava chips, moss agates, flint, no metates or doorsills. Stepped [off] a part [of the ruin]. Rooms larger. No stories visible.

These two slabs,* or posts of red stone, apparently sandstone, with prints of stops for feet, were lying outside of the main estufa. The height of the larger one agrees with the depth of the estufa, and both Adelaido and José Hilario declared them to be guacos, ladders![123] Farther east in the plaza there were also fragments of a lava post pointed, which at first sight appeared to be like a cross, but we could not make it fit. Descended into the Cañón del Alamo by a fearful trail covered with snow, where horses, and even the mule, fell. Juan José calls this the Cañada Honda, but José Hilario insists that it is the head of the Cañón del Alamo. We pass the night in a good cave. This bend is full of cliff-houses, some of them built outside. Not a trace of pottery or stone implements. Fine vegetation in the canyon and much grass.*

DECEMBER 3: Started from the canyon at 9:00 A.M. Warm. Got up to the lions at 10 A.M. and took two other views. Then, after sending Adelaido to Cochiti for meat, etc., we went to the Rito de los Frijoles, meeting on the way Luis (Shyu-ote) and another old man of the pueblo. Reached the Rito at 5 P.M. and took rooms in the "house of the cacique." Luis told me that the tradition is, the cacique of the Pueblo used to gather the común [tribe]. The others joined us soon. I asked them as to the traditions associated with the Rito, and they particularly insisted that this was part of the Teguayo.

The latter they identified with the q'ash-q'átreshtie [white

<hr>

123. Bandelier's recording here suggests a Spanish term though this could not be found in Velásquez. The phonetic form, wákos, may be preferable since it suggests an Indian, or specifically, a Keresan, term for ladder.

house] of the Navajo country, and distinctly added that the Mexicans call it *Teguayo*, thus implying that this name may be of Spanish origin, perhaps? One of them, Cristóbal, is about seventy years of age. He was at Santa Fe when they killed Perez, and says that the Abreus were killed by those of Santo Domingo by the roadside, where the pile of stones is erected. He also was one of those who guided the American engineers to New Mexico and hid the maps and charts in their chungas [chonga, or club of hair] or pig-tails, so that the Mexicans could not find them.

From here, they say the Jemez, Queres, Tigua, etc., scattered, settling as different pueblos; here they were all together as one people, after they had left the *Teguayo*.

Room of the cacique. Height 2.30 meters. The top is very smoky. Door. I found my pottery all safe and intact; also the stone implements. The night is very clear and warm, even, and as we sleep six in the room together, it is very comfortable. Opened the second can of beef this morning and also finished it completely.

DECEMBER 4: The rooms are remarkably well preserved in most cases, and much stonework used.* The goats have filled them with their dung. Went up west and examined the cliffs. Everything in its place. Snow ceased about 10 A.M., and we photographed the central part, the houses outside, and the projecting end with caves. These views were taken from the south side of the arroyo (the shady side), standing with the instruments in snow up to the ankles and with a fierce northwesterly wind blowing, making it necessary to hold the instruments.

Took dinner of tortillas and coffee without sugar; then measured the cluster of caves above the ruins and above the group of erosion cones. The climbing was difficult, but it is evident that little paths led up to every house. The floor is perfect in most cases, also the yellow plastering. The ceiling is generally smokey and sooty. Luis and the others left early for the top to cut brooms. José Hilario carried wood. Adelaido did not come. Our coffee is diminishing, and the sugar and meat are gone.

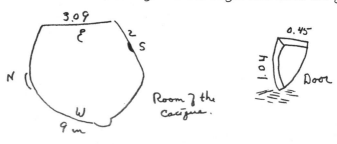

Room of the Cacique.

Not a trace of animal life, except crows and an occasional *sho-haqqa* [?].

There are, lower down, several of these large circular rooms like our present quarters. Were they estufas? The Indians say not; they are all houses, and the estufas were those below in the valleys. Asking them about it, I ascertained from them that at Acoma and at Taos, the gentes are still kept separate, and go to separate estufas in a body. The name of *Shipeue* [a kind of sage] is also found in Cochiti, but they do not know the meaning of it. They say that at Taos there are gentes of the eagle, bear, puma, etc. The pottery is prevailingly glazed. The men found several stone hammers in the caves west. In general the ruins are very rich in fine fragments of pottery and manos, fragments of metates, etc. also obsidian and lava.

But there are no traces of fields. There is a good deal of black and white pottery, too, but no indented and corrugated pieces at all. Tomorrow we intend to finish here. Then we shall try to reach Cochiti or the Cañada on Monday.*

Every room has its fireplace, except such as were evidently used as storehouses. The ruins are in groups, and the deep recesses and reentering angles of the cliffs are avoided, notwithstanding the numbers of caves which they naturally contain. The photographs, if successfully brought to Santa Fe, will be very good. It will not be possible for me to go higher up, although Juan José has assured me that there are two or three small pueblos in caves higher up yet. The ruins farther down are very well kept, and their walls are similar to those of the other pueblos. The round towers are, according to the people here, the work of the Salas [family]. But the date is not known.

The boy is chewing chiquihuite de pingue, *ne-etsh* [pine gum?], which is said to be very good for the chest. Tortillas gave out tonight, and no Adelaido. Prospects hungry. We have plenty of ocote for the night. Cristóbal went home.

DECEMBER 5: Last night Juan José himself came about 6 P.M. with every necessary provision. There is a difference of opinion in regard to the casa del común. Juan José says it is another house, farther east. I rather believe Luis and José Hilario. Am writing this at 3 A.M. (Juan José has been bragging terribly about his exploits.)

In general, the rooms of the eastern half are larger than those of the western section, there are even a number of very large ones. They are all plastered yellow, and smoky above.* Lowest ruin in the valley, about 30 meters north of arroyo, 640 meters southeast from round towers.* Double round tower. This tower is made of a double wall of pumice stone, and therefore double thickness. Two stories are visible, and so is the white plaster inside. The vigas [rafters] are round and still to be seen. It is partly well preserved, and evidently of Spanish make, as the tradition has it, too.

The lowest ruin stands immediately over the arroyo, and some places are well preserved, thus the northwest corner of one room is about 2 feet above the ground. Glazed pottery in large pieces; also black and white. This morning we went out to photograph west of our room, and took four views, all very good. Then I completed the eastern end, which is very rugged and almost impossible to survey owing to steep slopes and erosion cones, etc. Part of it I merely counted the rooms far below.

Many of the rooms contained carved walls, but while the carvings may have been made by Indians, they are certainly posterior to abandonment of the caves, as they are carved in the plastering. Stood in the cave all afternoon, talking.

DECEMBER 6: [The people of] Isleta near El Paso del Norte are in bad reputation as brujos (shyatz [shaiyak(?) hunt shamans] also). Started from the Rito early, and took a stereoscopic view of the Cañón del Norte, reaching the Cañada de Cochiti at sunset. Juan José left us at the foot of the Potrero de los Idolos. Was glad of it. José Hilario turned sullen also.

Stopped at the house of Luis Lucero. He was not at home, but his wife offered us hospitality. Gave up the idea of photographing the other lion. At night, Señora Lucero and José Hilario talked about the Pueblos. He is very positive about the fact that the inhabitants of Cuahpa retired to the Potrero Viejo

for safety from the attacks of the Tehua. The latter also attacked the Potrero Viejo, and the fight lasted all day. At night the Tehua were beaten back and the Cochiteños pursued them, driving them across the Rio Grande with great slaughter.

Telisfero and Herrera both do not recollect the time when the lion of the Potrero de los Idolos was not mutilated. They both positively assert that the round towers at the Rito de los Frijoles are the work of the early Spanish settlers. Lower down the Rito, on a bluff, there is another small ruin which I did not see, but Juan José saw it. No supper tonight, but an excellent warm room and kind reception. The conduct of Juan José is very childish. In the canyon of the Rio Grande my horse fell into a gulch, and I fell over his head, but without hurting myself or the horse—although both were very likely to happen.

DECEMBER 7: Took the view of the Potrero Viejo from in front of the house of Luis Lucero, stereoscopic. At 9 A.M. started for the Potrero Viejo on foot, the mule alone along, carrying the apparatus. Took the road to the ruin of the potrero south, and then ascended by a path, not as steep as the other paths, but still very bad, to the top. Along this whole side there are still walls of stones piled up, along the brink, dating back to the time when the pueblo was inhabited.

Photographed a section of the walls from the west side, and then José Hilario went down to the Cañada to get the horses, while we descended with the mule to the road to wait for him. There are two water tanks on the potrero also, but I did not see them. Reached the Barranca Blanca at 3:30 P.M., passing on the north and east side of the valley of the *Kolle* [Canyon] (In Queres, *Quetz-i-qaash*). This name is Queres, and signifies the descent into a room from above by a ladder. Reached Cochiti by 5 P.M. Very kindly received. Trip so far glorious. (My nose is again very sore. Wrote home.)

DECEMBER 8: (Written on the 10th.) Went to Peña Blanca; there received letters from Joe, from Dr. W. J. Hoffmann, and from Icazbalceta. Arranged with the Padre to get Bennett to Santa Fe. Leandro came with the ambulance. The bridge is fast falling to pieces, one of the vigas is down. The bridge over the Brazo is still entire, because the beavers have not touched it. In the afternoon I worked at the mantle of the malinche, after Bennett had left me, to stop at the Padre's until tomorrow night.

At night, Mariano Garbán, the gobernador of Cia, came, and he, Juan José, Hayohua, and another Indian stayed in my room till 10 P.M. talking loud, which troubled me a great deal. Finally all went except the governor of Cia, who slept in my room. I gave him two of my white serapes to use. I arranged with him to go to Cia next year and to stay at his house. He says that there are six ruins near Cia, all of stone, and that he will show them to me, and also go to Acoma with me. He saw the mantle of the *Tzimat*, and said that at Cia there was a similar one.

According to his statements, Cia contains 20 houses, 31 hombres de armas, and 92 souls. He enumerated the latter, so that I conclude his account to be correct. This shows the kind of work Librado [clerk?] Cabeza de Vaca has done. He and Juan José talked a long while about the robberies committed on the pueblos of Santa Ana and of Cia. It appears that their cattle are stolen, and that when they catch the thieves, these fire upon them. The agent, it appears, does not assist them. They are now going to have a general junta of the Pueblos to have their grievances placed before Congress. If they do not succeed, they will turn over the case to me.

DECEMBER 9: Worked all day at the mantle of the malinche. Mariano went for me to Peña Blanca and brought candles (and a letter from Norton). At night, I called on Victoriano, but he was gone. Mariano came again, but went off, because they were dancing in the pueblo—preparing for the dances of Christmas. In the afternoon, Juan José showed me how they fixed bows, anointing them with tallow, when they bend with the greatest ease. To smoothen the arrow sticks, they use a stone grooved lengthwise, and rub the stick through it up and down until it is smooth and polished. Hayohua came a moment to take some tobacco. He went dancing, and wore the maxtlatl, whereas otherwise he always wears pantaloons.

DECEMBER 10: Worked at the manta. Mariano left. Victoria, the sister of Juan José, came to invite me to breakfast. I went, but could hardly eat, as I had breakfasted before. The food, pozole of maize with chile, was very good, however. Better than the infernal chile. In the afternoon, I went to Peña Blanca and waited for Leandro. He finally came, but did not bring anything else than the box. He had not called on Bennett again. No money. Happily the Padre will help me, and José Hilario went to Santa Fe this morning. Thank God and my dear people for the box. We opened it deeply.

DECEMBER 11: The Padre lent me $35.00 this morning. Bought a serape, two tilmitas, and he gave me a beautiful tilmita and some pottery. He went over to the Cañada for the festival tomorrow, and took me along. The bridge is down in the water. Nearly all the horses are sick. Spent part of the night at Victoriano's, bought his guante [glove?], and his wife presented me with a tinaja. Began packing. Wrote to Norton, or at least began.

DECEMBER 12: All gone to the Cañada, and left me alone without food. I wrote to Norton and Morgan. In the afternoon the Padre came, and took along with him some loza. It is very lonesome. Wrote also to Dr. Bruhl and to Icazbalceta.

Juan José came home; the feast was a success, and they were still dancing—Mexicans only. Navajo in the pueblo, but they are very dear with their goods. At night, Juan José called and also Hayohua. They had been dancing Kachinas in the house of Juan Chavez, and he [Juan José?] frankly confessed that it was not permitted to see them, although he formally denied that they danced naked. He passed the night with me in the same bed. There has been a general meeting tonight, and Zashua, who came in and stayed sometime, had to go also being alguacil.

José Hilario returned with the things, but without money. George S. had none. How different is the Padre, and even Bennett! I shall see at Santa Fe. Hayohua wants to come along to Mexico with me, and I shall take him along. Hayohua says the Kachinas may perhaps be free to me when I return, and that they are perfectly decent.

DECEMBER 13: Began to take leave. Went to the governor, to the cacique, to Romero Chavez, to Quintana, to Juan Chavez, took leave of the sacristán, of the wife and sister of Victoriano, of the wife of José Hilario, of Merced, even of Agustín; of Señora Montoya, bought two chiquihuites.

Everywhere the friendliest wishes and greetings.

It appears that the junta of last night was again about Agustín and Juan José. The former now wants the latter to be punished by the Pueblo. Juan José very sensibly replied that the case was now settled, and that he had paid the cost. At dinner, horrible chile and onions, cold. Wrote card to Gatschet. Don Tomás Ribera came for me in the ambulance. Padres Truchard, Gromm, and Acorsini ate here. Ate well again, attended vespers, and spent a very pleasant evening till midnight.

DECEMBER 14: Last night the Padre bought from Hayohua, one fine tilma for $7.50 for me. After two early masses, service, High Mass, was performed at 10 A.M. I went behind the altar to sing with Hayohua and Zashua. Padre Acorsini led us, and afterwards the vicar-general himself came to assist us. The voices of the boys are uncultivated, therefore very raw, and they sing Dumont's masses, etc., more from memory and faultier "drill" than from anything else. Still there is something like corrrect hearing, for they stop whenever they find out that they are wrong. Padre Gromm sang the office with a very good voice, and Padre Truchard preached on the apparition of Nuestra Señora de Guadalupe. He has the voice of a stentor, and once had certainly a very handsome baritone.

After the service, a procession was formed. The church was full, and one-third more were outside. Nearly all the people of

Cochiti had turned out—men and women, girls and boys, in their best apparel. Many of Santo Domingo came also, and some of San Felipe; also Mariano from Cia. The governor of Santo Domingo was very friendly. He told me he was glad to get out of office on the first of January, having now been governor nine times. He complained about the weight of the office and wore a magnificent set of turquoises on his necklace. I had also the joy to meet Santiago Tenorio again. The poor boy was overjoyed.

He knew nothing of my being at Cochiti, until his father told him of it two days ago. He is as handsome as ever. No Indians took part in the procession, but they were very affectionate toward me. Victoriano was peculiarly affectionate, and his sister also came, very handsomely dressed. The women nearly all wore new mantles with red embroideries.

At 1 P.M., the padres left for Santa Fe. Gervasio, cousin to Hayohua, called me out in secret and sold me a small image, in alabaster, of a puma (*moqqat* [*mo-katch*]) which he says he found in the sierra. He confessed to me that it was the image of *Shyayaq*, and that they carried it in little leather bags, thus plainly confirming Pacífico Baca. He was very anxious to have me conceal it. Gave my knife to Santiagito Tenorio. Am tired and worn out. Eating, which was very good, does not fill my empty stomach, which always calls for more.

At nightfall I went out to see the races, which took place in the lane leading from Jesús Sena's house to the river. A considerable crowd was assembled, excited and shouting, Mexicans as well as Indians of Cochiti. When I reached them, they were just closing the race. Nearly all were more or less affected by liquor, and the whole crowd went into the house of Jesús Sena. The governor of Cochiti, Serafín, begged me, 10 P.M., before leaving, for a drink. At about 9 P.M., Juan José badly intoxicated, José Hilario on his white horse, holding its tail, and very tall drunk, dragged Zashua, beastly drunk, to the house of the Padre, asking him to take charge of the boy for the night. He refused, and they went off.

Manuel Montoya, who claims to be one of the heirs of the Rito de los Frijoles, told me yesterday that the towers were an heirloom to the Montoyas, made by the Captain, Andrés Montoya. The soil of the Rito was so fertile, that one fanega of frijoles gave ten to twelve fanegas, and maize yielded double. He also said that there was much old pottery, of very large size, still at Algodones and at Peña Blanca. The Padre also tells me that at Santo Domingo there is much less drunkenness than at Cochiti, but that he never saw the Indians of Cochiti going on a wholesale spree like the one of today. The whiskey was all bought at Jesús Sena's, as we ascertained by going to him in the evening in order to pay his bill. We surprised, involuntarily, the ladies dressing for a fandango. There was a great deal of noise in the tienda [store], and we retired without seeing Don Jesús, who had been sober until then.

DECEMBER 15: Zashua came for his serape, and the Padre told him that I had taken it along with me, but the boy did not believe him and stole into the house and got his serape. We went to Jesús Sena and settled his account—$77.25, so that, after deducting the $65.00 I paid Don Jesús, I remained owing the Padre $83.20. Don Jesús presented me with a fine Navajo tilmita. Left for Santa Fe about 10 A.M., the Padre himself driving. Señora Sandoval came along. Reached Santa Fe at sunset.

DECEMBER 16 and 17: At Santa Fe. Met three Taos Indians at the Indian agency, hideously painted. They call Taos in their idiom, Te-ga-ta, and Picurís, Ui-la-ta. Settled up all affairs and made my calls. Expenses finally $106.35 and $8.65 from board. This includes box for $5.00.

DECEMBER 18: Met Mr. Hough yesterday at Mr. Ritch's. Left Santa Fe 8 A.M. Had to take another engine at the junction to cross the Sierra to Glorieta. Covered vast fields of snow and quiet till Trinidad, which we reached about 11 P.M.

DECEMBER 19: Reached La Junta, Colorado, at 3:40 A.M.

DECEMBER 20: Reached St. Louis at 6 P.M. Attempted in vain to go to Highland; the train would not stop for me.[124] Thus went to Nan's and spent the night there. W. P. and A. D. W. after me. Expenses on the trip $19.50.

DECEMBER 21: Reached home safe at 9 A.M. Surprise complete. All well. Saw even old Aenni. She is very low. Everybody overjoyed [at my return].

DECEMBER 22: Slept well for the first time again, and perspired very strongly. In the afternoon went to the farm. Graffenried and Wachsmuth are still lazy, almost depressed, and always glad to go to bed.

DECEMBER 23: Wrote and mailed letters to Padre Ribera, to Juan José, to the vicar-general, Truchard. Called on Aenni in the afternoon and at the post office. The box came. The tinaja which I bought from Zashua is broken, and the piece of old glazed pottery is in pieces also; otherwise, all safe. Rosalie came in the afternoon. Went to see Maechtlin with the photographs. A petition was presented to me to deliver an address. Edward came home from Chicago tonight. Tonight Seybt came.

While at Peña Blanca, the Padre and brother-in-law, Jesús Sandoval, confirmed the former statement of Juan José about the original name of the Bajada as Majada. The latter means a place where cattle rest at night.

DECEMBER 24: Sent the photos to Norton. Had Eddy again in the morning. Always the same. Spent an hour at Weber's. Wrote to Gerdes. Afternoon at the priest's, and at several places. Weighed myself at H. Meyer's, 150 pounds. Very unpleasant day. Another cold. Christmas tree at Bertha's, fine; pleasant evening. Usual gossiping in town.

Governor Ritch told me that, at Santo Domingo, they had their naked dances at night and in darkness. He calls them the penitentes, and says that two Americans witnessed them, but did not care for more of it. Papa returned to the farm tonight to spend Christmas.

DECEMBER 25: In regard to the word heat, which I have as *oeroe-matze* and *oeroesh-quatshe*, this evidently signifies little

---

124. St. Louis, Vandalia, and Terre Haute Railroad.

and big warmth. *Oeroe-roeshquish* and *oeroe-mae-tsitsh.* Heat would therefore be *oeroe?*

DECEMBER 26: Quiet. Very sore nose. Indoors all day.

DECEMBER 27: Suffering very much from sore nose. Dr. Walliser gave me remedy. Decided to go east, and wrote to Norton and to Morgan about it. Letter from Morgan.

DECEMBER 28: Sent off letters to Norton and to Morgan. Worked at the *tzimat,* but Papa thought I should not go any further, so I went at the vocabulary. It is much more complete than I thought, and there are a number of names and words, also many more verbs and conjugations. In working at it I find much more regularity than I really expected, and the small words—interjections, conjunctions, etc., are confirmed and clearly expressed. The information secured from the Indians thus becomes of greater and positive value. It proves to have been truthful and reliable—principally what the young men, Hayohua, Zashua, and Juan Chavez told me. The language also becomes much more simple. There is no trace of the famous monosyllabism.

DECEMBER 29: Had calls from Pabst, and Hough, and from Gruaz. The lecture is to take place on January 5, Wednesday. Kept on at the vocabulary all day.

DECEMBER 30: At vocabulary all day. Went out in the afternoon to J. Scheule. Now improving rapidly. At night, meeting with Gruaz. No letters yet.

DECEMBER 31: Last day of an eventful year. Completed the vocabulary by 3 P.M. Mr. Balsiger dined with us. Letter from Hecker today.

Thus the most important year of my entire life draws to a close. Thank God, thank God for every blessing, every sore, for weal and for woe, which He has been pleased to dispense. So far, so good, and there is hope for better. Papa went out on the farm at sunset.

We spent the evening quietly at home, Widmer, Joe, Maly,

and I, talking. Took a bottle of white wine before going to bed. There is very little shooting, etc., going on in town. The brass band from Trenton came late, playing.

Have no reflections to record. Future action is all that occupies my thoughts.

1 8 8 2

THE BEGINNING of the year 1882 found Bandelier at home in Highland, Illinois, working on the 1881 Mexican material; reorganizing notes and painting water colors from sketches made during the 1880 trip to New Mexico; lecturing; and continuing library research in St. Louis. At the same time he was negotiating for further work in the Southwest.

During this period Bandelier expresses considerable concern over the health of his wife, Joe, and at the same time complains frequently about the bad weather in southern Illinois.[125] These factors, plus increasing tensions between Bandelier and his father, combined to make Bandelier all the more anxious to return to the Southwest.

Finally on March 13, 1882, he left with Joe for a rather leisurely journey by train across the plains to New Mexico. On the 17th of March the Bandelier family left La Junta, Colorado, for the final part of the trip to Santa Fe. At this point we resume the daily journals of Adolph F. Bandelier.

MARCH 17: Left La Junta at 12 midnight. Cars very much

---

125. As an illustration of his complaints, we quote from the journal entry of February 27, 1882, "Rain became very strong in the afternoon. Wind changing to the N.W. It is beyond all description. I never saw such a Winter before, and I hope it will be the last one. It is the meanest, most abominable climate ever heard of, and I cannot conceive how reasonable people ever could attempt to settle in such a country. There is no relief, nothing to invigorate, everything is depression, weariness, dirt, sloth, and ugliness. Oh! God bless the Tropics, in comparison with this awful mudhole. It is a mudhole physically as well as spiritually. The people, with very few exceptions, are mere moles and salamanders. Rain ceased at nightfall. Blustering from N.W. Cool."

crowded. Had to take sleeping-cars, and secured the drawing-room. Slept for awhile and awoke in the Ratones. The winter scenery is not as fine as the effects of summer. The grass is dry, the oaks and hollys also, the piñones alone, and the sabinos preserve some verdure. Coal-seams traverse the rocks; the miners' huts are occasionally visible. Twice I had a good view of the Spanish Peaks. They appear like an isolated double cone.*

At Willow Creek I was surprised to find how much the place had grown. Even a bank, the "Raton Bank," a rickety-looking frame shanty, by the way, is in the place. A large eating-house at the depot. The plateau beyond is very arid and as desolate as ever. At Wagon Mound, lava, brown and black, appears. The road passes them between two bold lava crags which rise abruptly out of the plateau. Large bold mesas appear beyond Springer. The high tops, snowclad, of the Spanish Peaks and of the Costilla, are very plainly seen, although the sky covers rapidly. Las Vegas has grown largely and has streetcars. Entering the Cañón Amarillo we passed by Pecos in sight of the ruins. Kingman has grown a little, so has Glorieta, but the buildings at Baughl's have all disappeared. . . . Reached Santa Fe at 7 P.M. and met with most cordial welcome from everybody. Ugly letters from the east. Professor Norton is acting very badly.

MARCH 18: Went out with Joe, who is feeling much better in the head. Everywhere the same cordiality. Jac. Gold has a magnificent collection of Indian goods. Got the lacking stereoscope views from Brown. Many Pueblo Indians here. I met a few from Cochiti. They told me that no changes had occurred, except in the usual roll of officers.

Day exceedingly quiet. Spent part of the afternoon at Governor Ritch's. He was very kind and showed me a pencil drawing made by a young Indian of Jemez, which I shall copy. It absolutely confirms the statements of Juan José Montoya about the mantle of Cochiti. Governor Ritch also told me that Antonio, the old Pecos chief at Jemez, told him that when the

Spaniards came (this was evidently in 1692 with Vargas), they took some Pecos Indians along to the heights of Santa Fe, but could not enter the town. That the old building near Guadalupe Church was the "house of the peones" and the church itself, the "church of the peones."

This would indicate that both really existed prior to 1680. If so, it is very important and interesting. Antonio also stated that the pueblo was then on the site of old Fort Marcy. But this may be doubtful. Saw the archives, they are still partly in disorder. There is a better feeling between the Americans and Mexicans than before. Ritch himself appears less bitter than usual. He takes great interest in antiquities. I wrote two letters to Parkman, one official, and one confidential. Also a few lines to Papa. Called on the Archbishop and on Father Eguillon, but they were not at home.

MARCH 19: [We] took a walk over the lomas around the foot of Fort Marcy and found obsidian right below the Fort. Went to the top of the lomas south of the Fort and the wind blowing stronger, returned about 11:30 A.M. It was a trial, and Joe stood it well. There must be a sandstorm in the Rio Grande Valley. The city has grown considerably. New houses have sprung up, some two-story, of stone and brick, some one-story of adobe, with metallic roofs. The latter houses are very fine and good-looking. Joe suffering from her eyes. It is the dust and wind. Saw Swope and spoke about trip to Tesuque. Met many friends, but principally wrote to the *Ausland*. Shall soon be through.

MARCH 20: Took a little walk with Joe, but the mountains west are hazy, and it appeared as if a very heavy sandstorm was blowing in the valley. I then called on Father Eguillon and on Father Gromm. They are very well pleased with times now. Had a very pleasant time. At home I finished the letter to the *Ausland* and mailed it. Then called on Dr. Thomas and Mr. Milburn. Very kind. Promised a lecture. Milburn told me that, at Jemez, they had the secret practice of shutting up a boy of fourteen years of age with a girl of twelve for forty-eight hours in a room!!¹²⁶ At the archives, I saw Ellison.

In the afternoon I went out with Joe to the south side of the city. Returned at 5 P.M. Meeting of the Historical Society. Not very interesting on the whole. Talk about the transportation of the puma from the Potrero de los Idolos to the city. Too much Ritch in the Society, at all events. Governor Ritch stated that Hosta had told him: "that all the Tanos were Tehuas, but not all the Tehuas were Tanos." Promised assistance [to Society].

MARCH 21: At Marsh's. He says that New Mexico contains about 260 species of birds, possibly 300. Worked till 5 P.M. Music at the Plaza.

Took a walk with Joe after dinner, it was beautiful. No letters at all. The mountains are magnificent. On the lomas, Mr. Holmes showed me a beautiful black and yellow salamander, which he had just caught in his yard while digging. Pauline came at 6:15 P.M. Wrote to *Ausland*.

MARCH 22: Went to Fort Marcy. View splendid, clear and bright. Found pottery, corrugated and painted black,* and also chips of flint, but no obsidian. Still there is no doubt of a settlement left up there as Jac. Gold has, himself, a collection of pottery from the same place. The pottery is ribbed rather than corrugated, but Gold has some corrugated too. Went to Governor Ritch and got pamphlets and bluebook from him. In 1778, 30 December, the Territory contained of weapons: 8 guns, one without carriage, and 84 serviceable muskets.

Stopped writing at 3:30 P.M. and went to the Curacy. Resolved to go to the Pueblo of Tesuque tomorrow. Received letter from Padre Ribera; shall go to him Saturday or Sunday. There is much electricity in the atmosphere; the hair is crackling strongly, and the stoves are imparting electric shocks. Took another walk with the girls [Joe and Pauline] at 4 P.M. Evening most splendid. Met Judge José from Taos. Joe is unwell.

---

126. Stories of this sort seem to have been common in the 19th and early 20th century and probably are due to a lack of real understanding of Indian religious and social activities on the part of untrained American observers.

MARCH 23: Ready for Tesuque. Joe is better. Yesterday the *Democrat* had my lecture announced. The *New Mexican* also has [a notice] about it. Have to take lunch again today, and am tired of that basket. Hope the roads will not be too bad. They are said to be sandy, but not rocky or rough. Leave at 9 A.M. with two horses.

Old José Maria (Ma-tihua) of Tesuque is blind but is a very intelligent old Indian, born in 1808; has been twice to the United States, and even as far as the Island of Cuba. He went to the U. S. first in 1852-53. I got [a number of Tehua names for the pueblos] from him in the upper story of a house, on the south side of the plaza of Tesuque, which house is occupied by his nephew Benítez Romero.

The road to Tesuque is through an arid cañada, the slopes overgrown with shrubby sabinos and cedars, perfectly dry now. The descent to the Rio Tesuque is very steep in part; there is a little group of adobe houses, picturesquely perched over the little rivulet of clear water, running down from the east, and winding its way towards the Rio Grande. Mr. Ed Miller, a German, intends establishing a summer garden about six miles from Santa Fe, above the Rio. He says that all sorts of fruit grow very well, apples, pears, grapes, etc. The soil is fertile but needs irrigation. At present it is but a waste of sabinos and cedars, much stunted in growth.

The pueblo of Tesuque lies ten miles north of Santa Fe, on the south bank of the Tesuque, not far from the high bluffs bordering it on the south. Its tillable lands are mostly on the north side of the river, and the acequia runs along the slopes of the northern bluffs. The pueblo is small and built exclusively around an almost square plaza. Houses, two-storied with ladders. They have an estufa, but it is decayed, as they let it go down and do not keep it up. José Maria told me that the people of Tesuque all descend from one ancestor, José Antonio Vigil, and that they have no gentes, but intermarry. Still he seemed to know what "generation" [clan] is but claims that the Tehua have none. The ruins at the Caja del Rio he says were built by people of his stock who have gone farther south. He intimates that they were not Queres and says there are also caves on the east side of the river. Says that this occurred long before the conquest.

I did not go into any details in questioning them, as they would not have told the truth anyhow. They had a great many very obscene figures of clay there, recently made. Chimneys, etc., as at Cochiti. The stand had three metates. In the middle of the room hung a cradle on four ropes. Most of the men, except the old ones, were working in the fields. There are fewer dogs here than elsewhere. José Maria told me there were many ruins about, on the bluffs, formerly occupied by the Tehua.

When we came, a child had just fallen down and hurt himself; the mother was very disconsolate but did not know what to do. Joe and Pauline washed his head with cold water. In the house, the husband and his brother have each married a young Mexican girl, both sisters, and are very good to them, so the mother-in-law, who is a Mexican widow living in the neighborhood, said. They told me that the old governor of Santo Domingo, Antonio Tenorio, is their uncle. This is doubtful. Spent a very pleasant evening at Mr. Gerdes. Joe is very well. Tired, but no trace of headache.

MARCH 24: Wrote to Padre Ribera and to Collet. Called a moment on Governor Ritch. Went to see Mr. Robbins' furniture store and was astonished at the variety and price of goods— comparatively low. An old gentleman informed me that at the Sierra del Valle there were large blocks of obsidian. Also that a fossil rhinoceros was found near San Ildefonso. Also bones of the mastodon at the Sierra de Sandía. Joe and Pauline left for Albuquerque at 3 P.M. Afterwards, went to the Archives. . . .

Stopped work and went home at 5:15 P.M. The Journal of Vargas is very interesting indeed. Wrote for the *Ausland*. At supper, I met J. C. Pearce, who had been to San Marcos, 18 miles south of here, and had stepped off a plat of the ruins there.*

Walls are of cobble stone laid in adobe. Stones laid at an approximate angle of 0.50°. Excavation 18 inches deep, 3 feet long, 2 feet deep. Much pottery about in heaps. We may possibly go to San Marcos Sunday by buggy. Wrote till very late.

MARCH 25: Stopped work at 4:30 P.M. and went home. At noon, I received a letter from Papa with good news so far. Thank God. Also a letter from Padre Ribera. The archives are very, very interesting. These different cases of witchcraft are of the highest value. Mr. Ellison says there are many of them. Bought myself a skull cap. Wrote to Joe and to Papa. Sent photographs to Papa. Spent a few minutes at Jacob Gold's. He has some fine axes of trap from the vicinity of Cochiti, and turquoise necklaces from Santo Domingo. In going through the archives, I become more and more convinced that the conquest by Vargas was made very easy by the preceding and persistent endeavors of Gironza Petriz de Cruzate. He was governor at El Paso twice.

MARCH 26: Went to the archives.

All afternoon at work with J. C. Pearce. At 7 P.M. went with Pearce to Judge Prince. He has a beautiful collection of antiquities. Among them is a splendid painted jar from the Casas Grandes of Chihuahua. The painting is red, yellow, and black, and very different from that of the Pueblos. The ornamentation is much more handsome, but it is not glossy at all. He also has gray carved pottery from Abiquiu, which is absolutely new to me. It is very thin and handsome, the color is ashy gray turning to yellowish.[127] He has many stone axes of beautiful granite, all from Jemez, Taos, and Picurís. They are similar to those from the Sierra of Cochiti. Large mauls from the Cerrillos. From San Juan, on the Animas River, he has a perfect skull, which was found in a grave near the pueblo. The skeleton was entire, and lay on the side, in a crooked position, in a stone chamber.

---

127. This was undoubtedly the ware known today as Potsuwi'i Incised (cf. Hawley 1950: 92).

THE SOUTHWESTERN JOURNALS

The skull appears to have a singularly narrow forehead, as if the temporal bones had been artifically compressed. It is strongly prognathic.

On the whole it was an interesting evening. Received a card from Joe tonight; it is all right, though they had some trouble. Judge Prince strikes me very favorably. His wife (he is newly married) is very pleasant. Senator Wadsworth from New York was here also. Returned at 10 P.M.; wrote awhile for the *Ausland* and went to bed at 11 P.M.

MARCH 27: Sent my shoes to the shoemaker and was thus kept in the room all day. Got letter from Collet today. Wrote at the lecture. Am much annoyed. No news from Padre Ribera. The room is cold, and I cannot go out. Got my shoes at last. Called on E. J. McLean and had a very pleasant hour. Met Brown; he told me that he was at my disposal as in former times. He also informed me that Stevenson was about to remove the pumas from the Potrero de las Vacas. This is very unjudicious and should be counteracted [prevented] if possible.[128] Wrote to Mrs. Morgan and mailed letter.

MARCH 28: Archives at last.

I went to Jacob Gold's in the morning and met two Cochiteños, Toribio and Salvador Arquero. Before them, Cleto, another one, had been in and had given to Gold a little dust or soil, telling him it was good to keep out the wind and prevent storms. The other Indians looked at it and laughed, saying it was *Ha-atze*, earth, and used also word *Q'ashia*, white.

At the archives I had a long talk with Colonel O'Neil, who has been in New Mexico for thirty-nine years. He says that, [early in] his time, the New Mexicans had hardly any firearms, that many of them even went to war with bows and arrows. Armijo had about 4000 men at Cañón del Apache, one single good piece of artillery taken from the Texans in 1843, and per-

---

128. Whether or not Bandelier ever transformed his sentiment into action is unknown. For whatever reason, the stone lions remain as one of the features of Bandelier National Monument.

haps two more old iron guns. It would have been, he said, sheer foolishness on his part to attempt to oppose the Americans. There are Indians of Jemez in town. Shall try to see them. My eczema is getting worse very rapidly. Spent the evening at Father Eguillon's very pleasantly. Mr. Ellison told me that there were ruins of an old pueblo five miles south of here, in the Arroyo Hondo. Shall go and see them.

MARCH 28: All morning at the archives. My eczema is fearfully ugly and irritating and gives me fever. It is as violent as I ever had it. Yet I am very careful about drinking. Leaving my pen, ink, and paper at the archives, I went to dinner. When I returned, Mr. Ellison had closed up and left. So I could not do anything during the remainder of the day. Eczema, besides, very painful. Lip badly swollen. Went to Governor Ritch at night. He was exceedingly kind with me. Made some confidential communications.

Received a letter from Joe. She is well and hearty. Also a letter from Frank Robinson. Nothing from Padre Ribera yet. After all, with my eczema, I am very glad he did not come. I would be very bad off in the pueblo. [There], no soft soap can be had at all. Dr. Sieber is not at home. Governor Ritch is of my opinion, that the removal of the mountain lions from the Potrero de las Vacas should not be permitted if possible, as it would injure further work among the Indians here. He took my biography.

MARCH 29: To the archives. It is bitterly cold in there, and almost unbearable. A fragment, of the month of November, but no year, certainly between 1821 and 1840, of a meeting with 3 Comanche chiefs, one of which was called Bordero, at the old pueblo of Pecos. (This was about 1835-36.)

MARCH 30: Most beautiful, but my eczema is awful. Saw Dr. Sieber; he prescribed like Walliser. Am shut up; dare not go out, it looks too frightful. Pain and inflammation make me feverish. Painted the Pueblo of Santo Domingo and left the painting, together with that of the enclosure of the pumas, with Governor Ritch for safekeeping. It is one of the most beautiful days imaginable, but my lip troubles me so that I am unfit for work.

Got a letter from Lizzie and one from Dr. Moore. Also a scrap from the *Rochester Democrat*. At night, friendly call from D. J. Miller. He confirms the fact of the existence of an old pueblo ruin at the Arroyo Hondo.

MARCH 31: Lip awful, but appears to be improving at last. A letter from Padre Ribera came early, and tomorrow I shall leave at last. Victoriano is in town, but he did not see me. The stepbrother of Padre Ribera, Alarid, told me that the Alarid killed near Agua Fria was Francisco Alarid, a relative of his, together with Ramon Abreu, and another Abreu. Wrote to Joe. Lip appears to improve at last; still I am not confident of it yet. Wrote to Papa. Met Victoriano on the street. He recognized me at once. The day is very beautiful indeed. Music at the plaza. Not many people. Met Indians of San Felipe and of San Juan.

Was told, as a positive fact, that a man made a bargain with a Pueblo Indian, an old man, for the sum of $5.00 for the use of his wife, a good-looking woman. The woman would not permit it but with the consent of the husband; then she gave in willingly and had to be used in the presence of her husband. The fact is given to me as undoubted, and was probably at Tesuque. This may be an instance of beastly depravation, but it may also be an old custom. Must investigate it closely.

Well, if nothing happens, tomorrow I shall be in the field again. Made arrangements with Henry Brown for photographs, if needed. Jacob Gold told me that the Indians of Cochiti never sell any puma skins. One of them sold him a puma skin once, but the principales of the Pueblo made him buy it back again. He never gets skins of skunks (*Mephitis*) either. These facts are more than significant indeed. The San Juan Indians have fine trailing leggings of buckskin. Lip getting better, still I am not sure of definite healing at all. Governor Ritch has a part of the

Journal of Vargas and of Otermín. The Vargas Journal is from
1693 and 1694 and complete. People are now coming in from
Peña Blanca; Marcos Vaca, Jesús Sena, etc., are in; so is old
J. D. McRae. The latter called upon me at night and stayed
some time. He is now at Golden, has coal (anthracite and bitu-
minous), iron, and gold. He is always the same good old man.
Tom Munn is with him. He says that there are large ruins at
Galisteo. Received a letter from Papa. Of course complaints
but what can I do? Enclosed a very nice letter from B. E. Hoffmann. Lip improving.

APRIL 1: After much delay, we left at 11 A.M. The plain is dry.
But the caña agria [dock, Rumex sp.] is sprouting. The Padre
told me that they used it for painting their pottery. The view
is always splendid from the mesa, and the Bajada very grand.
Arrived at Peña Blanca about 5 P.M. Reception more than
friendly. Letter from Cholula, thank God, and one from Mr.
Hebler. Eveything all right so far. Passing by the Pueblo Quemado I remeasured it.* The pottery is somewhat less, but there
is considerable gypsum about, even in large pieces. There was
nothing new at all at the Curato, except all very friendly and
very pleasant. He told me that Evans was here and went with
José Hilario to the Potrero de en el Medio.

APRIL 2: Started for Santo Domingo at 9 A.M. and attended
Mass. The Indians are exceedingly friendly. Santiago, the sacristán, and Santiaguito were particularly friendly. The latter is
married now. From Santo Domingo went to Wallace, or Armville, as it is now called. Father Ribera had to say Mass there
too. We stopped at the house of Mr. Wheeler and he was exceedingly kind, as were his family also. Got a letter from Mr.
Collet. It gave me a foolish impression and rather an unfavorable one so far. The old man becomes almost impertinent. I'll
forgive him, however. While at Wallace I sketched the sierra.
The place has grown, but there is a drawback. There is no water
at all, except what comes from the Bajada by the railroad channels, and from wells.*

After much delay, we left at 3:30 P.M. Reached Peña Blanca at 5 P.M.* Lip vastly improved.

APRIL 3: Adelaido came in the morning with a horse. The Rio [Grande] is very big; the bridge at Cochiti has been taken away and at Santo Domingo they will take it away soon and replace it in the fall, as the river would carry the bridge off anyhow. We passed through the river; it was deep and the current strong. Reception at the pueblo very friendly by everybody.

They are making pottery now. The clay is yellow. It is gray before they wet it. They build up the vessel, making first a bottom, and then wind strings of clay on top of it, keeping the clay moist, so as (if it is a tinaja) to give it the form of a wide-mouthed jug. It is properly a pile of clay sausages. The whole mass is kept wet, so that it can be shaped by pressure as they

like. The opening on top is kept open, large enough for the hand to get in. The vessel is placed in a flat basket. When the upper rim is done, all by the thumb, they scrape and smooth the outside and inside with the hand and a little scraper of calabash or wood. At the same time, by gently pushing from the inside, they make the sides bulge out so as to give the vessel the true form when it is complete. Then it is left to dry. When dry, it is smoothed, or scraped outside with a stone scraper, patched, if there are any cracks, and then painted, with guaco. This is a decoction of a plant which I do not know as yet—its juice is yellow, so is the color, but after burning, it turns black. The red color they make of red ochre, and burn it in. They burn only once, unless it should fail the first time, when they burn it over again. Before painting it with guaco, they put diluted white earth on it. That clay, which burns yellow, they get from the other side of the river.

I have a headache, which is not a good sign at all. Made arrangements for my wash with Luisa Mesta, and then wrote and painted. The height of the bluffs above the river-bottom is twenty-six feet about, and five feet higher from Mesta's house to that of Juan José. Cochiti, therefore, is about forty to fifty feet above the Rio Grande.

I saw them burn their pottery. They make a ring of stones, in the middle of which they put wood, and set their vessels on it. They cover it with a perfect vault of cow dung. Thus the clay is gradually baked all over.

APRIL 4: The garbancillo is in bloom, violet. They call it "pu-ya" and declare it very poisonous, but in October the donkeys even scrape out the roots with their hoofs to eat them.

The wooden shovel, used to clean grain, is called u-ia-shte-q'ume, and the wooden fork zash-tiome. The former is made of pinabete, and the latter of encino. They mix the clay [in pottery making] with sand, very fine volcanic (debris of pumice, probably) before beginning to work it. Knead it like dough, and then it becomes yellow. Again I painted different articles.

The pueblo is very quiet, most of the men being out in the fields. Next week they begin to sow wheat; now they are only irrigating. Padre Ribera planted his onions, his beets, and parsnips about 10 days ago. He is not satisfied with his essays [attempts] on potatoes. No wonder, for last year was exceedingly wet, so that he lost one-half of his hay, but the other crops did well. Every house is full of pottery; they complain of bad prices. But the metates are very high, as high as $10 apiece. And still they are so clumsy in comparison with the Mexican.

This morning, the war captain, Pomocena, showed me how they drilled the little bits of shell of which they make their necklaces. These shells are from the sea. It goes very quickly and they need but one hand for the drill, the other holding the shell, in a little concavity scraped out in a piece of wood. Went to the cacique and he gave me permission to paint all the objects for dancing. Also to survey the pueblo. Romero Chavez also was very friendly. His wife has sore eyes, but says she does not attempt to cure them at all. Juan José, after giving me the names of the kins [clans], said that, if a man left his kin, he still remained a member of the tribe. Saw Ha-io-ua; he is lonely, the poor fellow. Today, I had a new dish: fried eggs, cooked in red chile sauce. Egg is na-ua-q'a. This dish would be fair with more salt and less chile. Bears have gone away in part, but tarantulas are said to be frequent. Unwell again at night. This catarrh will simply not leave me. The people are coming in with presents. I verily believe they would give me a woman if I did ask for one. Eggs, wheat-bread, are coming in lots.

After night-fall, a change for the better occurred with me. I took some Virginia-Seedling which strengthened and kept me up. Soon my room was filled. Pacífico Baca, Juan Luis Lucero, Ha-io-ua, the governor, and José Hilario came in, and a talk on general subjects took place, until Juan José and Ha-io-ua alone remained. The former then repeated his previous statement, that clans were also at Tesuque, and that old José Maria had told me—a lie. I am not at all surprised.

After this, he told me a series of interesting things. It was a confidential talk, Ha-io-ua alone being present, and Juan José reposing much confidence in him. He began by describing their mode of fishing in former times, with long nets made of the threads of the Palmillo ancho (*Yucca baccata*) which were stretched across the river, weighed down by stones, and kept floating by guajes [gourds] and skins. One party, with ropes, dragged them up the river on one bank, another on the opposite bank. One man, with a rod, walked behind in the middle of the stream to keep the net from bursting. After they dredged awhile in this manner, it was hauled across by one party crossing the river and then pulled out of the water with the fish in it.

The thread of the Palmillo ancho was prepared as follows: In May or June, the governor sent out men to cut the leaves of the plants and gather them in "hands." Then they dug a hole in the ground (pozo) and kindled a large fire in it. After the ground had become thoroughly heated, the embers and ashes were cleaned out and the leaves placed in it carefully, covered with brush, then stones, and finally a layer of earth. On top of this, another large fire was built and left burning overnight; the leaves were, thus, well baked. Then the hands were carried to the pueblo, and, as the leaves became very sweet, the boys chewed them up, extracting the fibre (*Ha-tyañi-q'o-gomen*), which they carefully laid aside, each bundle by itself, returning it to the house where it belonged. That fibre was twisted into thread, and strips of netting made of it, which were handed to the officers, and then the whole net made. It was therefore, to all intents and purposes, a communal enterprise and work, and the proceeds were enjoyed in common.

Juan José further spoke of the fruits which they formerly ate, and still ate. He says that the fruit of the Palmillo ancho (the Latir, or "hush-q'añi") was about foremost, but that of late, while it grows in spring, it mostly rots now or is eaten by worms. This fruit the women went to gather in September and October, baking it until the skin could be taken off and the seed and fibres removed, then threw it into caxetes and mixed it thoroughly, boiling it alternately, until it came down to a firm jelly or paste. It was then spread into large cakes, about one inch thick and left to dry on hanging scaffolds, changing it and turning it over from time to time until perfectly dry. Then cut into squares, or rolled into loaves (Acoma and Laguna) and preserved. In spring, it was eaten in various ways: as paste, dissolved in water and drunk, or tortillas, guayaves, etc., dipped into the solution, thus using it like molasses or syrup. Among other plants which were used in former times he mentions the guaco (Uaq), the quelite(shq'oa), the verdolaga (q'a-eshye), the shi-pa (possibly cress?), the shu-ta-yaya, the shti-tshu. The guaco was baked and made into loaves, the [quelite?] also and preserved on strings. For New Year's Day, they sometimes made a mess of all these ingredients together, boiling them in one kettle as a *soupe a la bataille* [camp stew]. But their object in gathering these herbs and fruits was to have it in the spring when the crops gave out and previous to the coming in of new crops. Now, he says, they have become less provident, or more indifferent to such means of subsistence. This is a natural effect of the approach of civilization.

After Ha-io-ua had left, Juan José became more confidential. He told me that the cacique often, and even commonly, selected his successor while yet a boy, and then began to train him. If the cacique saw his end nearing, and that his successor was yet too young, he called for another man who enjoyed his confidence. He entrusted him with the secrets of his office and with the care of the young man. When the latter became fit for office, then his interim turned over the office to him. It thus succeeded at Jemez and at Cia. If the cacique died without naming his successor, the war captain (which position is also called *Masaua*) called together the Pueblo, and they appoint a new cacique. But the cacique never selects his successor from his own family. He is always very quiet and inoffensive, never attends any meeting outside of his own house, never meddles in any dispute or quarrel. If one of his household is accused of anything and punished, he does not interfere at all but lets the "law take its course." He is also the medicine-man of the pueblo, even for the Mexicans—this Juan José acknowledged finally; but he says that he never receives any pay for his services; although the Mexicans consult him frequently. I asked him whether the cacique fasted ever; he said he did not know it positively but that it was highly possible and even almost probable. On the day when they plant his corn (which is always planted first), he shuts himself up in an inner room for the whole day, alone. What corn is left of the seed which they take for his field, is distributed among the whole Pueblo by him, and they mix it up with their own corn-seed before planting their fields. When the corn is ripe, that of the cacique is housed first, and during the time they house and haul it, he shuts himself up again until the morning of the last day even if it lasts a whole week. During that time none of the other corn can be gathered, unless by special permit of the cacique, and even then it must not be hauled out of the field, but only put up in heaps, until the last ear of the cacique's is in. The cacique also has ayuntamientos [assistants?] of his own, but of what nature they are, he would not tell. The meetings of the governor are to be composed of all those who have once been governor or lieutenant-governor; those of the war-captain, of all those who have once preceded him or his lieutenant in the same offices. He calls these meetings "como jurados" [like juries]. This is very significative. The witnesses are examined under oath, and the officers also take an oath of office. These oaths are in Queres, and he will give them to me.

He says that there are at present two parties in all the pueblo: a conservative party, which clings to the old democratic customs, and a new one, which makes of the administration of justice rather a onesided affair. I have not become quite clear yet as to what constitutes the dignity of principal, but it appears as if only such as have once been governor or lieutenant-governor are henceforth regarded as such. The cacique certainly invests them, but as far as their election is concerned, I am yet in doubt about the role of the cacique. Our talk lasted till after midnight.

APRIL 5: Sent card to Dr. Engelmann with two plants, a garbancillo and one of the ugly, gray, flat-spined *Echinocactus* or *Cerei*. No letters at Peña Blanca as yet. The caña agria is only on the east side of the river, not on the west side. Also sent an *A-potz* [?] to Dr. Engelmann. Painted all day at the chimneys and tops.

Finally José Hilario came to call me out to see how the white guayaves were made. They are not the milk-guayave, but the atole-guayave (*Matzinyi-q'ashia* or *Matzinyi-chamutz*).

Corn is roasted, pounded, then boiled with atole. When cooled off, a fire is made under the stone which they call comal, and the solution rapidly spread over it. As soon as it begins to dry, another guayave is laid over it, and when the upper end of the mass on the stone begins to curl up, it is then seized and peeled off and laid on the others. I timed the whole operation and found it to last from twenty to thirty seconds. The comal [*yo'asha*] itself is a flat rectangular slab; [it is] about an inch thick, and it is prepared as follows: It is first well polished with a stone, then watermelon seed is crushed, boiled in water, and the upper surface of the block well covered with it. Afterwards a coat of fat and turpentine is spread over it and the stone is heated from below until the turpentine has evaporated, leaving a glossy, black surface, very similar to the painted pottery. This whole process is very significative, and suggests the idea that the so-called glazed pottery may have been made in the same way too. Shall follow this trail.

Juan José returned from his hunt with empty hands. He assured me again that corn would grow on the potreros where irrigation was impossible if the rains were ample. He also stated that watermelons, if picked while the seed yet clings to the flesh, will keep here till March. Once he even found watermelons that had wintered out and were very good in the spring. Last night I forgot to mention, that Juan José told me the hunters, etc., were the only ones who adored the shya-yaq, but that they also made a figure of the sun, painting it with almagre and marmaja (carbonate of copper).

Today I had: at 9 A.M. in the morning: Coffee, frijoles, and bread. At 1 P.M., tea, frijoles and bread, also eggs. At 7 P.M., tea, peas, and tortillas.

In regard to the dance he says that it is an intercession in favor of the crops to be planted and is emblematical, in the figures, etc., of the acts of planting and growing. The Kachina is secret, and celebrated in the sierra, except at Jemez, where Americans are allowed to assist.[129] But the other Pueblos do not like it at all. The remainder of his talk was particularly important and related principally to Santo Domingo. I condense it as follows:

The pueblo of Santo Domingo was formerly on the north side of the Galisteo Arroyo and was called Guipui (Compare Oñate). While in that position, a warlike tribe came from the east, called Quirauash (Querechos of Coronado) and threatened the pueblos from that side. Some ill-disposed people of Santo Domingo held secret intercourse with them and conspired to plan an attack upon the village. Every night, a coyote was heard to howl about the pueblo in a dismal manner, foreboding the coming of enemies.

---

129. It seems improbable that Americans participated in masked dances at Jemez.

José Hilario Montoya, frequently governor of Cochiti
Pueblo, who was Bandelier's guide and informant

Palace of the Governors, Santa Fe, as it appeared in Bandelier's day

Parade ground and post headquarters, Fort Marcy, Santa Fe, about 1890
The Palace Hotel, which later burned, is in the background

Pecos mission and monastery in 1846,
from a lithograph first published
in W. H. Emory's *Notes*
of a *Military Reconnoissance*

The massive stone walls of Quarai mission
and monastery, built about 1628,
after stabilization in the 1930's

The excavated ruins of the community house
of Tyuonyi, in front of the cliff dwellings
at Bandelier National Monument

The stone mountain lions in the Jemez Mountains,
associated with Cochiti ceremonialism;
the photograph is by W. Henry Brown

Painted Cave, Bandelier National Monument

Green Corn Dance at Santo Domingo Pueblo in the 1880's

Kiva at Santo Domingo, about 1882

The figure standing by the entrance is believed to be Bandelier

A view of Santo Domingo, dated 1883

Acoma Pueblo in 1883
This photograph is from the collection of the great photographer Ben Wittick

The renowned stone and adobe mission church at Acoma
It is perhaps the oldest of the Pueblo missions still in use

A rooftop view of a ceremonial dance in progress at Zuñi Pueblo
The photograph is by Ben Wittick

The great limestone ruins of Gran Quivira mission after partial excavation and repair

Girls of Isleta Pueblo in traditional dress
This photograph by the Cobb Studio, Santa Fe,
was made in the 1890's or early 1900's

One night the people resolved to catch him. Therefore they smeared one of their number with blood, and laid him out flat in the road, with arrows in his body and around, while the rest concealed themselves in ambush. The coyote came and began to speak to himself; "What has happened here?" "Is he really dead?" etc. After biting the man in the toes without eliciting any sign of life, he sat down upon the chest to tear out his heart. The man then seized and held him until the others came and made him a prisoner. He was brought before the cacique and set down in the center of the room. The cacique then bade him smoke a cigar. Thereupon the coyote threw off his skin, and showed himself as a *Quirauash* warrior, disclosing the whole plot. They set him free to return to his people, who, seeing that the plot had failed, abandoned it, and fell upon the Tano villages, destroying them all or nearly all. Thence they crossed the river with intent of attacking Cochiti, but were foiled. Finally they made an onslaught upon Santo Domingo but were repulsed with great loss and left.

This happened certainly prior to Oñate but, as Juan José says that it was after the first conquest, I infer that these Querechos were those who, a short time previous to Coronado, attacked Pecos, and with whom the Pecos finally made a treaty.

The next tale concerns the abandonment of *Guipui*. After Bartolomé Ojeda had obtained in 1689 the new grants for the Pueblos, through which Cochiti received the lands it now owns on the east bank of the river, they had just begun to open the acequia there. One morning they were startled by the song of a little bird calling out *Tihua-pu-pu*. The principales suspected that something wrong had happened at *Guipui*, and so sent four swift runners to see what was the matter. Halfway, they met three runners from *Guipui* who told them that the night previous the arroyo had swept away their pueblo, carrying off many people. So they sent out helpers, who assisted those of *Guipui* in collecting the bodies, burying them on the banks where they had been taken out of the water. The people of *Guipui* then removed to the present site of Santo Domingo and called it first *Uashpa-tzena*, and afterwards only Tihua.

APRIL 6: Rose late, as I had gone to bed at midnight again. Victoriano called and, afterwards, José Hilario. Breakfast at 8 A.M. Frijoles, bread and coffee. Dinner at 12 noon. Frijoles, bread and water. Painted the chimneys and the comal. [A sandstorm arose]; I painted on and wrote at my lecture, but painting was difficult on account of the sand. Letter from Joe. She appears to be very well and pleased. Juan José has been all day sewing a white shirt for himself. He does it well. I went to bed very early, being tired, and the wind making [me] drowsy. Supper at 7:30 P.M. Chile with bread in it, and tortillas.

APRIL 7: Cold, wind westerly. Impossible to make fire, as the smoke all goes into the room. Could not stand it. Breakfast at 8 A.M. Tea, frijoles, and wheat bread. My cold is bad again.

The corn is sieved after the second grinding, but at the time of the conquest they did not separate the bran from the meal. In September they make of maize, yet green, a food called *o-ya-tshape-ritz*. Green corn is boiled; then the grains are carefully cut off with a knife, ground, and mixed with salt. Then they build a large fire in the hearth, until the latter is thoroughly heated. Then they clear it of embers, coals, and ashes, place on the hot base-plate a layer of green maize leaves, bending the outer ones upwards. On this layer they place the dough to a thickness of about three inches, bend over the upturned leaves, cover the top with other ones, set a comal on the top, and build a fire on it, thus baking the mass to a kind of maize-cheese. Juan José says it is good, and I believe it to be.

Dinner at 3 P.M. Tea, *ruayli* [?] (very good), and bread. The little one has been baking wheat-bread all day. I painted and sent off a card to Joe. Also began to write to Monica. It was impossible to start a fire on account of the wind. Therefore I stayed in my cold room.

Juan José told me about olden times. He says that, previous to the years 1845 and 1846, there were schools at the pueblos,

under the direction of the Church. Five or six Indians of Cochiti could, at that time, read and write, but paper, books, and
ink, were extremely scarce, so scarce that the writing material
was mostly sheepskin or tablets of wood. To write their letras
upon it, they made a pencil by flattening and sharpening a ball
of lead; with this they drew lines, and with a quill they wrote.
When the tablet was full, they washed it off, and dried it again
for future use. The ink they made of pulverized charcoal, mixed
with water, saliva, or "slime" to bind it. Their inkstands were
deer-prongs cut off and one end stopped with a wooded prop.
Still they wrote and learned to write. The first teacher at Cochiti which he had was Meregildo Lucero. After the American
invasion [1846], the schools were gradually abandoned.

At 9 P.M., there was a horrible noise at the church, shouting,
beating, etc. The flagellants [Penitentes] were there performing. The church was closed, and the lights were put out. In
the dark night, it was lugubrious to listen to the dismal sounds.
The flagellants are from the Cañada mostly, all Mexicans. The
superstition is connected with the performance that it makes
the clouds form and thus brings rain. It is falling into disuse
now.

APRIL 8: Wind west-southwest, strong and room full of smoke.
Still had fire. Sowing wheat today. They say that wheat grows
without previous irrigation, but that it grows unequally. It
keeps without water for two months, but as soon as the lowest
leaves begin to turn yellow, it must be irrigated again, as it is
a sign of the ground drying up again. I painted all day and also
finished my lecture. Informed Governor Ritch of it by card.
Day beautiful, except the wind. The smoke grew so fierce that
I had to move into the front room. Breakfast at 8 A.M. Tea,
cornfritters, and bread. Dinner at 1 P.M. Tea, frijoles, and bread.
Supper at 8 P.M. Tea, kidney and stomach of mutton, and bread.

Before night, Ha-io-ua came and informed [me] that a Kachina was to be danced tonight at one of the estufas, and asked
me if I would like to see it. I declined, telling him that I did

not feel authorized to go, since it was my duty to publish every-thing I saw and as the dance was secret, it would be of no benefit to me and might injure him. So he went, telling me that tomorrow he would tell me all about it. At night public crying about the pueblo. The juego de gallos [rooster pull] is evidently an old Spanish game, not Indian. They have no name for it in Queres, but use the Spanish word gallos.

APRIL 9: (Easter) Baile de la Tabla [Tablita Dance]. About 3 P.M. went to the plaza. A drum with six or eight young men was stationed in the southeast corner. The drum was [painted with] yellow ochre, and the men were in clean, gaudy clothes. The dancers came in from the southeast corner. In pairs, two men preceding two women. (Crosses are men; dots women.) Meantime another cluster had formed and was gradually ad-vancing, 1., 2., then 3. so as to form 4. Then they went to the center 5. afterwards again and changing. Then 7. and finally 8. The men stamped and the women hopped. Every dance lasted about twenty minutes; thus, they alternated, changing drums each time. They invariably went out to the east, in the alley north of the house of the cacique, and came in by the southeast corner. The sight is very picturesque. Dance stopped at sunset.

The dress of the dancers was exactly as painted in General Simpson's Report. The men were naked to the girdle, the breast and arms painted white. The hair long and flowing, a tuft of green [parrot] feathers on the top of the head. Below the waist a scarf, originally white, and a kilt embroidered on the fringe like that of the Malinche. No leggings but moccasins with a skunk's skin about the heel. A foxskin hangs down from the waist behind. All carried a calabash rattle in one, and a green bough of sabino in the other hand. The women had nothing particular except the head-dress, O-pash-tia-uasht. At sundown I went back and painted again. At night Ha-io-ua came. He confessed that the Kachinas were an act of sun wor-ship, that there were many classes [types, or kinds], Shi-hua [Shi-wanna], Zuñi, Aha-ihi, etc. He denied strongly that any-

9th April 1882. (Easter.)

(Crosses are men   dots women.)

Mean time another cluster had formed & was gradually advancing.   x . x . x . x . x then (x . x . x . x . x) then   x . x . x . x . x so as to form (x . x . x . x . x) Then they went to the center. x. x. x. x. x. afterwards X. X. X. X. X. / X. X. X. X. X. again (xx   x . . x   xx) and changing. Then 7 and finally (x. x. x. x. x.) 8

thing obscene was practiced.[130] The other dances, he says, are imitations of the Kachina, and even have the same words. Juan José is very busy with a trial that the people of Santa Ana have with a Mexican, and in which he is going to figure as attorney. In general, he is a kind of country lawyer for the Indians.

APRIL 10: Juan José went to sow wheat again. I painted the head-dress of the women yesterday. I forgot to mention that Juan José had told me previously, besides other things, that in Taos there was always a man shut up in the estufa for one year. He saw it himself, that a big pine-tree was growing out of the estufa, whose branches completely shut the opening of the top. A woman told him that a man was confined in there, fasting, etc., for the tribe. The estufas rule the dance, and it is next to positive that the kins [clans] distribute themselves by estufas, thus making "phratries" of the latter.*

The dance began at 3 P.M., and there was but one party [society, actually] represented, the Koshare. There were in all about

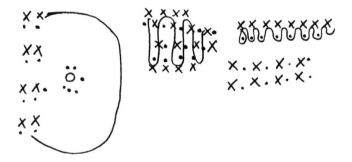

ten or twelve pairs. The women had a head-dress like that of the women yesterday, with the difference that it is slightly higher, and has a bow or arch on top of it and two points. The men had the same dress. But all the faces were painted white. There appear to be two sets of dancers in the pueblo: the Koshare and the Q'i-ranna [Kwerana]. This, coupled with the divi-

130. For details of the Cochiti Kachina Cult, see Lange (1959:467-510).

sion into two estufas, the *Tanyi*, or Calabash [Pumpkin], and the *Shu-amo* [Turquoise] indicates two phratries. I went to Peña Blanca at 5 P.M., returning about 7:30 P.M. The Padre wanted me to stay, but I could not delay. Had an Indian and his wife to ride ahead of me. Returned at night. Very strong wind from southwest which made me feel so sleepy, that I went to bed at 8 P.M.

APRIL 11: Painted nearly all day and with great success. Am improving daily. The dance began early, the dancers entering from the northwest corner and going out the same way. The flag (*Qash-te-tshume*) was carried in front. All had, on the left side of the head, a bunch of feathers of the sernicola [Sparrow-hawk]. They are all painted red, and they have the same head-dress as yesterday. The banner is said to be la [vera] bandera de Montezuma (the true flag of Montezuma).

I had some callers tonight, among them Ha-io-ua. When we were alone, I talked about the Kachinas. He said there exists a Kachina del sol [Sun Kachina], which he calls *shqoritze-goat* [round face], and that in it they use a round figure of the sun, painted yellow. He confirmed that they have images of stone, thirty to forty centimeters in height. The little figure of a man of alabaster he says is that of *Masseua* [Masewa], the war cap-tain. This might mean Montezuma! I asked him whether Montezuma had other names. He was undecided what to say, but finally answered that it might be, and that he believed it, but that he did not know it. This makes it quite certain that it is. The stone images he said I could not see. He also said that there was a Kachina to Montezuma. Wrote to Mr. Parkman.

APRIL 12: Rose at 7:30 A.M. In the rear of Juan José's house, in the store-room, there hangs on the south wall, covered up by a piece of calico, a quiver of hide, painted red, yellow, and black, 0.61 meter long and about 0.16 meter in diameter. It is cylindrical and has fringes of strips of hide at the bottom. This quiver contains a heavy object, evidently of stone, wrapped in white cloth and long straws, like a large bottle. What it is

I do not know, but it is evidently something sacred. Together with it was a collar, probably of bears' teeth, ground down to little plates. Also a breastplate of bear skin, and a hook-like object of wood. I regret the indiscretion, but it is committed now, and I have the remorse. Painted bows and arrows, clubs, rattles, etc. They have flutes of wood, painted red, green, etc., or rather Chirimías. They call them O-qatza. Had no dinner today.

Before the dance, Juan José told me how they prepared their calabashes or gourds to make vessels out of them. After cutting off the stem end, they cooked it with pounded seeds of watermelons. Then poured water inside so as to rot the flesh, grain, fibre, etc. When the inside is all rotten, they pour water again mixed with broken flint or obsidian and shake it well, thus grinding and polishing the inside, until no trace of a stench is left.

The dance began at 1 P.M. The dancers were all in one body, the flag at their head. They came in from the southwest corner, and their number was twice that of the last two days. At certain figures indicated on the diagram the flag was inclined over the heads of the dancers. Every move or change of direction in the promenade, was indicated by rattling, and the beginning of every dance, after a pause, by a shrill tremulous shout of the singers. The dancers themselves never shouted. Each dance lasted about twenty minutes, and the same figures were always repeated as in the diagram. Juan José told me that the stone rattles were the original ones and that the principales would not, at first, permit the metallic ones. The stone is gathered from the Cerro del Oso, twenty-eight to thirty miles west of Cochiti. The dance is closing up. Many small, very small, children danced along. There were old men who regulated the dance, putting the dancers in line whenever the younger and less trained ones got out of order.

I have now nearly all the features of the dance, except the words. These will be hard to get, if at all. I distributed some beads today and that "fetched them." They were overjoyed. The fact that one party went out by one corner and the other by another, is that the places where the drums are kept were in that direction. Thus Romero Chavez' [home] was the place where they painted themselves today. Their motions are clumsy, the men paw the ground, and women vibrate on the palms [balls of their feet], not on the toes. The singers generally do like the women, but today some of them stamped and pawed too.

I just saw Adelaido standing in the front room, stark naked up to the little *maxtlatl*, and his father and sister moving about as unconcerned as we would before the Venus of Titian. After all, what's the difference?

Juan José was very talkative. It appears that the Rio Grande is gradually eating its left bank. He made the very significant remark that it would be much better if the river would eat the pueblo, than to have it eat up its lands. The pueblo would soon be rebuilt, elsewhere! He then said that those of the estufa of *Shyu-amo* [Turquoise Moiety] were always against the Pueblo, and that in consequence of it, there had been constant squabbles between them and the *Tanyi* [Pumpkin Moiety]. (He belongs to the latter!) The Turquoise people went to Mexico to secure the citizenship of the Pueblo; he says that it was in times of Spain [prior to 1820]. The Pumpkins sent a delegation also, who reached the City of Mexico after the former had already returned home. The citizenship was revoked, but in the meantime the Mexicans had already occupied the lands near Peña Blanca, and the Pueblo was split up. Subsequently came the epidemic, then the surrender of the idols, which he also attributes to the *Shyu-amo*, and the Pueblo was so reduced that only twenty-five men-at-arms were left at one time. This fixes the founding of Peña Blanca between 1816 and 1819. It also shows that the estufa really indicates a phratry, or a cluster of gentes associating for purposes of dancing and, through custom, of government.

APRIL 13: Finished letter to Mr. Parkman. It is too ugly weather to go out, as it snowed till noon so I painted till late in the afternoon. Had crowds of visitors, and several slept very comfortably in my room. In the afternoon the governor, Victoriano, Zashua and his little wife, Ha-io-ua, two boys and two girls were here at one time. Had trouble with the fire again. Spent the evening with Victoriano. It is queer how the Indians defer to age, also how a man of 50 years is still called a muchacho. Age makes the man with them. Only an old man is hombre. I am yet only a muchacho. [Here, Bandelier recorded the words of the first Tablita Dance song, "the entrance."] We were interrupted by boys coming in.

APRIL 14: Rode to Wallace. It was bitterly cold at first, but grew slightly warmer as I approached Wallace. Found a letter from Papa. Good. Returned at 5 P.M. Juan José told me that the Tanos settled at Cubero after the Insurrection and that thence they went to the Moquis. Cubero is on this side of the river [San José]. The ceremony of the ant-hill is denied by the people here, but they say that it may possibly have been performed in olden times. Still Juan José very curiously asked for the day on which the Zuñis performed it! Met many Indians from Santo Domingo at Wallace.

APRIL 15: A very bad night. Cold and shivering all the time. My lip again threatening. I wish that the cold weather would cease, but they say that March and April are the coldest months of the year. Painted the quiver, oven, etc. Everybody at work on the acequia. They are very backwards with their work this year, and this they attribute to their governor. Other governors, they say, direct the sowing of wheat sometimes at the close of February, or even January, ordaining that those who should not sow then, would have to wait until after the work is done on the acequia. The governor has direction of these affairs, and unless he directs it, no work can be done previous to the cleaning, etc., of the acequia. Wrote till late at night.

APRIL 16: Rode to Peña Blanca. No letters. Met two Indians

from San Felipe. The dance there lasted only three days in all, and there were neither Koshare nor Kwerana. (They pronounce the latter word Que-ranna.) Their wheat was sowed two weeks ago already. [Here Bandelier continued with the words of the Tablita Dance which he began recording April 13.] There are two more songs which Ha-io-ua will give me also.

Ma-se-ua is the spirit of rain who dwells in the laguna of Shi-pap. This laguna is said to be to the north, beyond the Conejos [mountains], and is described to be very round and deep. Many streams flow into it, but it has no issue. Out of this laguna came forth the Indians and in it dwells Te-tsha-na, our mother, from which sprang the Indian race. Those who die go to heaven above where God judges them and while the bad ones go to perdition forever, the good ones return to their mother in the said laguna. They admit that God punishes even the good ones after their death, but that after that they still go to their mother. There is a singular admixture of Christian and pagan beliefs in this. There is another laguna on top of the Sierra de Sandía, whence the lieutenant war-captain [younger war god—O-yo-yewe] came. The whole is very symbolical of the course of the clouds and of rain and describes or rather invites the beneficial rain from both sides, to come.

At the Cura's there is nothing new. My nose and lip are both very sore again. I begin to grow uneasy, as it will not stop. It is most disagreeable and painful.

APRIL 17: Had a new dish, corn with chimajá. (Cham in Queres.) It is tolerably fair, though exceedingly aromatic. Had it again for dinner. Sent off, by Juan Luis Lucero, letter to Ausland, 17½ pages. Letters to Gregorio and to Monica, and letter and map to Mr. Hebler. Last night Juan José told me that the pueblos were almost depopulated in summer, nearly everybody going out to the ranchos, where they live till September or October. But few remain in the pueblo. Even the cacique leaves also for his huerta. Also sent off a letter to Papa, to Joe, and to C. S. Gleed.

Juan José this afternoon gave me a remedy of his own for my lip, Yerba de San Pedro,[131] ground and applied to the sores. It is true that it dries up with the greatest rapidity. It is a Mexican, not an Indian, remedy, but he says that the Indians have, in one of their plants, a specific against cancer, but keep it very quiet. At night I at last secured, through Victoriano, the much desired flute. It is of reed and gourds, with feathers.

APRIL 18: The medicine is at work. A fearful eruption in nose and lip is produced by it. I am too ill to go out. Still went to measure the lower estufa, shyu-amo, and afterwards painted it. The headdress of the Malinche is at Bautista's, but he is not at home, so that I could not do anything again. It gets obsolete. [This evasion becomes monotonous.] It is now two weeks since I have heard from Joe, and quite a month since I had anything from the Institute. What is the matter?

Feeling slightly relieved, I began the survey of the pueblo at 5 P.M., but it is almost too cold for it. I began at the northeast corner of Juan José's house and reckon the degrees east of north (magnetic declination to be added, 13½ east according to Mr. White). Could not work a long time owing to wind and cold.* [Series of declinations deleted; no tie-in with present-day features possible.]

The wind is piercingly cold and I am still very sensitive, although the nose positively healing, and very rapidly at that. The remedy appears to work well so far. I use it jointly with glycerine. [Here Bandelier inserted more Tablita songs.]

These songs are called ha-uina-a-ya. The ayash-tyu-q'otz is the song which is sung when they are in rows and Juan José told me that the estufas are always repaired. Only when they are fully destroyed, are they rebuilt in another place.

APRIL 19: Began northwest corner of the house of Juan José and sighted west, northwest, north, and northeast.*

---

131. From the description, this medicinal herb cannot be definitely identified. Possibly it is either retana (retama), Tecoma sp. or gordolobo, Solanum verbascifolium. Both herbs are used in north Mexico and the Southwest today and both are traded over distances of hundreds of miles.

There is an unexplainable deviation of the compass at the house of Ha-io-ua. It amounts to about 14 degrees. In general, the whole work is very unsatisfactory. Without spirit-level, it is next to impossible to do anything.

Ha-io-ua told me last night that the Kwerana had no wooden headdress, only a tuft of yellow feathers. There is a Koshare mayor who is for life, and he shares the custody of the ornaments jointly with the cacique. He also cares for the Kachinas.

Serafín came and brought me letters at last, from Papa, from Joe (she is sick), from Ratzel, Dr. Engelmann, and a card from Gold. Am dissatisfied with my work. Two Americans came, but I took little notice of them.

APRIL 20: Worked the whole day without success at the plat of the pueblo. My system is worthless and it is too blustering also. Besides, nothing to eat but tortillas and coffee. Wrote to Mrs. Morgan and began to write to Dr. Moore also. Strong wind from west with sand-whirls. At last, I obtained permission to paint the head-dress of the Malinche. The Koshare mayor himself, Juan Luis Moquino, showed me the article. Had to pay him for it. I was told that this was a great favor. His father, the deceased Bautista, would never have shown it. The Koshare mayor is a great principal. He is named to that office by his predecessor, like the cacique. He alone controls these articles, and no other officer has power over them. The matachinas are also danced here. They appear to be clowns. When I drew a sketch of the Mexican head-dress they at once said it was a matachín.

APRIL 21: Painted the Otatyusht [malinche head-dress], the Sha-atze, and began at the embroidery of the scarf worn by the Malinche. Everything came out finely. Wrote to Dr. Moore.

APRIL 22: Pedro is called Ha-yash, cloud; Adelaido, Tze-ua-tira; and Ignacia, Shai-tyu-o-tze.

Wrote to Joe, and sent off all three letters to Wallace by Juan José himself. Painted the whole day, and wrote to the Ausland, also to Papa. At night, Juan José returned. No letters. A beautiful night. Sat up late with Juan José and Ha-io-ua. Asked about the Amazons and about Quivira. They have no recollections of it.

APRIL 23: Went to Peña Blanca, crossing the river behind Juan José on the mule. In the afternoon everything was suddenly leafing out. *Cicindelas,* grasshoppers, etc., about.

Examined the canoe. Bottom (a., b., and c.) are three trunks

of trees joined together on the inside. To make it impermeable, they "cook" turpentine and when boiling, throw into it bark of the sabino (*Qui-pa*) and anoint the trees and fill the joints with it. On top of these trees they fasten planks and thus form a rim. The whole is a clumsy rectangular machine. As the wood grows old, it becomes very heavy, and moisture begins to penetrate through it. At the time of high water, three to four men are delegated every morning to attend to the ferrying across. They charge as they please, about 25 cents per person.

Got a letter from Joe. God bless her. Returned 2:30 P.M. on foot to the river. Nose better, but got diarrhea. Wallace is called *Qui-tshi-na* [east arroyo]. They cook and eat mushrooms, calling them *Ra-ty,* and also———[Bandelier's blank here]. Finished letter to Papa.

Juan José recollects the time when the people, old men, in

place of the *maxtlatl*, wore about the loins a piece of blue cloth, pushing it between the legs while sitting. He also knew two Mexicans who still wore pig-tails. Up to the time of General Vizcarra, the Mexicans wore their hair long like the Indians. At night, Victoriano came. It appears that for a lung-disease, *q'a-uitz-tihua-sa*, they use the froth of amole; for loose teeth, chewing of raíz colorado also chewing of willow-bark. The froth of amole is called *moosh-uish-pa-tzi*. The old man is getting rather tiresome. Wrote to Rosalie.

APRIL 24: Passed to Peña Blanca, with Don Benino Ortiz. I need a slight change and some rest. It is splendid otherwise. Many *Cicindelidae* about. Spent the day and night at the curacy, writing. Rather unwell. Terrible shave.

APRIL 25: Left the curacy at 2 P.M. and went to Eusebio Vaca. He told me that the Indians had idols, that he himself [once] took one out of a bag or satchel. It was small, of white alabaster, and represented a fox or a squirrel! He also told me that Miguel Montoya, of Zile [Sile], once surprised the Indians of Santo Domingo while performing a Kachina in the woods, and seizing the idol around which they danced, rode off with it. It was a mask of buffalo hide, yellow and black. Since that time, the Indians of Santo Domingo perform their Kachinas at the pueblo and guard all the outside.

Returned to Cochiti at 4:30 P.M., crossing the Rio Grande on a donkey behind the load. Cleto arrived with two letters. Nothing from Boston. Governor Ritch writes that he never received my card. Has the boy lost it? If so, he is a miserable liar.

At night, Juan José was very communicative again, but he did not speak any more of himself and of his prowess, etc. On the contrary he told me a long witchcraft story which he says happened at Cochiti since the arrival of the Spaniards and perhaps not longer than 100 years ago. The way we came to talk about it was by talking about corn. He told me various names for various grades of corn, and among others spoke of a certain brown or gray corn which was shunned by the people on account of its being maiz de brujerías [witchcraft corn]. It occurred as follows.

In a row of houses near the Peralta Arroyo, now abandoned, there lived (in Q'oyes) [cois?] two men, good hunters both. One of them was a sorcerer, the other not. The sorcerer and the other man's wife entered into a compact against the life of the other, in order that they might marry each other. So one night the [innocent] hunter was in the Cañada late and not wishing to return home before dark sat down in a rocky recess on the righthand side of the arroyo. While there, crows and owls began to alight upon the neighboring trees, and then change themselves into the forms of men and women. One of them approached the rock, without noticing the hunter, and the rock opened, showing a cave inside. Soon that cave filled with sorcerers and witches which all came in the shape of owls and crows. Among them were the friend of his and finally his own wife. She came late. When asked by the chief of the sorcerers where her husband was, she replied that he was still absent hunting but that she had placed his food on a certain shelf and that, upon his return, the brown corn would speak to him and inform him where the victuals were. It was then agreed upon to have the hunter killed in the morning by a deer, and for that purpose two of the sorcerers were sent out to fetch in the deer. They brought in the animal. It was called upon to sit down and a cigar was offered to it. After the deer had begun to smoke, it threw off its fur and was ready to talk. The task was then assigned to the deer, namely, to be on the other side of the arroyo the next morning, that the two hunters would come after it. Then the deer should [rush] upon the doomed one and kill him with its antlers. The deer wept, but said that, being once under the spell of the cigar, it could not refuse to obey although it was very wrong. It was led out again, and the listener stealthily went home.

There, indeed, the corn spoke to him. He seized it, dipped it into urine, and dashed it against the wall, then took a firebrand and examined the inner closet where he found, in a small painted cup, the natural eyes of his wife. These he also dipped into urine and replaced them, and then laid down. After midnight his wife returned, went into the closet, and remained there. At daybreak the traitor called him out; they went and found the deer as agreed. The deer rushed upon them but killed the traitor in place of the hunter who dextrously avoided the thrust. He then went home and found his wife sitting in the dark with her face covered. Seizing her by the hair he found that she had the eyes of an owl, not having been able to use her own. He threw her down, and she died.

Such stories appear to be current. Nambé and Isleta del Sur are great places for sorcery. During this talk Juan José unwittingly let out that the Koshare practiced medicine also, and that there were Koshare among the Piros too.

APRIL 26: Rode to Santa Fe with José Hilario. Collected the caña agria. It is used by the Mexicans for tanning; being mashed and the hide left in a trough with the plant and water. Afterwards salvado [bran] is used. Reached Santa Fe at 3 P.M. and dispatched José Hilario. Lecture for Friday night. Beautiful weather. Evening at Governor Ritch. Many letters. All right.

APRIL 27: Wrote and painted. Wrote cards to Joe, to Mrs. Morgan, Dr. Moore, Dr. Brühl, Dr. Engelmann, and [sent] bugs to Maly. Dr. Covert presented me with a beautiful old piece of glossy pottery, found in a walled-up cave in the Cerrillos, together with some charred tubes. Night at McLeans. Visits of D. J. Miller, Brown, Pearce, Ed McLean, etc. Every friendship shown. Dined at the Parroquia.

APRIL 28: Worked and painted. Wrote to Mr. Parkman in the afternoon. Dr. Thomas has a beautiful old stone-hatchet from Laguna, with handle. I have been rather neglectful of my duties in regard to my journal. It is a day of preparation for my lecture, and I trust to God for the result. He has been very good to me thus far.

Well tonight it will come off at last. But the prickle-heat bothers me. At 8 P.M. Governor Ritch called for me. The council chamber was full of people and the whole passed off finely. Revised the proof afterwards at the *New Mexican* office, and then although late, called at Mrs. Governor Sheldon. Bad news from the Chiricahua Apaches in the Southwest.[132]

APRIL 29: Disposed of everything for my leaving. Had some calls. Returned the money collected, except $7.50 which I kept for the hotel bill as originally agreed upon, the balance of $13.15 I returned to Ritch. Left at 3 P.M. At Lamy, waited for awhile. Train late. Met Mr. S. Eldodt of San Juan, a charming man. His talk is very interesting. He says there is but one estufa at San Juan, that they have the Baile de las Tablas and that the old church is inside the pueblo. From Lamy the country is peculiar. A wide undulating surface extends to the south; the hills are very rocky and crested with highly tumbled rocks. Hardly any settlements except along the road itself. The latter follows the Arroyo de Galisteo and crosses and recrosses it in its many windings. Extensive pile-work is resorted to for protection against the devastation of the creek, and a massive bridge with heavy stone piers buried in the sand, carries across the arroyo near Wallace. Reached Albuquerque at 8:30 P.M. All well. Bad news from the Navajo.

APRIL 30: Called on Padre Gasparri and then went to church. Old Albuquerque recalls the new Mexican towns of a better class. The town is renovated to some extent. In the afternoon, Will drove us out across the mesa, to within 6 miles of the canyon entering the Sierra de Sandía. The valley [of the Rio Grande] is very fertile, and considerably peopled.

---

132. There was considerable trouble in the area of the San Carlos Agency due in part to discovery of coal in 1881 and infiltration of the region by miners and prospectors. In April 1882 a group of some 60 Chiricahua who had fled to Mexico the year before raided their former territory. Some 20 settlers were killed, mostly in the Eagle Creek area, before troops under Colonel Schofield drove out the Indians.

MAY 1: Went to the new town twice. Spent an hour with Padre Gasparri and his excellent wine. He has, every year, about 1000 bottles. Showed me his garden. All kinds of fruit trees thrive. Apples, pears, but particularly peaches, quinces, and cherries thrive very well. Spanish and Italian grapes succeed perfectly. Also all kinds of vegetables. Strawberries will be ripe by the middle of May. But the late frost of this year has killed the peaches. At this time the mosquitos are terrible, but not one has stung me yet.

Sent the *Indio triste* to Mr. Parkman; also some papers to him and to Mr. Moore. Will tells me of an important ruin near Joseph's Springs, Taos. He dug out two skeletons, standing, at a depth of from three to six feet. He also speaks of a number of very small cells in rows, which he thought were graves. They were probably rooms. Arranged to go tomorrow to San Felipe.

MAY 2: Left at 5:30 A.M. The country flat, but well cultivated. Passed the little pueblo of Sandia five miles below Bernalillo. The latter town lies perfectly level, but the houses have orchards and vineyards.

At Angostura, between Algodones and Bernalillo, the sierra is nearest the river. Algodones lies flat. To the north of it the land rises gradually and the hills are of lava.

At 7 A.M. we reached San Felipe. The pueblo lies on the west bank at the foot of the mesa, which here is very high and close, frowning and dark. The pueblo is fine, nearly every house has two stories, whitewashed. There are two large round estufas and the church is at the southern end of the pueblo. Current of river very strong and its waters are turbid.*

Pueblo of San Felipe at the foot of mesa. At the northern extremity of the mesa stand the ruins of the old church in bold relief, and some heaps which look very much like the remains of the Pueblo of Pecos, and thus seem to indicate the ruins of the old pueblo. Its position was an excellent one for observation and defense, as on three sides it is utterly inaccessible. It

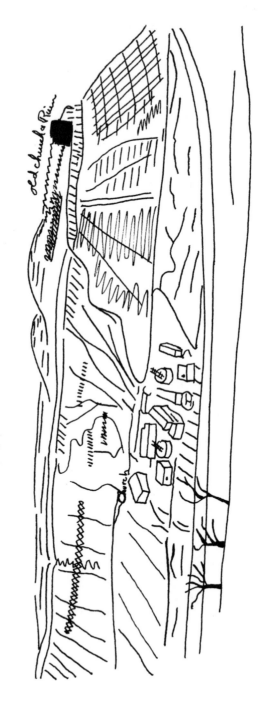

Pueblo of San Filipe at the foot of Mesa

stands about 300 to 500 feet above the river and the declivity is absolutely vertical for nearly 100 feet. The walls of the church are on the brink of the precipice.

The foundations of the church are of black lava; the walls appear to be adobe, light yellowish gray. Thus San Felipe, while the most southerly pueblo of the Queres on the Rio Grande, was separated from the Tigua by the bald mesa to the south. The Tigua appear to have occupied the fertile lowlands between the Sierra de Socorro in the south, the Mesa de San Felipe in the north, and the Sierra de Sandía in the east. The present pueblo of San Felipe lies nearly at the water's edge, but the descent to the river is steep. On this side (east) of the river are the fields, a narrow strip of terraced slope, steep but very fertile, artificially terraced, about three miles long, and perhaps, where widest, one half-mile wide. It is studded with well-constructed ranches and is almost one grove of quinces and peaches. One great bunch of vines was seen, utterly abandoned. The plots are small, but everything shows more care than at Cochiti. The river is clearly washing out on the east side, above the pueblo, nearly opposite the old church, where a low sandy bottom, covered with drift, lines it, and the fields are farther back. There the Arroyo de San Felipe, now dry, empties into the Rio Grande.

On the hills, lava, gravel, flint chips, and some obsidian are visible. We could not cross. The feast is over [May 1]. We saw the people come out of their houses in fine blankets and leave the pueblo on horseback, up the mesa. We soon found out that there was no possibility of crossing today. The bridge was down, and the men were floating the timbers on shore and saving and storing them all day. The canoe, of two logs, but longer than that of Cochiti, was lying in the pueblo, but it was leaking and they had not attended to fixing it. Early in the morning the public crier called out the men to gather turpentine. So the pueblo was almost empty during the day, except those who worked at the bridge. It was done with a great deal of shouting. The logs were tied with ropes, then drifted into the current and slowly pulled in by ropes to the shore. They got through by 4 P.M.

We spent the day in the fields and the nearest hills. Many cacti—some new forms. At sunset, all the chimneys began to smoke, and many people returned. The goats and sheep of the pueblo, which had been kept on the east side of the river all day, were driven across, north of the pueblo. The cattle, about 150-200 head, which had been driven to a pasture north of the village at the foot of the mesa in the morning, returned at night, and the steers, about a dozen, were driven into the river. They swam across, probably to be ready for work in the fields tomorrow.

They danced the Baile de las Tablas yesterday. We waited on the switch till the train came at 7 P.M., and returned to Albuquerque by magnificent moonlight. Very tired, but still glad. Joe stands it remarkably well. She is strong and healthy almost.

MAY 3: The 3 conical hills[133] west of the river and of Albuquerque are said by Willie to be burnt out volcanoes; at least the most northerly of them. I went to town and got a letter from Mr. Collet. Painted groundplan of orchards at San Felipe. Wrote up my journal. Called on Judge Hazeldine. Saw Mr. Provencher who gave me directions in regard to Acoma. Wrote the Garbancillo article and a letter to Father Brun.[134]

MAY 4: Went to East [New] Albuquerque and got letter from Mrs. Morgan. Decided not to return to Cochiti, but to stay until Sunday. In the afternoon I met three Indians from Isleta

---

133. Three of the five volcanic cones on the heights west of the Rio Grande above Albuquerque.

134. John B. Brun, French ancestry, brother of Mrs. Dumas Provencher, was ordained by Bishop John B. Lamy August 15, 1868. After serving briefly at Taos and Pecos, he was given charge of the churches and chapels of Cebolleta, Cubero, San Rafael, San Mateo, Laguna, Acoma, and Zuñi. Biographic material on Father Brun and on several other persons in the Acoma-Laguna area was supplied the editors by Dr. Myra Ellen Jenkins, formerly Archivist, Museum of New Mexico.

in the plaza and asked from them the names of the Pueblos. One of them was Domingo Abeyta, whom I had met at Lamy on the 17th of March. The poor man lost his plough by the railroad company. [There follows a list of Pueblo names given in Tiwa.]

They acknowledge that they understand the Taos somewhat, but principally the Picuries [Picurís]. They have no knowledge of the Tano pueblos, and no names for them in their own idiom. They say that those of Senecu are Piros, but those of the Isleta del Sur are Tiguas and speak their own language. Their pueblo they also call *Tshia-hiu-pa*. Their cacique is speechless now, owing to infirmity, but this does not invalidate him.

They [?] have a fine live magpie in the house, black and white. Sent plants to Dr. Engelmann, a cactus. Wrote to Collet. Went to town and got pass and compass. Saw a magnificent Navajo blanket. Left the washing with a Chinese as follows: 3 white and 2 gray shirts, and 1 night-shirt, 1 undershirt, 1 pair drawers, 2 pairs socks, 4 handkerchiefs, 6 collars. Spent the night pleasantly. Resolved to leave day after tomorrow.

MAY 5: Went to town to arrange for tomorrow. Drew salary and $100 [for future needs]. Got letters from Papa and from Dr. Engelmann. Went to W. A. Smith and bought pottery, shipping it to St. Louis. Bought shirts, etc., also paper. Went to the Parroquia and met Father Personnet also. They have old books at the Parroquia, but they contain little as far as I can see. Wrote to Mr. Parkman. Also to Papa, sending him $84.00 and the bill against Mr. Collet for $16.00 for collection. Wrote to Juan José, etc. I thus gradually prepared everything for tomorrow. My stay at Albuquerque has not been without effect, of course. There are church books which may be of interest but, after having looked for them in vain several times, I got them when it was altogether too late. Saw Mr. Provencher and took a card from him to his wife.[135]

---

135. Mrs. Dumas Provencher, a sister of Fr. John B. Brun of San Rafael. Provencher, a settler of French ancestry, with various other members of his

MAY 6: Left at 5 A.M. for the new town, as there was no car, had to walk. Left Albuquerque at 6 A.M. Ran south, crossing the Rio Grande above Isleta and then passing the pueblo which is large, well-built, and surrounded with vineyards and many orchards. It lies flat and level, though on ground sloping down to the Rio Grande. After Isleta the road gradually bent to the southwest and west. The Rio Grande bottom and the first valleys above are fine, green, covered with blooming verbenas with *Rumex* [dock; caña agria], and much grass. But they are totally uninhabited.

In the distance the Sierra de Socorro appears distinct. The first hills are of black lava, and they soon merged into the mesa formation, very highly developed and characteristic. Approaching the Rio Puerco, barrenness set in again, and the rocks became red, like red sandstone. Some of the distant mesas appear very high. The Rio Puerco is a very dirty, inconsiderable stream. Beyond it, vegetation reappears, and the change from the red into the black rock is very sudden and very picturesque. The mesas appear rising. It is the most characteristic mesa landscape I ever saw. In the northwest the Sierra de San Mateo (Mount Taylor) rises. There is still snow on its summit.

Reached Laguna at 8:50 A.M. It is perched on a high slope, rocky, the houses appear large, the rooms small, the stories low. It looks like a regular old pueblo. The valley of the Rio Puerco [of the West, or better known today as the San José] is fertile although the stream is small and turbid, and there are many ranchos about, occupied by Indians. Beyond Laguna the road enters into still narrower passages though there are no high cliffs. At a distance columnar rocks on conical hills, like basalt, figured in Fremont's Report, appear. Some of the distant mesas appear high and very extensive. Between Cubero and

---

family settled in the Ojo del Gallo or old Fort Wingate area about three miles south of Grants after the Navajo campaign of 1862-64. This region, long claimed by the Acoma Pueblo, was renamed San Rafael in the early 1870's.

Provencher was shot and killed on November 7, 1888, while acting as an election judge at San Rafael.

McCarty's, on the promontory jutting out from a low rocky plateau, to the left of the railroad (going up) stands a group of one-storied Indian houses of stone. This is Acomita, the summer village of the Acoma tribe. The road passes through the lands of Acoma. From Cubero, the pueblo is seven miles off to the south, from McCarty's six miles south-southeast. Reached Grant [Grants] (Los Alamitos) at 11:05 A.M. There is a store of tentcloth, kept by the brothers Bibo,[136] a station-house, a section boarding-house kept by Gaspar Perret, where I dined, and a saloon. Navajo blankets cheap here.

The valley is growing up, willows in leaves. But it is very cold, rain in drizzle mixed with icicles, and snow flurries on Mount Taylor, which is plainly visible through a valley on whose left side (northwest) are some high, vertical cliffs. Rock dark, possibly trap. Grant is two-and-one-half miles from San Rafael, which lies almost south-southwest. The very good wagon road makes a long bend on account of a lava flow between. This malpais is pure black scoria, terribly burnt, forming cauldrons with recesses and cavities, and high dykes and rims. It is wild and craggy, but covered with vegetation. Of cacti I saw only *Opuntiae*, though I miss *Clavata*. Many new species of flowers, and much blossoming verbena.

Left my things at Grant and walked on to San Rafael on the excellent wagon-road. Was overtaken by Mr. Lavery who told me about the shooting affair yesterday. The boy wounded in the ribs by his brother (in self-defense) is Román Ortiz. San Rafael is a small village, formed about seven years ago, ex-clusively by Mexicans and Navajo captives and some few Americans. It lies in a broad flat moist valley. There are piñones and sabinos, and the soil is deep and appears fertile. Rocky

---

136. These men were undoubtedly Simon and Nathan Bibo, German-Jewish merchants who came to New Mexico during the 1860's and later established stores at Fort Wingate, Laguna, Cebolleta, and Grants. (Bibo 1922, Parish 1960: 13) Later they were joined by a third brother, Solomon, who married an Acoma Indian, settled north of the pueblo and was for a time governor of Acoma.

eminences protrude over it. The valley is long and swampy. Reception cordial, and I stayed at Mrs. Provencher's. They are somewhat uneasy about the Navajo and say that the Apache come very near; particularly last year, when they murdered Domingo Gallegos near Cibolleta [Cebolleta]. South of Acoma the country is very unsafe. They say that, as long as the killing of Navajo by Americans continues, trouble must be anticipated, particularly if one of the chiefs should be hurt. The Navajo almost implicitly obey the orders of Manuelito, their head chief. In regard to Acoma they say the mesa is small and about 200 feet high. There are four rows of houses forming three streets. Some of the houses are three stories high. Two estufas are used, and when they dance the tablas there are two camps, one wearing but twigs of sabinos. They speak of a third estufa, that of the gobernador, which is secret, and only used for Christmas dances.[137] Last Christmas, when they visited the pueblo, they found the people in tears. A woman had given birth to three children, and they regarded it as a sign that the tribe would soon become extinct.[138]

In summer only a few people remain; the rest go to Acomita and the other ranchos. They are strictly Catholic but very independent, and will make use of their cliff against obnoxious intruders. They do not know the cacique here. Father Brun says that the people of Laguna are a branch of those of Acoma, who separated from them on account of overcrowding and settled at Laguna. Subsequently, those of Acoma and Laguna had quite a fight about a saint's image. Now those of Acoma think of removing their pueblo, but they are divided. Some

---

137. There continues to be some variance in opinions regarding the number of kivas at Acoma. Hawley and White designated six, whereas Stubbs mapped seven. Bandelier (entry of May 10, 1882) recorded that an informant told him there were seven, and in a later entry, Bandelier noted that he, himself, counted seven. (For a summary of this discussion, see Lange 1958a: 39-40.)

138. For further information on Pueblo Indian attitude toward multiple birth, see Parsons (1939: 95 et seq.).

want to go to Acomita, others to McCarty's. They would still leave a few old people at the pueblo in order to attend to their fine peach orchard, which lies near the pueblo. On the mesa they have two or three natural cisterns, eroded in the rock, and in winter, when the snow is deep, they make big snowballs and roll them into these concavities, where, melting, they form with the rainfall, a supply of water in case of need. Otherwise, their water is distant. In regard to the ruins of other pueblos they say that at Cibolleta there are considerable ruins, and that in general to the south there were many. In the canyon of the Agua Azul [present-day Bluewater] there are ruins with distinct walls, and at the same time other places with much pottery, broken, and in heaps.

MAY 7: From the Cura I gathered that Pahuate [Paguate] is an Indian town pertaining to the Laguna tribe. Mrs. Provencher told me of a superstition current among the Mexicans, and, she says, also among the Indians. They say that whenever any child through its appearance, strikes a woman favorably, that child will certainly fall sick or die. As a protection they spit in its face. This they call enojarla [vexing it]. I asked about the llorona [female ghost] and about the muerto [spirits] but nobody knew anything of them. Only they believe that when a person dies, he announces his death in the neighboring houses by making noises at night. Neither do they know about the coyote or the owl.

Two Americans, unknown, came to the house at night and were put into my room. One of them has been kicked by a horse this morning and is suffering from the effects of the kick. He is in much pain but is quieting. Went to Mass early, and took dinner with Mrs. Provencher, and supper with the Padre.

The male termination is also tihua and the female, itza.

Libro de Entierros, San José de la Laguna, 1777 to 1846, in May, 1805, 28 Indians were buried without the priest "por no me llaman los Indios" [for the Indians didn't call me].

Went afterwards to J. L. Telles.[139] He told me that he had witnessed the Baile de los Entremeseros at Laguna, in the month of November, and had noted the same ugly actions and performances which I had seen at Cochiti in 1880. He also stated that once, at Laguna, he had inadvertently entered one of their estufas while they were gathered there, but that he hardly had set his foot on the last round of the ladder when the Indians rushed upon him and hustled him up the ladder again. He noticed that they were worshipping a very ugly idol painted on the wall, representing a beast. It was of a gray or brown color. At Zuñi, they celebrate their dances in the plaza, night and day.

Navajo rumors afloat, of course, but nothing positive as yet. My things came from Grants early in the morning. Tomorrow will start for Acoma. Prepared card for Joe.

MAY 8: Left at 8 A.M. for Grants where I bought an ordinary Navajo blanket and some few other trinkets for my use. The lava flow starting from the volcano of Agua Azul is about 25 miles long and sometimes two miles wide. It runs between rocks of white limestone or sandstone, very distinct, and forms like a frozen and bulged up jet-black river. Terribly broken and burnt. It follows the railroad and furnishes excellent opportunities for surprises and ambushes. Last year the Navajo killed many people there.

Coming down to McCarty's we broke the buggy. Took horses at McCarty's. Very cold and windy. The road winds to the south-southeast along the foot of high cliffs. Potreros like those of the environs of Cochiti, but the valley is broader, covered with sabinos of a higher size. The soil is fertile, but there is no water. We crossed a narrow divide and descended into another level basin. Turning into a high plain thickly studded with high sabinos, Mount Taylor burst into full view.

---

139. José León Telles was one of several settlers of the old village of Cebolleta who moved into San Rafael about 1875. For many years he was justice of the peace.

The view is very extensive, the plain is level and looks like an immense orchard.

At 5 P.M. we reached the southern brink of the high plain and stood almost vertically above an oval deep basin, surrounded by vertical potreros, and open to the northeast, with isolated mesas on perfectly vertical rocks. I judged the mean elevation to be about 200 to 400 feet and the walls almost vertical with a few narrow canyons descending into it. In the southern half of that basin stands the Mesa of Acoma. It is the most remarkable sight I ever saw. Huge isolated groups of rocks rise in front of the potrero; in passing at their foot, it looks like huge monuments or enchanted pillars. They are about 100 to 150 feet high. The ascent is from the north. Immense masses of sand are drifted, principally from the southeast side. The ascent is very difficult. Toward the top there is a narrow path, very rocky, and the steps are made of beams of wood. Then a path is followed between two rocks and the plateau is reached. It is very windy and cold up here.

The mesa is totally barren, nothing else but the mere bare sandstone rock, of a dark and dirty yellow color, much worn by rain and wind. The church and convent stand on the south side. The pueblo forms three streets or rather three rows of houses running east and west. They are all invariably three stories, and only the upper stories have low doors, the others all trap-doors. In many cases the second story also is entered through a trap-door. The windows are very small, and mostly of gypsum sometimes irregularly round, and without crosspieces. The plates of gypsum are larger than those at the other pueblos. Steps of mud and wooden planks or of stone plates laid in mud, lead into the upper stories as a rule, but while the ladders are generally below, there are also ladders leading up into the third story. The walls are similar to those of Pecos, and mended with adobe. The largest portions of them are [made of] broken stone.

The ascents are all from the south; the north side of the

wall is mostly unbroken. No estufa is visible; they are all built inside. The church is an immense building, the walls are 2.25 [meters?] in thickness. It has two bell-towers of stone and adobe. The convent is said to contain about 40 rooms; [with the church, it] forms a hollow rectangle around which on the inside is an enclosed corridor. In front of the church, to the east, is the churchyard, with a dry stone wall. The earth for the burials was all carried up from the basin, and it is said they worked 40 years for that purpose. Found a piece of glazed pottery near the church, also some obsidian in the churchyard. On the east side, [there is] a footpath, along which the women and men carry loads. It is very dangerous and vertiginous. Many have been killed there by falling. Another footpath, similar in steepness, comes up from the southeast. There are lower plateaus both southeast and north. The end of the former is 200 meters from the northern rim of houses.

We stopped at the house of the governor, in the second story, and were well received, but hardly any [of the Indians] understood Spanish. Their idiom is very little different from that of Cochiti. In place of *Go-uatzen-a*, they say, *G'uatze*; in place of *pesare*, *pe-sare*. In general, they accent the penultimate syllable. It is tolerably clean in the houses.

MAY 9: The people here are much ruder and coarser than at Cochiti; only a few understand Spanish, and the younger men appear particularly rude and suspicious. Mass at 8 A.M. Most of the people are at Acomita, and the Governor alone came. There was trouble between them, owing to a Zuñi boy wishing to marry an Acoma girl. She has no father, and her mother consents although neither of them understands the other. The chiefs were against it, saying that the boy was unknown, etc. The priest's advice prevailed, and they were thus married. There were ten baptisms in church after Mass. While these baptisms were taking place, one of the old men, Martín, told me that the potreros were full of old ruins, that even on the Mesa Encantada [Enchanted Mesa] there was an old pueblo. [He also said] that the Acomas had come from the north in two bands, and that, meeting at the spring in the basin, they concluded to settle there, or rather, on the rock.

It was afterwards arranged that I should live with Andrés Ortiz,[140] a young man who speaks fair Spanish. His wife is very sick, but he assigned to me the family room, at least for a time. He is better provided with furniture, etc. than Juan José but cannot read. Has been to the United States.

I was told that the cacique of Acoma died four years ago. May be? At all events, the people here are very, very rude. The padre told me that they bury with the child a bowl of milk, meat, and other vegetables or food. Many of their marriages take place simply before the governor and the principales, not one-half before the Church. He knows nothing about the ceremonies performed there. Have learned that the name of Francisco (Ha-io-ua's brother), is Tzemat-tihua.

So I am at last quartered at Acoma. It looks much like an enchanted castle. The rattles, Q'atzanyi of Cochiti, they call here Shti-ri-na. Among themselves, they are very cordial. When any one enters a room, he passes around and shakes hands with all. I painted the big drum, in the house of the gobernador, as it had some peculiarities different from those of the Cochiti drums. It was more regularly made.

The woman here is very sick; her face speaks death, and the parents seem to care well for her though none of them professes to know her disease. They use the remedies of the country, but I do not know them yet. About 4 P.M. her father and mother prayed with her in Queres for a long time. I thought [that I] noticed the words "Jesus" and "Amen," still am not sure of it.

Went to church, and measured the wall of the churchyard, that is, its height. Found it to be, where it was highest (north-

---

140. Andrés Ortiz was Interpreter for the Pueblo of Acoma in the 1880's and, like many Indians of that Pueblo, opposed to white visitors because of the difficulties over the surveys of the grant in 1877 and 1883 in which the Indians had been defrauded of lands around the Ojo del Gallo (San Rafael) by white encroachers.

east corner), eight-and-one-half meters, not including the parapet. The southwestern corner of the church stands 80 meters from the brink of the highest platform. Farther west a fearful cleft opens, and through it one of the paths descends by which the plain can be reached. It is a vertiginous path, partly made by fixing billets of wood in the stone, and certainly very dangerous. Still the Indian women go up and down with the greatest ease and serenity. Tonight, they made *nish-tamal* at the house of Andrés Ortiz's father-in-law. They call them *maqatgonya.*

The father-in-law of Ortiz who speaks very indistinctly, told me again that the people of Acoma came from the north. He mentions two brothers, one of whom settled at Cia while the other went ahead to the south, and found the spring near Acoma. The settlers at Cia soon became much disturbed and harassed by venemous insects, and thus [the leader] moved south with the rest of his people, until he met his brother's crowd at the spring of Acoma, where both settled. Afterwards, those of Laguna separated from the Acoma tribe.

The children here are remarkably free with me, and the dogs unusually quiet. When he left, I handed Padre Brun one post-card for Joe and one for Papa. At night, Andrés has not yet returned, and the question is as to whether I shall sleep in this room with the dying woman or not. I would rather not, if possible. There appears to be a dance tonight, at least the drum is beating. The drum is heard from the southwest and my supposition is confirmed. Shall not go. Night very cold but starry. Was put into the 3rd story for my bedroom, with plenty of fresh air through fissures from the northwest.

MAY 10: (Andrés returned late last night.) I slept fairly well, although often disturbed by the people going in and out. I went out to see "the country," and Andrés went with me. Mount Taylor, here called the Sierra de San José (in Queres, *Shpi-nat*) is north 6° west of Acoma. He led me to the northern tank. It is a very romantic spot and recalls to me, [leaving out] vegetation and the waterfall, the "Pool" of the Franconia Mountains. The steps to go down are partly hewn in the rock, but the basin itself is natural. Pure erosion. It lies about north 4° east of the course of first alley (from east, to west of third row of houses). Its water is very green, though not deep now, and the rocks surrounding it rise about 60 feet above it. On the northeast side opens a narrow gorge, through which the eye plunges into the vertical chasm. The women carry their water up the vertical steps without stopping at all.

We then went to the church, and he showed me, south of the church, and northeast of it, the remains of the ruined houses of the old pueblo of Acoma, but I could not ascertain whether this was before the church was built, or afterwards. Probably before. I got much obsidian and old painted pottery. The other natural tank is about south-southwest of the church. Andrés appears very friendly. He ran off to get me an old stone-axe.

He confirms the statements of his father-in-law about the tradition of the Acomas. When the tribes began to separate in the Teguayoque [Teguayo] the oldest brother left first, and he settled in Mexico and Ha-ton. Then followed the second brother, called Hua-toro, and when the mother of all the Indians asked him whither he wished to go, he replied: to Acoma, which he [thought] to be south. So he left with his people, and a younger brother, Hua-Esteya. Ojero (I give the names as I heard them) followed him to Cia. Both afterwards met at Acoma and founded the pueblo. But upon second inquiry I find that there is a confusion in regard to the reconquest. The events of the reconquest are mixed up with those of much anterior times. Thus he called the oldest brother Hua-toro, Ojero, then afterwards said there were four in all. The oldest one who settled at Acoma first, and Geronza who came from Cia, José Popé, from Cia [Taos], and Catité, from Santa Ana [Santo Domingo].

This explains the whole tradition. The story of a double migration looks like a recollection of the reconquest, for Popé and Catité are well-known, and Geronza is evidently Gironza Petriz y Cruzate. [There is] a recollection of his capture of Cia and the subsequent issue of grants to the Pueblos. Thus historical facts may become mixed with tradition, absolutely foreign to their real object and import.

I talked with my man further. He told me that there were seven estufas in all but did not know whether I would be permitted to see any. I must go slow with my questions at all events. Asking about pottery, he says the clay is found in but one place, southwest of the pueblo, and that all the colors, black, red, yellow, and white, are mineral paints. . . . He says that the oldest pueblo of Acoma is on the road to Cubero. I decided to go to Cubero tomorrow and to examine that point at least.

I have to prepare my work slowly and without arousing their suspicions. So I took the bearings of the church while alone. [Bandelier then recorded compass bearings on the church and on the rows of houses.]

So far everything is pleasant, but I have to be careful and on my guard. At noon, Andrés first denied that there were any *Hanutsch* [clans] but soon acquiesced. He was foolish enough to say that he did not belong to any. Says there are no *Shyu-amo* but a few left of the *Shya-uate*. There are *Tyami* [Eagle], *Moq'shatsh* [Mountain Lion], *O'shatsh* [Sun], and nearly all those of Cochiti. (I went out again at 2:30 P.M. [for more compass readings].)

Seeing that most of the first-story rooms are unoccupied, I asked Andrés what they were used for; he said that they were mostly empty, and that only when much corn was raised, the surplus of it was stored there. The people commonly occupy the second story, and the third. The estufas do not belong to a particular clan, and the clans do not live separately. As I am still uncertain as to whether I can measure the pueblo, I stepped off the northern row, and find it as follows.*

MAY 11: Wrote to Joe, to García Icazbalceta, and to Parkman. Also to Papa. Went to bed very early. The night is splendid, and not too cool.

MAY 12: Left very early with Andrecito on foot. It was about 5:30 A.M. The boy soon showed bad will. He was sulky and mute. The plain to the ascent is about four miles wide, the ascent wild and romantic, two tiers of sandstone rocks, and the highest tier is surrounded at its base by blooming verbenas. The basin itself preserves the sight and appearance of a magic or enchanted valley as always. The Mesa Encantada is particularly bold in relief. From the top the Sierra de Sandía and the Huérfanos stand in bold relief in the far east, and the Sierra de San Mateo is plainly visible. Its sight, still freckled with snow, is very remarkable. It awakened slumbering and melancholy, though intensely sweet, reminiscences of Mexico!

The Mesa is a low orchard of sabinos (Q'anyi). Many flowers blooming. Its width is at best 9 miles. We crossed the canyon and reached Acomita at 10 A.M. It lies pleasantly, on the northwest corner of the mesa, on the rocky slope. The white-washed houses, clean inside and comfortable, are of stone. The fields extend on both sides of the valley and the railroad. There are two ruins on the mesa above Acomita, but the brutish, infamous boy positively refused to lead me to them. I got angry and left him—saw Napoleon[141] and strutted along to Cubero.

It lies to the north of a high peak of black lava. The Queres name of Acomita is Te-tyana, for the Cabao Mountain, A-quitsh-q'ote. Reached Cubero at 11 A.M., the distance to Acoma by the way I came is about 17 miles, but by the Cañada de la Cruz about 14 or 15. Cubero is a Mexican town, much scattered and decaying. Since peace has become established, many of its inhabitants have gone to San Rafael and to the Rio Colorado. Mr. Dearmond [De Armand][142] received me very kindly. There is a Mexican at his house, Trinidad, who speaks

---

141. Possibly a Napoleon Pancho who in 1883 was a principal of Acoma.
142. Probably José de Jesús de Armand of Cubero, another individual of part French ancestry who had settled in the area in the early 1870's. There were various members of this family in the region around Cubero. A spring called "De Armand" is found approximately ten miles northwest of Cubero and the old De Armand family cemetery is located in the village.

the Acoma language handsomely. Napoleon sent a horse for me at night but I preferred staying with Mr. Dearmond. The day is delightful.

Cubero is an old settlement, but the church is only 50 to 60 years old. The soil of the plain extending to the foot of Mount Taylor is fertile but lacks water. The distance in a straight line is about 20 miles, to San Mateo about 18. Mr. Dearmond and Trinidad both confirm the story that the Acoma first lived on the Mesa above Acomita. Had a very pleasant evening. Trinidad told me that the prayers which they offered for the sick woman were incantations, and that their remedy was mostly a bluish powder dissolved in water. They are now sowing the Trigo Sonoreno [spring wheat?], but they acknowledge it to be late. The A-qutsh-q'ote is 12° southwest of Cubero. Mr. Dearmond affirmed me that there is a whole string of pueblos south of Acoma, clear to the Rito Quemado. He gives credit to the Acoma for [as much as] $100 sometimes.

MAY 13: At 9 A.M. Diego Antonio, son of Martín Valles, came with a horse and we rode to Acomita, where he showed me a very old vessel which came from the ruins. It is very odd.* There are two holes on the top on each side of the opening, just as if made for a string or leather strap to pass through. The bowl is painted white, the ornaments are black and recall forcibly the ornaments on old pottery about Cochiti. I then went to the other settlement, called Pueblito, where Martín and José Miguel live. Crossed the railroad track to see Martín in the fields. The old father is a very nice man. He spoke to me of the ruins, and I hunted them afterwards but could not find them. Walking along, the boy came up after me. I again tried to coax him to show me the ruins, but he refused. I grew very angry but kept my peace until we reached the foot of the Mesa of Acoma, about 3 P.M. Then he tried to mislead me in the medanos [dunes], and I gave him a piece of my mind, both in Spanish and English.

We went up as we had gone down, by the padre camino [the

priest trail], thus called for the reason that the first priests took it. At the same time I ascertained the height of the Peñol. It is 65 heights, or about 126½ varas, or 347 feet. This settles the much disputed question about the height of Acoma. Reached home, tired and sunburnt, about 3:30 P.M.

Andrés told me that, before they knew the use of the clay and pottery, they used vessels of stone, and showed me one which he called Yao-sha-qa. It is of black lava and formerly used for cooking. Similar stone vessels, only larger, were used for other purposes. . . .

The wife is very bad off and will probably die. José Miguel called on me tonight. He is a handsome old Indian, the best looking one I have ever seen as yet.

MAY 14: The wife died about 6 A.M. amidst floods of tears of the family, the husband included. In consequence of it I had nothing to eat until 4 P.M., 21 hours fasting. There is much sincere grief in the family; the husband is crying, so are the sons. The female relations of her kin [clan] came in one after another and raised lugubrious yells and howls. It is only the kin who mourn. Her kin is Tya-mi [Eagle], the husband Andrés is Ya-q'a-qu-quanye (Red Maize), and there is also a kin called Ya-q'a-q'otshenyi (Yellow Maize). Kins alone intermarry. Another kin is Qo-ha-yo [Bear].

The infernal boy, Andrecito, had gone for wood without knowledge of his father and so the burial was delayed until about 2 P.M. It was very simple. Her father with a bundle containing probably food, went ahead, then followed the husband, that boy [Andrecito], the son-in-law, her brother, and the relative of hers living with them, bundling about the corpse, which was in a plain serape. Nobody else went with the body. The women, who had until then been about the house yelling and howling in official grief, went home. I did not follow the corpse. The ceremonies lasted about an hour in the cemetery, but I do not know of what they consisted, beyond that the girl carried water in a tinaja to the graveyard, which water was never returned, nor the tinaja either. During that time they were perfuming [fumigating or better, purifying] the room with [burning] sabino, cleaning out the room and finally cooking or boiling sabino in water. This all the family drank and thereafter vomited strongly. They call it purifying. At intervals, they burst out weeping still, after one of them recited a song or chant. It is very stifling [below, in that room].

Andrés pains me. He feels the loss of his wife greatly, but consoles himself with: "Solo Dios" [the will of God]. When "that boy" came home with the wood, a girl unloaded it; that is, he threw it up to the first story and the girl carried it up. There was a man (the one who is constantly eating, and has such an enormous snout) sitting on the first step all the while, but he merely beckoned the girl to get the wood, and did not stir himself. It may be that he was too lazy. Looks just like it. Painted groundplan of house A. [no further details].

MAY 15: Sunday. The Acomites are not very pious, for all morning the pregoneros went about shouting and calling the people to church. Painted all day. The skirt, the room, the little drum, the chimneys.

The place where Andrés' wife died is kept sacred for four days. A bottle with water and a little quilt, probably with food, is there, and Andrés told me, that the soul remained in that particular spot for four days, eating and drinking of that food and water during the time. At the end of the four days, the soul would be with God. In the morning Andrés and his father-in-law each spoke a piece, and then the wholesale weeping recommenced. It looked as if they were singing a death-song. They are very friendly, but eat cooked food only twice a day.

General meeting of the people today. Andrés went, so that I shall know what it is about. He complains very much about the backwardness, etc. of the people. Got my drawing paper and shirts. There is a long general meeting today, about the caballada. Here they appoint 6 men, weekly, to take care of the horses. The men gathered on one of the western rocks to play a game which I did not understand. I again asked for the number of *hanutsh*, and they positively asserted they did not know exactly how many.

At supper they placed by the side of the little quilt the same food which we all ate. I then asked Andrés whether there was not a little figure between the quilts and he confessed that there was, that it is called *q'ush-tu* and is intended as a portrait of the deceased, and at the expiration of the four days is burnt up. When I am asked, "Where to?" I reply now, "Andrés *q'a-mashti*"; or if I want to say, "my house," "*Sa-mashti*"; house being *tza-ma* or *sa-ma*, it follows that *ma* is properly the word for house.

The game which they played is with 2 little sticks. Two camps are formed, and in each camp, a champion is picked out who chooses one or two companions, and the play consists [of each of those 2 champions trying to kick] his stick the farthest. *Ha-ue-qo* is its name. Andrés told me that they placed a bowl of water and some victuals on either side of the corpse, in the grave, and that they dressed the dead person in his best.

MAY 16: Last night I got paper and shirts by Express from Mc-Carty's. [At this point Bandelier inserts a series of measurements on the pueblo.]* Worked all day at the plat of the pueblo and peñol and am succeeding very well. (Of course, the infernal boy has not returned yet. He is a nuisance to all intents and purposes.)

MAY 17: Painted at the map all day and happily finished it (but my eyes have suffered a great deal). Weather splendid. We had a really fine dinner. (Broiled liver, coffee, and splendid bread.) Today is the last day of mourning. They are singing often, and crying.

There are seven estufas in all. I counted them. Their distribution is irregular. They are all small, and in the first story [of the houses]. Last night I got letters, pipe, and tobacco.

MAY 18: We counted 14 *hanutsh*, with Martín Valles. He is a lovely old man. Early in the morning a lot of women came in with amole and washing bowls. I was prohibited from entering the room below. Left at 6 A.M. with Santiago, a bright boy of 10-12 years, for the ruins southwest of Acoma. We descended one of their tremendous veredas into the plain. Very sandy. Stunted sabinos, and many flowers. Lovely cactus. But no trace of culture. About one mile south-southwest of the peñol, proceeding along the foot of high vertical columnar walls of mesa, I found, nestling in cavities in the base, or in crags, about five to twenty feet over the path, a series of eight ranchos of stone. The work is similar to that of today. [The structures] are small and really cliff-houses, built of stones [and in bad repair]. They are not very high, some of them closed natural cavities. There is little pottery about and hardly any obsidian at all. In front of the cliffs is a broad valley, studded with young sabinos, and traversed by dry arroyos. The soil is sandy or at least appears so, reddish, but probably fertile. No trace of cultivation, and the Acomas appear confident that they never cultivated it, and say that the houses are "de cuanto hay" and were built by the people of their own stock who went south first, from the mythical Teguayo. Among the cliffs there are, in a slightly concave rock, fresh looking paintings which I copied. They are in a rocky mass about 60-70 feet above the base, easy to climb, although the rocks are smooth and steep. The boy, when he showed them to me, called out, "Koshare."

I found at the foot of the cliff or rock two little sticks of wood, painted blue at the end, with a feather attached to the painted end, and the other side slightly and bluntly tapering. Also a little stick painted red.* When I showed them to Andrés he threw them away with some haste, stating they were playthings of the boys, and that the boys also had made the paintings. This I doubt very much. Martín Valles subsequently told me that nobody knew who had made the paintings, that they were very old. Finally we came to a high cliff in a large recess. On top of it, in a cave, is a complete house. The upper part of the ascent is on a perfectly smooth greyish sandstone. I took off my shoes,

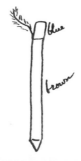

but even then the ascent was very dangerous. Without the help
of the boy it would have been impossible for me to ascend. It
was the most dangerous thing of that kind I ever saw. Hardly
any pottery and no obsidian. I found some little obsidian at the
entrance to the gorge, and it looks as if that entrance had been
closed by a wall of large stones, but I am not sure. The house is
well plastered inside and outside, and the stones are so broken
as to form a fair piece of masonry. But the walls are neither
vertical, nor square, nor level! Still it is plain that the stonework is better than at Acoma, and better while bare than if
plastered. Plastering has made it more uneven.

In the gorge I saw many flowers. Some distance to the northeast of it I met with a large tumbled rock about four feet wide
and six to eight [feet long] covered with rude carvings. The surface of the rock is corroded with iron and therefore dark, but the
carvings have the original yellow color, thus showing that the
rock was already corroded when they were made. No tradition is
attached to the sculptures beyond that they were made by the
predecessors of the Acomas "los de cuanto hay, cuales pasaron
al sur" [the ancient people who went to the south].

Returned at 9 A.M. highly pleased. The mesa along whose rim
are the houses, is encompassed by vertical walls like those of
Acoma, and the people say there is no access to it, and that
there is no pueblo on top. Still I believe that one must be there.
They also say that there is a pueblo on the Mesa Encantada.
They call that mesa, Q'atzima, and say that a very steep and
dangerous path leads to the top of it.

At home I found everything cleaned up. All had washed
themselves from head to foot and were in the room below, and
Andrés sang the song in tears. (I noticed the refrain: he-e-ti-na,
he-e-ti-na often.) Then the father, the mother, the son-in-law,
and the daughter, all tearfully recited in succession. Finally
those women sitting apart [each] recited a long piece, one
after another. One of the women's [recitations] was particularly
lengthy. [She] cried and howled most abominably. When all

was over, the two women rose and took leave of every one, shaking hands in turn, and the party who shook hands breathed on her hand (like kissing it) at the same time. Lastly they came to Andrés, and the chief weeper raised him up by both hands, embraced, and kissed him most fervently, afterwards spitting out on the floor, as if she had been sucking something out of his mouth.

He then accompanied both women out of the house. When he returned, he began to distribute the wife's goods. Two trunks-full went to his wife's parents; then, to her brother, to the abominable fellow with the hoggish snout, he gave a shirt, which he immediately put on. It was a calico jacket, trimmed a'la Dolly Varden. His wife's uncle also got something. The house-hold folks, as far as I could see, got nothing. All this was done with much crying. After all had departed, quiet was restored again.

I went to Martín and painted his shield. Among the 14 clans of the Pueblo we counted *Sho-ha-ga* and *Shu-u-i*. Toribio brought me a specimen of black very spongy lava which they say they used in olden times to smooth the hides. They call it, *Za-na-Za-na-ga*. [I] called on José Miguel. He is non-committal. Andrés is very cross and ugly.

I ought to have had the 17th yesterday, but am out of reckoning. Started on horseback with Andrés. Galloping down from the pueblo, my mule fell. Andrés very sassy, until I flew up and stopped him. He told me that, in former times, he heard of one engagement between the Apache and the Acoma. The old pueblo* is in a well fortified position. It is above the Cañoncito, which descends towards the Cañada de la Cruz. On both sides of the latter there are pueblos, and José Miguel told me that there was the first pueblo of the Acoma. There is also a ruin above the Pueblito, and above the cuevitas [little caves]. I found much obsidian, in small bits, and very little pottery. Went to Cubero, found letter from Joe and card from Dr. Engelmann. News that 500 Navajo Indians have broken out to join the Apache. Heard for the first time that the Secretary of

Ireland had been assassinated.[143] Day fine. Painted plats and maps, etc.

MAY 19: Drove down to Cubero with José María de Armond.[144] Reached McCarty's at 10:30 A.M. Met Juan José Torres, who told me there were many ruins about San Mateo, 25 miles from here. Country reported unsafe. Mrs. McCarty[145] confirms that the cacique, Juanico, died three to four years ago, and that he has no successor as yet. But she says they go on the rabbit-hunt for the cacique every month. Reports customs of sowing and planting for the cacique as at Cochiti. When they celebrate Christmas, they place a large, fine, painted caxete in the church, in it are all sorts of little clay animals and birds, and in the center a piece of bakery white [bread] like a *Hostia* [wafer]. These forms sell at no price. Encarnación also told me that about the Mesita Redonda there were ruins. I went out and found them, three to four miles from the station, on the foot of the mesita. I was also told that on the top of the mesita there was an extensive ruin. For the rest, I surveyed closely the mesa tops around and found no trace of buildings of any kind.* It lies on a very gentle slope and overlooks an extensive bottom of the Bluewater Creek, and also the malpaís.

The ground is fertile.* The chips, etc. were all black lava, with very little obsidian among them. About 200 to 300 meters northwest of it there are faint traces of another ruin and very low rubbish heaps, about four meters in diameter and with some little pottery.

143. From the New York *Times*, May 7, 1882: "Lord Frederick Cavendish, the new Chief Secretary for Ireland, and Mr. Thomas Henry Burke, the Under Secretary, were assassinated early this evening while walking in Phoenix Park, Dublin. The early dispatches received here stated that the two gentlemen had been shot, but later information shows that they were stabbed."

144. José María de Armand of Cubero, a brother of José de Jesús.

145. Apparently the wife of Matthew McCarty, another settler on disputed Acoma lands. On October 18, 1884, McCarty testified for the San Rafael settlers, stating that he had lived on his ranch for twenty years. A station on the Atlantic and Pacific Railroad some fifteen miles west of Cubero within the limits of Pueblo-claimed land was named for him. Today, this is an Acoma village.

I returned at 5 P.M. and painted the rest of the day. Encarnación Lucero is well-posted. He told me that, besides the important ruins at Cebollita, there is another one half-way between McCarty's and Cebollita. Mrs. McCarty told me that on the slopes, etc., around McCarty's, across the railroad tracks, there were ruins of little houses and that pottery had been dug up almost entire. (I spent the night at McCarty's.)

MAY 20: Reached Grants in time, together with Father Brun. Found letters from Papa and from Mr. Parkman. Rode over to San Rafael on horse of Rafael Chavez. Painted all afternoon. Am yet undecided as to whether I shall go to Cebollita or not. The railroad has changed time, which makes it very inconvenient.

MAY 21: Last night I wrote to Mr. Parkman, to Papa, to Prof. Norton, to Mr. Ritch, and to Prof. Ratzel. Finished my third letter to the Ausland. Wrote to Dr. Engelmann, sending plants, and to Padre Ribera also. Went to the top of the mesa. It is covered with a comparatively dense overgrowth of sabinos. No traces of pottery, etc. Soil good, and in places dark. Ascended the highest point, whence a fine view is enjoyed upon the Sierra de Sandía in the far distance. In parts there are flint rocks protruding; some knolls are of a fine gravelly conglomerate of dark brown sandstone. Many flowers. Sphinx lineata is abundant, but no beetles. To the west and southwest the view appears as over a flat mesa without mountains, but thickly studded with sabinos. Shall leave tomorrow for McCarty's on foot.

MAY 22: After arranging with Father Brun about my baggage, I left about 8 A.M. Traversed the malpaís. It is rugged, of course; there are deep holes like funnels, crevices, and breaks, but still there is vegetation. The lemita is blooming white, verbenas are fastened in the crags, and a red blooming cactus with double flowers attracts attention at once.

(At Grants I mailed my letters and the plants for Dr. Engelmann; took leave and then started along the railroad track.) About seven miles from Grants where the malpaís closely hugs a mountain spur from the north, I had a friendly chat with an Irish section-boss. Wherever the lava comes in proximity to the sandstone, the latter appears somewhat tilted. The mountains to the north are also sandstone, capped with black trap. Sandstone same as at Acoma and apparently horizontal. There is a marked difference between the scantiness of vegetation of the sandstone, and the fresh green of the lemitas on the lava beds. Both sides of the flow are bordered by a treacherous swamp in which I very nearly got mired twice, but at last came out very dirty and exceedingly tired. The red cactus is numerous and very, very beautiful indeed.

After much trouble and many exertions, I finally reached the Mesita Redonda and ascended to the top. The slope is steep, almost vertical, for 20 heights, then comes a rim of vertical rocks of two heights. There are a few sabinos on the slopes, but the top, although perfectly bare of soil, grows a dense grove of low sabinos. The ruin lies on the north half, where there are no trees almost, and is interesting owing to its central feature, which appears like a round tower or an interior estufa. Looking down on the south side, I was surprised to find very large ruins beneath. After collecting whatever pottery struck me, I clambered down through a fissure and surveyed the ruins. It strikes me that, in this instance, the communal house is smaller, that a greater number of buildings compose the pueblo, and that the rooms are, sometimes, larger. Would this indicate a progress in architecture? Among the pottery I also found several specimens which are glossy, but the gloss is less bright, or rather less glue-like or resinous, than that of the Rio Grande pottery.

The color of these pieces is flesh-red. At all events, there is an important point about here, and I must look out.* The objects which I found are only flakes and some rude mallets; all of lava or trap. Obsidian* is very scarce, and neither transparent nor translucent, and of a pitchy gloss.

Reached McCarty's at 4 P.M. very tired. Very kind reception. Arranged to start with the boy, Encarnación, day after tomorrow for Cebollita and the Ventana. Wrote a short letter to Joe.

MAY 23: Painted all day till 2 P.M. It appears now that there are three groups of ruins about here besides the Mesita Redonda; on the mesa to the southwest, across the railroad tracks along the heights to the northwest, and on the road to the Rinconada de Cubero northeast. I started for the last after 2 P.M. and found about 15 houses along the mesa base. They resemble the summer ranchos, but some of them are larger, and the rooms, though larger than those of the north, are still [small]. Examined the top of the mesa, but found no trace of ruins. Pottery mostly black and white, or black and gray, some black and red, and much corrugated and indented. Found the leg of a pot of indented pottery, a fine and rare piece, perhaps so far unique. Shipped my pottery to Joe. The architectural features need very close watching. Important results may be ahead. Shall see Cebollita.[146]

MAY 24: Shall leave today for Cebollita. The Acoma call Cebollita *Qa-ui-na* and McCarty's *Ti-tzi-a-ui-na*.

Left for Cebollita about 9 A.M. At first took the path towards Acoma, but soon struck off to the right, ascending to the top of the mesa. The mesa is very broad, perfectly level, thickly studded with sabinos, and without water. Galloped across it in about two hours, towards the close of which time the bushes or shrubs of sabino began to grow into timber of piñon. There is one or perhaps two ruins up there. They are small rancho-like. Then a gentle descent began into a laughing plain, surrounded by mesas on two sides, by a high ridge on the south-southwest, and an immese dark malpaís on the west. Spurs of sandstone wander, so to say, into the llano. The sight is very pretty and realizes that often repeated dream of mine, seated on a horse and galloping across a plain of that kind, with the dread of Indians before me. On the east side of that plain are the ventanas, a rock showing a natural bridge, in a recess. This bridge is the opening of a pool of dirty water.

---

146. This is Cebolleta Mesa south and west of Acoma *not* the Cebolleta to the north on the flanks of Mount Taylor.

The perimeter of this entire plain is studded with ruins. It is an intermediate between the rancho of today and the large pueblo house of today. Pottery, here, very thick, and shows enamel-like traces. Painted black and white. Crossed over to the lavabed, and there found very interesting ruins. The malpaís here is very broken and bad. Almost on the edge of it I found a circular depression like an estufa, about eight feet deep, which I measured and found to be fifty-five feet across. Along its rim were four buildings.* Near by were scattered about six disks of sandstone generally two feet in diameter and seven to eight inches thick. They look exactly like mill-stones, and are well [made] and fairly rounded. In one place two were superposed and their size fitted well. Two of them each had a figure carved on it.* One is a lizard, the other the print of a small foot. The carvings, originally not deep, are now much weather-worn and almost obliterated. Both are painted by me. I cannot imagine what was the use and object of these stones.[147] About 20 paces southeast of it there is a circular heap of rubbish. 275 steps from it, about 36° northwest, is an important heap of ruins of which I painted the groundplan. The section is as follows.* Wall is 2.40 meters high, and at a. the mass is about five meters. How much of that is natural hill I could not detect, but it looks as if there were three tiers, each of one story, along the slope of a natural mound, which would give the following restoration: (b. and c.) look like round chambers similar to estufas, or at least like very large chambers, but they are so much ruined that it is impossible to detect anything without excavations. The wall standing is 32 inches (0.81 meter) thick, and very well made; its outer and inner faces appear straight and vertical, the stones are thin plates of sandstone, altogether according to the natural cleavage, but their outside face, while not hewn, is still smooth, though not polished. There was much pottery about,

---

147. Bandelier, here, was probably in the ruins of a great kiva. The disks mentioned were used to support (as pedestals and/or capitals) the wooden columns that held up the kiva roof.

mostly of gray and black and of the corrugated kind. There is some red and black too. The chips are of lava, and very little obsidian of the dark opaque kind. On the llanito of the ventana, over a plain about two miles in diameter, there are about 20 to 30 single ruins scattered, along the slopes. Perhaps there are more. This might accommodate, at most, about 100 families or 500 people.

We left about 11 A.M. and plunged into a wooded canyon. Timber growing higher, road badly broken and the country very romantic. Hugging the rocks on the left side, we finally came out on an open plain. The rocks formed a round corner, an astounding mass of vertical rock, perfectly smooth, and really grand to look at. I never saw anything as appalling. We swept around at full gallop, and entered the beautiful Cañada de la Cebollita, a handsome plain, about one mile across, bordered by steep mesas, particularly on the left where behind the lower sandstone rocks very high mountains capped with trap are towering up. It is very picturesque.

There are many caves in the sandstone, but only one, on the level of the plain, is closed [by] a wall with doors and windows. It is of stone and plastered, 11 inches thick and well-preserved. The walls of the cave are well-preserved, and somewhat blackened by smoke, but no alteration has been made in the interior of the cavity itself. Found nothing inside. The foot of the masonry is five feet ten inches above the soil of the plain. About two miles from it the Cañada turns to the left and narrows. Nearby were the ash heaps of the camp-fires of the soldiers, embers still were glowing. The Cañada terminates abruptly two miles farther on. It is beautiful. Much oak-timber, piñon, and sabino. Tumbled rocks. A very picturesque spot.

High mesas, crowned with trap, frown upon the gorges, and from the south gushes down a limpid murmuring fillet of clear water. It is charming, but there are too many flies. At the place where the brooks turn into the Cañada, on a bare hillock, stands the deserted rancho of McBride with a corral. The owner left it out of fear of the Apache. Solitary as it is, it recalls bloody Indian surprises and romantic adventures. I was much fascinated. On the right side a ledge of steep rocks, about 20 feet high, overlooks the brook. On that ledge, hidden by shrubbery and timber, are the ruins of the pueblo.* The outer walls, 18 inches thick, are still standing. The masonry is of the most splendid workmanship. The stones, nearly of equal size, appear dressed with care.* On their faces the marks of cutting with a sharp instrument appear. Still it is not to be overlooked that the cleavage of the reddish sandstone is thinly tabulated and might perhaps, through natural wear create some of the marks as they are. Still it is too uniform, not to appear artificial. The face of the wall looks perfectly vertical, and there is no better piece of workmanship in the territory. The blocks are about 0.45 by 0.30 [meter?]. The cells are small and the buildings appear to have been one-story. The outside forms an irregular polygon with rounded angles. There are two entrances, with beautifully straight sides. On the whole it is stupefying work. As a piece of house architecture, let alone decoration, it is very superior to Mitla.[148]

But the Indian peculiarity is shown in the irregularity of the directions. There is much shrubbery and cactus about the ruins, but little pottery. The latter is white and black, gray and black, red and black, corrugated, and indented. There is evidently

---

148. It is hard to believe that Bandelier could actually be serious here. Possibly his acceptance of the Morgan point of view that Mexican Indians were not really "civilized" forced him to minimize differences between Mexican high culture and the Southwest. Even so, his own statements on Mitla a year earlier show the deep impression that great Oaxacan site made—see Introduction and White (1940: II, pp. 242-243). It seems that here, as in other cases, Bandelier was capable of fine reporting but, when under the spell of a theoretical point of view, could make statements that his own evidence proved wrong. Something of the same sort of thing appears in his attitude toward Indians. Though he, himself, documented many cases to the contrary, Bandelier apparently held firmly to the view that the Indian was essentially a savage. This was, of course, the attitude of much of the Latin American upper class of Bandelier's day. Nevertheless, it does contrast the more or less easy acceptance of this point of view by Bandelier with the rigorous examination of conflicting evidence by such contemporaries as Franz Boas.

a change in architecture about here. If now I can find the ruins in the Cañada de la Cruz, and if these exhibit forms like those of the Rio Grande Valley, then an important point will be gained. As a site, the pueblo of Cebollita was well-placed. Close by running water, with fine timber about, and a fertile, well-irrigated valley, it was admirably chosen. For defense it was also well-situated. The rocks fall off vertically, and on the side where the mountains rise, the outer wall is built. The latter follows the sinuosities of the rock in bending and in going up and down. Encarnación did not like to stay here overnight, so we left about 4 P.M. directly along the brook up to the high mesa. Path steep, long, difficult on account of the loose lava. Near the top of the mesa, the oaks disappeared, and the plateau presents the same appearance as all the others, with sabinos and an occasional piñon. Up there we found a laguna with dirty water, and some cattle. Crossed the mesa and descended into the Bajada de Acoma. Some small oaks appeared occasionally, but on the whole it was all coniferae. Reached the level pastures about six miles from Acoma near sundown and found three herds of sheep. Camped with the shepherds, and ate fine atole and excellent meat. There is a laguna about one-and-one-half miles off, and an "ojito" [small spring] about four to five miles. My serape is barely large enough. Am tired. We have ridden, mostly at a gallop, about 35 miles. There are some stone ranchos along the Bajada, but the pottery appears to be Acoma and recent.

MAY 25: Our horses were gone, and until 10 A.M. could not leave. An Indian finally caught them and brought them back. Left alone, down the Cañada, a very good path, high cliffs bordering it on both sides. Vegetation is sprouting, but there is as yet no water. Struck the Acoma trail, and nearby several ruins of the same small houses. Three rooms about ten by three meters. Pottery black and gray, black and white, black and red (scarce), and corrugated. Am sure of at least four such ranchos on the slope of the mesa, that is, on the foot, toward the railroad track. Reached McCarty's tired. The boy, Manuel, brought me specimens of pottery from the hills opposite. He says there are two small houses there, and each one of several rooms. Pottery, black and grey, black and white, etc. Painted all afternoon. Encarnación returned tonight with a steer.

MAY 26: Finished my paintings. Left for Cubero on foot at 2:30 P.M. (Heavy wind and bitterly cold.) Found at least four pueblo ruins, houses of three to six rooms each, scattered on the plain between McCarty's and San José. Pottery alike. Reached Cubero 5 P.M. Pleasant chat and kind reception. Shall stay here for a time. My boots are gone [worn out?].

MAY 27: Manuel Baca offered to get me to the Cebolla. He says there are many ruins, and among them one exactly like the Cebollita, and the stone equally well dressed. Shall go to Albuquerque, possibly tonight. Wrote to Mr. Parkman and to Mrs. Morgan. No Indians from Acoma yet. It appears now that there are several ruins around here.

We visited one about one mile west of Cubero, on a hill whose top is lava or trap. My compass is broken. The walls appear to have been of large blocks of lava; at least at the bottom.* There is much pottery, black and white. Some red and black, also corrugated. Many flint-chips, also a fragment of metate. The brow of the hill seems to have been lined with very large rocks of lava. On the whole, these ruins recall to me those on the left bank of the Rio Grande, below the Caja del Rio.

Afterwards we called on Plácida Romero, and conversed with her awhile. She is pleasant, young and very resolute. Rather pretty. But her story strikes me as doubtful in some points.

There appear to be lots of ruins around here. On the outskirts of the place, about one-quarter of a mile northeast, there are the remains of three small houses, each of three to five rooms, about eight to ten meters long, and two-and-one-half to three meters wide. Pottery black and gray, black and red, not glossy. No Indian from Acoma. The fools are always the same.

MAY 28: With Mr. De Armond I went to the Pueblito one mile
to the north of Cubero, in the level cultivated plain, southwest
from the steep Picacho. The hill of rubbish formed by the ruins
is about three meters high, and the ruins are very extensive. They
are built partly of sandstone, with some blocks of lava. Much
pottery, obsidian, and flint. Found a number of metate fragments, also manos, all of porous lava. Flint chips are very frequent, also lava chips of all sizes. In regard to the pottery, the
following types are found.

1.) Corrugated and indented, very frequent. } probably the
2.) Plain gray, coarse.   { same kind.
3.) Black and white, striated. Not glossy.
4.) Black and red. Not glossy (?). Doubtful (!).
5.) Glossy, of various colors.

This ruin is highly important. It is of the plain pueblo type,
without estufas, and rather resembling the one at the Mesita
Redonda, although more compact, and with the quadrilateral
plainly indicated. It lies about north-northeast of the pueblo of
Acoma. Everything indicates that the two kinds of architecture,
and two kinds of pottery, are here impinging upon each other.
If now I can secure the surveys of the ruins in the Cañada de la
Cruz, a great point will be gained, and the line of demarcation
about fully established. The importance is patent. The walls of
the ruin are about 0.35 [meter] thick, but this is still conjec-
tural, as the walls are much ruined, and only portions, traces,
left of the foundations. In fact the whole is but rubbish-
mounds. Mexican herders have constructed stone enclosures,
among the ruins, out of its very stone-material.*

I spoke to Mr. De Armond about digging, for I believe that
excavation there might yield something. This is the third ruin
within reach of Cubero and a radius of one mile. There are said
to be other ruins at the Encinal, two miles northeast of the
place. Shall go there this afternoon if I can. Tomorrow the
Cañada de la Cruz and then at night to Albuquerque.

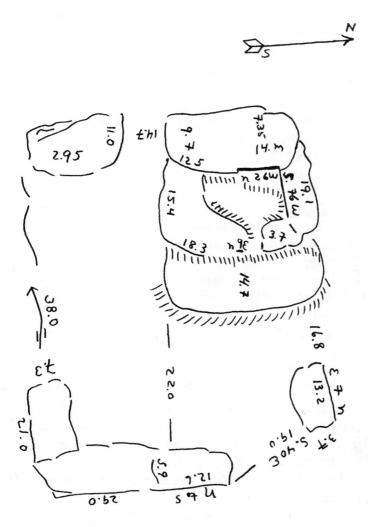

Packed up my pottery as follows: From the Pueblito: in the coat and on the top. From the Ruins on Lava, in the pants. The fragments of metates, etc., from the Pueblito at the bottom and the pottery from the small houses near San José and near Cubero in the stocking. Encinal is about 8 miles; too far to walk this afternoon! On the lava range of the Picacho, people assert there are no ruins.

When writing about Cebollita, I forgot to say that there are traces of small doors entering from the walls. This is the case in the polygon. All these doors enter from the inner court. They appear to be about 0.75 [meter] wide, and 0.50 [meter] above the ground. Saw no doorplates. In the cave, the lintel was composed of the usual three sticks or poles of wood, bark peeled off. Wrote to Prof. Norton.

It appears that we are here only two days' journey, on horseback, from the Rio Chaco and its very important ruins. Got my letters; Papa, Joe, and De Costa. Replied at once to De Costa, authorizing publication of my lecture as asked for, though not as an original contribution.

Fine night. Wrote to Papa. José Paisano, a Laguna Indian, came late at night. He disputes the claim of the Acoma, that the Lagunas were but a branch, and says they are a settlement of Acoma, Zuñi, and of cuanto hay.

MAY 29: Left Cubero at 9 A.M. and walked across to the railroad track near the pueblito of Laguna, and thence up the mesa to the right. I examined carefully every part of it, but found no trace of pottery or of anything else like ruins. Wandered across the mesa, crossing the Cañoncito, and there are no ruins to be seen. The same result at the Cuevitas. There are ruins there, but they are recent, and the pottery is entirely modern. Thus far the whole thing has been unsuccessful.

I then walked over to McCarty's, and on the road met a fine rattlesnake, long and slender, and still with but one or two rattles. Shot it, but it escaped under a tie.

The potreros from beneath Mt. Taylor recall forcibly those of the Rio Grande. About three or four years ago, there died in La Rinconada de Cubero, a man of 137 years of age, called Salvador Candelaria, in a state of absolute infancy. He had been married 5 or 6 [times!], the youngest child being then about 40 years old. At 10 P.M. I left McCarty's by rail. Met Provencher and Col. Fletcher.[149] [No entries for period May 30 through June 1.]

JUNE 2: Reached Albuquerque at 4 A.M., May 30. Mouth very badly swollen. Painted most of the time. Report in. Cured my mouth at last. Violent remedies. Went to call on Father Gasparri at 2 P.M. [and copied a document].

I got through with the manuscript about sundown. Wrote to Mr. Parkman and mailed letter.

JUNE 3: Wrote to H. Brown. Went to new town twice. Packed up my stone implements. Called on Father Baldassare and examined the books of the Church. They are only *Partidos, Cartas Cordilleras*, etc. Nothing for me.

Willie proposed a trip to the Cañón del Oso for tomorrow, and of course we all said it was all right. I hope thus to see the interior of the Sierra de Sandía. Bought a splendid little object from a bar keeper. It is beadwork of the Indians of Isleta, the handsomest thing of that kind I ever saw.

JUNE 4: Started at 6:30 A.M. with a four-horse team. Mr. Peter Weber was along, and Mr. Holton of Lancaster. Mr. Holton was our driver. We followed the railroad track till beyond Don Adolfo Otero, and then turned due east. Rabbits (Jack-Rabbits), *Tusas* and many *Phrynomys* about, numerous beetles. Could not find any traces of habitation and do not believe there were any at all. Soil good but there is no water. Many cacti blossoming. *Opuntia clavata* very common. Saw the red and violet blooming *Echinocactus*. The Sierra de Sandía is very bold, and its western declivity very rugged, the lower slopes seem to be formed of more immense debris. Enormous masses of granite, gray, with little mica, and bands of fine-grained also greenish and red granite. Cañón del Oso splendid. Grand scenery. But man never could have inhabited these cliffs. It is almost fearful to look up at them. Fine brook and small water-

---

149. This is possibly Winfield S. Fletcher who had extensive mining interests in New Mexico in 1882. During the administration of Gov. L. Bradford Prince, 1889-93, Fletcher was territorial Adjutant-General.

fall. In the lower part of the canyon, the cacti are large and varied. Large leaved *Opuntia*, *Echinocactus*, and *Opuntia arborescens* prevail. *O. clavata* disappears. *Papilio turnus* common and handsome, also *Hesperidae*, *Varessa urtica*. Many lizards.

The interior of the canyon is very beautiful. Sights changing at every step. Grand views of the near mountains and of the main ridge in the east. The latter looks like a mural band at the top. Up to that band, the slope is green, studded with strips of pine trees. The bottom of the canyon is covered with a very rich growth of brush and smaller vegetation, occasional large cottonwoods and pines. Vegetation is quite varied. Flowers very plentiful. Thistles (blue), white violets, verbenas, oak, holly, sumac. But the cacti disappear whereon the other plants prevail. Many cattle. It was hot, but not at all oppressive. No wind, only a gentle breeze. Everywhere granite alone appears.

We left at 4:30 P.M. after spending a charming day. Everybody is pleased and tired. The distance is 16 miles at least, and we returned in 2 hours, against a fierce west wind, and clouds of dust and sand. While we felt quiet and comfortable in the mountains, it had been blowing all day at Albuquerque. Resolved to go to Bernalillo tomorrow. Pauline fell ill at sundown. About 1 A.M. Willie called at our door. Everybody sick; had to get the doctor.

JUNE 5: Left Albuquerque at 6 A.M. with emigrant train. River and valley very beautiful in its green groves and fields. Reached Bernalillo at 7:30 A.M. and went to house of Don José Gutiérrez. Well received. While there, met Juan Truxillo from Sandia whom I had seen at Santo Domingo in 1880. He told me that the ruins north of the bridge were those of To-re-una. I also found out that Pua-ray lies about one mile south of it. The bottom of the river is low, much flooded, but exceedingly fertile. Ascertained the following sites of pueblos: Where the curacy stands. Near the Tresquilada. At Cangelones about 1 mile above

To-re-una, opposite Algodones. These would be six out of the 12 of Coronado.

Left with Martín Lucero. Crossed the eastern bottom and the long wooden bridge, then turned to the right. Ruin on the banks of the river, which all along the west are composed of steep bluffs of gravel and deep, fine sand. These bluffs are very abrupt and appear about 25 feet high. The pueblo is strewn over with pottery, glossy prevailing. But there is also some plain smoked. Only the dark stripes are glossy, the red and gray is plain. There is much obsidian, mostly opaque, dark, but transparent in thin splinters. Moss agates, flint chips, lava, trap, broken metates, manos, etc., very abundant. The manos are made of lava and compact quartz, the metates of trap. Found splinters of turquoises. The pueblo has been partly of adobe, partly of stone, but adobe prevailed. The southern foundations appear of adobe, the northern of rubble set on edge, large gravel. No trace of estufas.

The Rio Grande is very broad here. Current swift. Found many and new beetles. Telegraphed for drawing paper. Made fair collections, much pottery. There are no walls standing at the ruins, but the foundations are still remarkably well traced; particularly where the walls were of adobe. Truxillo told me the name was Tigua, but it sounds rather too much like the Spanish Torrejón [tower]. The width of the foundations is very irregular, from seven to ten and 15 inches, varying from one partition of one chamber to another, and even the opposite walls of the same room being different. So it is also with the size of the rooms. But on the whole it was a large pueblo, built of adobe. The stone heaps about it are gravel and rubble, mostly quartz and broken lava.*

It appears to have been a pueblo of the regular form, that is: a quadrilateral, open to the east. From what I hear, all the ruins are located on the river bank or near it.

Ground rising, sandy, barren, dotted with low sabinos, occasional bare hillocks.

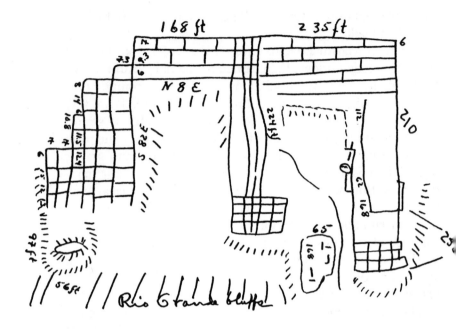

I brought home an arrowpoint of obsidian. Saw the pottery of Sandia. It is black and very thick. They made no other kind. It is burnt with cow-dung (buñiga), after having been smoothed with a fine stone or a wooden spoon or spatula. They make a vault over it with the dung as at Cochiti. The clay, previous to burning, is red. Señor Gutiérrez says that they mix no paint with it. He also says that the people are considerably advanced as far as cleanliness is concerned. They have an estufa, but he does not know whether it is a round or square. They use it as a lugar de juntas [gathering place].

Went to the Curacy, but the Cura was absent in Las Vegas, and he will not return before Wednesday. Wrote to Prof. Norton. It seems evident that the 12 pueblos of Tiguex were all around here and on the right bank of the river. The ruins of this morning contain no corrugated or indented pottery at all. Mention is made of a ruin near Sandia, but I doubt it very much.

On the whole, Bernalillo is a very pleasant place. Fine residences of the Otero's, Perea's, many shade trees. It is singular that no watercourses run down from the west slope of the Sierra de Sandía. No aboriginal population is to be expected therefore on that side of the river, until near the cerrillos, where the Tano were located. The sierra from here presents really a terribly grand appearance. Its bold crags, vertical walls, and immense cliffs are appalling. Padre Ribera was truly right: *C'est une montagne terrible!* [It's a terrible mountain!]

The pottery is mostly painted inside and outside, but it is coarse, and the figures very rude and badly done. A Sandia Indian showed some green and blue copper ore today, calling it chalchihuitl.[150]

The Indians of Sandia make handsome willow baskets, and sell them very cheap. Also their pottery. A large caxete, 15 cents; a smaller one, 10 cents. Wherever the glossy paint wears off, it turns gray. One piece is perforated. I also found a little fragment of pearl shell. Possibly dropped recently. Formed the acquaintance of Dr. Harrison.

JUNE 6: Among the pottery fragments there is one, narrow-striped inside but glossy, which recalls the pottery from the Mesita Redonda, Ventana, and Cebollita. It is bright red, thin, and appears well made.

No letters and no paper. Annoying. Started for Puaray. Bottom of river wet, still passable. Across the bridge, to the left, on the top of high bluff, a space covered with bits of pottery, some obsidian, and with rubble stone. The latter is not a sure sign, however, since it protrudes on every loma above the river bottom. The mounds or low rubbish heaps show as follows.*

About 300 feet to the southwest of it, there are other mounds, very low, which present the following shape.*

No rooms or cells are visible in any of these ruins at all.

Crossing the medanos and the lomas, finally the road to the jarra, we found the ruins of Puaray on the left side of that road,

---

150. (Spanish, chalchihuites) Nahuatl or Aztec word for jade (or precious stone), normally used to mean turquoise in the Southwest.

in a similar position as the pueblo of Toreuna, on the brink of a high sandy hill of gravel overlooking the river-bottom. Distance to the river about one-half mile.*

The pottery is all glossy, and black, there is no corrugated or indented piece. Much transparent obsidian, fragments of flint and of moss agates, metates and manos. Among the glossy pottery there are green pieces and one perforated bit of turquoise. The pueblo must have been large. The two buildings A. and B. may have been church-edifices, but B. has small adobe chambers. At G. there is a small mound. I was informed that a skeleton had been dug out here, that there were two pueblos at the Alameda, nine miles south of Bernalillo, and that on the site of the school and church of Bernalillo many skeletons and turquoises had been found. Otherwise, there are no pueblos on this side of the river, but on the opposite bank there appear to be many.

Returned after 11 p.m. Was told that the Indians of Sandia celebrated a Kachina [dance] on Thursday and Friday of Holy Week, at their estufa, on which occasion they placed guards around the pueblo. That, like those of Acoma, they put a jar with water, and some food alongside of the body while burying it, and that they mourned three days for the dead, combing themselves on the fourth day.

On my return to Bernalillo I met Pacífico Vaca at the Tresquilada. He is herding sheep here. Packed my things in the afternoon and expressed them back to Albuquerque. Failure of getting my letters and the paper, lack of money, etc., compels me to return quickly.

Am well satisfied on the whole. Castañeda proves very reliable. Of the 12 pueblos of Tiguex I have now found nine: all close together. The Mesa del Cangelón is northwest of the Pueblito, as the people here call To-re-una, about two miles from it. Pua-ray is called Pueblo de Santiago. The Alameda is on this side of the river, below Sandia. The ruins found near the church contained also ollas, filled with maize-meal, and metates. Also burnt sticks and posts of wood. It looked as if the place had been

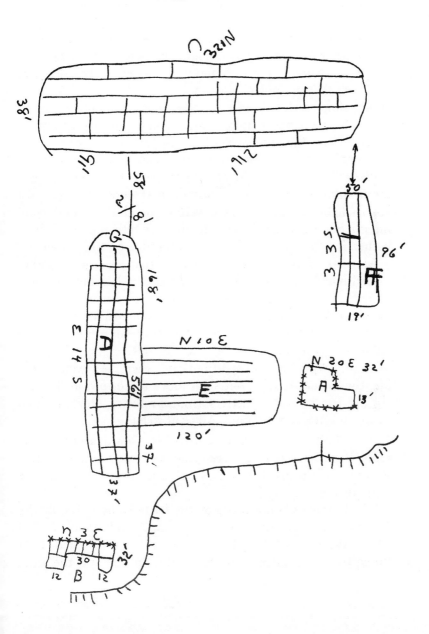

Puaray

destroyed by fire. All the west bank of the river, above the bottom, is very arid. The bottom begins right at the bridge, and widens out to about one-half mile. Very fertile ground. Am lazy or tired.

The list of ruins of the Tigua so far ascertained would be:
    East bank of the Rio Grande: Bernalillo, Alameda—two
    West bank: opposite Algodones, Cangelón, Toreuna, two
        at the Tresquilada, Puaray.

In all, nine scattered over 12 miles in length from north to south. Beetles appear quite frequent here, although they are nearly always the same species.

Went out to foot of bluffs on east-side. Returning, saw two Indians of Sandia trying to coax or coerce a third one, who was drunk and very noisy and boisterous. It ended in the most beastly fight I ever saw. There were six in all, three more coming up. Such beating, kicking in the face, etc. Three of them bathed in blood, and one was left insensible on the ground.

Met Mr. Nathan Bibo. He told me that there was another ruined pueblo on the east bank, but that it had been washed away by the river. It stood in the northern part of Bernalillo. He also told me that 40 miles from Rito Quemado, west, there were important ruins, and that the Zuñi Indians are in the habit of walking, once a year to the Sho-lo River, 65 miles south of Zuñi, to perform superstitious rites there. All well so far. Slept with Joe tonight, but shall move tomorrow, as it is decidedly too crowded. Letters from Professor Norton, from Brun, and from De Armond. All right so far.

JUNE 7: Left at 5 A.M. and went to Mr. Girard, and took my room there. It was nice, very clean, but badly aired. Only a skylight. Still painted two diagrams, one of Toreuna, and the other of Puaray.

The beadwork is not made by the Isleta Indians, but by the Comanche. They use it to carry an [awl?] and money. Call it *Mu-u*. Went to see Joe at 3:30 P.M. and got drenched. Poor thing, to be separated from each other in one and the same place! Met Mr. Latta. Speaks of extensive ruins north of his place and about the volcano.

JUNE 8: Painted all day. Joe and Pauline came, and Joe stayed for dinner. She slept awhile in my room. Wrote to Brown, to Reed, to Sivers, and to De Armond.

JUNE 9: Went out to Old Town, saw Joe, and took home some of the pottery with me. Then called on Mr. Mass who promised to do for me what he could. Dined with Sanders. Packed up my things in a box, ready to ship to Papa. Mailed pamphlets. Called on Mr. Quetil, and he was much pleased with my paintings. Mr. Quetil showed me some splendid work of his and gave me some very good advice. Shall be able to leave Sunday night at all events. Took a stroll about town after nightfall. On the platform of the depot I asked an Isleta Indian if there were ruins about the pueblo. He said yes, and mentioned the name Tu-a. He also said that the Moqui were called M'bu-que. Shipped my box to Papa by express. Wrote to Papa also.

JUNE 10: Letter from Papa. All well. Went out to Joe. She is well. Was lazy all afternoon. Wrote to Papa and to J. D. McRae. Shall start tomorrow at all events. Joe will go to San Pedro.

JUNE 11: Settled up at the Hotel and then went over to the old town. Procession this morning. Willie sick. Dined at [Father Baldassare's?]; spent the afternoon chatting and pre-paring my things. Talked to some Isleta Indians. They confirm the statements about the ruins near Isleta and also say that they are called Tu-ay. The Rosaries they call Rosa-yo. One of these with silver crosses costs as much as $25.00 to $50.00.

Left Albuquerque at 8:20 P.M. On the train I met Don Cristóbal Armijo and Mónico González; the latter from San Marcial. He told about ruins at San Marcial, 14 miles north of the Jornada del Muerto, which possibly are the most south-erly ones on the Rio Grande. Also told me that the same Apache who killed Plácida Romero's husband, killed his mother, son, daughter, and nephew. He said that there are many springs artificially closed (filled up) by the Indians who, when they abandoned them, covered them up with wood and mezcla [mortar?]. They discover such springs about every month. They are only thin fillets sometimes. Decided to go to San Marcial also. Reached Socorro at 11:45 P.M.

JUNE 12: Splendid morning. Went and saw Mr. Shaw who gave me some very general information. Went out to the Ojos Calientes, three miles from Socorro. The place itself (3000 souls) is much scattered, but the plaza is large, and the mixture of buildings, Mexican and American, is not unpleasant. It lies at the edge of the river bottom, has many trees, mostly cotton-wood and ailanthus, and is the greenest spot I have yet seen in New Mexico. The river is about one-half mile to the east. Beyond the river low ranges of arid and highly tumbled volcanic rocks rise one behind the other. They are often conical. On the west, three miles away, rises the Sierra de Socorro, an enor-mous lump with steep terraced slopes, often vertical, to the north of it the Sierra de los Ladrones. On the narrow foothills with very steep ascent, the buildings of the mines nestle like small huts. It is very picturesque. Toward the south the sierra of Socorro terminates in high volcanic mesas, very steep, with no foothold along their slopes for pueblos. The latter must have been therefore between their base and the river. The Ojos are three miles to the south-southwest on the foot of the mesa, which towers boldly and ruggedly above it. The ruins are southeast and east of the springs, south of the crushing mill of Señor Vigil, on low rocky slopes, slanting to the east. The tradition is that the lands thereto lay to the southeast of them, which is very probable. Vegetation treeless, as also the mountains, not even sabinos. But *Opuntia arborescens* flowers beautifully. A small shrub, the mesquite, makes its appearance here. A high westerly wind blows across this low tableland, but the sand does not fly; there is not enough of it. Everywhere traces of mining.

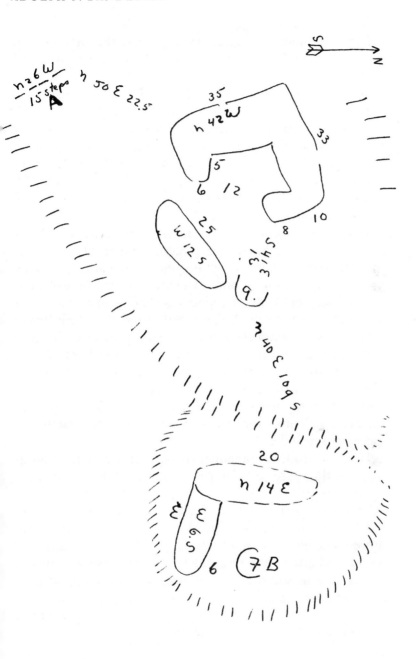

The ruins are not large.

The dimensions are given in steps, and the step at 0.735 meter. These ruins are covered with bluish-red and yellowish flint-chips. There is some obsidian, but little of it. I found some few small bits of pottery. Red and smoked, but there is hardly any at all, and nothing painted or figured. At A. and B. there are distinct foundations, and these appear to have been of rubblestone. Otherwise the ruins only consist of mounds, low, and obliterated. I was told that five miles north of Socorro, on the top of the mesa or loma, there are fine ruins. On the mesas west there are none nearer than 30 miles. This is very important.

Called on Mr. Longuemare. He has fine collections. Showed me the following interesting pieces. A fragment of an iron cuirass and of an iron falconet dug out by him at La Joya (east bank) five feet in the ground. Evidently from the time of Coronado or Sosa, or Oñate. A copper vessel of Spanish make, from a pueblo near Socorro. A fine metate from the Black Range. A fine black jar, complete, from the same region. Stone-hammer also. Showed me the pottery. It is glossy, and black. No indented pottery is found along the river here, except at one place on the east bank where, at 15 feet below the surface, he found, beneath the ruins of a pueblo with painted pottery, pieces of indented and corrugated vessels. This exactly corroborates my find at Pecos.

He showed me an ornamented pipe, of dark talc, from 47 miles to the southwest. He states that, from the Bosquecito, 35 miles south of Socorro, on the east bank, a string of ruins extends to opposite La Joya. Some are also on the west bank, but the majority on the east. West of the river bottom, the nearest pueblo is 35 miles. He says that they are small and round, and generally 3 to 4 miles apart. He has a fine metate from cliff houses in the Black Range where these appear to be very numerous. Shall start tomorrow morning for two ruins across the river, about two miles away. Good work ahead. Fossil buffalo found in the limestone.

June 13: Slept long and late, so that I could not leave before 9 A.M. The ruins are said to be situated on the left side of the Cañada de las Tinajitas on the east bank of the river. I crossed the river bottom after much trouble. It is low, sandy, and covered with a thick shrubbery of cottonwoods and willows, interspersed with some large trees. The current of the river is very strong here, and its waters are turbid. Crossed on the ferry. Deep sand also on the other side.

Right above the landing is a high sandy bluff, on top of which broken pottery, black and white striped, not glossy, but the regular old style which I found at the Ventana and elsewhere. The space on top of the bluff is small, indicating a small ruin. I then proceeded to the north, past the abandoned adobe houses, across the mouth of the Cañada, to the northern bluffs thereof. The top of these does not form a mesa, but a series of ridges, narrow and steep, jutting out towards the river and leaving but a very narrow bottom. The Cañada, however, is not that of the Tinajitas but one farther south about one mile. I still was two miles from the place without knowing it. On the tops of these spurs I found about six ruins, almost obliterated, of little houses with rubble foundations.*

Farther on there was another one, on another ridge, and along its northern rim, which there descends very abruptly to the narrow ravine.

One ruin had some very small fragments of gray pottery, and beneath a bush there were pieces of a broken caxete, gray and black, exactly like the pottery of the Ventana. But it looks so new and freshly broken that I am suspicious of it. Still it is not modern pottery. On one of the ridges, composed of red clay, descending very abruptly and partly tumbled, I found traces of another small stone dwelling, and near it a piece of corrugated pottery made of red clay, which is micaceous. Farther on I found traces of three more small buildings, but no pottery. Little white flint about, and no obsidian. Returned about 3 P.M.

The Feagle brothers, who have the ferry-boat, told me about

the ruins at the pueblo (35 miles west of here). They say that there is no ruin between it and the river, and that its pottery is glossy. Called at Father Bernard's. He told me that at the Escondida de Limitar [probably, hiding place of the Limitar family] there are good ruins. Shall go there tomorrow, early.

At last found Mr. Longuemare. He said he had analyzed the pottery, but found no alkali in the paint and no silex. But it invariably contained phosphoric acid, which is a proof of the existence of animal matter. Speaking of the barro blanco [white clay], he suggested it might perhaps be kaolin! He also states that, while all the pottery is micaceous, the clay itself is not micaceous at all. At night he showed me the pottery from the Sierra de las Gallinas. It is absolutely like that of the Ventana in all its varieties, and there are two pieces with their glossy stripes, showing that the glossy kind is scarce.

But I begin to doubt the accuracy of Mr. Longuemare's recollection of the pieces. He says that he dug out three skulls and many bones from the cliff houses there, all of adults, and all very small. Even the cliffs are very small. In the Sierra de los Mogollones, the pottery becomes very thin, very handsome, glazed (?) on both sides, and with the patterns of the Casas Grandes. Very important if correct. Talked a good deal tonight. Heard that Adolph Mermet was here. The mesquite bush is common here. Longuemare says that the Spaniards made much pottery on the cliffs which I visited today. [The present] Socorro dates from 1816, and the churchbooks from only 1820.

JUNE 14: Started at 6:30 A.M. on foot. The road leads due north through the bottom, which there is open and cultivated. Reached the two houses (one of Vivian Baca) at the foot of the loma at 7:30 A.M. There the loma, which behind Socorro and northwest of it is but a foothill to the mountain, sweeps in a curve to the river front, and hugs it so closely, that where it terminates, there is but room for the acequia and the railroad track alongside the river. Then I ascended to the top of the steep, gravelly mesa, about 50 to 75 feet high. On the right side of the road, very near the brink, stand the ruins. They can be plainly discerned and show all the rooms distinctly. They appear to have been of rubble, very irregularly broken. Pottery, glossy and black, is strewn over them in moderate amount. There is some flint and jasper, and a very little obsidian. I measured them very satisfactorily.

This place is called El Barro, and there are no traditions current about it. Below it is the ferry. Juan Domingo Sylva, the boatman, showed himself exceedingly pleasant and kind in every way. He gave me much valuable information, stating that his own house stood on a large pueblo, called Pueblito de la Parida, and that a still larger one was on the top of the loma above it. He went with me to his house and showed me everything.*

This plat or sketch is very imperfectly made but the bearings and the figures are of sufficiently accurate approximation to permit a more perfect copy to be based upon it. These ruins stand on the loma, about 500 steps from the pueblito to the east, on a height of about 50 feet. There is much mesquite at the bottom, and some on the top. Whereas the ground is red below, it is lighter above, and sandier. The pottery at the pueblito is painted and glossy, similar to that of the barro, but the stripes may be somewhat smaller. It is also black, smoky, and plain red. On the loma it is gray with black stripes, and corrugated and indented. Sylva told me that, at the foot of the hills, southeast of his house, he found a Campo Santo [cemetery]. The bodies were laid flat, head to the south, feet to the north. They did not appear to be with stone cists. Mr. Longuemare told me that in every instance in New Mexico, he had found the dead in a squatting position. His statement includes cliff dwellers.

At one point, I found a lot of charred corn, dug out. The loma appears to have been a settlement of small isolated houses, and the pueblito one of the regular pueblo form. Sylva also confirmed to me the existence of the ruins on the north of the Cañada de las Tinajitas and says that the other ruins on the river bank consist of small houses as on the loma, and with the same pottery. Returned along the railroad track about 1:30 P.M. with a fierce wind blowing against me.

Mr. Longuemare told me that the big ruin in the Cañada de la Parida was four miles inland. This would make three or four regular pueblos on the east bank, opposite Socorro, besides the small houses. There is also a ruin with a church at the sabino, two miles above the pueblito. On the whole, I am pleased with my stay. The fact is ascertained, that both architectures are represented here, and each with its corresponding pottery sharply and clearly defined. There is no impinging of either upon the other.

Saw Adolph Mermet about sunset. Friendly. Shall leave tonight if possible. San Marcial is my *Ultima Thule* this time. There appears to have been a pueblo on the very site of Socorro itself. Mr. Longuemare says that it was a very large one. But his statements need caution. He is extravagant in figures. Left at midnight for San Marcial.

JUNE 15: Reached San Marcial at 1 A.M. and took lodging at the Station Hotel. It is poor, but kindly attended. Slept badly.

The new town is small; so is the old town, about one-half mile to the southwest of it. River bottom fertile. The river has a very strong current. The mountains on the west are high and bold; on the east they recede, leaving a dark, bold mesa, very abrupt, on the southeast of the town, and east of the great railroad bridge. This mesa is about 400 feet high and has very steep, almost perpendicular, craggy slopes. The rock is black lava or trap.

I went to Mónico González, and he again confirmed his statements about the ruins on top of the mesa, and at the house of Esteban González. So I went on through the fields and clambered on top of the high mesa. It was very difficult, although I ascended through a cañada. The top is perfectly level; the rim is strewn with sharp lava and sandy soil. Mesquite is the only shrub. No tree visible all around; the mountains are barren beyond all description. To the southeast the mesa gradually sinks to a plain, and the mountains leave a gap there. This is the direction of the Jornada del Muerto which begins 14 miles away. I wandered, with great trouble, over the whole mesa, and examined it carefully, but found not the slightest trace of habitations; not even pottery. The soil is very sandy, and the lava protrudes in spots. On the north side corrales of lava appear. Evidently modern.

My right shoe being completely worn out, I descended on the north side, where there is deep sand. On the northwest the mesa hugs the river closely. On the top I saw two mountain partridges, very handsome, and at the foot, there is a row of cottonwoods planted. Four quadrupeds, one of which [was] a gray squirrel, started from the trees and ran up the slope. Three of them were so large, that I took them to be foxes. Found a fine beetle. Then I went to the north of the town and found the ruins at the house of Esteban Gonzáles. They had been uncovered through his making adobe; the foundations are of rubblestone, pottery black and red, indicating the glossy kind. North of the ruins, which I measured, are embankments which show traces of a rectangular building, and the soil now covering it appears to have been formed by decay of adobe walls, as at the Pueblito de la Parida. I then went to Mr. Spears' barroom and painted there. Left by the emigrant train at 9:45 P.M.

JUNE 16: Reached Albuquerque at 5:30 A.M. Everything all right. Went out to Joe, then returned and painted and slept. Very tired. Painted till 10 P.M.

JUNE 17: Letter from Papa, and papers from Rochester. All right. Painted and went out to Joe. Pass matters yet unarranged, which is very annoying. Had to write to Brown not to come until Monday. My room is very hot. Wrote late, and painted too. Shall try my hand at figures. Had my shoe fixed and soled. Called on Judge Hazeldine. Very busy as usual.

JUNE 18: Received a letter from Frank Smith this morning. Heel and mouth are both sore. Joe spent the day here and sat in my room while I painted. She returned about 4 P.M. after a severe blow had passed over.

JUNE 19: Went out to Joe and found her sick. She took cold, evidently, but is recuperating fast. Good letter from Mrs. Morgan, with one of her enclosures. Day so far all right. Letter from Mr. Norton and from Lizzie. At night, Superintendent Smith arrived, also both Brown and Bennett. Hope to take Joe along tomorrow.

JUNE 20: Very [little] success at the railroad office. Half-fare tickets were all we could get, and the permission to use freight trains was flatly refused. Very angry, but what is the use of it? Joe cannot come along. So we left at night, I very much disgusted. Night clear and splendid. Shall try to do our best at Acoma, but not go any farther.

JUNE 21: Reached Cubero at 2:30 A.M. and camped alongside of the railroad tracks. At sunrise I walked to Cubero, and then took breakfast, returning with Trinidad and a two-horse team for the artists. The excavations at the Pueblito have not yielded a single unbroken piece as yet. We left Cubero Station about 9 A.M. and drove up the Cañada del Agua Escondida which is the one east of the Cañada de la Cruz. It is very level, somewhat sandy, and the nearer we come to Acoma, the more craggy and picturesque become the rocks.

Trinidad told me about the tribe. He says that the singular being whom I once met at Acomita is Mariano Amugereado, and that there are about four of such amugereados [amujerados, or effeminate persons, transvestites] in the pueblo, and two at least in Santo Domingo. They have no inclination for women, but pay men to sleep with them. When such propensities show themselves in a man, the tribe dresses him in a woman's dress, and treats him kindly but still as a woman. It is affirmed by him to be a custom of the Pueblos, who call such people qo-qoy-mo.

Trinidad also affirmed that, at Acoma, married women would

secretly sell themselves or their favors, and that undue favors from a girl might be occasionally obtained by application to the father of the family. He affirms that, at the rabbit hunt, illicit intercourse with women is allowed the whole day until sunset and taken advantage of during the hunt, etc. He was never allowed to see a Kachina, but always shut up in his room as long as they danced it. When we approached Acoma, fires arose on top of the rock and it became apparent that they were celebrating a Kachina. Indeed, José Miguel soon presented himself and bade us to wait below until the Kachina was over. We photographed the cliff and pueblo from the north side, and then he led us to the foot of the cliff, where we sat down, sending Trinidad home. Soon others came to greet us and then went and got us food. At about 4 P.M. José Miguel said it was time to go, and the whole procession started from the rock by the Camino del Padre, our Indians carrying the luggage. Andrés insisted upon all of us staying with him, and so we took quarters.

Towards evening the boys played *to-tya-note*. Two pegs are rammed in the ground about four inches apart, and the play consists in shooting a large ball through them, at the same time caramboling another. The player who does this scores two, and the one who gets ten first, wins. They play in parties or sides, and both with large and with small balls. One of the players sits near the pegs and pushes the balls with a scraper or little shovel of wood.

Next Saturday is Saint John's Day, which they will celebrate extensively. José Miguel repeated his statement in regard to the fact that they came originally by the Cañada de la Cruz, and Trinidad, who once visited an estufa, says it is square, and that the fire (of encino) burns in it night and day, and is constantly cared for by an Indian. The lieutenant governor and Diego Antonio accompanied us all around. In regard to Montezuma Rock they say that, as the grass or weeds on top of it grow in spring, so the crops will be later in the year and that the rock is prophetic in that respect. Of the Mesa Encantada he repeats the story already told, of three young men who climbed on the top and, unable to get down again, had to starve to death there. Slept on the roof in the open air.

June 22: At noon Encarnación Lucero came up. He is in pursuit of three robbers, who stole two horses from him last night. Day most splendid, and [Brown and Bennett's] photographs very successful in every respect. They took a number of photographs, but as it clouded in the afternoon . . . , they failed in getting the general view from the top of the church.

June 23: Sky cloudless in the morning. They began photograph-ing from top of the church at 8 A.M. It was very hot and I re-mained at home to write and to paint. Painted the basket or *O-tanyi*, and began on the tinaja or *shtionyi*. They finished taking views at noon and came back. At 3 P.M. Trinidad arrived, and we went down to leave. Took another view from the bot-tom. Trinidad told me they called a meeting today, jointly with the Laguna, which meeting was held on the cliffs of the Acoma lands, close by the Laguna lands. It was held to deter-mine damages owed by the Laguna for destruction of corn by their horses. The Navajo call the pueblo of Acoma *A-go-ho*. We reached Cubero at night.

June 24: Tired. Mr. De Armond more friendly [than] ever. Stayed there the whole day and painted Acoma pottery. It was Saint John's Day, and the Mexicans began rooster-pulling. Fighting soon ensued. Returned to Cubero Station at 7 P.M. and took the train at 10:34 P.M. It was crowded with returning tie-cutters. Very tiresome and uncomfortable.

June 25: Reached Albuquerque at 4 A.M. All well. Letter from Boston, etc. Joe well off. Grew terribly hot. Wrote to Mrs. Morgan and to Mr. White. Shall leave soon. Joe is tired, and I too. Bennett and Brown still here.

June 26, 27, and 28: Wrote to Prof. Norton. Took leave [on the 28th of June] and Joe came down to sleep in the new town. Shall leave tomorrow for Santa Fe.

June 29: Train eight hours late owing to rain and consequent

ditching of a locomotive two miles from San Marcial. Went out
to Indian school and were well pleased. Fifty-six children of
both sexes are there, among them six Apache. Train at last
arrived at noon, and we left. At Lamy, west of the depot, Ed
McLean led us to a group of small house ruins. Pottery gray
and black, corrugated, also one piece of red and black, not
glossy. The ruins consist of mounds and stone heaps as follows:

The ruins are much obliterated. At (a.) and (b.) there are
possibly foundations of walls; these foundations indicate that

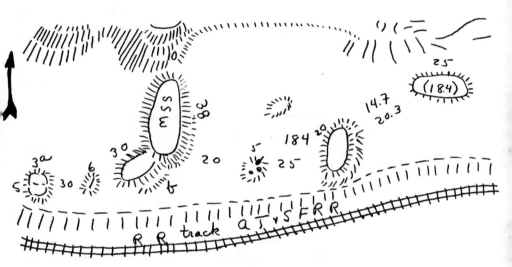

limestone was used, in the shape of cobble-stone. Found some
flint-chips and also some obsidian. There may be more houses
yet. The whole settlement seems to have been built on the
slope of hills whose tops are rocky, and covered with sabinos,
whereas the places where the houses stand are destitute of
shrubs or of trees. It was a typical small-house settlement.

Met Sheriff Martinez and Amado Cabeza de Vaca. All well at
Peña Blanca. Reached Santa Fe at 6 P.M., found letters from
Ratzel and Greenleaf. Joe is very sick. Headache terrible. Saw
nearly everybody except Governor Ritch who is very, very sick.

Judge Downs told me of ruins, small houses, with black and white pottery, etc., 12 miles southeast, on the Pecos Road.

JUNE 30: Painted all day. We took some walks [toward evening]. I examined the recent pottery from San Ildefonso. It is red and black, rather handsome. Cochiti also is beginning to paint its pottery red.

JULY 1: Went to Dr. Thomas and got his stone-hatchet from Laguna. There were six or seven Navajo there and I asked them their name for Acoma, Zuñi, and Isleta. They call them respectively: *Ha-qo, Na-tesh,* and *Na-to.* Some Cochiteños came in. They were overjoyed. Are making great preparations for the 14th and expect many people. Painted all afternoon. At Marsh's saw three very interesting articles from San Juan—a fine head-dress, a peculiar rattle, and a ring of cornhusks, for the head. All from the dance, buffalo dance, he says.

JULY 2: Took a walk with Joe about the base of old Fort Marcy. Finished painting the hatchet at noon and although it thundered and looked threatening, I returned the object to Dr. Thomas. He told me that, once, there was a disagreement between the principales of Isleta and their cacique, concerning the election of governor, the cacique being in favor of one man and the principales of another. Dr. Thomas was called upon to compromise, and he went to Isleta and called a meeting. That meeting was at last convocated, but no agreement was reached. Dr. Thomas then proposed to confer with the cacique alone, at the latter's house. At this conference, the cacique insisted upon having another man present, whom he declared was his right-hand man, who was entitled to know the same secrets which he knew himself, and Dr. Thomas had to yield the point. Then they finally came to an agreement about the matter and the person.

Arranged for trip to Santa Fe Canyon tomorrow morning. Saw Governor Ritch.

JULY 3: Started for the [Santa Fe] canyon at 8 A.M. It is more beautiful than the Cañón del Oso. The slopes are covered with large pines, and picturesque rocks of granite jut out everywhere. Many flowers. From the lower part of the canyon the Sierra de San Mateo is seen very distinctly. A very pleasant ride. Met some Indians from Santa Clara. They had black shining pottery, platos [plates], which they call *saua-pi-i,* and little pitchers of yellow micaceous pottery, called *sam-be.*

Got note from Dr. Thomas stating that Indians from Jemez are here. I went there after dinner and met, to my greatest delight, Mr. Walter G. Marmon of Laguna.[151] He gave me a good deal of valuable information. He said that the Laguna are evidently of Acoma stock, but that there are admixtures of Navajo and of Zuñi Indians. There is a tradition that, at one time, the Laguna lived at Zuñi on account of some warfare. In regard to their descent he says that everything is very indefinite. They have a number of clans, the most numerous of which is *Yaq'a* [corn]. There is also *O-shatsh* [sun], *Tya-me* [deer], *Shru-u-i* [snake], *Qo-hay-o* [bear], etc. He does not remember everything. There are a number of medicinemen whom they call *Tshay-ani,* but there are four principal ones, *O-shatsh, Ha-qanyi* [pine], *Haatze,* and wind. The cacique was the head of the medicinemen, but the office is now abolished, since the dissension which broke out in 1872. These dissensions were caused by a Zuñi Indian who married into the Laguna tribe and began to establish a new faith. This faith was said to be

---

151. Walter Gunn Marmon, civil engineer and surveyor, born in 1841, served in the 87th Ohio Infantry during the Civil War and was taken prisoner at Harper's Ferry. He came to New Mexico in 1869 to survey the Navajo Reservation. In 1871 he opened a trading post at the Pueblo of Laguna, and from 1871-75 was a government teacher at the pueblo. In 1875 he returned to trading and, with his younger brother, Robert G. Marmon, also a resident of Laguna, did extensive surveying of land grants for the Surveyor-General's Office. Both Marmons married Laguna women and their descendants are still important in affairs of the pueblo. Both were Laguna governors, Robert in 1880, Walter in 1886. In 1883, Walter secured a patent to a homestead south of Laguna still known as the "Marmon Ranch." He died in November, 1899.

similar to Protestantism, and [dates back] to the missionary Gorman.[152] It is taught and symbolized in a dance called the *chacuan* [*chakwena*] in which they wear black masks with white beards. (Compare the rock-paintings near Acoma!) He saw nothing indecent in the Kachinas at all; they are symbolic dances representing traditions and beliefs only. At present, the pueblo is quiet and orderly, and there are no religious dissensions. I agreed to go to Laguna upon my return and to study the people there. I then met an Indian from Jemez who gave me the names of the pueblos in their languages. [Roster of names deleted.] Jemez: *Tu-hoa* also *Je-ua*. But he says that the former is more properly the name of their chief estufa in which they celebrate their main dancing, etc. The pueblo of San Diego has the same name.

I then went back and got the head-dress and rattle from Mr. Marsh and painted all day. Many people coming in from all sides.

JULY 4: Overnight, Joe had a very violent attack of vomiting, diarrhea, and cramps. She is very weak. I consulted Dr. Eggert, who says she ought not to travel at all. Gave her medicine. The city is crowded with people. Even from Cubero, Gregorio Otero. Albuquerque is finely represented. But it is terribly hot. Sultry and cloudy. Joe up again. Handsome uniforms. Procession at one o'clock. Painted all day. Meagre fireworks at night. The plaza is crowded with people. Music. Spent evening with Gerdes.

JULY 5: Joe much better. Returned the objects to Mr. Marsh and bought his stone-axes and arrowheads. Saw Dr. Covert and

---

152. Samuel Gorman came to New Mexico in 1852 under the auspices of the American Baptist Home Mission Society and was one of the first Protestant missionaries to Pueblo Indians. From 1852-59 he lived at Laguna conducting services and maintaining a school. From 1859-62 he was at Santa Fe, returning east with other Union sympathizers in 1862. While at Laguna, Gorman was a frequent and vigorous spokesman for that Pueblo against white encroachers and in disputes with other Indian groups. His house is now the residence of the Walter K. Marmon family.

got his old vessel and pottery. It is very handsome. Saw Father
Defouri, very pleasant. He has a splendid painting, on copper,
of Nuestra Señora de Guadalupe. A beautiful group of minia-
tures. Called on Mrs. Sheldon, also on Mrs. Brown. All ready
for tomorrow to Galisteo. Mr. Ellison spoke of a very important
paper speaking of an early expedition to Zuñi by Juan de Oñate's
father.[153]

JULY 6: [mislabeled 7th in journals] Left at 8 A.M. and went
to Lamy where we took dinner. South of Lamy a treeless plain
gently slopes to the south and southeast, where the Arroyo de
Galisteo forms its limit.

When we reached the arroyo, a fearful storm was upon us.
Rain and wind made the horse and me powerless, and I had to
stand still in the middle of the arroyo, while we got fearfully
drenched and the wind lifted and almost upset our buggy. At
last I drew the horse across in the blinding storm and as soon
as we reached the high bank, [the storm] relaxed. We were
about one-half mile from Galisteo, a small scattered village of
adobe buildings, on the southwest side of a ridge. It is picturesquely situated, but almost without trees. To the east of it
spreads an entirely barren treeless plain.*

[Sylvester] Davis was not at home, so, thoroughly wet, we
went to Don Nicolás Pino, who received us most handsomely.
His house is spacious; we got a very good room, and the treat-
ment was excellent. His daughter, Donna Trinidad Pino de
Pino, speaks English; so does Mrs. Beckwith.

I at once started for the old pueblo of Galisteo which lies
about one-and-one-half miles (airline) north-northeast of the
new town, beyond the crestón [outcropping] and the arroyo, on
the latter's right bank. The soil is dark red, loamy. The de-

---

153. Cristóbal de Oñate, father of Juan de Oñate, the conqueror of New
Mexico, arrived in the New World in 1524 and was commander in Nueva Gali-
cia during the Coronado Expedition to the Southwest, 1540-42. In the late
1540's he became one of a small group of entrepreneurs who founded the mining city of Zacatecas. As far as is known, the elder Oñate never visited the
Pueblo area.

clivity of the crestón is very rocky, but the arroyo eats on its north bank, so that the gentle slope is on the south side. There is also an old ruin there, and they say that this was the old pueblo of Galisteo. Pottery not glossy, but painted and black. The ruins of the pueblo show many traces of combustion, much of the painted pottery even appears charred and burnt. There is a rotten beam lying on the ground, and I secured the piece of a pole, with the cut end charred. The pottery is mostly glossy, some of it green, other with red and black lines, the black lines glossy. Then again pottery all red, and also all black. There is much obsidian, very handsome and transparent, little flint, lava in blocks and chips. The foundations are plainly visible in places, but no estufas appear, although there are huge depressions between the rows of houses. It was evidently but two stories high, and very extensive. The foundations were partly of stone and partly of adobe, and the latter show themselves as at the ruins of the Pueblito de la Parida and of Bernalillo. No estufas are visible.

There appears to have been a wall along the banks of the arroyo. The latter has eaten fearfully, and has scattered pottery, etc., not only along the northern [bank] but also carried it over the southern bank in part. There appear to have been some excavations made at two places. The whole is on the large house plan, very complicated, the directions are difficult to define, and the measures can only be approximated.

Spent the evening very pleasantly. Don Nicolás showed axe of stone, which one of his herders had brought up; probably from the Pueblo Colorado. The pueblo of San Cristóbal was probably abandoned last of all. It lies five miles east of Galisteo at the foot of the mesa. Shall go there tomorrow if the weather allows.*

JULY 7: Started at 8 A.M. The road traverses the plain to the east, along its entire width, about four miles at most. Then the rocks seem to close, the Arroyo de San Cristóbal comes down from the rear side of the mesa of Pecos in a winding course, and the

last spurs are rocky hills of sandstone, large boulders lying
scattered about the slopes, and the tops being very craggy. In
a bend formed by the arroyo, about one-half mile east of Eaton's
ranch, almost shut in by hills, nestles the pueblo. The church
is partly standing, the choir is entire, but the roof is gone. The
walls are about 18 feet high, 32 inches thick, and composed of
thin plates of sandstone superposed with adobe mud between.

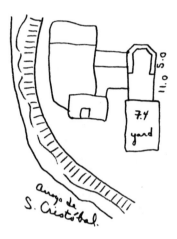

The front part is entirely ruined. The walls run east and west.
In front of the church is the old cemetery enclosed by a stone-
wall, and to the south are yards and the foundations of buildings.
The church is 500 feet from the eastern curve of the arroyo, and
on the south side of the arroyo lies another pueblo.

The large pueblo is composed of a number of ruins, large
mounds of debris. From what I could see, the houses were nowhere more than three rooms at the base. In two cases the front
rooms were opened, showing the walls. They were eleven inches
thick, and, like the church, of thin plates of sandstone with
adobe mud, and so broken as to present a smooth wall on both
sides. Could not find any trace of plastering. Neither was there
any mica to be seen. Some pieces of wood, sticks and poles of
the roof, lying about. Very few manos and no fragments of

metates at all. The manos are flat, mostly of gneiss and similar to those of Galisteo. No axes nor arrowheads, but a great many pieces of very handsome obsidian. It is perfectly transparent and of a smoky color.*

I only measured the church alone, and not the annexes. Thunder-clouds were coming up from the south, with distant thunder, and also forming in the north. It would have been imprudent to risk the storm in the narrow basin, and the sun was too hot. Of course, if Joe had not been along, I would have risked it, as the ranch is only one-half mile away from the ruins.

The letters (b^1.) (m.) and (1.) refer to points on the north and south portions of the general plan. The places within the mounds are very deep, but on the north side the ground is much higher. (Z. and b^1.) are evidently refuse-heaps similar to those on the north side of Acoma. They are covered with more broken pottery than any other part of the ruins.

Towards the church the ground slopes much, so that the northern part of the ruin is much higher than the southwestern. The creek runs around the church, and another branch of it along the west and northwest of the ruins.*

. . . the creek has evidently taken away a part of the pueblo in former times. The banks are not only vertical, but over-hanging even. The creek eats on that side. The pottery is similar to that of the other ruins, but there is less of it, and the condition of the mounds indicates their abandonment at an earlier date. In the other ruin, the main one, I found a small piece of corrugated pottery, much smoked. The black pottery is sometimes micaceous too.

At 12 noon we left, and reached Galisteo in 40 minutes. Joe being unwell, we decided she would stay tomorrow, while I would go to San Lázaro which is five miles from here. The Pueblo Colorado is five miles south, Pueblo Largo three miles southeast, Pueblo de Chelle four miles south-southwest, and the other Pueblo Largo three miles south-southwest.

Saw Sylvester Davis. He is very talkative. Joe unwell again [tonight]. It appears that San Cristóbal was abandoned within

less than 80 years ago. The whole ruins recall Pecos to me.
There is an air of similarity between the two places.

JULY 8: In yesterday's report I forgot to mention the peculiar
double wall of stone, running along the south side of the pueblo
of San Cristóbal. It is evidently composed of two walls of stone,
parallel, and about one and one-half meters apart. It looks as if
there had been a path between the two walls, wide enough to
walk single file only, and as the passage is very tortuous, following the lowest brow of the hill, it suggests the idea of a covered
way. It cannot have very well been a water channel. In general,
while the pueblos are composed of a series of more or less
connected rectangles, the houses are still more scattered and
frequently connected by stone enclosures which have evidently
been similar to that of Pecos. Thus the lack of size in the houses
was compensated by these walls for purposes of defense.

Left at 8 A.M. Distance six miles to the west. Lost my way of
course. Followed the railroad at about one-half to one mile,
crossing the Arroyo de Galisteo to a stone rancho then turned
south about two miles, between two rocky ridges of sandstone,
crossing two arroyos. Found the pueblo on the south side of
the Arroyo del Chorro, on bluffs, slightly overgrown with few
sabinos and large flowering *Opuntia arborescens*. The bluffs are
not steep and appear to be of gravel leaning against sandstone.
The bed of the arroyo winds at the foot of the ruins; the sandstone above them is eroded in little towers and cliffs, jutting out
promiscuously along the slopes of the hills.*

There is much lava in chips, and some bits of obsidian also.
The pottery is similar to that of the other two pueblos, but I
also found three pieces of black and white striped. This can be
accounted for by the proximity of caves, of which there is no
doubt. They are said to be at the very pueblo and along the road,
but I did not see them. Returned at 12:30 P.M. Spent the remainder of the day pleasantly, partly at home, partly at the
Plazita.

Father Mailluchet is here. He speaks of a ruin about seven

miles west or northwest of Pecos, on a high mesa, which he has heard of recently. He says that the ruins are small houses. Don Nicolás spoke to me of the mining prospects. Insists that the Placeres are rich in gold, but lack water. In regard to silver he says that an uncle of his wife, the Vicar-General Razgón from Chihuahua, made an attempt at the Nuevos Placeres, which attempt was very successful, but lasted only about six months. After he was recalled by the Bishop Zubiria to Durango, the mine which he had opened was gradually abandoned as nobody understood how to work it.

JULY 9: Left at 7 A.M. Ambrosio [Pino?] had arrived the night previous. He says the distance to Quivira is 114 miles, and confirms the statement that the four pueblos, Largo, Colorado, Chey, and Blanco are of the large-house type. They appear to be the identical pueblos of the Tano, which the Q'uirauash destroyed, according to the tradition related to me by Juan José at Cochiti.

We reached Santa Fe at noon. The road is completely without water and without trace of habitation. The *Opuntia arborescens* is about through blossoming. Called on Governor Ritch. Joe is all right, although the last drive, 25 miles, has been a very hard one. The road is fairly level, except about the railroad and thence rising up to the tableland adjoining the sierra, on which stands Santa Fe.

JULY 10: Spent [day] in painting the ruins and their pottery. Called on Mrs. Sheldon. Went to Fort Marcy with her and Miss Daton of Steubenville, Ohio. That lady has spent some time in the southwest, in the Sierra de Mogollones. She describes one ruin on top of a mesa, evidently large-house type. It forms a number of connected cells around an oblong depression. A rectangle of the pure original type, with the court in the middle. The fragments of pottery are corrugated and ribbed, but while they are thicker and painted red inside, the indentations and corrugations are very fine and delicate, much more regular than those of the northern ruins. It is of far superior and nicer workmanship. The painted pottery is not glossy, the ground appears white, the paintings brown, but the decay is so strong that the original color can hardly be discerned. Still the designs appear somewhat more artistic. Spirals are plainly visible.

At the fort we found a great deal of pottery, all corrugated and indented smoky, grey and white and black and white, but no glossy fragments. Evidently a small-house pueblo. On the southeast side of the old fort a ring of stone seems to indicate foundations of a building similar to an estufa. There is a depression, but it may be the result of contrast only. In general, any ruin up there must necessarily appear doubtful, on account of the remains of the old fort and its annexes. Mr. Cole found a small arrowhead. Obsidian is scattered there also. The remains are not confined to the eminence on which Fort Marcy stands, the tops of other adjacent lomas also are covered with them, showing the former existence of a small-house settlement like that of the Parida. Faint traces of foundations are also visible. We enjoyed a very glorious sunset and went home at nightfall.

JULY 11: Overnight Joe had a severe attack again, but it passed off well. Mrs. Sheldon and Miss Daton going to Cochiti, and Bennett came up from the Cerrillos. Hai-ou-a in town.

JULY 12: The ladies ready for tomorrow. Day as usual. Bought provisions for the trip. Gold is coming along, on his own hook.

JULY 13: Left at 8 A.M. with the three ladies, Bennett and Mrs. Brown following in another carriage. The trip very pleasant, though hot. Reached Peña Blanca at 1 P.M. Reception very cordial. Left with the Padre and Mrs. Sheldon and Miss Daton at 5 P.M. for Cochiti. The Rio Grande is very treacherous. We had to cross it five times and always with difficulty. It changes its bed almost daily. At the pueblo all is noise and bustle, but the people are always the same in friendliness. While there, the Rio de Santa Fé suddenly came down in a violent stream, flooding part of the valley opposite Cochiti, and then suddenly subsiding. After vespers, which were accompanied by a violin, we returned home, crossing the river again. The valley was still partly flooded. At night, fires were lit on the church towers. The horses of the pueblo were in the sierra, so that no escaramuzas [contests] could be arranged for tomorrow in honor of Mrs. Sheldon. Lost my hat on the road.

JULY 14: Gold got to Cochiti this A.M. The storm caught him at the Bajada yesterday, and he had a hard time of it. We reached Cochiti about 9 A.M. Took up quarters with Juan José. The pueblo is gradually filling with strangers. As far as I can see, the following Pueblos are represented: Cia, Santo Domingo, San Felipe, Santa Ana, Jemez, Sandia, Tesuque, San Juan, Santa Clara, San Ildefonso.

Men and women on horseback, and such a display of turquoise and of Navajo blankets, silver trinkets, Navajo bridles, skirts, etc. One woman of Tesuque had a peculiarly handsome and very large turquoise on her breast. Every house was open and each one entering was at once fed. Mass was said at 10 A.M. A great number of Mexicans were here too; among them was Miguel Montoya of Zile. He confirmed the idol story, but said that it had gone to waste since. He said also that the Indians of Santo Domingo had offered him $100 and a good mule for it.

At noon the three Koshare, among whom [was] Julán Luis, almost naked and painted as at the Baile de los Entremeseros, opened the dance as usual, singing "Ho-a." Previously, the procession had gone forth and placed San Buenaventura in a little niche made with green boughs and Navajo blankets at the edge of the portal of José Hilario's house. As the dancers delayed, I went with Juan José to the estufa of Ta-nyi where they were dressing up and painting. The sight was a very picturesque one. The singers were squatting on the floor, singing and beating the drum. Each estufa had its banner tied to the ladder, above the roof. At last, about 2 P.M., the estufa of Shyu-amo made their appearance, about 25 pairs, dressed and painted as [they were] this spring; they did not go to the plaza [but] directly to the churchyard, and danced in front of it, surrounded by an ellipse of about 200 Indians on horseback, all gaudily dressed, presenting a very striking appearance with their gay handkerchiefs and blankets. Soon after the Ta-nyi arrived also; then the former left for the plaza. The latter danced in front of the churchyard and then followed to the plaza again, where the remainder of the dance was conducted during the day.

All the while, the three Koshare were cutting up their capers, sometimes very filthy, though not properly obscene. The ladies left about 3 P.M. with the Padre, while Bennett and I remained to photograph. This was a hard job. We got the three Koshare, however, and one plate of the dancers. But the weather was very unfavorable and the people in a great hurry to dance, so that the Koshare who had the management of the floor in every respect, took the groups away from us whenever they formed. Much work and very small profits. For the rest, the dance was identical with that of Easter time. The horsemen filled the entrance to the plaza and made it look very gay.

Jac. Gold bought pottery, old things, Victoriano's shield, and rubbish in general. About 5 P.M. rooster-pulling began, but it was a tame affair, and only led to squabbles between the Indians and the Mexicans, and among the Mexicans themselves. I saw some whiskey flasks circulating on the sly, but otherwise there were no disorders. We left at sunset, in time to cross the river by daylight. Remained up long with the Padre. The ladies pleased.

JULY 15: Left at 5 A.M. Contented and happy. Got on top of the Bajada well and slowly, and reached Santa Fe at 11 A.M. Letter from Pauline. Joe is tired but well. Brown is sick, but pleased with the negatives. Began to pack up.

JULY 16 AND 17: Packing up and taking leave. At Dr. Thomas', I got the statistics of the Pueblos of 1880. [List of the Pueblos with population]: Tesuque 99. Pojuaque 26. Nambé 66. Sta. Clara 212. S. Juan 408. S. Ildefonso 139. Taos 391. Picuris 115. Jemez 401. Cia 58. Cochiti 271. S. Domingo 1129. Sa. Ana 489. S. Felipe 667. Laguna 968. Acoma 582. Isleta 1081. Sandia 350.

Zuñi 1608. This makes for the Queres 4164, Zuñi 1608, the Tiguas and Taos 1937, the Tehuas 950, and the Jemez and Pecos 401. Total 9060. But the figures for Acoma and Cia are hardly correct.

At night letters from Mrs. Norton and Parkman. Gold got a fine shield.

JULY 18: Left Santa Fe early by train, Miss Daton coming along. Four months of recollection go along with us, many of which are very pleasant. Homeward bound again. Joe is well and happy. The day delightful and the Pecos valley remarkably handsome. On the train met Mrs. Root, who is now keeping house at Glorieta. We got off at Las Vegas and while the two ladies rode out to the springs, I called on Mr. F. Kihlberg. Missed the train for the springs and had to remain in town.

Las Vegas was founded in 1835, as a small settlement up the Rio Gallinas. It had to contend greatly against wild Indians, until in 1835 the Apache and Jicarilla, which were the most troublesome, were surprised and slaughtered by the Mexican volunteers in the sierra. Since then it has been quiet. Its population is 7000. Situation much more pretty than Albuquerque and while its buildings are equally fine, everything promises more solidity and a more healthy condition. Called on Father Personnet, who is sick, and on Father Mara. Met Father Defouri with whom I spent the night at [Father] Coudert's. Father Defouri told me he had a document speaking of a massacre of Spaniards by Missouri Indians on the site of Fort Leavenworth about 1716. Promised a copy.

JULY 19: Went out to the Springs. Hotel splendid and everything arranged in first-class style. The canyon of the Rio Gallinas itself is very handsome and picturesque; the river is clear, and dark, fine pines grow on the slopes. It is not the grandest (not by far) but the most lovely and the most romantic scenery I saw in New Mexico; the Cebollita always excepted. Many flowers. Left the Springs and got to town at noon, leaving about 1 P.M. The plains, now green, present a handsome appearance.

JULY 20: Thrift and prosperity visible at every step as soon as we pass Fort Dodge. The Arkansas bottom, however, although green, is still comparatively barren.

JULY 21: Awoke in Kansas City. The surprising growth of vegetation, its luxuriant green, etc., is charming. We traversed Missouri which appeared like a vast beautiful garden. We reached St. Louis at 6 P.M., George, Gustav, and Hubert receiving us at the depot. Went home with George. Everything all right so far.

JULY 22: Beautiful day. Did not go out except to Beckers. Left at 6 P.M. for home. The country a perfect paradise in the lovely golden hues of the setting sun. Never saw it so beautiful as now. At the depot, Papa and a whole crowd. All well. So glad to be home again!

FROM HIS ARRIVAL HOME, July 22, Bandelier spent a quiet summer—visiting with relatives and friends. He painted and worked at his notes and manuscripts and also corresponded with Professor Norton and others in regard to his future plans. A week after his arrival, he noted, "There is an air of peace and repose which strangely recalls to me the summer of 1852, the happiest time of my life. To live thus would be only too good; I would become spoiled. God will speak."

The daily entries in the journal continue through August 8, in much the same vein but with several complaints concerning his father's quarrelsome moods. From August 8, the journal skips to an entry of October 31 in which Bandelier summarized the highlights of the preceding weeks.

Bandelier remained on the farm until early September when his father became increasingly quarrelsome and Rosalie, his sister, became too domineering. Other members of the family were occupied elsewhere and consequently, Bandelier "volunteered to keep the books for a month." He added, "It was the most pleasant month I ever spent in Highland." He and Joe had numerous visitors; he appeared at the Historical Society in St. Louis, September 19. From the 12th to the 24th of October he made a trip east to Rochester. The remainder of October was spent finishing bits of correspondence, visiting friends, and packing.

On the 1st of November, Bandelier wrote, "Took leave of Papa! Poor Papa, if he could only control his temper and be less egotistic than he is. It was hard to leave him, but the hardest is yet to come. . . ." This last was undoubtedly in reference to the next day when he left St. Louis—departing in the evening after spending the afternoon "quietly at home with Joe. . . . Leave of Joe very, very sad. Poor, dear, little wife. But it must be!"

We resume with the entry of November 4, Bandelier being enroute to New Mexico.

NOVEMBER 4: Through the lonesome and tiresome plains of Kansas. I noticed that *Yucca angustifolia* appears near Larned. Mr. Reed told me that in his time (1876) antelopes and even buffalos were common in southwestern Kansas. On board the train I found a gentleman from Raton, Mr. McKowan, who informed me that there were probably ruins near Anton Chico and Puerto de Luna. That I shall ascertain at Vegas.

NOVEMBER 5: In the Ratones. Met Señor Romero, who told me that the proper name of the Spanish Peaks was Los Huajatoyas, an Indian name. Reached Vegas at 1 P.M. Went to Father Coudert, who received me in the kindest manner and insisted upon [my] staying with him. He said that the Cienega of the Pecos was probably Las Vegas, the little arroyo running through the town being still called Arroyo de los Pecos, and there are traces of three pueblos almost in town. He went out to inquire. (Saw Frank Kihlberg.) Wrote to Joe.

Had a long talk with F. O. Kihlberg. He also states that

there was a pueblo at the Plaza Nueva. Moved to the Cura at
5:30 P.M. Subsequently Padre Leone from Watrous, Padres
Rossi and Masset [?] came. Pleasant evening. The pueblo stood
about three miles from town. Metates were found there, but
the place is built over now. There may have been also a pueblo
at the Alamos, in the Valles de Gerónimo between here and
Pecos. But it is doubtful in regard to Anton Chico.

NOVEMBER 6: Left for the Plaza de Arriba with a letter for
Don José A. Baca, at 9:30 A.M. Went down to the railroad
crossing and then following up along the Rio Gallinas reached
the house of Don José Baca, a large two-story adobe with
porches in front.*

The lower part of the Plaza Arriba, where the house of Don
José Baca stands, is on a low bluff northeast of the Rio Gallinas.
Its height above that stream is equal to two heights (?) or eleven
feet, 3.30 m. The hill is of gravel, and the whole is rather a
tongue. It appears that along the whole of this tongue remains
were found of small stone houses. Skeletons were dug out but
unfortunately not preserved. Much pottery, stone implements,
metates, etc., were found. The pottery he describes as corrugated and indented, also painted. He promised to send me some
pieces. The following gives an idea of the location.*

The [area] south of Don José Baca's, across the Gallinas, is
a barren hill. There I found the upright foundations. They are
of lava rock, and only faint. Near them a big hole is dug. I begin
to suspect that these small houses have been the innocent cause
of many a mining enterprise, the remains of them being taken
for remnants of old mines. I found, scattered over the brow of
the hill, flint chips, one little piece of obsidian, and two pieces
of pottery, one of them finely striated black-on-white. It would
indicate the former presence of small houses. Nothing else was
found. Neither could I detect any traces on the other hills
bordering the Gallinas on the west and northwest. It thus appears that the settlements on the Plaza de Arriba and that opposite were about the only ones in that direction. Returned

home about 2 P.M. and Padre Navet then suggested that we should go to the Valles de San Gerónimo, 18 miles west of Vegas, on the Tecolote.

So we started about 3 P.M. with the black ponies of Padre Coudert and his topbuggy, and drove to the depot where I found my trunk, to my great delight. Took out the photographic apparatus and we started finally at 4 P.M. driving south. Then we turned sharply into the mountains to the west, passing through a gate of rocks. We crossed the Rio Tecolote after dark, losing our way previously, so that Padre Navet had to walk ahead for awhile to hunt the road.

At 7 P.M. we reached the village of the Valles de San Gerónimo. The sight from the heights above with the lights of the little village below (about 400 souls) is very handsome. We went to the house of Juan Antonio Atencio and were very kindly received. The lord of the mansion told me that there were two ruins, one on the north end of the plaza, and the other on the loma in front, on the east side of the Tecolote. Metates had been found in both places. San Gerónimo was founded in 1838, and until 1846 the Apache were very troublesome. They made it almost impossible to exist, carrying off stock and children, and killing adults. Even the Navajo extended their raids into the vicinity.

NOVEMBER 7: Went over to Pueblito, the place north of the plaza, a barren hill of granite, and some fields east of it along the Rio. I found denuded spaces with scattered stones, but only a few small bits of nondescript pottery, one of them very micaceous. Also smoked pottery, but this is evidently recent, as the Indians of today sell it to the people. I returned to the village, where meanwhile the election had begun. Mass was on and I took Simón along. He told me that the place north of the plaza was always called Pueblito and the ruins were scattered over the hill, etc.*

Ruins in the field of Pueblito, upright stones set on edge. I found these foundations in the field east of the granite hill.

Photographed the view twice. Don't like the result. Returned home. Señora Atencio told me that, on the hill opposite, she had been present when a small house of two rooms was dug into. A hearth was found, and close by it a tinaja of black ware with indented figures containing some yellow clay or dust. The house was small. There was also a metate, concave, and with three feet. It is now lost. Everything indicates small houses. Simón also told me that about two miles south of the town, on the slope of a high hill, he once found a piece of obsidian.

We left at 11 A.M. and from the brow of the hill I again photographed the charming view of the valley. We returned by the Agua Zarca, a charming gorge and a few huts with a tendejón [perhaps store, or commissary tent]. The Puertecita, of highly tilted rocks, is very picturesque. Near the Puertecita where the road sallies into the plain of Vegas, there are ruins of an old Spanish town, with a round tower. Reached Vegas at 3 P.M. and found that Father León Mailluchet of Pecos was here. (We handed the plates to Mr. F. E. Evans, who promised to develop them.) Father Mailluchet spoke to me of the ruins at Kingman, also at Glorieta, where there is a round tower. Of Quivira he says that the houses are much scattered. He is of the opinion that an earthquake destroyed the place, because the houses were fallen in and many skeletons found beneath the roof, all with the heads toward the door, as if they had been crushed during the attempt to flee.[154] Election today. Very noisy. Result uncertain. Had a very pleasant evening. If only Joe could be here.

NOVEMBER 8: Last night, about 10:30, we were called out to a man who had just died of the smallpox. Stumbled about Las Vegas for a whole hour, and then finally could do nothing, since the undertaker had taken the matter in hand. Went to bed after midnight and slept rather poorly.

Went to the depot and got my things out. Then to Mr. Evans. Plates in the trunk badly broken. Out of 12 only 5 left.

---

154. This is possible as the Rio Grande area is a fault area.

Took out the 4 plates used and put in 5 new ones. Mr. Evans will develop and print. He told me that 10 miles southeast of here, on the top of a high mesa, there is, according to Mr. Sulzbacher, a ruined pueblo. Wrote card to Norton. Sent a bag of piñones and letter to Joe.

Election returns coming in. Americans here generally downcast in politics and in business. They grumble a great deal and seem to comprehend that they cannot force anything. Saw F. O. Kihlberg. It looks as if the tide of settlement was going to Lake Valley and Kingston, and as if Las Vegas and Santa Fe were going to be depopulated. Railroad schemes are of course afloat, amongst them one from Kingman up the Pecos Valley by the Plazita. Also a large hotel scheme for the ruins of Pecos. Schemes and scheming, and nothing else.

Father Coudert returned at noon. He tells me that the Sierra de los Jumanos is north of Quivira, and east of Cuaray [Quarai] and Abó. After mailing card and piñones to Joe, I painted. It is a great pity that José Albino Baca has not sent his pottery, but yesterday it was the election in which his son-in-law, Manzanares, was involved, and besides Miguel Montoya of Cubero has died, so that he had to go to his funeral. Called on Mr. and Mrs. F. O. Kihlberg. Afterwards pleasant evening at the Curacy with the doctor. Much smallpox in town. Got my blanket.

NOVEMBER 9: Called on Dr. Emmelheinz who gave me the prescription against smallpox. Left at noon, but was called back, as news had come that ruins with pottery were at the Vigiles, 5 miles from town, on the left bank of the river, and at the foot of the crestón, about one mile this side of the Springs Hotel. I accordingly left with Manuel García, in his wagon. At the very foot of the crestón between it and the Vigiles, is a large expanse covered with rocks and boulders. There is much flint also, and I soon found some flint arrowheads and also black pottery, black and white, and a small-house type clearly indicated. It is a field now, covered with sunflowers, level, and directly above the Gallinas River. García told me that it was all timber 20 years ago, as well as the loma and the cerrito. No foundations.

We went to the town, and there met the sacristan, Ramón Mes, who has lived here a long time. He showed me a metate of quartzite and a doorsill of syenite which came from the ruins. The metate is large, has no feet, and is hollowed out in the middle, not concave or curved as they commonly are. It has no shape, but is merely a large block worn out by grinding, a kind of transition between the mortar and the grinding slab. He said that the manos are short, elongated pebbles, and not larger than eight inches to one foot. Very crude. He then told me that the village was composed of small houses, irregularly scattered, and that it had a single estufa, the place of which he showed me. The foundations were of rubble stone, which are still lying about profusely. They were set in the ground to varying depths. Doorsills of stone, fragments of metates, all very crude, are lying about also.

Ramón told me that while there were only foundations at the Vigiles, at the Plaza Arriba, where the house of José A. Baca now stands, the wall was [within memory] still about 0.50 meter high. It was mud, made in a box, and on foundations of rubble. The walls were not thick, about eight to ten inches. There were two villages, one on the Plaza Arriba, and the other at the Vigiles, each containing about 30 homes and an estufa. Now everything has disappeared. These ruins, he says distinctly, are the only ones along the Rio Gallinas down to Las Vegas. There are none in the canyon of the Springs. There are still pots and pans buried at the Vigiles. Stone axes and hammers were also found. I gathered many arrowheads. The pueblo stood on good soil, very fertile, but wooded with fine trees.

Don Ramón then told me that he had lived long among the Tehua and knew their language. The Tehua have one, two, and three estufas, according to the numbers of the population. They have a cacique which they call ?? (Forgot to ask!) Returned

home very well satisfied. Evening pleasant with Dr. Emmelheinz and Mr. Penda[ris?] The latter says there are no ruins at
Tecolote. [Bandelier later learned this was erroneous.]

NOVEMBER 10: An old man came and was closely interrogated
by Padre Coudert. He states that there are ruins at the Allender
[?], 20 miles south-southeast of here, and also traces at Romero.
There are also small houses near Las Vegas (south); none at
Tecolote and none at Anton Chico. But at the Agua Negra near
Puerto de Luna there are, and in the Cañada Pintada, ten miles
northwest there are [ruins].

He then described the manner in which the Pecos Indians
hunted eagles. There were many eagles here; at the confluence
of the Arroyo de los Pecos and the Cañada Azul, they had a large
woodshed and came there every summer to hunt the eagle. They
dug pits and covered them with boughs and straw. Outside of
the small hole which was left, a dead rabbit or rat was tied to a
string, and near it a live eagle was also fastened. The eagle saw
the dead animal, and it began to flap its wings and make an
effort to reach it. This and his shrieks would attract another
eagle to the spot, and the two invariably engaged in a fight.
While thus fighting, the Indians in the pit reached out and
seized the wild eagle by its legs. Then they pinned him to the
ground with wooden tongs, thus securing him. This was done
every summer.*

Pottery all black-on-white, and some of the coarsely corrugated kind too; gray obsidian and much flint.

After that old man had gone, another came. He assured us,
Padre Coudert and me, that halfway between the Plaza Arriba
and the Vigiles, there was an estufa, out of which pottery was
taken. This makes three pueblos on the Rio Gallinas above Las
Vegas. Then there are pueblos near Romero, also at the southeast corner of the Ratones, but I could not get any description
of them. Left at 12 A.M. (hurriedly since the coach was late).
They wanted to keep me at all hazards, but I slid out, although
the hospitable room will be greatly missed by me. Mr. Evans
showed me the only good view of mines [?] which is the last one.

Arrived at Pecos Station at 2 P.M. and thence on foot to San Miguel where I was very well received. Padre Fayet at once arranged for me to go to Pueblo, where there are three pueblos. Then I went to Mr. Guérin, who directed me to a ruin. . . . It is above the banks of the Rio Pecos, and two rooms are still perfect. The walls are 0.30 meter thick, and the stones are well broken and fairly laid. Pottery all of the small-house type. Still the building is large and may have been two stories high. Near by is a high hill, very rocky, on the top and slopes of which much pottery is found, also corrugated specimens. San Miguel was formerly a site of Indios genízaros [Hispanicized Indians]. The church was begun 86 years ago. It is rather pleasantly situated, but extremely windy. Father Fayet is extremely friendly. So is Mr. Guérin, and all the people. Tomorrow I go to Pueblo to relatives of Father Ribera. I was also told there are ruins at the Chaperito, 20 miles south of Vegas, on the Rio Gallinas.

NOVEMBER 11: Left for the pueblo at 8 A.M. The height above the river is 36 meters, of the ruin itself 6.4, of which however a part is of the rock, and only about 3 meters of mounds.*

Ruins of the pueblo, left bank of the Rio Pecos, opposite the Plaza del Pueblo. Pottery coarsely corrugated, little obsidian. I rode to Pueblo. It is a very handsome ride.

The valleys dotted with sabinos and cedars, on the dark red ground, with the handsome mesas all around, are very striking. The place is small, houses all of adobe. I stopped at the residence of Don José Lino Ribera. His brother, Francisco, was at home alone.

Started for the ruins very soon. There is a large ruin north of the town, on the banks of the river. Walls are uncovered in part. They were of stone, the red sandstone of the mesas, but also of mud, made probably in a frame. They are only nine inches thick and not of adobe brick. Pottery smoked, white painted black, handsome, not glossy, but there is like a thin glaze over it. Much flint.

Crossed the river; then a field 200 meters wide; and then

almost vertically up to the mesita, 32.0 [meters] high. It is rocky, and has sparse cedars and piñones. The ruins are on the brink or southern point of the plateau. The declivity south and west is vertical for three or four meters, shelves of bare rock jutting out, then it is almost vertical farther on, to the river edge. The situation is admirable for defense as well as for culture [occupancy?]. The beautiful river at its foot, fine fields between it and the mesa, north of the point, and the timber once full of game. No wonder they selected that spot. But it is terribly windy.

The ruins are but an immense rubbish pile, stone having been used formerly for the construction. A small plaza, now oblong, occupies the center. I found traces of rooms. Pottery black-on-white, very good, smoked, and corrugated. Many handsome arrowheads of white flint. But these are only flint, and one little piece of obsidian. The wind blew awfully from the northwest with occasional snowflurries. Could hardly photograph. At last got an exposure, largest diaphragm, 2 seconds time. Returned soon (at 12 noon).

Painted in the afternoon. A party brought me 2 handsome axes, one particularly beautiful of green serpentine. Don José Lino Ribera came at nightfall. Very pleasant and kind. He told me that he believed there was a ruin at Tecolote. Lost my revolver. Found it again. At the Cañón Blanco, 8-9 miles south of west on the road to Albuquerque, there is a pueblo. This might have been the route of Castaño?[155]

NOVEMBER 12: Never had such cold hands and feet before.

---

155. Gasper Castaño de Sosa, the Lieutenant Governor of Nuevo Leon, with some 170 colonists marched north in the year 1590 on an unauthorized expedition to settle New Mexico. He forded the Rio Grande, perhaps in the Eagle Pass area, moved past the Pecos junction and, if the suggestion of Hollenbeck (1950: 57-58) is correct, across the Davis Mountains to eventually rejoin the Pecos which he then followed to the Pueblo of Pecos. Castaño turned westward, probably through the Galisteo Valley, finally establishing a settlement on the Rio Grande near present-day Santo Domingo. This colony was short lived for an expedition from Mexico soon arrived, arrested Castaño, and returned with him to Mexico City.

Last night it took me three hours to get my feet warmed up. Photographed the pueblo (Plate 3). Exposure 1 second, largest diaphragm. Beautiful, but terribly cold. Could hardly write, it is so cold. But there is not a cloud in the whole sky, and there is a sky of rare beauty.

Ruins of the Pueblito north of the town.*

Wall, where exposed, of mud, not adobe-brick. Mounds about 2.0 meters high. They are of earth with scattered stones and very little pottery. Hardly any flint. Afternoon splendid, but bitterly cold. It never thawed all day. All puddles remained frozen.

About 3 P.M., I went to see Don Jesús Ribera. His father came here in 1805 and built the first house, San Miguel being already settled. The Apaches were very troublesome. The tradition is current as a fact, that the Indans who lived here, when they abandoned this point, joined the Pecos. There are still descendants of the Pecos Indians, called Pequitos, in this neighborhood. Here there are two pueblos. Another one is one-and-one-quarter miles south of here, at the Garamuya. With the two villages at San Miguel, it makes five. The presumption is, therefore, that the Cienega was here. Two pueblos are still lacking. There is one at the Cañón Blanco, 8 or 9 miles from here, in a place called the Cañada del Pueblo. When Don Jesús was still young, his father had him at work on the acequia, east of the present mounds, along the whole length of the eastern wing, and there the ground was studded with skeletons, showing that the dead had been buried there. The bodies occupied little space each; all the bones were gathered in a heap, including the skull, which indicates that they were buried in a sitting posture, facing (the) sunrise. As at Pecos! Opposite the Pueblito, on the east bank, there was a thicket and a fine ciénega!

Don Jesús told me that he saw the Jumano; they were savages and regarded as a branch of the Comanche. Their faces were striated [painted?]! He says that Quivira is on top of a mesa. While talking, I heard them use the word, "es muy quiviro." It means that he speaks the language imperfectly.

This word is interesting. We afterwards looked it up in the Dictionary of the Academy (an old edition) but did not find it. It strikes me as if the word had something to do with Quivira! In that case it would be important.

From what I could learn, between the Cañón Blanco and the Sierra de los Jumanos, there are no ruins. Don Jesús says that the fields of the Indians were on the east bank, at the foot of the pueblo, and strung along the acequia which hugged closely the rocky bluff. Many metates were dug out, also flat stones with round concavities, serving as mortars. The manos were small, flat, and of quartz or granite. Some of the metates have feet. Called on Don Urbano Ribera, who formally presented me with the axes. He said that a maul of serpentine had also been found, but he lost it. Smallpox very severe here and at the Cuesta, six miles south. Painted at night. My feet are much warmer. The people here show me the utmost kindness. They do all in their power, and refuse all pay.

NOVEMBER 13: Don Vicencio López told me that, two miles from San Miguel, and close by San José, there is a circumvallation similar to a circus, and inside were signs of an Indian ruin. Arrowheads were found there. Near San José a tinaja was found —white, painted black, with red bottom. This would be the sixth pueblo in this vicinity. Left on foot at 9 A.M., for San Miguel, leaving my things to be sent after me.

Previously, I had been informed that there was a pueblo at the Chaperito, which is directly east of the pueblo. The ruins were where now is the plazita. Reached San Miguel about 10 A.M. Padre gone, but reception none the less friendly. Visited the river front again. No trace of villages beyond the one I saw Saturday or Friday. Called on Pedro Durán. He told me that there was one here, two at the Pueblo (not counting the one at the Garambuyo), one at San José, one at the Cuesta, one at Fulton called El Gusano, one at Kingman called Las Ruedas, and the Pueblo of Pecos. He says that when the Comanche destroyed San Cristóbal, the people fled to Pecos and to Cochiti. This must have been 60-75 years ago.[156] He came to this place from Alameda. Photographed the plaza, and painted. There is a ruin near the depot, left side of the station, or depot, of Pecos. On the whole I am quite satisfied that Castaño took the road through here. Old Durán asserted that there were pueblos all along the Rio Pecos down to Texas. This is doubtful.

NOVEMBER 14: Yesterday, the Rio Pecos was frozen firm along the banks, and heavy ice ran along the middle. Photographed the church to suit the Padre. He well deserves that much attention through his great kindness and hospitality. Light splendid. Exposure 5 seconds of time. There are two young Indians from Sandia here, trading.

Pueblo west of station at San Miguel.

Pueblo of Kingman.*

Missed the ruin opposite the depot. It is one hundred steps from it, and one hundred steps from the river. Hardly distinguishable mounds compose it. The pottery is black and white, but there is also red and black, and considerable of it. Before the train left, Don Francisco Ribera from the pueblo came up. He had a little boy last night; mother and child OK.

Left at 2 P.M. railroad time. Ramón Archuleta is at Vegas; so is Mariano Ruiz. But the sons of the former gave me a room, and I arranged for meals at the Station House. Went at once to see the ruin. It is about one-fifth of a mile east of the railroad in a kind of bottom, above the arroyo. Densely wooded hills surround it. The spot is sheltered and also secluded. A small plain slanting toward the arroyo surrounds the ruin on the west. The building was made of plates and blocks of sandstone. No walls are visible, only rubbish mounds. Little pottery; flint and obsidian. Pottery smoked and plain, black and white, red and black, and corrugated.

---

156. This date is probably not early enough. Actually the Galisteo Basin was largely deserted by the early 18th century (cf. Riley 1951: 237-243). The Domínguez report of 1776 mentions a mission at Galisteo with 152 persons. These had removed to Santo Domingo by the early 1790's (Adams and Chavez 1956: 217 et seq.).

The banks of the arroyo are steep, about 3.0 [meters] high, and at 0.30 to 0.40 [meter] from the top there runs a seam of charcoal bits; plain, smoked, and corrugated pottery. I begin to believe that this seam is a remnant of the old rubbish-heaps and of the pottery-hearths combined, nearly all the pottery being very much charred. The pueblo had three plazas with two visible entrances to the east, facing steep wooded hills. Depressions still indicate former rooms. No trace of estufas. In the center of the southern plaza is a round structure, built of dry stone, and of Mexican origin. The people here are kind. The young ones, however, do not know anything about the pueblo. One of them recalls Pecos, three years after it was abandoned. There were three stories; they lived in the middle and upper ones—the lower one being dark and vacant. They used chimneys like the Mexicans of today. Their pottery was white, painted with black, also glossy, the glossy lines being sometimes brown and greenish. They had many metates in frames in the middle and upper stories. Painted late.

NOVEMBER 15: It remained cloudy until noon, and then, at last, seeing that there was no remedy, went and photographed the ruins from the southeast. Time 5 seconds, smallest diaphragm. Painted all forenoon, three pieces of pottery. Photographed the ruins at noon; could not do any better.

Left at 4 P.M. At Lamy met Don José María Telles, and Don Lorenzo Abadia. The latter repeated to me that the Jumanos were a branch of the Comanche,[157] and that the Mesa Jumana

---

157. The "Jumano problem" has never been conclusively solved, but the facts seem to be as follows. The Jumano were noted as early as 1582 at La Junta de los Rios (the modern Presidio area) where they were in contact with the sedentary Patarabueye. In the next two centuries they ranged a territory from La Junta to the Colorado River (Texas) southwestward to the Gulf Coast and perhaps as far south as Coahuila. During the 17th century the Jumano were bitter enemies of the Apache, but during the 18th they allied themselves with Apache groups and may eventually have merged with them. The Jumano were migratory and lived either in tents or in some form of easy-to-construct dwelling. Their linguistic affiliation remains a mystery, but it is unlikely that they were related to the Comanche as stated here. Aside from the Jumano

was Quivira. There are no ruins at Gran Quivira.[158] Arrived at Santa Fe. Reception most friendly. Spent an hour at Dr. Eggert's. Letters from Joe, Prof. Norton, Mr. Parkman, Dr. Engelmann, Mr. Collet. Wrote to Joe. God be with her.

NOVEMBER 16: South and west of Anton Chico there are ruins at Cañón Pintado, thirty miles south of Anton Chico at Agua Negra, seven miles [from] the Pecos. To the point of the Sierra del Capitán, and around the mountain, at forty miles from the Pecos River. Apparently connected with this, to the west, around the base of the Sierra Blanca and extending to near the malpaís of the Carrizo. There are many ruins there. From the Capitán south, evidences of ruins on both the Rio Bonito and Rio Ruidoso. Those two join, forming the Rio Hondo; no ruins noted there.

Twenty-five miles south to the Sierrita Pajarito, ruin, fortifications on top of volcanic breccia. Has noticed nothing south of it, except mounds of stones along trails leading to water. He observed that custom almost everywhere among the Indians of New Mexico. Between San Juan and Picurís there are pueblos. Northeast of Picurís there are ruins which the Picurís Indians claim as those of their villages. All along the Rio Taos and up to the Conejos there are ruins also, claimed by the Taos Indians as their own. This is information from Mr. Willison, who spent the whole evening with me in the kindest manner possible.

I paid visits, and wrote to Joe, dear Joe. In the afternoon, all of a sudden, Mr. Stephenson dropped in. He told me that, in the Cañón de Chelle, he had visited forty-six cliff villages, and that he had seen upwards of fifty in all, but that some of them were so high up as to be out of reach, and there is no access to them at present. In these cliff-houses he found hand-

---

proper certain other groups, including the Taovaya, Wichita, Pawnee, and Havasupai have at one time or other been called Jumano, a term cognate with "rayado" (painted or decorated). (Cf. Kelley, n.d.; also Bandelier 1890-92: I, 85 et seq.)

158. A puzzling statement in view of the mission church and large ruin. The site referred to by Bandelier as Gran Quivira was probably Humanas.

some things. Mummies, in a squatting posture, enveloped in fine bags of white film, not cotton. (Probably pita?)[159] Rope and cloth of the same material. Sandals very well executed, moccasins of twisted work of the same fibre. The pottery is handsomely painted, even blue color being used, and the ring is very metallic. The houses are mostly small, but they are also several stories high, the stories being carried up, not in terraces, but in one straight wall. Stone work excellent. He is very enthusiastic.[160] It appears that the handsomest specimens of pottery and tissues are found in Arizona. Mr. Gustin, the artist of the corps, showed me some sketches and watercolors, which are magnificent. The houses may yet be with retreating stories [stepped or terraced]. . . . I dined with the Vicar-General Eguillon. Had a pleasant time, Father Parisis being here from Bernalillo.

NOVEMBER 17: Mr. Gustin came and stayed with me all afternoon. I painted pottery. Spent the whole night with Brown developing plates. Glorious. Out of five, four are good, and these are excellent.

NOVEMBER 18: Painted. Colonel Haren, Mr. Baxter, etc., arrived. Nothing new. Last night I had a letter from Joe. Thank God. She is well, and Papa is well. Dr. Eggert had the kindness to invite me to Prof. Gorman [?]. Pleasant evening. Letters from Dr. Brinton and the German Consulate.

NOVEMBER 19: Prints of photographs splendid. Mr. Evans called. In the afternoon called on Mrs. Stevenson. She has recovered and is pleasant. My prints of photographs please me very much. But the constant calls and disturbances dissipate me. This morning the chambermaid took refuge in my room,

---

159. Basketmaker burials in the de Chelly area have been found wrapped with a mass of yucca fiber and then enclosed with a fiber (usually yucca or apocynum) or skin blanket or bag. Bandelier's suggestion that the material might be pita (fibers of the agave) reflects his familarity with Mexico where this material was used in various ways.

160. The beautiful Canyon de Chelly (Navajo tsegi=canyon) of east central Arizona is famous for archaeological Pueblo sites, many still very well preserved.

the head-steward having attempted to outrage her. Wrote to
Collet and also to Brinton, accepting the editorship of the
Anales.... Met Evans again. Wrote to Joe and sent the medicine. Colonel William was here all evening. He states that [?]
is seven miles southeast of San Ildefonso. Offers a man to guide
me through the country. Dr. Eggert shakes his head at the
proposal.

NOVEMBER 20: Had plenty of callers: Colonel Haren came and
asked me to see Mr. Brumley. I called on him therefore. Colonel Haren asked me to go with them to Tesuque tomorrow.
Evening at Governor Ritch's. Lent Marsh $15. Spent the eve-
ning not very profitably, but still well enough. Received a letter
from Prof. Norton, painted, and wrote to Joe, and to Mr.
Parkman. Prints of photographs turned out very well, indeed.

NOVEMBER 21: Set out at 9 A.M. Photographed the view from
brow of hill at 10 A.M. Reached Tesuque at noon. Well received. Could not gather much information besides [a few
vocabulary items]. Failure to photograph Tesuque, twice, from
my own awkwardness. Returned at 5 P.M., thoroughly frozen.
Developed photographs with Brown at night. The general view
is excellent, the others out of focus. Arranged with Mr. Evans
to go to the Arroyo Hondo tomorrow at 10 A.M.

NOVEMBER 22: Mr. Evans came at the appointed time, but
soon suggested that we should drive out with Judge Sloan, instead of walking. So we left at 10:30 A.M. driving south. We
missed the road, however, driving too far east, and so struck
the Arroyo Hondo above the canyon. Right where the road
crosses and to the right of it, are the ruins, a rectangle of connected mounds. There is much loose stone on it, but little
pottery. It is black, smoked, slightly corrugated, indented, and
painted black and white. No traces of a gloss. The situation is
a good one. The arroyo on the south has a thin film of limpid
water, running freely, and the soil is very good. Deep and black
loam. It is well sheltered from the west and south by wooded
hills. There is no outlook to the west, but on the east the

southern mountains of Santa Fe loom up conspicuously. The spot must be warm in winter and rather pleasant in summer. The ruins are small and could not contain over two hundred people. On the east side, the mound is 5½ meters above the road, and on the north side, 3¼ meters. On the west, it slants down and on the southwest also, as the section shows. There are low cedars and sabinos about. I photographed it twice, with apparently good results, and was about to return, when a Mexican told me that the main pueblo was one-and-one-half miles west, or lower down the arroyo, at the outlet of the canyon, and that it was larger. So we followed the arroyo down, until it became a rocky and exceedingly picturesque gorge. On the north side it rises about 1000 feet almost vertical. About one mile to the west, the country suddenly opens and affords, beyond the dark clefts, a splendid view of La Tetilla and of the Sierra de San Mateo, deeply covered with snow, in the far-off western sky. It is a magnificent view.

I photographed it and with the greatest difficulty secured 2 plates. But it was almost impossible to hold the instrument, so steep was the slope. We did not proceed any farther, as the sun was fast declining, but returned to Santa Fe. There, Colonel Willison told me, that the largest ruins were indeed one-and-one-half miles lower down, and that they cover about two-and-one-half acres. It is evidently a large house pueblo, but looks to me as if it had been occupied and abandoned long before the conquest. John Pearce told me that near the eastern Tularosa, on the lava or malpaís, he found much pottery, white and black, red and black (small-house type of Acoma), also metates, but no distinct ruins. When we developed the plates at night, the 2 first ones were excellent, but the 2 gorge views are entirely lost. Pity. Returned at 9 P.M. and went to bed early. Tired. Purchased articles at Gold's and at Mr. Marsh's, so as to have collection for the Berlin Museum.*

NOVEMBER 23: Painted, but with indifferent success. The piece

22nd November 1882.

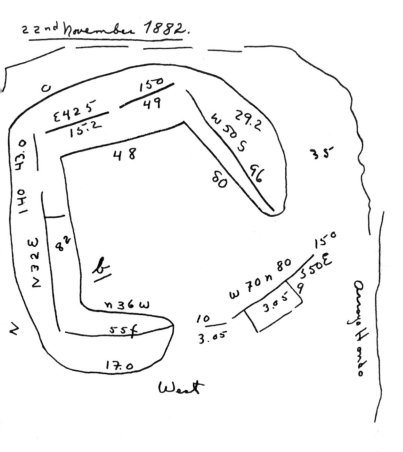

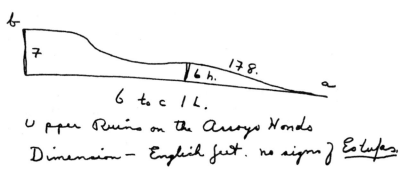

6 to c 1 L.

Upper Ruins on the Arroyo Hondo
Dimension — English feet. no signs of Estufas.

is difficult, and I am growing weary. Wrote to Dr. Gerlich, Dr. Engelmann, to my wife, and to Dr. Walliser. Nothing new. Sent word to the Padre at Peña Blanca. Clouds lowering. Prints coming out fine. Gold shipped his goods. Dr. Eggert insisted upon my charging $300 for them, and gave good reasons for it. Bought the ornament of the matachinas, blankets, etc.

NOVEMBER 24: Had a beautiful letter from Joe last night. Thank God for it. Received a letter from the Padre who sent me his carriage. Shall start tomorrow. Bought some more things. Sent photographs to Dr. Gerlich, 20 select ones. Very beautiful. Also a piece of turquoise in the rock. No possibility of taking photographs for Brown, from the top of Fort Marcy. Too cloudy. Saw D. Miller. He gives good report of José Olivas. The horse is not suitable, having a sore back. Drew $100 (November salary) and paid $50 to J. Gold and $20 to Marsh. Shall start tomorrow. Bought woolen jacket for José Hilario, and [?] for the Padre. Marsh brought me pottery from Triapi, and from the site of Nuestra Señora del Rosario at Santa Fe. The latter is old, black-on-white. Sent photographs to Parkman and Norton. Eight views. Passed [the time of day?] at Brown, and then went to Dr. Eggert. Everything ready for tomorrow.

NOVEMBER 25: About the time we reached the Cieneguilla the fog began to lift, after a heavy cold flurry. We stopped at the house of José de la Luz Romero, to warm ourselves. He assured me that there was not only one, but that there were several pueblos at and near the Cieneguilla, that many ruins were originally met with on the site itself, that metates, pottery, turquoise, etc., had been found, and that there were still old men living, who recalled the name of the pueblo. I arranged with him to stop at the place on my return. Photographed the Bajada, the sky having cleared sufficiently. Arrived at Peña Blanca about 3 P.M. and was received with the customary cordiality.

The Padre lives perfectly alone, and takes his meals at Don Nicolás Lucero's. There is to be a grand wedding tonight, the daughter of Don Nicolás, with Hilario Ortiz of Santa Fe. Rómulo Martinez is [their padrino?].

The wedding took place in church, and the Padre spoke very well. Then we followed to the house of Don Nicolás, where refreshments were extended. Don Nicolás told me that there was indeed a pueblo at the Cieneguilla, and that it was a well-known fact. The name he could not recollect. About the ruin of Santo Domingo he is very positive also, and he affirms that it took place after the reconquest. Juan José intimated between 1689 and 1692. Don Nicolás lived a long time among the Tehua and says that Yunque is the name given to the region about San Ildefonso. He mentions it as: El Reyno de Yunque [the community of Yunque].

NOVEMBER 26: The day being magnificent, I photographed the valley from Peña Blanca, looking north. After Mass I stayed with the Padre. At 2 P.M., José Hilario suddenly came. He was overjoyed. We returned to Cochiti together. Day splendid. Reception most friendly everywhere. Juan José is gone to the Rito with Mr. Gustin. Hai-ou-a [has gone] to the States. But the rest are here and the same good old friends as ever. Santiago, the governor, led me to an old Piro Indian of Senecu, a sentero, who gave me a good deal of information. He says that Teypana was at Cuaray, Trenaquel on the northern spur of the Sierra Blanca, that Cuaray was a pueblo of the Piro, Tigua, etc., that the pueblo of San Marcial was of the Manso. That the Zuma, as the Piro called them, were of the Apache, and still lived in small houses of adobe like the Mexicans, but they were more strictly sedentary. Quivira, he says, was not destroyed, but abandoned by its people owing to fear of a giant. All this is incongruous and suspicious.

Of the pueblos from Socorro (called San Miguel!) to San Marcial he affirms that they were inhabited formerly by those who went south.[161] There is an evident mixture of facts from the time of the reconquest with others of subsequent date. He says that some of the Piros of Quivira now live at Jemez. Santiago also told me that the people of San Marcos were Tanos, and not Queres. José Hilario also told me that the little amulets of alabaster are called *gua-puy*, and promised me three or four to paint.

There is to be Baile de los Entremeseros next Thursday, and the Baile de los Matachinas at Zile, on the 4th of December. Plenty of work before me. The Padre has a little amulet of alabaster, with a crucifix on it, which was found in the ruins of the Bajada. This might be looked upon as significative, but I have some doubt about its genuineness. Santiago tells me that the Cieneguilla is called *Hañi-china* [east arroyo].

Wrote to Joe. The infernal pen is making a good deal of trouble. It is a humbug after all.

It is interesting, how eager they are here for plumas de guacamayo [macaw feathers]. They insist . . . *que hacen mucha falta aqui* [that they are much needed here]. Pedro tells me that, when a boy and girl are engaged, it is customary for the boy to sleep with the girl every night. Adelaido indeed goes out every night.

NOVEMBER 27: Wrote to Henry Kaune. José Hilario, as usual, very late. Victorio brought me pozole and guayaves. Left at last on foot, without José Hilario, at 9 A.M. for Peña Blanca. Arrived at the Curacy at 10 A.M., the Padre being on the point of leaving for Wallace. Gave him my letters, and then waited for José Hilario.

---

161. Quarai was a Tiwa pueblo some 30 miles east of the Rio Grande near the present-day town of Manzano, New Mexico. Trenaquel was the most southerly Piro town on the west side of the Rio Grande, on or near the present-day site of San Marcial, south of Socorro, New Mexico. The Manso probably lived originally in the area of Las Cruces, New Mexico. Their linguistic affiliation is uncertain. The Zuma mentioned here is possibly Oñate's Zumaque, perhaps a southern Piro village. Gran Quivira probably was the old Humanas, the southernmost of the Salinas Piro settlements, some 28 miles due west of the modern town of Corona, New Mexico.

Size of the cradle: width 0.09 [meter]. Length 0.30 [meter].
Name in Queres: O-a-tze-me. The cradle suspended is called:
A-esh-to-tze. Wrote to Professor Norton at night. José Hilario
did not come to Peña Blanca until noon, and we returned at
noon. Painted the cradle. It strikes me that I had very bad success with my writing and painting. The latter principally is
incorrect. I believe it is because I am too hasty, too impatient.
In the evening I wrote to the Ausland. It is better for me to
keep up this correspondence, even if it is troublesome. José
Hilario and Ventura Ortiz came in tonight. The entremeseros
are practicing at the estufa.

NOVEMBER 28: Last night, the boy Ventura stayed until late.
He told me many things about the Koshare and the Kwerana.
There is a qu-share-nauaya, or Qu-share-Mayor, and a qui-rana-
nauaya, or Querana-Mayor. Both are for life and elected. José
Hilario told me that Romero Chavez was the Chayane [chai-
añi] of the sun! Ventura also told me that the boys and girls go
to sleep together in presence of their parents, if the girl likes the
boy. But he does not say that actual cohabitation follows. It
looks like a decent Kiltga [German, Kiltgang]. He asked for
money "to go to sleep with the neighbors' girl." Thus it seems
that presents are given, expected, and received.

At last we started, at 10 A.M., towards the Potrero de
los Idolos. I found some nuggets of obsidian in the pumice.
Measured the height of the cliffs. 58 heights = 1.60 x 58 =
92.80 meters or 304 feet. The vertical around the top is from
10 to 60 feet high. The ascent of the cliffs is rugged but not
impracticable, through a rill or gulch or slide on the south
side. Top oblong, and covered with stunted piñones and sabinos. Ruins in about the same condition as in 1880. Photographed the potrero from the loma on the south side of the
Cañada, and the sculptures on the top. Plate # 6 is the last.
Exposure 8 and 9 seconds. Light delightful. We returned by
way of the Cañada, stopping at the house of Doña Juliana
Lucero, wife of Luis. He was not at home. Saw Martín. (Telis-

fero died.) They denied that the Cañada had ever been called Cieneguilla. Took the wagonroad home, fine view over the Santa Fe mountains.

They are building a roof on the house. The adobes (very irregular) are up, and a number of boys throw dirt up with shovels, while men and boys equalize and stamp it on the roof. Women and girls carry water in large tinajas, caxetes, etc. A fire is burning near, and it is a source of enjoyment rather than of toil. It is communal work, and the workers change in and out as they please. Some of the principales appear to superintend it.

Called on Francisco and his mother; they have good news from Hai-ou-a, who is at school in Carlisle, Pennsylvania. The day on the whole was exceedingly pleasant, but we could not reach the Colle; it was too late. Tomorrow shall stay at home and paint if I can get the cradle again. It appears that the soil of the Cañada is very rich, except for [growing] wheat. José Hilario and little José Lucero came to spend the evening. They stayed rather late, but I was glad of it. Juan José and Mr. Gustin are at the Cañada tonight, and will be here tomorrow. José Hilario faithfully promised to get me the cradle for tomorrow again. He will probably forget it, but no matter. I shall get another one or the same through somebody else. Went to bed after 11 P.M. tired and with a cold.

NOVEMBER 29: Rose very late. I painted at the cradle, and was greatly surprised at the good results. The blankets are excellent. Mr. Gustin and Juan José returned at 1 P.M. He is full of the Rito and his sketches are very beautiful. He visited the Rito, the Cueva Pintada, the Potrero de los Idolos, and the Potrero Viejo. We walked over to Peña Blanca at 2 P.M. and found Colonel Stevenson. He is much elated with his trip to Chihuahua. It was of course not scientific. Is much incensed at Cushing. We returned on foot to Cochiti, crossing the bridges at sunset. Had a talk with Juan José, but elicited nothing new. Whitney and Hernandez left Peña Blanca this morning for the Rito.

The pen is a decided nuisance, and I have no other. It is almost impossible to write with it as the ink will not flow down. José Hilario called for a short time.

NOVEMBER 30: Last night I had still another call, Francisco Pancho, brother of Hai-ou-a, called for about an hour. While he was here the drum beat, and they told me that it was the Koshare who are going out to practice. It appears to be a rehearsal, at which only the members can assist. Pancho's wife is a Koshare while he is nothing.

At 9 A.M. the chorus of singers opened the dance by passing before the house of the cacique to the estufa of *Shyuamo*, singing. Before the Colonel and the others got in, I had finished painting the cradle. After they got in, we went around. At intervals, some of the Koshare (commonly nine men and four women) came singing into the plaza, and formed in a row, alternately on the south and the north side. They held twigs of sabinos and bowing down all together seemed apparently to plant corn; although it was hardly intended for it at all. It was 3 P.M. until the dance proper began, and it was an exact repetition of the figures and also in part of the obscenities practiced in 1880. The whole is a filthy, obscene affair. Drinking urine out of the bowls and jars used as privies on the housetops, eating excrements and dirt, ashes and clay, washing each other's faces with urine and with every imaginable dirt, imitating cohabitation and sodomy, were the principal "jokes" of the abominable leaders of the Koshare. The dancers were all painted in a sinfully ugly manner, white and black prevailing. The malinche had her face painted blue. Santiago, the governor, had his body painted light indigo blue. Red was not visible.

I succeeded in getting a very poor photograph, as no persuasion could induce them to stop any length of time. The three leaders seemed particularly anxious to prevent my taking any view. Left at 4 P.M. on foot, and photographed the pueblo from the other side of the river. The wife of Mariano Pancho is *Shutsuna* [*Shrutsuna*=Coyote] and is a Koshare. I have thus far secured the following divisions of the clans [into moieties, or phratries]. To *Tanyi: Tanyi, Huashpa, Hiitshani, Yssi, Tzitz*, and possibly *Tyame*. To *Shyuamo*, are *Shyuamo*, and Kwerana are *Tanyi*. But not all the *Tanyi* are Kwerana, neither also the Koshare, comprise all the *Shyuamo*. Returned at night and called on Victoriano. Sent my photographs to Santa Fe.

DECEMBER 1: Went over to the house of Juana and copied the other cradle. It has a very rotten appearance. Juan José went out after his cows. In the afternoon I painted the *opash-tya-nasht*, or loom for small girdles and garters. It is tied to a post and thus stretched with one hand, while with the other hand they twist and weave. The large loom, for broad girdles and for scarfs, is tied to a stake stuck into the floor, and the man sits down to it, stretching his legs in the direction of the stake. Zashua stayed with me most of the time. At night Juan José returned, tired and sleepy. Could hardly elicit any information from him. I painted the whole process of pottery-making and began at the fabrication of baskets. Painted so long that I grew perfectly dizzy and in consequence of it had a sleepless night. Bad cold besides.

DECEMBER 2: An abominable night. Perfectly sleepless. Painted the baskets, making but little headway. Left on foot for Wallace at 2:30 P.M. and Peña Blanca at 3 P.M. The road being exceedingly sandy, I traveled only with great difficulty. Got to Wallace about 4:30 P.M. and found Mr. McIlvain who gave me a letter from Prof. Norton. Good so far! Took quarters at the Railroad Hotel, got shaved, and then went to Manuel Montoya. Was received and treated in the kindest possible manner. He affirms that there is a ruined pueblo two-and-one-half miles east of here, above the Galisteo arroyo on the north side of the railroad track, and that the old pueblo of Santo Domingo is one-and-one-half miles south of the present village, on the Rio Grande and not on the Galisteo, as I had been informed.

I met Mr. Aoy, a Spaniard, who had been to Yucatan with

Stephens and Cabot, and who recollects much of it. He even speaks Maya somewhat! Very interesting indeed. Got my plates and many letters. From José, from Collet, from Mr. Garrison, Mr. S. P. Ely. Called on Manuel Baca. His wife is daughter of Nazario González. She says that the houses of the Cieneguilla are not the old pueblo, and that there is no pueblo at the Ciénega proper. Thus the Ciénega and the Cieneguilla are in fact but one place, the latter being the village, and the former scattered houses only. Also called on Juana Lopez.

Went back to the Hotel. The railroad agent showed me a painting of Santa Bárbara, on buffalo-hide which came from the old church of Pecos. He has got a half-grown Grizzly— alive, tied to a post in front of the Hotel. Wrote to Joe, to Professor Norton, to Mr. Garrison, and to Mr. Ely. Very good night.

DECEMBER 3: Am somewhat elated by my photographic successes, and greatly relieved of my cold. Returned on foot to Peña Blanca and ate dinner at Jesús Sena's. After dinner we drove over to Zile, a little hamlet in the sandy but fertile bottom opposite Peña Blanca, where the Rio Grande is divided into five narrow and swift running branches, brazos.

There is to be a rehearsal of the matachinas at 4 P.M. They came at last—eight matachinas, El Monarca, La Malinche, and El Abuelo. Sometimes there are twelve matachinas, two abuelos, and one torito [Little Bull]. The abuelo is the clown and devil of the piece, flitting to and fro, and at the same time master of the dance. The arrangement is as follows:

a. x	a.) *El Monarca*
c.	c.) *The Fiddler*
b. x	b.) *La Malinche*
	. . . . *The Matachinas*

The monarca, the malinche, and the fiddler are seated, the others stand up or kneel on one knee. The whole is a symbolical cotillion, graceful and very decent.

I photographed it, giving at least 20 seconds of time, owing to increasing obscurity. The people were all very kind and exceedingly willing to stand for me. The matachinas wear white trousers, are muffled up in shawls, a headdress, or cupíl, decorated with gold and silver trinkets and a bead fringe in front. They are so muffled that only the eyes appear. All the finery of the women is evidently borrowed for the occasion. They have a three-limb palma of wood in the left hand, and a small rattle in a handkerchief in the right, with which they accompany the fiddle. The monarca wears an imperial crown, also with ribbons attached to it; he is equally muffled. The malinche, a bridal dress with a wreath of artificial roses. The abuelo only a mask of sheepskin. For most of the time, the monarca and the malinche are seated. It is an evident Mexican importation from the time of the conquest, and very graceful and handsome. Spent the night at Peña Blanca.

DECEMBER 4: Drove over to Cochiti with Don Jesús. Photographed the cacique and his loom, the family of José Antonio and of Salvador, the room of Juan José and my own, and packed up things. Called on Mauricio Mesta and on his wife to take leave. They told me a good deal about the idolatries of the Pueblo. It appears that Romero Chavez and Rafael are the head medicinemen.[162] They wear a species of cotones with wide

---

162. It is unfortunate that Bandelier was not more precise here; again, one senses a basic lack of interest in the details of the theocratic structure and functioning of the tribe. In view of his announced intention to study the prehistory of these peoples, such omissions are understandable but nonetheless regrettable.

Lange's study of the Cochiti (1959: 457) lists among the caciques, "Rafaelito Herrera (known also as Semilla and Guayave de Leche): Coyote Clan, Pumpkin Kiva, born 1864; Flint Society, Ku-shá-li Society; became cacique in November, 1911, and died in office 12/22/14."

This quite obviously is not one of the men to whom Bandelier referred. Since the cacique who died in 1914 would have been only eighteen years old in 1882, it is most unlikely that he could have achieved the status Bandelier ascribed to this person at that time. If related at all, it would seem that Rafaelito might have been the son, grandson, or nephew of the Rafael mentioned by Bandelier. The other prominent medicine man, Romero Chavez, does not appear in any of the medicine or other secret society rosters compiled by Lange. The rather

sleeves, the cacique wears it with black and red stripes. Their chief idols are of skin or hide, brown, the bust of a man with short feet, and the claws of a bear. They also have stone idols, and small ones of gypsum. Luis Moquino showed me a trinket of obsidian, similar to those which I saw at Calpan, perforated to be strung up, and in the shape of a bear. When I asked what it was, his wife told me Qohayo. Luis winked at her not to tell, but it was too late. I told him that I had two of alabaster, and he asked me, "Porqué no me lo vendes?" [Why don't you sell them to me?] He appeared eager to get them. Luisa told me that it was principally at night that they committed their festivities, that there was an old "qoye" where they kept their idols, and that one night she met a procession of Indians, men and women, walking on all fours behind some kind of an animal. Left at 4 P.M. with David Baca. The leave-taking was sad, Juan José almost cried. Night at Don Jesús! Wrote letter to Padre Rómulo.

DECEMBER 5: Left at 9 A.M. Had a very pleasant companion. He told me that, on the north side of the Galisteo, one-and-one-half miles east [west?] of Wallace, there is an old pueblo which he says was probably the former pueblo of Santo Domingo.

Photographed the Bajada from below, and also the top. About one mile east, on top of the mesa, and facing La Tetilla [at the Bajada], there are faint traces of a ruined pueblo. Foundations of rubble. Lava blocks deeply sunk into the fertile sandy soil, but no trace of pottery or flint or obsidian. Photographed the view from the mesa above the Cieneguilla. The old pueblo then stood [where] the plazita is now, on the left (south) bank of the river. Its former name was Chi-na-ma.

Reached Santa Fe at 5:30 P.M. Chilled through and through. Found letters from Joe, from Dr. Gerlich, and from Mr. Evans.

---

consistent practice of referring to individuals by their office or by only a given name was a habit of Bandelier's that is extremely frustrating to anyone attempting to reconstruct the broad social structure of any of the groups with whom Bandelier was living.

Worked up the photographs, and only three of them good. All the interiors are lost. Worked with Brown until midnight. Hotel full. N. B. [no bed?] The cacique of Cochiti told me, that the Tano were also called *Shyumutz.*

DECEMBER 6: Bought my things from Gold, and had him pack them up. Wrote a long letter to Dr. Gerlich. Met José Olivas. He told me that the Jumanos were a kind of sedentary Comanche, and that he met them in Texas. Their language, manners, and customs were like those of the Comanche, except that they lived in huts, long, and made of branches and reeds, and had garden plots. Their faces were painted with red and blue stripes. Spent the evening at the Vicar-General's. Very pleasant. Mr. Gerdes bought a horse for me for $50. Wrote to Joe. Mr. Gustin is here; he called on me.

DECEMBER 7: I painted nearly all day, except in the forenoon, when I went to the cathedral and photographed the interior. Time ten and one-half minutes. Barely an outline visible. At night painted, and then went to see Dr. Eggert, whom I met at old Dunand's, and dragged him over to the room, to read him my letters to the *Ausland.*

DECEMBER 8: Went to the cathedral at 11 A.M. Set up the instrument and then dined with Padre Eguillon. After an exposure of 40 minutes, I closed the objective. Plate bad. Returned and set up the instrument again: 35 minutes. Picture fair. Evening very cold. At home painting. Visit from Mr. Bigler.

DECEMBER 9: Took two views of Santa Fe, but they were both bad on account of the plates. In the evening at Brown's. Pleasant. Got a letter from Mr. Parkman. All right in regard to Olivas and to the horse. Bought some silver trinkets at Gold's, and painted at the axe from San Miguel de Pecos.

DECEMBER 10: Met Mr. S. Eldodt of San Juan. He told me that there were no obscene dances in public, but that they had their secret meetings at the estufas. One very dark night, while going about the pueblo, a band of Indians came past him in single

file, running at full speed to the vega [fields]. He went to the
estufa and saw that a man stood guard before the little window.
Soon after, he met the same band again returning directly to
the estufa, where they disappeared. They are of course idolaters.
They have a cacique. Invited me to San Juan.

Afternoon took a stroll to the plaza with Pearce. Day very
beautiful. Mr. Bigler called again at night. He told me about
the ruins of the pueblo at Joseph's Springs. The pueblo is on
the top of a mesa, above a creek, which is reached by a detour
of one-half mile. There are several large estufas in the plazita.
The pueblo is three-fourths of a mile from the Ojos Calientes.
Painted at night.

DECEMBER 11: It being the festival of Nuestra Señora de Guadalupe tomorrow, large preparations were made everywhere. José
Olivas came and told me his story. He has had six people sick
from smallpox, and two of them died. He had consequently to
borrow from Mr. T. B. Catron $50 which he wants to repay
him. After information taken I concluded to refund the money
to him. Catron was impudent and exorbitant, and asked $5 to
cover a loan of eight days. So I simply paid Catron. Upon returning I met Mr. Mahler. I was overjoyed, and broke up work
and invited him to dinner with me.

After taking leave I went back and painted the axe. At night
I went up to Guadalupe church and witnessed the functions,
Bishop Salpointe of Tucson officiating. (I had met Father
Brun of San Rafael previously.) Called on Padre Defouri afterwards, and after a short chat, returned with J. C. Pearce, and
then to Dunand's where I met Dr. Eggert and Joe Meyer who
treated me to punch. It was very silly on my part to accept it.
Got letters from Papa, such a good letter, from Engelmann, and
from Professor Norton.

DECEMBER 12: Feast of Guadalupe. Went up to Padre Defouri's and found my drawings which I had lost the day before.
Dined with Mr. Mahler again and then went to Padre Defouri
to take leave of the priests. He showed me his manuscript,

"History of the Catholic Church in Kansas." Very interesting, but no original documents.

DECEMBER 13: I was very pleasantly surprised, at 9 A.M., by the visit of Captain Pradt[163] of Laguna. He is a quiet, attractive, and therefore a very pleasant man. He told me that the *Chacuan* was a modern kachina, formed at Zuñi by a white man for the purpose of gradually abolishing the immoral practices among the Pueblos. He says that, while at Laguna the obscene dances are abolished, they still continue at Zuñi. The morality of the Pueblos is very evidently fearfully low. At Laguna there are 2 parties, resembling the Koshare and the Kwerana, or rather the *Shyuamo* and the *Tañi*, one of which is the progressive party, and the other, the *Qapaitz*, is the old conservative party. The former one is fairly moral and clean; the latter clings to old customs and to immoral practices. These practices, besides obscene dances, consist in promiscuous intercourse of unmarried people, prostitution with women who have succeeded in aborting, and abortion itself. Illegitimate children are called: *Dios-sa-uishte* (children of God) and there are such at Acoma. He told me that, while at Acoma, his own father-in-law called upon him at night to visit these prostitutes. He refused to go. Is not very much taken with Cushing, nor with Dr. Menaul. Says Protestantism has no effect upon the Indians. Shall stay with him at Laguna. It was a very pleasant meeting altogether. In the afternoon I at last finished both axes, and in the evening quietly remained at home, preparing to pack up my specimens. It is a fearful job and one which exasperates me at the mere thought of it.

---

163. George H. Pradt, surveyor and close friend of the Marmons, came to New Mexico in 1869 to survey the Navajo Reservation. He had served with the 40th Wisconsin Infantry in the Tennessee campaign during the Civil War. In 1872, he was on the staff of the Surveyor-General's Office in Santa Fe, but in 1876 went to Laguna, married into the Pueblo, was governor, and homesteaded to the south. In 1882 he organizd a company of Laguna volunteers against raiding Apache and Navajo. He also conducted surveys for the Surveyor-General and held various county positions.

DECEMBER 14: Began to pack. I finished 18 cigarboxes of pottery before nightfall. My collections are much as I had expected, and in many cases the specimens are much handsomer. But it is a great trouble, besides being bothered by constant calls. I finished a long letter to Mr. Parkman, and also mailed him my drawings, 13 pieces. Wrote to Dr. Gerlich, and to George J. Engelmann, to the latter a very saucy letter. Am gradually getting over my cold. In assorting the pieces from the different pueblos about Cochiti, I find the small-house pottery represented everywhere, and found exclusively at the Potrero de la Cañada Quemada, at the Cueva Pintada, and in the small houses on the Potrero Chiato. At the Rito de los Frijoles the glossy pottery is largely represented and so everywhere. I cannot paint the pottery from Triape, nor that from the Ojos Calientes de José.

At night I was presented to Mr. John Gwin who promised to let me look at the Merced of the Bajada tomorrow. A Tehua Indian on the street told me that the name of the Pajarito was *T-re-ge* [*Tscherige*].

DECEMBER 15: Called on Mr. Gwin at 10 A.M. and he very kindly lent me the document with papers annexed to it. It is one of the oldest grants existing, but only a copy, and there are very great discrepancies about it in dates. The year 1658, for instance, appears several times, and always in connection with Pedro Rodriguez Cubero! There is an evident mistake of the copyist. It results from the new Spanish houses opposite Cochiti, which were abandoned after 1680, and the ruins of the Bajada, the Ciénega and the Cieneguilla.

DECEMBER 16: Shipped the six boxes in the morning, took a bath, had my photograph taken, but Brown was not satisfied with it. Packed up my old clothes to send them home. In the evening took oysters with Eggert, Pearce, and Meyer, some wine at Dunand's and at 9 P.M. went with Bennett to the Gallery. He talked good sound photography to me for a long time. My plates have come and they are well paid for. They are Cramer and Norton's, better packed than Eastman's and guaranteed to be more rapid. Got a charming letter from dear Joe tonight. The Doctor and companions wanted to get me "out" at night, but I stoutly refused, and thank God for the strength he gave me to remain solid. It is all his work, not mine. Sent $50 to the Padre for mantle.

DECEMBER 17: Ed J. McLean paid me a visit. I shipped the box of clothing home, and then went home to have my photograph taken again. Result beautiful. Then went to Father Eguillon and confessed. Afterwards finished letter to Joe, packed up photographs for Mrs. Morgan, Mr. Parkman, and Rev. Adams, packed the valise for Belen, wrote to Father Gromm, and then spent a pleasant supper at Governor Ritch's. I was going to Dr. Eggert, after having read a very favorable letter from Dr. Gerlich, when Fathers Mailluchet and García came in on a visit. So I went with them to the Vicar again and had a very pleasant evening. Father Mailluchet has restored and cleaned up the cemetery at Pecos, planted a cross where the original one stood, and surrounded the whole with a wire fence to protect it from vandalism. On the 15th the ceremony took place, a *Libera me Domine* being sung on the premises, in the presence of 300 people.

DECEMBER 18: Ready to go by 10 A.M. Valise shipped to Belen. Letters, etc., all mailed, debts all paid. Ulster sold to bishop for nine dollars. Started almost at a gallop. Horse splendid, fierce, lively, and still tame. It was almost a gallop to the Arroyo Hondo. Before leaving Santa Fe, I got my watch again. I had at first left it at Peña Blanca, afterwards it was brought back to me by David Baca. Then I left it Saturday at the bath, and this A.M. it was brought back to me by a boy who found it beneath a bath-tub. Bought a knife and comb.

We reached Galisteo at 3 P.M., and were cordially received by the Pinos. Father Mailluchet soon afterwards arrived at Davis and bought my apparatus. He tells me there is a Saint here from San Cristóbal, and an old painting from 1648. Vespers of Nuestra Señora de los Remedios tonight. Illumination on the hill. The new church will cost $1200. At supper Don Germán Pino told me that there was an old pueblo at the Ciénega. Tomorrow we will go to San Cristóbal.

DECEMBER 19: I went up to the Padre's. He showed me the saints of the church, several of which are painted on buffalohide. There is the old San Cristóbal of that pueblo, a horrid picture, and a better-executed painting, of Nuestra Señora de Begonia, 1608. This I photographed, giving 25 seconds.

Ramón Chavez told me that in 1780 the Indians of the old Pueblo of Galisteo (perhaps San Cristóbal?) left for the Cerrillos on account of the Comanche. They went to the old place at the Cerrillos, where the smallpox killed them all, except a few who escaped to Santo Domingo. About 1810 the first settlers appeared here, and in 1834 or 1835 the present church was built. The San Cristóbal painting was gathered from the Cerrillos (an indication that it was the Indians of that pueblo, and not those of Galisteo who fled thither). The Nuestra Señora de los Remedios was carried to Santa Fe to the church of San Miguel and thence back to the church here.

There were formerly two detachments of troops, one at the old pueblo of Galisteo, and the other at San Cristóbal, both against the Comanche. We left for San Cristóbal at 11 A.M. Got the photograph under many difficulties, 15 seconds of time. Returned, almost blinded by the snow and violent gusts of wind. Took the photograph of the place from above, south of the church, medium light, 12 seconds.

I now have the following plates—all taken today. 1.) Lost. 2.) Nuestra Señora de Begonia, 25 seconds. Light bad. 3.) San Cristóbal, nom. 15 seconds. 4.) Galisteo, 12 seconds. Wrote to Joe. I could not let the opportunity pass to write to her from the same room which we had occupied in July. Tomorrow I shall leave with the Padre to the Chorro.

DECEMBER 20: We changed our minds again, and in place of going by the Chorro, decided to take the lower road, passing south of the Cerro Pelón so as to visit the Pueblo Largo on the way. Traversing the plain to the southwest we struck the southeastern point of the cerro. The plain of Galisteo is bounded, on the south, by another crestón, almost identical in shape, number and size of openings, and direction and height, with the northern one. There is a dry arroyo running into the valley out of the plain. About eight to ten miles from Galisteo, and three miles from the Pelón lie the ruins, on both sides of the arroyo, in a position very similar to that of San Lázaro, hidden, not very good for defense. There appear to have been two pueblos, the southern one, like that of San Cristóbal, having been partly washed away by the arroyo. The latter, however, is dry at the present time. It looks as if the southern pueblo was the older one. Where the walls are exposed, they are like those of San Cristóbal, of thin plates of sandstone, about ten inches (0.25 meter) thick. In some instances the coating, of brown clay (not gypsum), is visible on both sides of the wall, and there is no trace of them having ever been whitewashed. In distinction of the other pueblos of the Tano, there are estufas in three of the six plazas. The northern pueblo is now larger than the [southern?] one, but there was originally little difference.* Saw no obsidian, but on the contrary much black lava in the shape of chips and unfinished axes. Pottery all glossy, and exactly similar to that of San Lázaro, Galisteo, and San Cristóbal, also San Marcos. Here it was that an ivory part of the Franciscan rosary was found, which Father Mailluchet secured. The skull on one side has the legend: *Ecce finem* [Behold the end!], the legend on the other side we could not decipher. But it is characteristic of a Franciscan rosary. However, there are no ruins indicating a church there. But the pottery is very markedly like that of the other Tano pueblos already explored by me.

There is a very singular feature in the southern plaza of the northern pueblo. To the northeast of the estufa, a row of apparently hewn blocks of trachyte are set standing as follows:

a. is a hole dug to get out the slab (or?) stone set there. That stone is 0.75 [meter?] long, and they are in general from 0.30

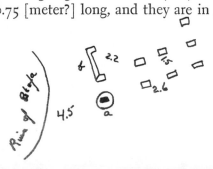

to 0.40 wide by 0.20 to 0.30 broad and thick. They are evidently but cleft and not hewn, and similar stones crop out on the height surrounding the pueblo. b. is a row of thin slabs, of sandy rock, set upright to communicate between two upright blocks. The blocks are set in the earth about two-thirds of their length or height, and thus protrude above the ground from 20 to 35 centimeters. There is nothing in their surroundings indicating for what purpose they were.

We finished about 2 P.M. and then drove on. The road is exceedingly picturesque but absolutely desolate. High piñones everywhere. On the left is a barren mesa, where antelopes still herd in great numbers. We passed between the New Placeres and the Sierra de San Francisco, two colossal and very grandly indented mountain-groups, with the Sierra de Sandía before us, wrapt in icy mist.

Rounding the northwestern edge of the San Francisco chain we reached the Real de San Francisco, or Golden, a hamlet in a deep mountain valley, slopes covered with piñones, houses of boards and adobe irregularly scattered on the steep banks. Grand mountain scenery. These mountains are full of mines, all said to be very rich, but there is as yet great scarcity of water. Still there are big wells, and at 500 feet the water rose to 300. I ascertained that there are two pueblos very near, one of the Tuerto and the other of Valverde. Farther northwest is the pueblo of Tunque. There is a good road, of 22 miles, around the north point of the Sandia chain to this place. The nearest pueblo to the south is at San Pedro, eight miles, but there are ruins southwest and southeast and nearer.

Wrote to Joe. An old man showed me pottery from the Rio Mimbres. It is black and white striped. Stay at Agustín Ramírez.

December 21: I forgot to put down yesterday that I took the view of the ruins on the south side of the dry arroyo about 2 P.M. Plate #6. Time 20 seconds. The walls are in shadow. The immorality of the people here is said to be great. We left at 9 A.M. We passed toward San Pedro, the new place, in a valley on the northeast side of the Sierra de San Pedro. The houses are all of boards and some of logs, mortised and well made. The hotel is a large house of planks. The valleys are covered with piñones and sabinos, and the whole would be very handsome were it not for the snow and the general cloudiness of the country. The arroyos are all dry, and it appears that few of them have water. That water all remains on this side of the Sandia Mountain, and when they [the arroyos] enter the Rio Grande Valley, it disappears in the sand. There are springs almost everywhere along the mountains, and near them are ruins. Thus there are two at Golden, the pueblo of Tunque and the pueblo of Valverde. Turning southwest from San Pedro, we entered the valley between the Sandia and the San Pedro ranges, it running almost directly north and south. It is broad, covered with piñones and, although somewhat narrower, it resembles the valley of the Pecos. It is decidedly handsome. To the northwest, the view extends to beyond the Tunque and the Tejón, in both of which places there is a pueblo.

We crossed the Arroyo (or Rio) de San Pedro, a little deep stream running in a barranca hardly four to five meters deep. It runs from south to north up to the old, now abandoned plazita, or rancho, of Don Sebastían Ramírez. He came up from Chihuahua previous to the American invasion and settled here. He was one of the prominent men of New Mexico. He built not only the rancho but a little chapel or church by the side of a large house. The place, called "Old San Pedro," is situated on the point where the rio is entered by a dry arroyo from the west.

At that very point stands the earth-enclosure. It is a narrow embankment of stones and earth, about two to two-and-one-half meters high. I found very few pieces of pottery, black and red. To the south of it, and clear up to the rancho, extends a flat rubbish mound with posts of wood sticking up as if set in the ground for some purpose. Probably old corrales, and the old pueblo may have become converted into one of them. South of the rancho extends an open plain, the former fields of Señor

Ramírez. There are still visible the acequias running through it. The arroyo runs on its eastern border, and timber skirts it on the south and west. About one-half mile south of the plaza or rancho, there is the large pueblo.* It stands on the edge of the timber-belt. Large rubble-blocks compose it. They are not broken to fit, but appear to have been selected to fit. The rooms appear to have been tolerably good-sized. Three estufas, and at least three large corral-like structures as at San Cristóbal and at San Lázaro. The mounds are from two to three-and-one-half meters high. There was so much snow on the ground that I did not see a bit of pottery or other artifacts, though [I noticed what seemed to be] fragments of imperfect axes. The ruin is largely overgrown with high *Opuntia*, and the work in deep snow was very difficult. Photographed, but Plate #7 would not go up, so I let down #8 and could not move either. Had to take them out, kicked over the instrument, split the wood, cursed amazingly, and finally took the view again, 11 seconds time. But am afraid my camera is spoilt.

On the opposite side of the arroyo there are signs of other ruins too. Finally, in the plain, about 100 meters from the main ruin, there is another pueblo, somewhat smaller. The embankments are somewhat higher.* I only approximated the sizes, as I was completely frozen, and considerably mad. From there to San Antonio, where we arrived at sunset, it is all low timber, and the valley is narrowing. A dry arroyo, in whose bed it is terribly cold, is to be crossed before we reach the miserable little hamlet of San Antonito, where we took quarters with the wife of Manuel Crispín. He was not at home. It is a miserable place, with a little tienda where I could get with difficulty some glue to fix my camera. The cold intense, and on an average one foot of snow on the ground. We are at the foot of the Sandias, and to the north we see the Placeres and the Cerrillos. The hill is low and bare. People very much behind the times. Supper: coffee, eggs, and tortillas. Room fair.

While from here the arroyos all empty into the Rio Grande, losing their water before they reach the valley, farther south

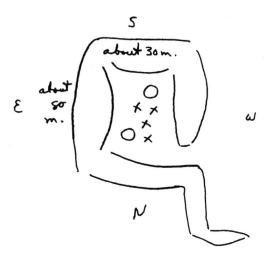

they run east, and empty into the Salines where they disappear! There is no good water, in fact, no water, beyond it, to the Rio Pecos; this explains the settlements here, near the headwaters of the arroyos, where there is water. It is a cold region, productive of maize, frijoles, but no chile. From what Señora Crispín (daughter of Sebastían Ramírez) says, the ruins at the rancho are not those of a pueblo, but simply of the houses of peones. She was born there. The pottery of the ruins is described by her as pinta glossy, and of many colors! In the plaza of the second pueblo, there appeared boulders or upright blocks, similar to those at the P[ueblo] Largo, particularly one, which was very large and heavy. Along the Rio Grande on the east side opposite Belen and south of it, lack of timber. People get their firewood from the west side. Another impediment to settlements!

DECEMBER 22: Started at 9 A.M.

At the Gallego there is a sawmill run by steam, belonging to Pablo Crispín, and two Americans are engineer and mechanic. Thence we rise to the heights above Chililí, . . . [which is] a little hamlet in a nook on the eastern slope, well sheltered and open to the east, certainly a favorable spot for spring and summer. There is an arroyo running through it, the Arroyo de Chililí, which flows all the year around. There is a chapel, and the old pueblo stood on the east side of the arroyo. They find arrowheads of flint, metates, black and glossy pottery. We stopped at the house of Juan Griego and were well received, but everything very high. The horses were very well treated. We had a hard day of it in general, because the cold is awful. The snow is deep and frozen. Filled up my [?] with plates. Corn, chile, and beans, grow well here. This is 25 miles from San Antonito.

DECEMBER 23: Smallpox just reached here. There are a considerable number of bears about in the mountains. The people here know the Yerba de San Pedro well. They tell me that the Indians of Sandia keep and worship a snake in the sierra. Even Captain Pradt believes the same thing of the Indians of Laguna. The day broke cloudy, cold, but quiet; no light for photographs at all. There is a dull yellowish hue or glow which bodes no good. Mr. Dow, son-in-law of Mr. McAfee, gave me an interesting account of the course of the arroyos here. They fill up their own beds. Thus the Plaza Vieja of Chililí was originally one-and-one-quarter miles lower down, but the creek gave out and so they fitted up their village here. The same happened at the ciénega, and near the boquilla of the Rio Bonito.

Found pottery. Photographed from the west side, 10 seconds. Light fair. Left at 11 A.M. I called upon Inez Armiento, who told me that the old plaza was about one-half mile east, and that the only pueblo was the one on the west side of the creek. It is all built over now, only the ruins of the small chapel are visible on the east side. Fine pottery, red and black. The road winds to the south over wooded ridges whose passage is very chilly, and in sight of the vast salines in the east and southeast. The tops of the Sierra del Manzano peep over the woods in the southwest and west. No water courses.

We reached Tajique at 2 P.M.; it is in a valley similar to that of Chililí, but the place is larger. Stopped at the house of

Antonio Chavez. Very kind reception. Pottery glossy, also one piece black and white.

The pueblo was of stone, the church of adobe. Don Antonio Chavez told me that there are a number of ruins of small houses

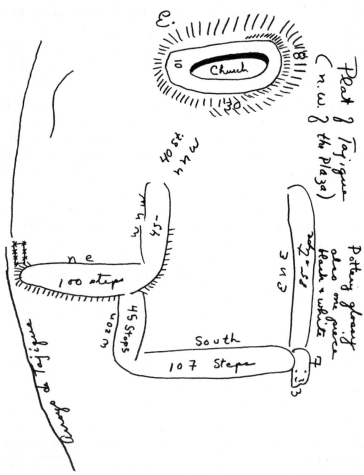

in this vicinity, houses of stone containing two and three rooms, etc. They are scattered in the fields and along the banks of the other creeks, which are mostly dry now. Photographed at 3 P.M. 10 seconds (#2) looking northwest. Light good. Cold, much

wind. On the whole, we are treated very well here. The place
is now San Antonio Tajique, formerly San Miguel. I tried in
vain to obtain information in regard to Tabira [Gran Quivira],
Tenabó [Abó], and the other pueblos. The people tell me, that
there is a pueblo at the Mesa del Camaleón, and in the Sierra
Blanca but one: the Nogal. One at the Torreón also; they
speak a good deal of the Pueblo Blanco and of another ruin near
by. About the Quivira there are various reports, but it seems
that the nearer we come, the smaller it gets! There is said to
be water six miles from it.

DECEMBER 24: José made a mistake of $10.00 yesterday with
Juan Griego. The good fellow rode back at 3 A.M. and returned
at 9 A.M. with the money. A man told me that at the Cañón de
José Largo above the Rito Quemado, there are large ruins. Their
walls are of adobe with loopholes and low, narrow doors. Above
the Torreón there are ruins of small houses, at the Rancho del
Cochino, one-and-one-quarter miles west, up the canyon. The
country from here is across ridges, rather barren, except an
occasional sabino and piñon. We are on the very edge of the
valley of the Salines. The Sierra de Santa Fé is in sight north
and the Sierra Blanca south. This is the famous region where
the eleven pueblos of Chamuscado[164] lay. They range around
it in a half ellipse, beginning with Chililí and Tajique. At the
bottom of the valley southwest lies the Manzano with the
Pueblo del Ojito, and at the farthest northeasterly point of
the Mesa Jumana lies the Pueblo Blanco. The arroyos all enter
the valley, but disappear at the lagunas.

---

164. The expedition of Coronado did not bear immediate fruit but the
Pueblo area remained in the minds of Spanish explorers and administrators.
The explorations of the middle portion of the 16th century gradually pushed
the frontier northward into the Durango-Zacatecas, Chihuahua-Coahuila region.
Finally in the year 1581 a small party (3 missionaries, 9 soldiers, and a handful
of Indian servants) led by Fray Agustín Rodríguez and Francisco Sánchez
(Chamuscado) moved up the Conchos to the Rio Grande and then on into
Pueblo territory. This small expedition returned in 1582, Chamuscado dying
on the trip home. The Rodríguez Expedition and the Beltrán-Espejo Expedition
of 1582-83 paved the way for the eventual conquest of New Mexico by Oñate.

Reached the Manzano at 1 P.M. It is at the bottom of the valley or rather at its head, where two little gulches meet. The source is about one-quarter of a mile above the place. On the hill, at the northwest [?] point, stands the house of the penitentes. This abominable practice is very strong here and at Chililí. Padre Louis Bourdier received us with open arms and insisted upon our staying here, at the Curacy. He complains bitterly of his people, says that they are extremely ignorant and brutish. He also complains of the climate in winter as exceedingly cold. In summer it is very pleasant. There is no irrigation here; the crops depend upon rain for their growth.

We photographed the place from the right. Plate #13. Time eight seconds. Light fine. The town is full of rumors of treasure. The people run after me with their stories. One fellow told me that at the Torre on the Rio Bonito there are caves with Indian paintings. Of course there is a big story about treasure connected with it. What I can ascertain is that there is a pueblo near here, since there is still the apple-orchard of the Franciscans, which is certainly 225 years old, and there is one lower down also. There is another at the Ojitos; and one perhaps opposite. At the northeastern point of the Mesa Jumana there is the Pueblo Blanco, and there is also a Pueblo Colorado. On the Mesa Jumana there are said to be many. About the Quivira there is more talk and wind than I almost can stand now. Treasure, treasure, gold and silver, is all that these ragamuffins dream of. It is a wretched people, and they all came from the Rio Grande here. The distance to Tajique is twelve miles, not nine. It looks like it.

DECEMBER 25: Very handsome day, but I could not enjoy it. My lip and nose are in bad condition, inflamed and full of pustulae. Used the Yerba de San Pedro with good effects. It is an excellent remedy. I painted the pottery of Tajique. Quiet, and nose is improving considerably. At sunset, another Mexican, Roque Candelaria, whom the Cura says is reliable, said and affirmed, that the ruins on the Mesa Jumana were those of small scattered ranchos! There were two pueblos at the Manzano, one on the hill of the penitentes, one on the south side of the creek, near the lower arboleda, one opposite on the loma, and one at the Ojitos. They have been small pueblos of large houses! He spoke of the Pueblo de la Parida, Pueblo Colorado, etc. At Abó there is a complete tinaja, black and white, dug out of a ruin. There are two pueblos near Abó. Some of the metates dug out near the Manzano are mere blocks of stone, with a [?] in the middle.

DECEMBER 26: I painted all day, and got much information. There is a good deal of lying going on in the village, but there are still some truthful people about. Roque Candelaria told me that there are the following pueblos: near the Ojo, and above the arboleda. Near the Ojitos. Opposite the Ojitos, on the north side of the arroyo. Besides, they all speak of little houses (ranchos) scattered mostly over the Mesa de Jumanos, so that it appears that I am in the home of the small-house. We also went to the Postmaster Kriss (of German descent), who showed me the sculptured beams of the church of Quivira, and also some of the pottery. It is absolutely different from all that I have seen in New Mexico, gray, with black and red designs, and almost recalls the tinaja of Cochiti which I brought to the Museum of Cambridge two years ago. It appears that at Abó they found an entire tinaja painted black and white which is still preserved at Abó.

DECEMBER 27: Painted all day. The Padre came with Manuel Luján of the Torreón, with whom I made an arrangement to drive us to the Quivira next Wednesday. He asks $2.00 per day. He says that on the mesa there are numberless small-houses. There is a pueblo at the Mesa del Camaleón, and one on the malpaís. But there is not the slightest recollection here of the Jumano, nor of the names of the pueblos as told in Oñate. Made arrangements to go to Cuaray tomorrow. At the Camaleón there is painted pottery.

DECEMBER 28: Left at 9 A.M. The road goes over hills, wooded and with occasional pinabetes. Cuaray is, in a direct line, six miles from the Manzano, southeast, and close by the edge of the Salines, in a beautiful spot, near the banks of an arroyo, in a valley very similar to that of Chililí and of Tajique, well sheltered. The church is a grand structure, 104 x 50 feet, and at least 25 feet high. It is all built stone plates, red sandstone, very well-laid in adobe mortar. The walls are 1.17 [meters?] thick, and the whole presents an imposing appearance. It is situated on the northeast corner of the pueblo, which latter consists of high rubbish-heaps, with about a dozen rooms exposed. These are built like the church, but they are only 0.25 to 0.30 [meter?] thick, and on an average 3.0 or 3.5 to 5.0 [meters high?]. In many places it looks as if the pueblo had been three stories high; it was certainly two. I photographed the church from the south, 10 seconds. Light good. Afterwards the pueblo and the church from the northwest. Light splendid, time 8 seconds. The first is #4, the last Plate, #5.

There are two or three new ranchos about the earth, and a large rancho of stone, now abandoned, on the south side of the pueblo. The pottery is red, corrugated, and principally glossy. Owing to the deep snow, I found but little pottery, but the pieces are characteristic. I was through at 1:30 P.M. and we returned home, well satisfied, and content. Painted all afternoon. Then wrote to Joe, to Father Gromm, and to Mr. Bigler. Mr. Kriss told me (as well as Luján) that the Quivira is not as large as the Manzano. Father Bourdier, who is charming always, gives me a letter to Abó. There are several ruins there and it will take me several days.

DECEMBER 29: I fixed my camera with glue at Kriss's and we started at last for Abó at 11 A.M. Reached Abó at 3:30 P.M.* The distance is about 20 miles to the southwest. We crossed over the usual ridges covered with piñones and few pinabetes. Reached the top of the ceja [summit] about noon and then traversed a level plain, very cold. La Ciénega is a small hamlet with a church or chapel. The cold is intense, and there is much snow. The people told me there are no ruins around here. There is a fine view of the Sierra del Manzano. Traversing the level plain, we reached the descent to the Puerto de Abó. On the right, fine cliffs of red sandstone protrude out of the heights, and the valley expands, with the Mesa de los Jumanos on the east, an independent mesa south, and a high sierra southwest and west fronting Socorro. As we descended in a narrow valley dotted with piñones and sabinos, snow began to decrease. Reached Abó at 3:30 P.M. It lies in a deep valley or cañada, shut in on two sides, with two arroyos passing through it to the southwest. These empty into the Rio Grande at La Joya, but the water never reaches the river. It loses itself in the sand.

The sierra is in sight from north to northeast. In the center is the church, a handsome structure, made of thin plates of red sandstone with adobe mortar. It is more ruined than that of Cuaray, but the stonework is more intricate and therefore more handsome. The pueblo is on the west and northwest of the church and was large. There are few foundations left, and it appears that it was made of sandstone, but not as handsome as the plates of the church. It is made rather of rubble than plates. I saw estufas. The pottery is glossy, black, and red, thin and clumsy too. It resembles in every respect that of Cuaray and Tajique, etc. They found a large tinajón in one of the cells; it was empty, but large, about three feet high. They broke it, and I am promised the privilege of seeing the pieces. An escudilla [porringer] is also said to be here, entire. They affirm that there were many, many stone axes and stone arrowheads (black and white).

I photographed at 4 P.M. Plate #6, 20 seconds time. Light good. The ranchos here are built into the ruins, and out of the stone of the ruins. These ranchos were founded in 1869 (April) by the father and father-in-law of Manuel Cisneros. They had formerly settled at the Saladas six miles below, near where there is also an arroyo and a ruin of a pueblo. There are also scattered ranchos all over the hills. They raise corn and wheat, chile and beans. Corn is planted in April, wheat sown in May. It is much warmer here than higher up, and there is hardly any snow. Distance from here to Quivira 25 miles, to Belen 45 miles. Eusebio García came in tonight also. As to traditions, there are none to be had; everything is too recent. I shall measure tomorrow, and take another view, perhaps two, if weather permits.

DECEMBER 30:* Last night, I still had quite a valuable conversation. The report is, that the pueblo was originally three stories high, the lowest of which is regarded as a basement or as subterranean. There is but one arroyo, which has water within 500 yards of the pueblo; the other one, on the northwest side, is dry at this time. Beyond it, are the ruins of another pueblo, which appears much larger than that of Abó proper. At a short distance south-southeast and southwest are scattered ranchos.

I measured the recent pueblo first. It is not very large. They tell me here that in the small rooms which still were found intact, when they first unearthed them, entire skeletons were found intact, not buried, but lying on the [?] floor. Also that there were many signs of combustion, even in the church itself. I noticed that on some of the few beams still at the latter edifice, there are marks of burning, so that it looks as if the people had been slaughtered and the place burnt.

I photographed the church, but it was a very difficult operation. I almost froze. Time 18 seconds. Then measured the old pueblo. Its pottery is identical with that of the other, glossy and thick, black, and smoky. It is three times larger than the new one, but the mounds are flatter and decidedly more ruined.*

They state that many stone axes are found in the ruins, arrowheads, etc. I myself found obsidian.

I painted the two pueblos, and then Don Ramón went with me to the lomas directly south of the place. They form a broad hill, flat, overgrown with sabinos and with but little snow. The ground, for about a square mile, is dotted with the faint traces of small-houses. They are from two-and-one-half to five-and-one-half meters on each side, distinct to indistinct foundations. But

there is an immense amount of pottery about, and it is extremely characteristic for the small-houses. Black and white, and
red and black, and corrugated, entirely different from that of
the pueblos. It is an extremely interesting and valuable find.

We descended to the Cañoncito de la Pintada. It is a wide
canyon, with steep rocky sides 50 to 100 feet high, which form
recesses, in which a number of paintings are found. They are
in red, yellow, white, green, and black, and some of them are
fairly [well] made. Many recall the Cueva Pintada. I copied
some; and returned at 4 P.M.*

DECEMBER 31: José declared it was too cold to leave [for the
ruins], and I really felt like it. Nevertheless, after painting for
some time, I started to photograph the church. Plate #7 failed,
I forgot to put it back to the focus. Plate #8 was all right so
far, that is, if no light entered the camera, time 18 seconds. But
the cold is almost insupportable.

Don Jesús Aragón of Valencia came, completely frozen, from
the ciénega. He says that the vigas of the Quivira are gone, but
that a hut was made out of them, which affords shelter. He says
that the ruins on the mesa are mostly small-houses. In the
afternoon, I went with Don Ramón Cisneros to the Cañón de
la Pintada. The paintings are all on the north side. I examined
the south side also, but there are no paintings. The arroyo in the
canyon is dry, but the whole is eroded. The strata are hardly
disturbed, and the rock is red and variegated sandstone. The soil
on the loma is very good, and light, and the air is warm there.
But [while the arroyos are dry] with rocky beds; where [they
are], there must have been water once! In many ruins wide
sabinos grow now. These small-houses look much older than
the pueblo.

The night was spent at home (?). And at home also are my
thoughts! God be thanked for all his blessings. May He bless
Joe, Papa, and all. May He lead me back again home, in body
and in heart. The year is past, and an eventful year it was too.
Tomorrow a new period begins. I wish I was at home.

GLOSSARY

Spanish words used by Bandelier

abuelo - grandfather
acequia - irrigation canal
acostar - to lie down, to go to bed
álamo - poplar tree, cottonwood tree
albañales - dikes
albejones - peas
alguacil - constable or other minor official
almacén - storehouse
almagre - Indian red
amole - soap-root
amugereado (*amujerado*) - effeminate person, transvestite
apellido - family name or surname
arboleda - a woodland or wooded area
atole - a watery mush made of maize
ayudante - assistant or adjutant
azoteas - rooftops
baile - dance
bajada - descent; the *bajada* referred to by Bandelier, however,
   may have been originally *majada* - sheep fold
barranca - canyon
barro (for *loza*) - pottery clay
barro blanco - white clay
boquilla - literally "little mouth"; sometimes used to refer to
   the opening of a canyon or valley
bosque - forest or woodland

brazo - arm, also used for a channel of a river

brujo - witch

cabildo - a town government, also the building used to house it

cacique - chief or headman in the pueblo, the religious leader

cadenas - "chains" of ten meters

calentura - fever

campo santo - cemetery

cañada - canyon or glen

carrizo - reed grass

castruenza - military chapel

cavador - wooden hoe

caxete (*cajete*) - bowl

cedro - cedar

ceja - summit

cerrito - small hill or mountain

cerro - hill or highland

ciénaga - a marshland or swamp

cienaguilla - a small marsh often used as a place name

cimarrón - mountain sheep

comal - a flat earthenware pan for cooking tortillas

como jurados - like juries

común - tribe

convento - convent

corral - a yard or enclosure

cosecha - harvest

cotón - printed cotton

crestón - outcropping

cuartel - a district or ward of a town, sometimes a single dwelling

cuarto - room

cuesta - cliff

cura - parish priest

chalchihuitl (*chalchihuite*) - turquoise (this and several other words in the glossary are borrowed from Nahuatl, the language of the Aztecs)

chamizo - a piece of burned wood

chaparro - the evergreen oak
chiquihuite - basket
chiquita - small girl
Dios - God
encina - oak
encinal - oak wood
enojar - to vex
enseñar - to show or teach
escalera - family or household (literally ladder)
escaramuza - contest
escudilla - porringer
espiga - ear or head of corn
estanque - reservoir
estufa - stove, also used to refer to the underground ceremonial
  rooms or kivas of the Pueblo Indians
falda - slope
fandango - a Spanish dance or the music for this type of dance
fanega - measure of land; measure of grain
fecha - date
fiebre - influenza
fieros - terrible
fiscal - one of the Pueblo Indian village officers
fósforos - matches
frijoles - beans
gamuza - antelope skin
garbanzos - chick-peas
gobernador - governor
guaco wood - bee-weed stems
guaje - gourd
guante - glove (?)
guerra de los Gachupines - war of the Spaniards
hermano - brother
hombre - man
hombres de armas - warriors
huerta - orchard or garden
Indios genízaros - Hispanicized Indians

jarra - jug or pitcher
jaspe - material used as whitewash (literally jasper)
jícara - basket
juego de gallo - rooster pull
junto - together, united
laguna - lake
librado - clerk
loma - hill
loza - pottery
llanito - small plain
llano - a plain or flat basin
llorona - female ghost
malacate - windlass
malpaís - badlands
mano - hand, hand stone for grinding corn
manta - a blanket or over garment
mantel - altar cloth
más bonita - prettier
maxtatl - kilt
medanos - dunes
merced - grant (of land)
mesita - small mesa or flat-topped hill
metate - grinding stone for making maize meal
mezcal - mortar (literally mixture)
milla - mile
monarca - king
muchacha - little girl
muerto - corpse
muy curiosa - very odd
muy malo - very bad
nopal - nopal cactus
ocote - pitch-pine
oficial - official
olla - jar
paeso - peso (the Mexican coin) alternate pronunciation
panocha - wheat sprout pudding

para *platicar* - to talk
pariente - relative
partido - party, group division
peñol - large rock
peón - sharecropper or other rural laborer
pinta - painted or marked
plato - plate
poniente - west
por *contento* - satisfactory
portal - porch or entryway
potrero - pastureland; in New Mexico, a tongue of high ground
pozo - waterhole or pond
pozole - a boiled mixture of beans and barley or sometimes
    maize
pregón - public announcement
pregonero - crier
primicias - first-fruits
primo - cousin
principales - head men of a town
puerta - door
punche - tobacco
¿Quién sabe? - "who knows?"
rancho - ranch or ranchhouse
relámpago - sheet-lightning
rezar - to pray
rincón - corner (or a room, cliff indentation, forming miniature
    box canyon)
ristra - a string of green chile
sabino - juniper
sacristán - sacristan or sexton
St. *Iago* - Santiago
salvado - bran
sandía - watermelon
sangría - bleeding or blood-letting (used by Bandelier, however,
    to denote a small irrigation canal)
serape - a blanket worn across the shoulders

sernicola - sparrow-hawk
shaparro - see chaparro
taparico - gate
tembladas - chills
tendejón - store (or perhaps commissary tent)
tepalcate - potsherd
tienda - store
tilma - blanket
tilmita - a small blanket or cloak
tinaja - an earthenware jar
tío - uncle
torito - little bull
torrejón - tower
trigo - wheat
tuna - fruit of the Opuntia cactus
vara - a rod or pole, also a cane of office given to Latin American town officials
vega - field
venado alazán - elk
verdolaga - purslane
vereda - trail or path
viga - rafter
vívora - snake
yeso - gypsum
zacate - grass or hay

BIBLIOGRAPHY

Adams, Eleanor B., and Fray Angelico Chavez, trs. and eds.
  1956. The Missions of New Mexico, 1776: A Description by Fray Francisco Atanasio Domínguez. (University of New Mexico Press, Albuquerque)
Bandelier, Adolph F.
  1877. On the Art of War and the Mode of Warfare of the Ancient Mexicans. (Tenth Annual Report, Peabody Museum, Cambridge, pp. 95-161)
  1878. On the Distribution and Tenure of Lands, and the Customs with Respect to Inheritance, among the Ancient Mexicans. (Eleventh Annual Report, Peabody Museum, Cambridge, pp. 385-448)
  1879. On the Sources for Aboriginal History of Spanish America. (Proceedings, American Association for the Advancement of Science. St. Louis Meeting, 1878, Salem, Massachusetts, pp. 315-337)
  1880a. On the Social Organization and Mode of Government of the Ancient Mexicans. (Twelfth Annual Report, Peabody Museum, Cambridge, pp. 557-699)
  1880b. Rau's Palenque Tablet. (Review in The Nation, Vol. 30, June 3, pp. 423-425)
  1881a. Historical Introduction to Studies among the Sedentary Indians of New Mexico. (Papers of the Archaeological Institute of America, Vol. I, no. 1, pp. 1-33, Boston)
  1881b. A Visit to the Aboriginal Ruins in the Valley of the Rio Pecos. (Papers of the Archaeological Institute of America, Vol. I, no. 2, pp. 34-133, Boston)

1884. Report of an Archaeological Tour into Mexico in the Year 1881. (Papers of the Archaeological Institute of America, Vol. II, Boston)

1885. The Romantic School in American Archaeology. (Papers of the New York Historical Society, February 5.) (Also in 1885 reprinted by Trow's Printing and Bookbinding Co. 14 pp.)

1890-92. Final Report of Investigations among the Indians of the Southwestern United States, Carried on mainly in the years from 1880 to 1885, Parts I and II. (Papers of the Archaeological Institute of America, American Series III and IV)

1892. An Outline of the Documentary History of the Zuñi Tribe. (Journal of American Ethnology and Archaeology, Vol. III, Cambridge)

1904. The Cross of Carabuco in Bolivia. (American Anthropologist, VI, pp. 599-628)

1910. The Islands of Titicaca and Koati. (The Hispanic Society of America, New York)

Bandelier, Fanny Ritter.

n.d. Recollections regarding the early years of Adolph F. Bandelier. (Archives, Museum of New Mexico, Santa Fe)

Bartholdi, Albert, ed.

1932. Bandelier, in Prominent Americans of Swiss Origin. (James T. White and Co., New York, pp. 193-197)

Bibo, Nathan.

1922. Reminiscences of Early Days in New Mexico. (Albuquerque Evening Herald, June 11)

Bingham, Hiram.

1914. Bandelier. (The Nation, Vol. 98, March 26, pp. 328-329)

Cather, Willa.

1927. Death Comes for the Archbishop. (A. A. Knopf, New York)

Cole, Fay-Cooper.

1952. Eminent Personalities of the Half Century. (American Anthropologist, Vol. 54, no. 2, pp. 157-167)

Edmunds, Brother Cassian.
1937. Adolph Francis Alphonse Bandelier in New Mexico, 1880-1892. (Unpublished M.A. Thesis, Manhattan University, New York)

Erasmus, Charles John.
1950. Patolli, Pachisi and the Limitation of Possibilities. (Southwestern Journal of Anthropology, Vol. 6, no. 4, pp. 369-387)

Espinosa, J. Manuel.
1940. First Expedition of Vargas into New Mexico, 1692. (University of New Mexico Press, Albuquerque)

Goad, Edgar F.
1939. A Study of the Life of Adolph Francis Alphonse Bandelier, with an Appraisal of His Contributions to American Anthropology and Related Sciences. (Unpublished Ph.D. Dissertation, University of Southern California, Los Angeles)

Hackett, Charles W., ed.
1923-26-37. Historical Documents Relating to New Mexico, Nueva Vizcaya, and Approaches Thereto, to 1773, Collected by Adolph F. A. Bandelier and Fanny R. Bandelier. (Carnegie Institution of Washington, Publication 330: I, II, III)
1942. Revolt of the Pueblo Indians of New Mexico and Otermin's Attempted Reconquest, 1680-1682. Parts I and II. (University of New Mexico Press, Albuquerque)

Hallenbeck, Cleve.
1950. Land of the Conquistadores. (Caxton Printers, Caldwell, Idaho)

Hammond, George P., and Edgar F. Goad.
1949. A Scientist on the Trail. (Quivira Society. Vol. 10, Berkeley)

Hawley, Florence M.
1950. Field Manual of Prehistoric Southwestern Pottery Types. (University of New Mexico Bulletin, Anthropological Series, Vol. 1, no. 4, revised)

Hobbs, Hulda R.
    1940. Bandelier in the Southwest. (El Palacio, Vol. 47, no. 6, June, pp. 121-136)

Hodge, Frederick W.
    1914. Bandelier Obituary. (American Anthropologist, Vol. 16, no. 2, pp. 349-358)
    1932. Biographical Sketch and Bibliography of Adolphe Francis Alphonse Bandelier. (New Mexico Historical Review, Vol. 7, no. 4, pp. 353-370)
    1940. Unpublished manuscript of paper presented at a Memorial Conference, August 6-8, 1940, in Santa Fe, as a part of centennial celebration of Bandelier's birth. (Archives, Museum of New Mexico)

Hooton, Earnest A.
    1930. The Indians of Pecos. (Yale University Press, New Haven)

Kelley, J. Charles.
    n.d. Jumano and Patarabueye Relations at La Junta de los Rios (ms.)

Kidder, Alfred V.
    1924. An Introduction to Southwestern Archaeology. (Yale University Press, New Haven)
    1928. Adolph F. A. Bandelier. (In the Dictionary of American Biography, Charles Scribner's Sons, New York, Vol. I, pp. 571-572)
    1931-36. The Pottery of Pecos, I, II. (Yale University Press, New Haven)
    1932. The Artifacts of Pecos. (Yale University Press, New Haven)
    1958. Pecos, New Mexico: Archaeological Notes. (Andover, Massachusetts: Phillips Academy, Papers of the Robert S. Peabody Foundation for Archaeology, Vol. 5)

Lange, Charles H.
    1950. Notes on the Use of Turkeys by Pueblo Indians. (El Palacio, Vol. 57, no. 7, pp. 204-209)
    1952. The Feast Day Dance at Zia Pueblo, August 15, 1951. (Texas Journal of Science, Vol. IV, no. 1, pp. 19-26)

1958a. The Keresan Component of Southwestern Pueblo Culture. (Southwestern Journal of Anthropology, Vol. 14, no. 1, pp. 34-50)

1958b. Recent Developments in Culture Change at Cochiti Pueblo, New Mexico. (Texas Journal of Science, Vol. X, no. 4, pp. 399-404)

1959. Cochiti: A New Mexico Pueblo, Past and Present. (University of Texas Press, Austin)

Leonard, Irving A.

1932. The Mercurio Volante of Don Carlos de Siguenza y Góngora, An Account of the First Expedition of Don Diego de Vargas into New Mexico in 1692. (Quivira Society, Vol. 3)

Lummis, Charles F.

1914. Death of Bandelier, an irreparable loss. (El Palacio, Vol. I, nos. 6 and 7, April-May, Santa Fe)

1916. In memory. (In The Delight Makers, Second Edition, by Adolph F. Bandelier; Dodd, Mead, and Co., New York, pp. xii-xvii, reprinted 1954)

McCreight, W. T.

1927. Major George H. Pradt. (New Mexico Historical Review, Vol. 2, no. 2, pp. 208-210)

Morgan, Lewis Henry.

1869. The Seven Cities of Cibola. (North American Review, Vol. 114, April)

1871. Systems of Consanguinity and Affinity of the Human Family. (Contributions to Knowledge, Smithsonian Institution, 17, Washington)

Newspapers.

Die Highland Union—Reisebriefe, March 25-August 19, 1881. Weekly Telephone—July 9, 1884; Nov. 5, 1884; May 6, 1885; June 2, 1885; June 9, 1885; June 14, 1885

Parish, William J.

1960. The German Jew and the Commercial Revolution in Territorial New Mexico, 1850-1900. (New Mexico Historical Review, Vol. 35, no. 1, pp. 1-29)

Parsons, Elsie Clews.
  1925. The Pueblo of Jemez. (Yale University Press, New Haven)
  1939. Pueblo Indian Religion. 2 Vols. (University of Chicago Press, Chicago)
Rau, C. C.
  1879. The Palenque Tablet. (Contributions to Knowledge, Smithsonian Institution, 22, No. 331, Washington, ix and 81 pp.)
Riley, Carroll L.
  1951. Early Spanish Reports of the Galisteo Basin. (El Palacio, Vol. 58, no. 8, pp. 237-243)
Spencer, A. P.
  1937. Centennial History of Highland, Illinois. (Centennial Commission, Highland)
Stubbs, Stanley A., and W. S. Stallings, Jr.
  1953. The Excavation of Pindi Pueblo, New Mexico. (Monographs of the School of American Research and the Laboratory of Anthropology, Number 18. Santa Fe. 165 pp. illus., figs., maps, tables)
Taylor, Walter W.
  1948. A Study of Archaeology. (Memoirs of the American Anthropological Association, No. 69)
  1954. Southwestern Archaeology, Its History and Theory. (American Anthropologist, Vol. 56, no. 4, pp. 561-570)
Underhill, Ruth M.
  1958. The Navajos. (University of Oklahoma Press, Norman)
Waterman, T. T.
  1917. Bandelier's Contribution to the Study of Ancient Mexican Social Organization. (University of California Publications in American Archaeology and Ethnology, Vol. 12, no. 7, Berkeley, pp. 249-282)
White, Leslie A.
  1932. The Acoma Indians. (Bureau of American Ethnology, Annual Report, Vol. 47, 1929-30)
  1935. The Pueblo of Santo Domingo, New Mexico. (Memoirs of the American Anthropological Association, No. 43)

1940. Pioneers in American Anthropology: The Bandelier-Morgan Letters, 1873-1883. (University of New Mexico Press, Albuquerque. Two volumes)

1957. How Morgan Came to Write *Systems of Consanguinity and Affinity*. (Papers of the Michigan Academy of Science, Arts, and Letters, Vol. 42, pp. 257-268)

White, Leslie A., and Ignacio Bernal.

1960. Correspondencia de Adolfo F. Bandelier. (Instituto Nacional de Antropología e Historia, Seria Historia, VI, México)

Winship, George P.

1896. The Coronado Expedition, 1540-1542. (Fourteenth Annual Report, Bureau of American Ethnology, Washington, pp. 329-613)

Wissler, Clark.

1914. Bandelier Obituary. (El Palacio, Vol. 1, nos. 6 and 7, p. 8, Santa Fe)

REGISTER OF PERSONS*

ABREU. SANTIAGO, Delegate to Congress, Mexico, 1824; Governor, New Mexico, 1831-33; RAMÓN, Prefect, First District, New Mexico, c. 1837; MARIANO, August, 1837, unrest at Santa Cruz over administration of Governor Albino Pérez led to plot and pronunciamiento; August 3, engagement and defeat of Pérez near Santa Cruz; August 8, assassination of Pérez, prisoners taken and some executed; Mariano and Ramón Abreu apparently killed August 9; Santiago Abreu killed August 10.

ACORSINI, REVEREND J. A. Assistant priest at Mora, 1882; in December, 1882, Archbishop J. B. Lamy appointed Father Acorsini pastor of a new church at Springer.

ATKINSON, GENERAL HENRY M. Surveyor General, New Mexico, 1876-82; "capable, honest, popular"; U.S. Surveyor General, 1882-83; resigned 1883; helped reorganize New Mexico Historical Society, c. 1880; died 1886.

BACA, AMADO C. DE. Mentioned by Otero as living in Peña Blanca with David and Valentin C., all cousins [nephews?] of

---

*This list of persons, with varying amounts of data on each, has been compiled from a file gathered by Dr. A. J. O. Anderson while he was a member of the Museum of New Mexico staff and in this capacity was doing preliminary research regarding the Bandelier journals. The data, extracted from the Anderson file, are presented here as supplements to footnotes and other comments in order to provide additional information concerning the individuals Bandelier met and with whom he talked or corresponded. Unless otherwise attributed, quoted material is from Dr. Anderson's data.

Don Juan María de Baca of Upper Las Vegas. In 1872, the Baca boys returned to Peña Blanca and New Mexico for vacation after schooling in the East.

BLAKE, CAPTAIN F. A. Las Vegas Coal and Coke Co., 1882; agricultural, livestock, mining, and newspaper interests in the Las Vegas and White Oaks areas; also operated health resort and boardinghouse at Beulah, 20 miles northwest of Las Vegas. Served as postmaster, Vera Cruz, Lincoln County, c. 1882.

BRUHL, DR. GUSTAV(US). Born in Prussia, 1826; educated in Germany, became physician. Came to U.S. in 1848, to Cincinnati, Ohio, St. Mary's Hospital. Editor, *German Pioneer*, 1869-71; Examiner, Cincinnati Public Schools, 1874. Writer of prose and poetry. Interested in archaeology of the Americas, United States, Mexico, Central America, and South America. Died 1903.

CATRON, THOMAS BENTON. Born 1840, in Missouri; earned A.B. and M.A. degrees at Missouri State University; served in Confederate Army. Read law; admitted to bar; came to Santa Fe, 1866. District Attorney, Third Judicial District; settled at Mesilla, Doña Ana County. Married Julia A. Waltz; five children. Attorney General, 1869-72; U.S. Attorney, 1872. Legislative Council, four sessions; Mayor, Santa Fe; President, Santa Fe Board of Education, 1895. President, New Mexico Bar Association until 1896. Leader in Republican Party. Shared political power with Otero-Luna group. U.S. Senator, 1912. Died 1922.

CHÁVEZ, DON AMADO. Born Santa Fe, 1851; ancestry extended to 1692, to General Chávez, with De Vargas. Educated at St. Michael's in Santa Fe, and at business college in Washington, D.C., Georgetown University and National University Law School, diploma 1876. Employed by Interior Department, Washington, D.C. Returned to New Mexico, 1882; attorney-at-law, sheep raiser. Elected House of Representatives, Territorial Assembly, Speaker, 1884; Superintendent of Public Instruction, 1892; established education in New Mexico on firm basis; second appointment, 1904-05. New Mexico-Texas boundary litigation, 1912. Married Kate N. Foster, née Nichols, 1892; three children.

COLE, E. L. Elected secretary, first meeting, Eighth Territorial Education Association, 1886; Principal, Preparatory Department, University of New Mexico (at Santa Fe).

DAVIS, SYLVESTER. Native of Massachusetts, probably of Puritan ancestry. Came west, Santa Fe and Bernalillo, when about 20 years old, 1859. Married Joseta Ortiz, daughter of Juan, 1860; lived in Galisteo except for prospecting in Sandia and Manzano mountains. Operated Ramón's sawmill at San Antonito, in the Sandias; later acquired Cadial Grant near Galisteo. Became sheep grower; operated saloon, post office, and store with government commissary at Galisteo. Died at age of 76.

DEFOURI, REVEREND JAMES H. Born La Palud, France, 1830; ordained 1854; came to U.S. 1856, various missions among Plains tribes; Kansas, in 1862; Bishop Miege's Vicar-General, 1875-80; private secretary to Archbishop Lamy and priest at Guadalupe Church, 1881; rebuilt the church and built parish house. Wrote several historical items: *Mes de María; Historical Sketch of the Catholic Church in New Mexico; History of the Apparition of the Holy Mother of Guadalupe; Historia de los Mormones.* Moved to Las Vegas, where he died.

EGGERT, DR. WILLIAM. First homeopathic physician in New Mexico Territory; in Santa Fe throughout the 1880's and 1890's, specializing in women's diseases. Came to Santa Fe from Indianapolis; Governor Sheldon appointed him to seven-man territorial medical board; served as secretary since its organization in 1882. Aided in writing new bill on the practice of medicine which passed in 1895. Ranked high in his profession; medical writer of national reputation.

ELDODTS, MARK, NATHAN, and SAMUEL, brothers. Natives of Westphalia, Germany. Nathan came to U.S. in 1851, and to Santa Fe in 1862, with Mark; Samuel, to U.S. and Santa Fe in 1868 (aged 18); merchants. Nathan to Conejos, 1878; Colorado senate, 1890; died 1908. Mark moved to San Francisco,

c. 1901. Samuel became partner in brothers' firm in 1882; Treasurer of Territory of New Mexico, 1894-98; delegate to Constitutional Convention, 1910; mercantile business in Chamita, New Mexico, as late as 1911.

ELLISON, SAMUEL. Born in Kentucky, 1817; to Cincinnati and then to Texas, 1837; Army until mustered out, 1840; deputy sheriff, San Antonio, Texas, 1840-49; then to New Mexico, marrying Francisca Sánchez. Interpreter, secretary to Colonel James Monroe; civil and military commandant, 1849-51; secretary, translator, interpreter, for Governor William Carr Lane, 1852-53; for Governor David Merriwether, 1853-56; for Governor Abraham Rencher, 1857-61. Appointed clerk, Superior Court and First Judicial District, 1859-66; U.S. Commissioner, 1868-69; farmer, 1866-81(?); legislature, 1856, 1865, 1866; Speaker of House, 1865-66; Territorial librarian, 1881-89. Wrote sketch on behalf of H. H. Bancroft for *History of New Mexico and Arizona.* "Governor Pile completely blackened by archives affair—ignorant, knave, fool." Sold archives as wrapping paper to merchants; forced by citizens to recover it (at much cost); dumped papers in a room (chicken roost, damp); Governor Wallace had them put in room next to parlor and had Ellison, as librarian, look after them. Archives in cardboard boxes, 2" x 10" x 15", according to subject; 135 boxes. Manager, New Mexico Historical Society; died 1889.

FELSENTHAL, CAPTAIN LOUIS. Came to New Mexico in 1855; joined Historical Society in 1859; donated some Spanish arms to the Society; was clerk in legislative House during this period; active in Historical Society until Civil War caused it to suspend activities; was a veteran of the Civil War. Helped reorganize New Mexico Historical Society, c. 1880. Appointed Adjutant General for New Mexico by Governor Sheldon, December 31, 1881.

GASPARRI, REVEREND DONATO M., S.J. Born in Biccari, Province of Naples, 1835. Entered Society of Jesus in Salerno, 1850; went to France in 1860 (revolution in Italy); ordained, then went to Spain. Was one of five Jesuits brought to New Mexico in 1867 by Lamy; replaced Father Truchard in Albuquerque, 1868. Superior of Jesuit Mission, 1869-76; printed books for the church and mission, beginning in 1872; edited *La Revista Catolica* for a time; known as "The Walking Encyclopaedia" by people of New Mexico; was active in the establishment of Las Vegas College before returning to Albuquerque as parish priest; brought Sisters of Charity to Albuquerque in 1881. Died there, December 18, 1883, of a stroke following two weeks' illness, aged 48; buried December 22 in side chapel, San Felipe Church, Old Albuquerque.

GRIEGO, JUAN. Justice of the Peace, Chililí, New Mexico, 1882.

HAREN, COLONEL ED. A. ". . . the congenial passenger agent of the A., T. & S. F. Railroad, came down the road yesterday and stopped at the Palace [Hotel]. The Colonel has come to Santa Fe to enjoy a rest. He is still somewhat lame." *Santa Fe Daily New Mexican*, June 29, 1882.

JOSEPH, JUDGE ANTHONY (ANTONIO JOSÉ). Born in Taos, 1846; early education in private schools, Taos and Santa Fe; Webster College, St. Louis, Missouri. Married Elizabeth M. Foree, Clark County, Missouri, 1881. Member, Territorial Assembly; Delegate to U.S. Congress, 49th-53rd Sessions, 1880's. Lived at Ojo Caliente, Taos County, where he had general merchandise store and served as postmaster; also ran winter resort, Los Ojos Calientes, "sure cure for many diseases." Vice-President, New Mexico Historical Society, for Ojo Caliente; led in building the public roads in Taos County; was instrumental in erection of capitol building, since known as Federal Building, Santa Fe (not used as capitol). Worked for admission of New Mexico as a state; succeeded in establishing Court of Private Land Claims; succeeded in obtaining annual appropriations; President, upper branch, Territorial Assembly, 1896; Died at Ojo Caliente, 1910; buried in Santa Fe.

KOZLOWSKI (KOSLOSKIE), MR. AND MRS. ANDREW. Had farm-ranch in Pecos area from 1858 (1 mile south of pueblo ruins and 4 miles south of Pecos town) which was sufficiently important to have been included on U.S. Army Engineers' map in 1870's. Union artillery had used ranch in 1862. "A Polish gentleman," Kozlowski was owner of first store in Rowe, a main stop for the Barlow & Sanderson Stage on the Santa Fe trail. Ranch house and corral were at spring "in deep copse." Kozlowski reputed to have used timbers from Pecos pueblo and mission ruins in building ranch.

LEONE, REVEREND ALEXANDER, S.J. Born Sorrano, Italy, 1838; entered Society of Jesus, 1855; to France, 1860, on expulsion of Jesuits from Kingdom of Naples. Continued studies; taught in colleges; took orders in Spain; stationed in Belgium after ordination for his third probation. Was sent to New Mexico with Father Tomassini on Lamy's request for a Jesuit mission—the first to be sent. Arrived in 1870. Secretary to Lamy; local superior at La Junta, Colorado, and at Isleta, Texas; Apostolic mission work primarily; preached in almost all parishes of New Mexico, El Paso District, and Chihuahua; a noted speaker (in Spanish). Opened Church of the Sacred Heart in 1900 where he remained three years; aided in publication of *La Revista Catolica*, Las Vegas. Then returned to Sacred Heart parish; died in Albuquerque, July 26, 1913.

LONGUEMARE, CHARLES. Mineralogist, Socorro; employee of Otero, Sellar, & Co., in later 1870's, "one of the commission-house boys"; the "recognized geologist of the firm," though apparently not too highly regarded by Otero. "Jaunty little Frenchman," from celebrated school of mines near Paris, France. Intense enthusiasm, but never found any paying deposits, either near Las Vegas or near Socorro. Publisher and editor of *The Bullion*, mining paper, located at northeast corner of plaza, Socorro, 1884-85.

MAILLUCHET, REVEREND LÉON. From near Porrentruy, Franche-Comte, France, Was parish priest in the Pecos-Las Vegas area during the 1880's; lived with his brother and family.

MARMON, LIEUTENANT COLONEL WALTER GUNN. Came to Laguna, 1868; married into the tribe; Civil War veteran; worked as surveyor, at times in government employ. Wm.

F. M. Arny (Pueblo Indian Agent, 1868-72) appointed him government teacher in Laguna, 1871; served until 1875 when school was taken over by Presbyterian Church. As colonel, led Pueblo Indian soldiers, 1st Cavalry Regiment, 1883-85, Apache wars (with Major George H. Pradt, also of Laguna).

MARSH, CHARLES H. Taxidermist and dealer in curiosities, Santa Fe, in the early 1880's.

MENAUL, DR. JOHN. Missionary and government teacher. Sent by Foreign Board, Presbyterian Church, to Navajo Mission, 1870-75; later to Apaches also. In 1876, chosen by Reverend Dr. Sheldon Jackson to succeed Marmon as government teacher at Laguna; mission school started at Laguna, October, 1876, with 30 pupils; school lasted there 20 years (supported by Church Society of Albany, New York, and later, by Women's Executive Committee, Presbyterian Church). Earlier Reverend Samuel Gorman established mission there, 1852-59, and after Gorman's death, Laguna Governor continued school, 1859-61. No Protestant mission in Laguna, 1861-76, due to resistance of the priest. Menaul established printing press and translated and published McGuffey's First Reader in Keresan; other publications, some in Spanish. John M. Gunn wrote that Menaul, after ten years, "left in 1887, loved & respected by all." Captain J. G. Bourke, however, stated that such men as Menaul were "almost invariably bigoted, mendacious, unscrupulous and illiterate tricksters who do the cause of Christianity more harm than can be corrected by the efforts of a score of honest, sincere and hard-working servants of God."

MILBURN, DR. GEORGE R. Lawyer and property holder in Santa Fe, according to assessment roll of April, 1882. Served in the Indian Office, Santa Fe, in the early 1880's, then resigned to practice law.

MILLER, CAPTAIN DAVID J. Translator and chief clerk, U.S. Surveyor-General's Office, Santa Fe. Exchanged letters with L. H. Morgan concerning fieldwork among Pueblo Indians; his field notes (Taos) and an interview with Pecos Indian (from Jemez) and one from Zia are in Morgan Archives, University of Rochester. "Meager and of little value," L. A. White. Active in New Mexico Historical Society, chartered in 1859 but died soon after because of the Civil War; helped organize a New Mexico Historical Society in 1880; Corresponding Secretary, 1882-83.

PÉREZ, DON ALBINO. Colonel, Mexican Army; Governor of New Mexico, sent from Mexico, 1835. Came to enforce provisions of new constitution, departmental rather than territorial. Had reputation for honesty; to enforce tax laws. Election of Ramón Abreu as Prefect of First District brought about Rebellion of 1837 at Santa Cruz. Pérez went to meet rebels; was unexpectedly attacked and routed; fled to Santa Fe, but not welcomed; killed by Indians, August 8, 1837.

PERSONNET, REVEREND SALVADOR, S.J. President, Las Vegas College, 1878-82; known to New Mexicans as "The Vanisher of Sadness"; dignified, benevolent, had faculty of making people cheerful. Succeeded Father Gasparri as parish priest, Albuquerque, 1882.

PINO, DON NICOLÁS. A conspirator, 1846-47; not involved with Taos Revolt, however; took oath of allegiance after imprisonment; afterwards, loyal to U.S.; joined with Colonel Price in attack on Taos. Mentioned as living in Galisteo, 1855, 1857; Nicolás and Miguel [a brother?] Pino fought on Union side, Civil War. Pinos were in Territorial legislature continuously. Nicolás died in 1896, aged 77; a wealthy man; buried at Galisteo.

PRINCE, LEBARON BRADFORD. Born Flushing, Long Island, New York, 1840. Founded Flushing literary society, 1858; member, Queens County Commission, 1861; A.B., Columbia University, 1866. Delegate to state conventions, 1866-78; delegate to national convention nominating U. S. Grant for President, 1868; active in New York State politics, member of State Legislature, 1870, 1871, 1873-75; State Senator, 1876-77. Delegate to national convention nominating R. B. Hayes. Refused appointment as Governor of Idaho Territory, 1878; appointed Chief Justice, New Mexico, 1879; resigned 1882. Married Mary

Katherine Beardsley, 1881 (one son, surviving, 1925). President, University of New Mexico, Santa Fe, 1881; Vice-President, New Mexico Historical Society, 1882-83; President, 1883-1923. Appointed Governor, New Mexico, 1889-93; member, Legislative Council, 1909; Chairman, First Republican State Convention in New Mexico, 1911; President, New Mexico Spanish-American Normal School, El Rito, 1902-12. President, Board of Regents, New Mexico Agricultural College, 1899-1904. Active in securing statehood for New Mexico. Died in 1923.

QUETIL, CHARLES J. Civil and mechanical engineer, architect, surveyor, New Albuquerque, 1882.

RIBERA, REVEREND JOSÉ ROMULO, at Peña Blanca; one of priests added to New Mexico church by Lamy. In the 1880's, DON TOMÁS, his father, together with his mother, kept house for Father Romulo at Peña Blanca. FRANCISCO, JESUS, JOSÉ LINO, and URBANO RIBERA, all of El Pueblo, San Miguel County, all related to Father Romulo. José Lino, operated general store and raised livestock; was postmaster; mentioned, in 1886, as nominee, on Democratic ticket, for County Commissioner, Third District, San Miguel County. Urbano, blacksmith and wagon maker.

RITCH, WILLIAM G. Born New York, 1830; to Michigan in 1855; later to Wisconsin; held various public offices; had Civil War service; State Senator, Wisconsin; later, Presidential elector (for Grant). Newspaper editor; went to New Mexico for his health in 1873; appointed agent for Navajos at Fort Defiance in relief of Wm. F. M. Arny. Became Secretary of the Territory in 1873, three terms. Acting Governor, New Mexico, 1875. First President, new New Mexico Historical Society, 1880, serving until 1883. President, Bureau of Irrigation. Active political life; prolific writer. Died Engle, New Mexico, 1904.

SENA, MAJOR JOSÉ DONATEO. Born Santa Fe, 1836, the son of Don Juan Sena, trader from Mexico. Family traced to 17th century in New Mexico (Don Bernardino Sena, who came to

Santa Fe, 1654); soldier, orator, lawyer; Union forces, Civil War—Captain, 2nd Regiment; Distinguished Service at Valverde; promoted to Major. After 1865, in charge of rebuilding Fort Marcy; resigned soon after. Served as Sheriff, Santa Fe County, 12 or 14 years. Several years as private secretary to F. R. Gallegos, Territorial Delegate to Washington (Republican); skilled interpreter in courts, 20 years of service. Died in 1897.

SHAW, JOHN M. In 1882, noted as oldest American resident in Socorro, having been there since 1851. A county commissioner; lawyer in firm of Moore and Shaw, attorneys-at-law. Indian Agent, Ojo Caliente, during Apache troubles, 1874-76. Recognized authority on Indians.

TELLEZ, HONORABLE JOSÉ LEÓN. Of San Rafael, Valencia County. Mentioned as 1st Lieutenant under Major George H. Pradt in Indian campaign (Apache), 1885. Services commended in letter from Pradt to Lieutenant Colonel Walter G. Marmon, Laguna, July 10, 1885.

THURSTON, J. D. C. Employed in Indian Bureau, Santa Fe, c. 1880.

TRUCHARD, REVEREND J. AGUSTÍN. One of six young men brought to Santa Fe from France, 1856. Ordained, Santa Fe, December 12, 1856. Listed as "Commissioner of Schools," Santa Fe, 1877 and 1882, probably serving for several years about this period. Rector of the Cathedral, 1879. Returned to France because of failing health, sometime before 1898; died 1911.

WALDO, HENRY L. Born in Missouri, 1884. (Father was a freighter; killed in Taos Rebellion.) Lawyer in interest of Stephen B. Elkins, of Catron & Elkins, the latter then New Mexico delegate to Congress, 1873. Appointed Chief Justice, 1876; resigned 1878. Law firm of Waldo & [Wm.] Breedon. Served as New Mexico Attorney General, 1878-80. Solicitor for AT & SF Railroad, from 1883 to about 1908 or 1909. Dissolved partnership with Breedon; brought AT & SF branch to Santa Fe from Lamy. Had reputation for honesty in all dealings.

WILLISON, COLONEL ROBERT B. On assessment roll as property holder in Santa Fe, April, 1882. Civil and mining engineer; real estate interests also.

WITTICK, BEN. Of Wittick & Russell, "photographers and New Mexico views for sale," early 1880's. Accompanied archaeological survey under Colonel Stevenson sent to Fort Wingate by Smithsonian Institution in 1882; went to Moqui (Hopi) country, Canyon "Dechelle," "cliff-dweller country"; later, to Acoma, Peña Blanca, and Cochiti.

INDEX

Aragón, Don Jesús (Valencia), 391
Archaeological Institute of America:
files examined by Goad, 6; Norton,
Pres. of, 16n8; supported Bandelier's Southwest research, 21;
Papers of, 26n19, 27; provided
photographic apparatus, 38; major
interest in E. Mediterranean, 49,
49n31; Bandelier dropped from
payroll of, 50; *Report* of, given to
Padre Ribera, 160; mentioned, 22,
27, 266
Archives, Santa Fe, N.M.: Bandelier
journals now in, ix; Bandelier
gained access to, 26; destruction of,
by Gov. Pile, 73, 74, 410; neglected by Gov. Arny, 74; Ellison to
search for Cochiti entries, 88; Keres
census list, 144; Journal of Otermín, 180; condition of, 239;
Journal of Vargas, 242; mentioned,
72, 181, 410
—church records: Bandelier proposed
research in, 21, 22; examined by
Bandelier: Haassavas, Sonora, 40;
Sonora, 41-42; El Paso, Tex., 53;
Juarez, Chihuahua, 53; Vatican,
53n36; Albuquerque, 72, 277, 309;
Santa Fe, 73, 74; Peña Blanca, 91,
126, 127, 129, 131; Laguna, 281;
mentioned, 82, 309, 322
—examined by Bandelier: Santa Fe,
40, 41, 143, 144, 180, 240, 242,
243, 244; La Paz, Bolivia, 57;
Lima, Peru, 57
—examined by Bandelier and Fanny
R. Bandelier: Lima, Peru, 58, 60;
Madrid, Seville, and Simancas,
Spain, 64
—Mexico City, D.F.: 41, 52, 55-56;
transcriptions of *Archivo General*
presented to Carnegie Institution,
64
—civil and ecclesiastical, La Paz,
Bolivia, 58, 60
—Spanish: transcriptions of, pre-

sented to Carnegie Institution, 64;
source of Hackett's volumes, 64
—*See also* Bandelier, as archivist;
Documents and/or Manuscripts
Archuleta, Ramón (Pecos area), 355
Arispe, Sonora: Bandelier at, 40
Arizona, 2
Arkansas River: 70, 343; insects, 70;
vegetation, 70
Armand, José de Jesús de (Cubero),
289, 289n142, 290, 297n144
Armand, José María de (Cubero),
297, 297n144
Armand, Mr. De (Cubero), 306,
316-317, 328
Armiento, Inez (Chililí), 383
Armijo, Don Cristóbal, 317
Armijo, Gov. Manuel, 75n61, 84,
244-245
Armond, De. See Armand
Armville, N.M. See Wallace, N.M.
Arny, Gov. W. F. M., 74, 75n61,
181, 183, 412-413, 415
Arquero, Salvador (Cochiti), 244
Arquero, Toribio (Cochiti), 244
Arroyo de Chililí: Bandelier at ruin
on, 383
Arroyo de Galisteo (Galisteo Arr-
oyo): Bandelier at, 132, 272, 333,
337; geology, 132; climate, 333
Arroyo de la Cañada (Cochiti area):
Spanish ruins in, 139-140, 147;
Bandelier at, 139-140
Arroyo de la Cuesta Colorada
(Cochiti area): Bandelier at, 203
Arroyo del Cañón de Pino (Cochiti
area): Bandelier at, 202
Arroyo del Chorro (Galisteo area):
ruin of San Lázaro, 337; vegetation,
337; Bandelier at, 337
Arroyo del Nombre de Dios (Chihua-
hua): Bandelier at, 40
Arroyo de los Pecos (Las Vegas):
Bandelier at, 344, 350
Arroyo de Pecos (Pecos): Bandelier
at, 71